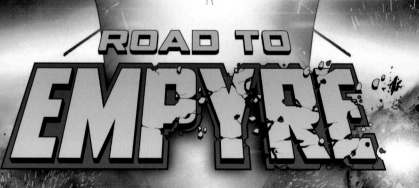

ROAD TO
EMPYRE

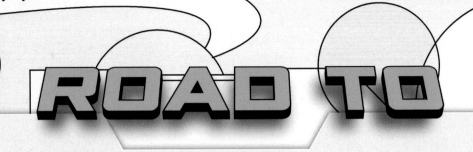

ROAD TO

INCOMING!

WRITERS, ARTISTS & COLORISTS:

PAGES 1-4, 21-24, 69-72 & 81-84 .... **Al Ewing, Humberto Ramos & Edgar Delgado**
PAGES 5-8 .... **Chip Zdarsky, Jorge Fornés & Jordie Bellaire**
PAGES 9-12 .... **Kelly Thompson & Mattia De Iulis**
PAGES 13-16 .... **Kelly Thompson, Carmen Carnero & Rachelle Rosenberg**
PAGES 17-20 .... **Jason Aaron, Andrea Sorrentino & Jay David Ramos**
PAGES 25-28 .... **Matthew Rosenberg, R.B. Silva & Israel Silva**
PAGES 29-32 .... **Greg Pak, Annie Wu & Tríona Farrell**
PAGES 33-36 .... **Eve L. Ewing, Kim Jacinto & Espen Grundetjern**
PAGES 37-40 .... **Al Ewing, Joe Bennett, Ruy José & Dono Sánchez-Almara**
PAGES 41-44 .... **Ed Brisson, Aaron Kuder & Michael Garland**
PAGES 45-48 .... **Donny Cates, Ryan Stegman & David Curiel**
PAGES 49-52 .... **Saladin Ahmed, Javier Garrón & David Curiel**
PAGES 53-56 .... **Tini Howard, Jim Cheung & Romulo Fajardo Jr.**
PAGES 57-60 .... **Jonathan Hickman, R.B. Silva & Marte Gracia**
PAGES 61-64 .... **Dan Slott, Luciano Vecchio & Espen Grundetjern**
PAGES 65-68 .... **Dan Slott, Francesco Manna & Edgar Delgado**
PAGES 73-80 .... **Dan Slott, Carlos Pacheco, Rafael Fonteriz & Morry Hollowell**

LETTERER .... **VC's Travis Lanham**
COVER ART .... **Patrick Gleason & Morry Hollowell**
SPECIAL THANKS TO .... **Jordan D. White**

ROAD TO EMPYRE: THE KREE/SKRULL WAR

WRITER .... **Robbie Thompson**
ARTIST & COLORIST, PRESENT DAY SEQUENCE .... **Mattia De Iulis**
ARTIST, FLASHBACK SEQUENCE .... **Javier Rodríguez**
COLORIST, FLASHBACK SEQUENCE .... **Álvaro López**

LETTERER .... **VC's Joe Caramagna**
COVER ART .... **Phil Noto**

ASSISTANT EDITORS .... **Shannon Andrews Ballesteros & Martin Biro**
ASSOCIATE EDITOR .... **Alanna Smith**
EDITORS .... **Tom Brevoort**

EMPYRE

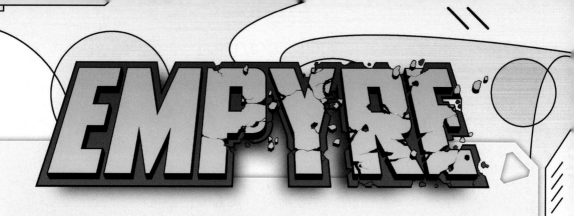

EMPYRE HANDBOOK

HEAD WRITER/COORDINATOR .... **Mike O'Sullivan**

ASSISTANT COORDINATORS .... **Anthony Cotilletta**, **Carl Farmer**, **Mike Fichera**, **Jacob Rougemont** & **Luc Kersten**

WRITERS .... **Ronald Byrd**, **Jeff Christiansen**, **Anthony Cotilletta**, **Daron Jensen**, **Luc Kersten**, **Rob London**, **Chris McCarver**, **Marc Riemer**, **Jacob Rougemont** & **Stuart Vandal**

IMAGE REFURBISHMENT .... **Carl Farmer** & **Mike O'Sullivan**

DESIGNER .... **Jay Bowen**

COVER ART .... **Ron Lim** & **Israel Silva**

EDITOR .... **Brian Overton**

SPECIAL THANKS TO ....

Tom Brevoort, **Chris Buchner**, **Shawn "Keebler" Byers**, **Jocquelle Caiby**, **Russ Chappell**, **Patrick C. Duke**, **Al Ewing**, **Katie Santa Ana Farmer**, **Antonio Gaviño**, **Demetria Hatcher**, **Elissa Hunter**, **Joshua McMahan**, **Gerard McMenemy**, **Mark & Patti O'Sullivan**, **Roger Ott**, **Jacque Porte**, **Jamie Sitzler**, **Al Sjoerdsma**, **Nick Smiles**, **Vic & Jan Sneed**, **Douglas Wolk**, **Jeph York** & **Kristin Zelazko**

LOVINGLY DEDICATED TO .... **Patricia McCarver** (1946-2018) & **Ricky Rougemont** (1958-2019)

NOTE: COVERAGE FOR THE PROFILES IN THIS HANDBOOK STOPS AT THE END OF *INCOMING #1*.

COLLECTION EDITOR **Jennifer Grünwald**

ASSISTANT MANAGING EDITOR **Lisa Montalbano**

EDITOR, SPECIAL PROJECTS **Mark D. Beazley**

LAYOUT **Jeph York**

SVP PRINT, SALES & MARKETING **David Gabriel**

ASSISTANT MANAGING EDITOR **Maia Loy**

ASSOCIATE MANAGER, DIGITAL ASSETS **Joe Hochstein**

VP PRODUCTION & SPECIAL PROJECTS **Jeff Youngquist**

BOOK DESIGNER **Jay Bowen**

EDITOR IN CHIEF **C.B. Cebulski**

EMPYRE: ROAD TO EMPYRE. Contains material originally published in magazine form as INCOMING (2019) #1, ROAD TO EMPYRE: THE KREE/SKRULL WAR (2020) #1 and EMPYRE HANDBOOK (2020) #1. First printing 2020. ISBN 978-1-302-92588-8. Published by MARVEL WORLDWIDE, INC., a subsidiary of MARVEL ENTERTAINMENT, LLC. OFFICE OF PUBLICATION: 1290 Avenue of the Americas, New York, NY 10104. © 2020 MARVEL No similarity between any of the names, characters, persons, and/or institutions in this magazine with those of any living or dead person or institution is intended, and any such similarity which may exist is purely coincidental. **Printed in the U.S.A.** KEVIN FEIGE, Chief Creative Officer; DAN BUCKLEY, President, Marvel Entertainment; JOHN NEE, Publisher; JOE QUESADA, EVP & Creative Director; TOM BREVOORT, SVP of Publishing; DAVID BOGART, Associate Publisher & SVP of Talent Affairs; Publishing & Partnership; DAVID GABRIEL, VP of Print & Digital Publishing; JEFF YOUNGQUIST, VP of Production & Special Projects; DAN CARR, Executive Director of Publishing Technology; ALEX MORALES, Director of Publishing Operations; DAN EDINGTON, Managing Editor; RICKEY PURDIN, Director of Talent Relations; SUSAN CRESPI, Production Manager; STAN LEE, Chairman Emeritus. For information regarding advertising in Marvel Comics or on Marvel.com, please contact Vit DeBellis, Custom Solutions & Integrated Advertising Manager, at vdebellis@marvel.com. For Marvel subscription inquiries, please call 888-511-5480. **Manufactured between 8/12/2020 and 9/8/2020 by LSC COMMUNICATIONS INC., KENDALLVILLE, IN, USA.**

10 9 8 7 6 5 4 3 2 1

INCOMING!

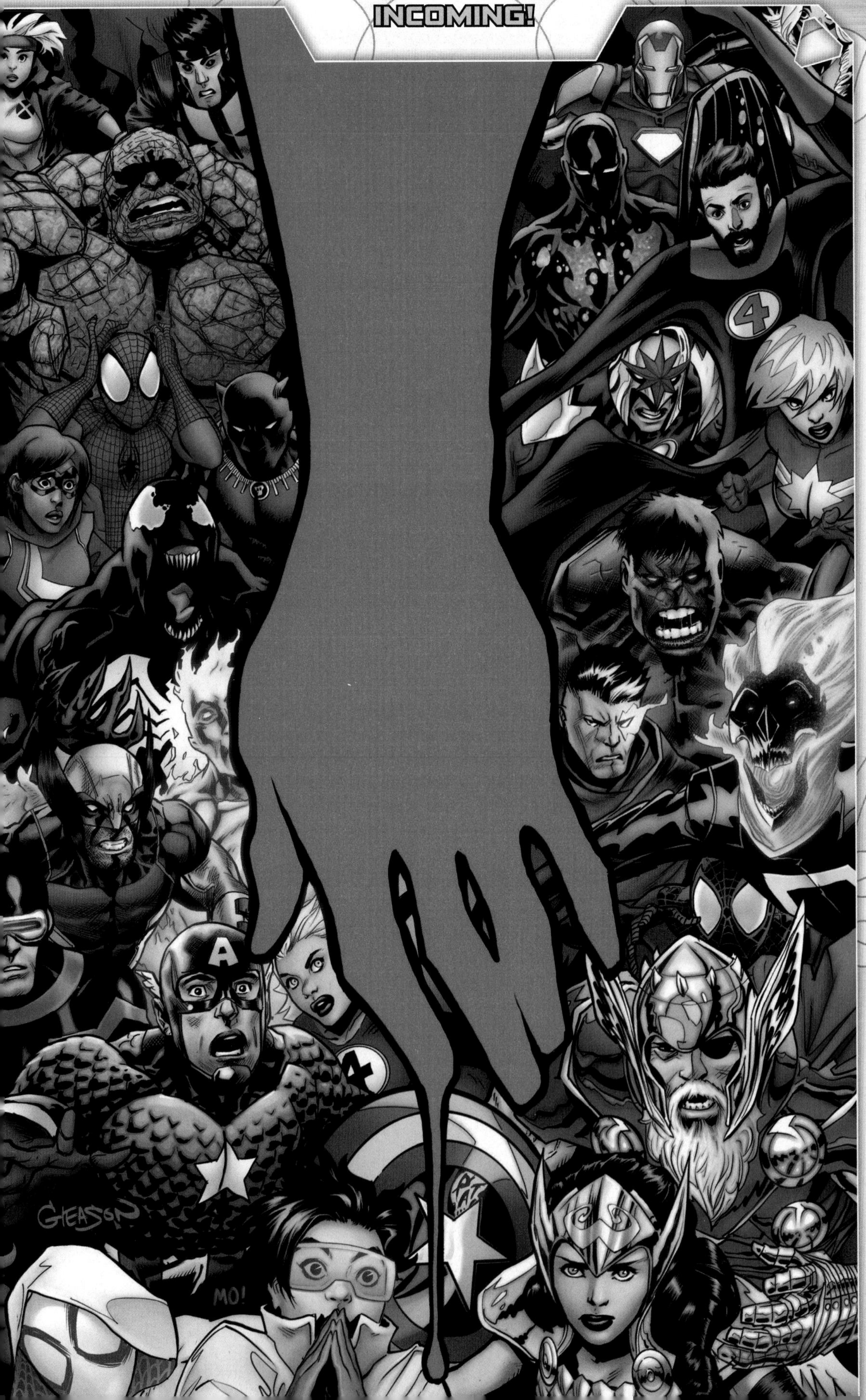

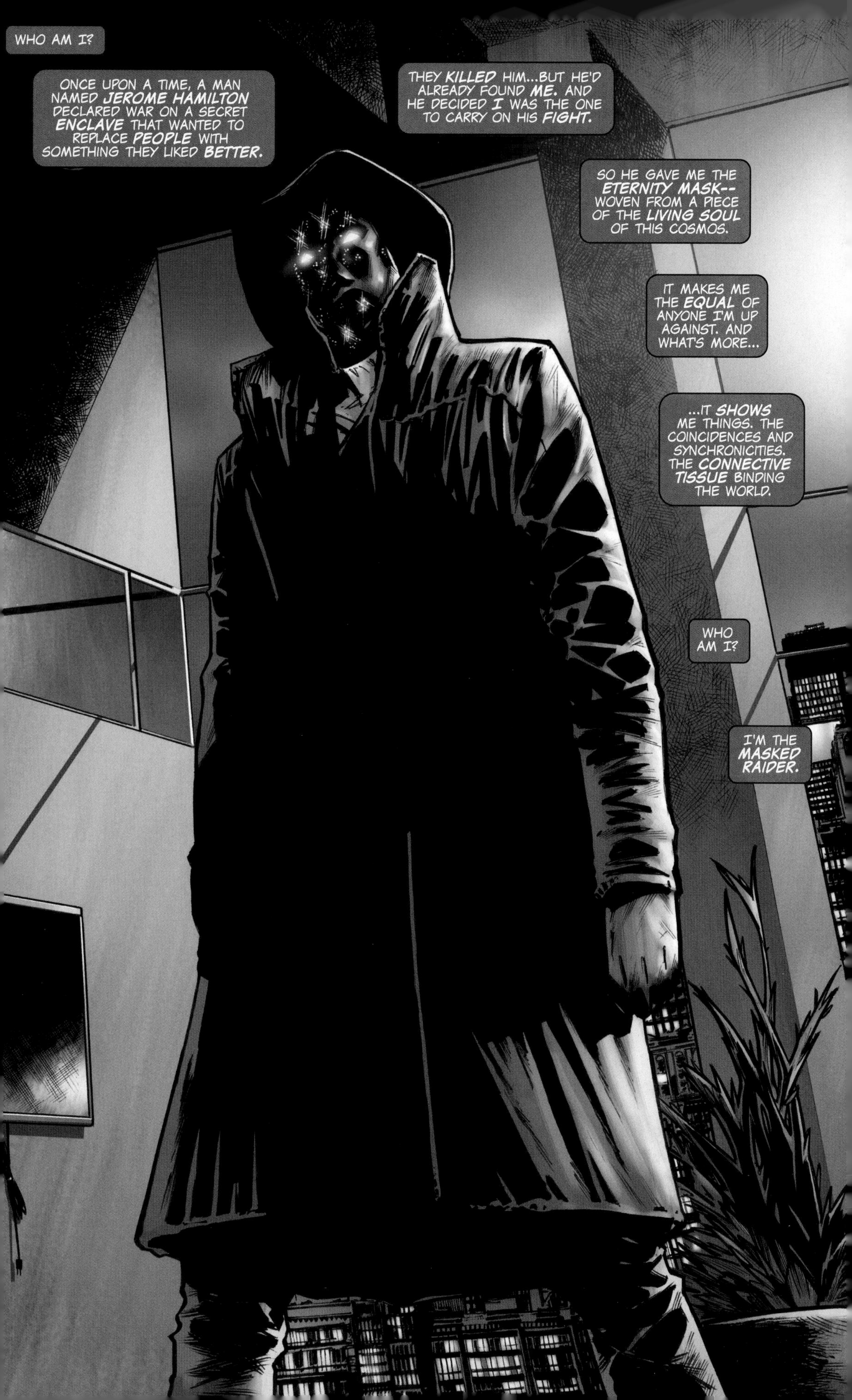
WHO AM I?
ONCE UPON A TIME, A MAN NAMED JEROME HAMILTON DECLARED WAR ON A SECRET ENCLAVE THAT WANTED TO REPLACE PEOPLE WITH SOMETHING THEY LIKED BETTER.
THEY KILLED HIM...BUT HE'D ALREADY FOUND ME. AND HE DECIDED I WAS THE ONE TO CARRY ON HIS FIGHT.
SO HE GAVE ME THE ETERNITY MASK-- WOVEN FROM A PIECE OF THE LIVING SOUL OF THIS COSMOS.
IT MAKES ME THE EQUAL OF ANYONE I'M UP AGAINST. AND WHAT'S MORE...
...IT SHOWS ME THINGS. THE COINCIDENCES AND SYNCHRONICITIES. THE CONNECTIVE TISSUE BINDING THE WORLD.
WHO AM I?
I'M THE MASKED RAIDER.

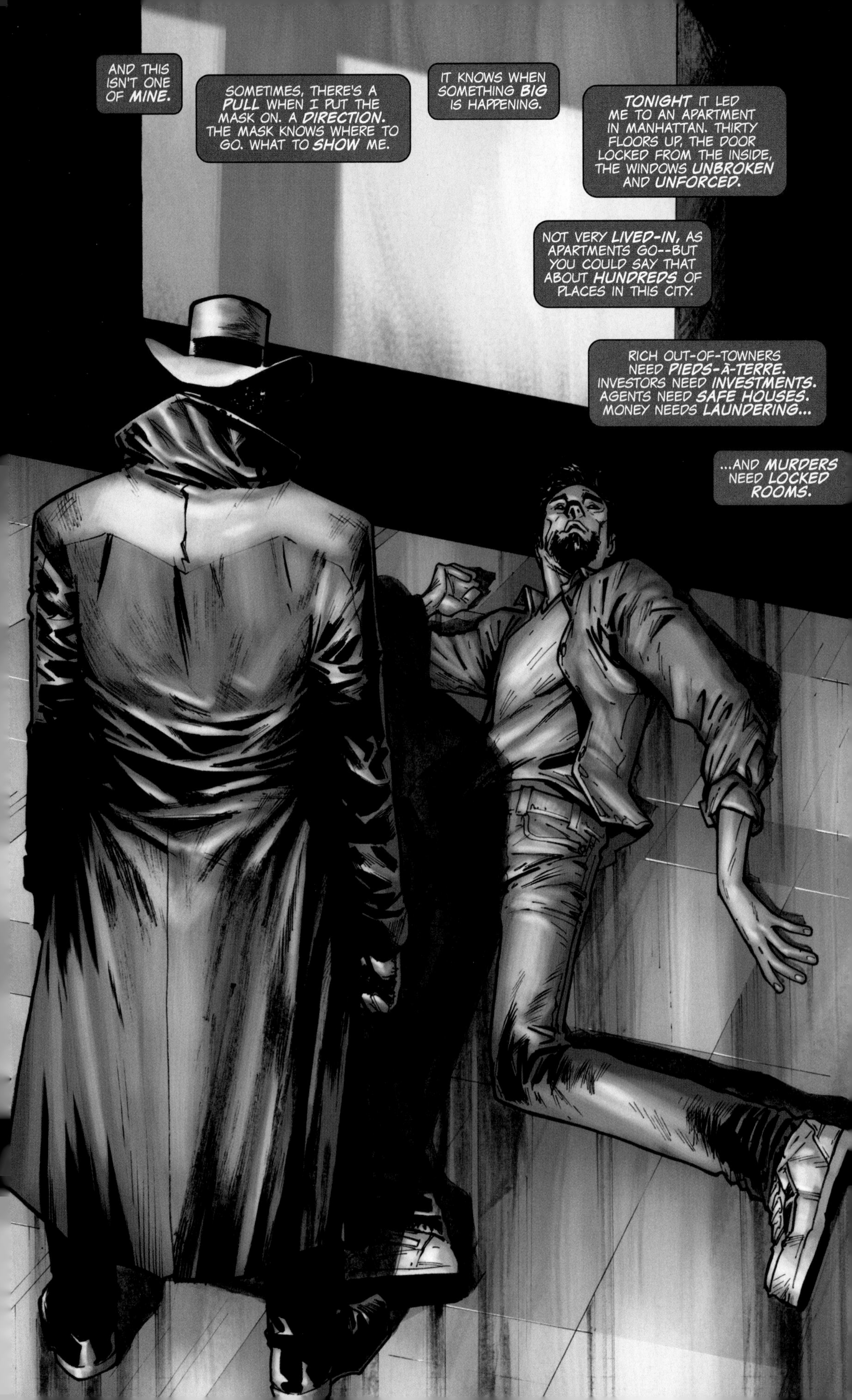
AND THIS ISN'T ONE OF MINE.
SOMETIMES, THERE'S A PULL WHEN I PUT THE MASK ON. A DIRECTION. THE MASK KNOWS WHERE TO GO. WHAT TO SHOW ME.
IT KNOWS WHEN SOMETHING BIG IS HAPPENING.
TONIGHT IT LED ME TO AN APARTMENT IN MANHATTAN. THIRTY FLOORS UP, THE DOOR LOCKED FROM THE INSIDE, THE WINDOWS UNBROKEN AND UNFORCED.
NOT VERY LIVED-IN, AS APARTMENTS GO--BUT YOU COULD SAY THAT ABOUT HUNDREDS OF PLACES IN THIS CITY.
RICH OUT-OF-TOWNERS NEED PIEDS-À-TERRE. INVESTORS NEED INVESTMENTS. AGENTS NEED SAFE HOUSES. MONEY NEEDS LAUNDERING...
...AND MURDERS NEED LOCKED ROOMS.

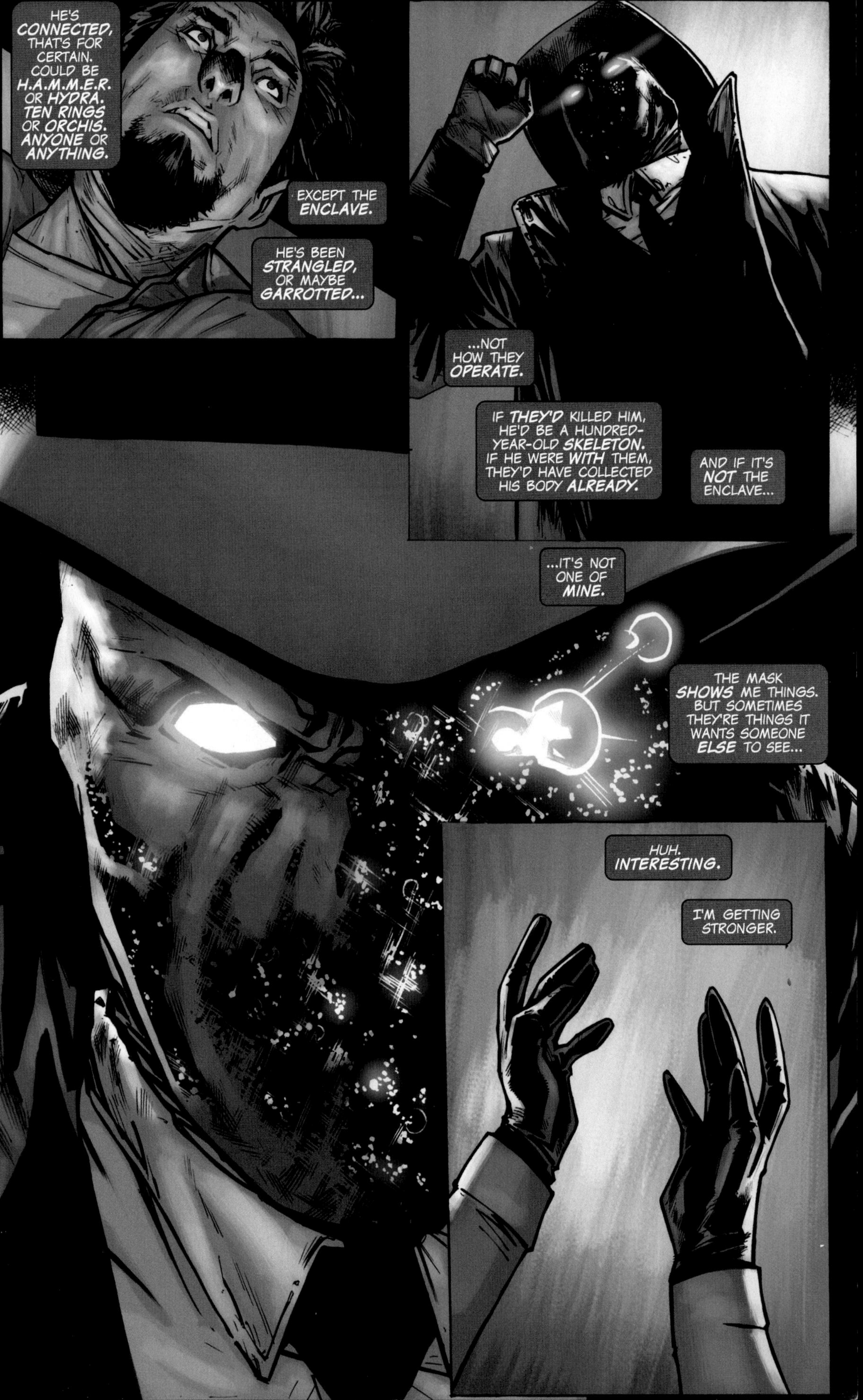
HE'S CONNECTED, THAT'S FOR CERTAIN. COULD BE H.A.M.M.E.R. OR HYDRA. TEN RINGS OR ORCHIS. ANYONE OR ANYTHING.
EXCEPT THE ENCLAVE.
HE'S BEEN STRANGLED, OR MAYBE GARROTTED...
...NOT HOW THEY OPERATE.
IF THEY'D KILLED HIM, HE'D BE A HUNDRED-YEAR-OLD SKELETON. IF HE WERE WITH THEM, THEY'D HAVE COLLECTED HIS BODY ALREADY.
AND IF IT'S NOT THE ENCLAVE...
...IT'S NOT ONE OF MINE.
THE MASK SHOWS ME THINGS. BUT SOMETIMES THEY'RE THINGS IT WANTS SOMEONE ELSE TO SEE...
HUH. INTERESTING.
I'M GETTING STRONGER.

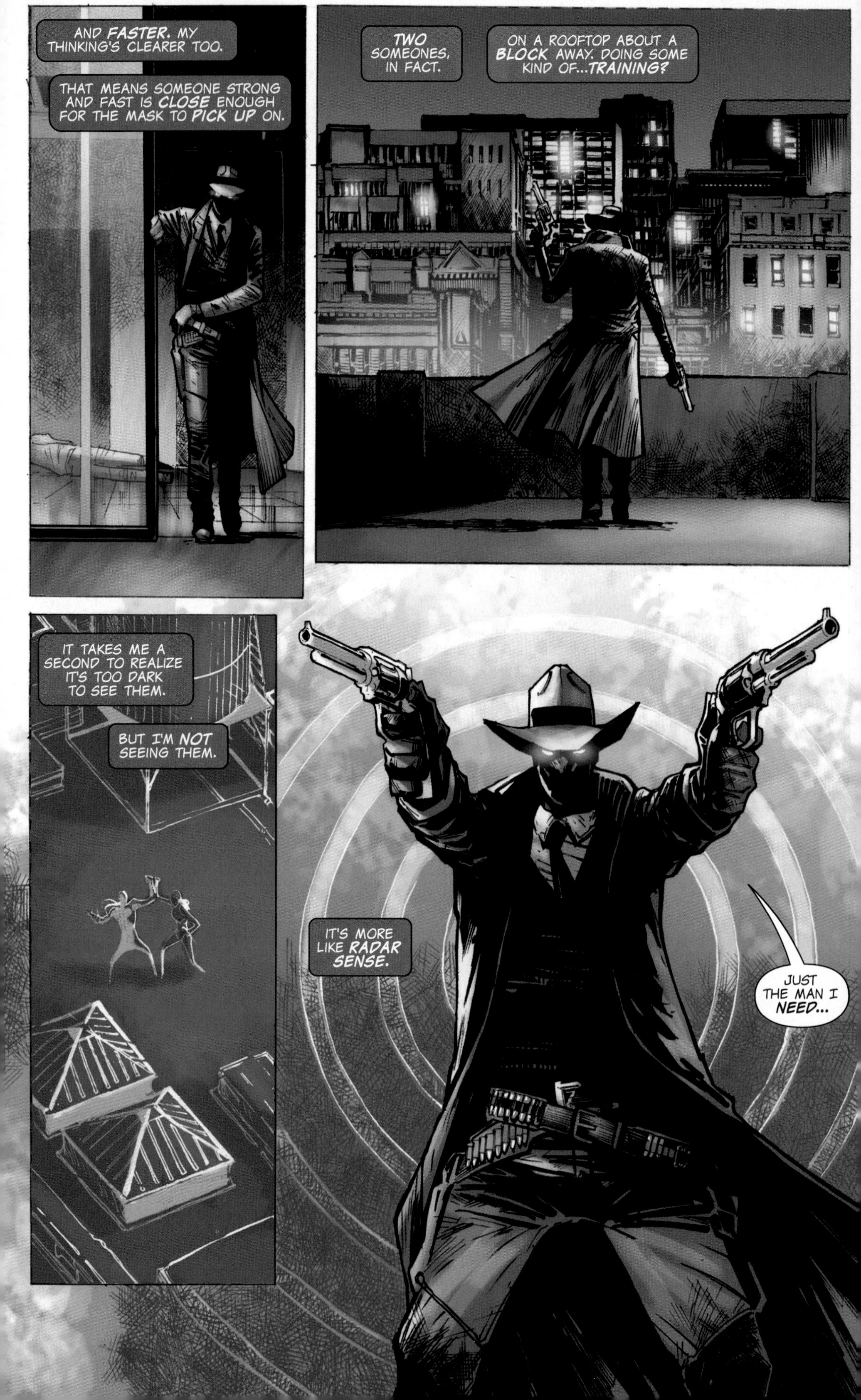
AND FASTER. MY THINKING'S CLEARER TOO.
THAT MEANS SOMEONE STRONG AND FAST IS CLOSE ENOUGH FOR THE MASK TO PICK UP ON.
TWO SOMEONES, IN FACT.
ON A ROOFTOP ABOUT A BLOCK AWAY. DOING SOME KIND OF...TRAINING?
IT TAKES ME A SECOND TO REALIZE IT'S TOO DARK TO SEE THEM.
BUT I'M NOT SEEING THEM.
IT'S MORE LIKE RADAR SENSE.
JUST THE MAN I NEED...

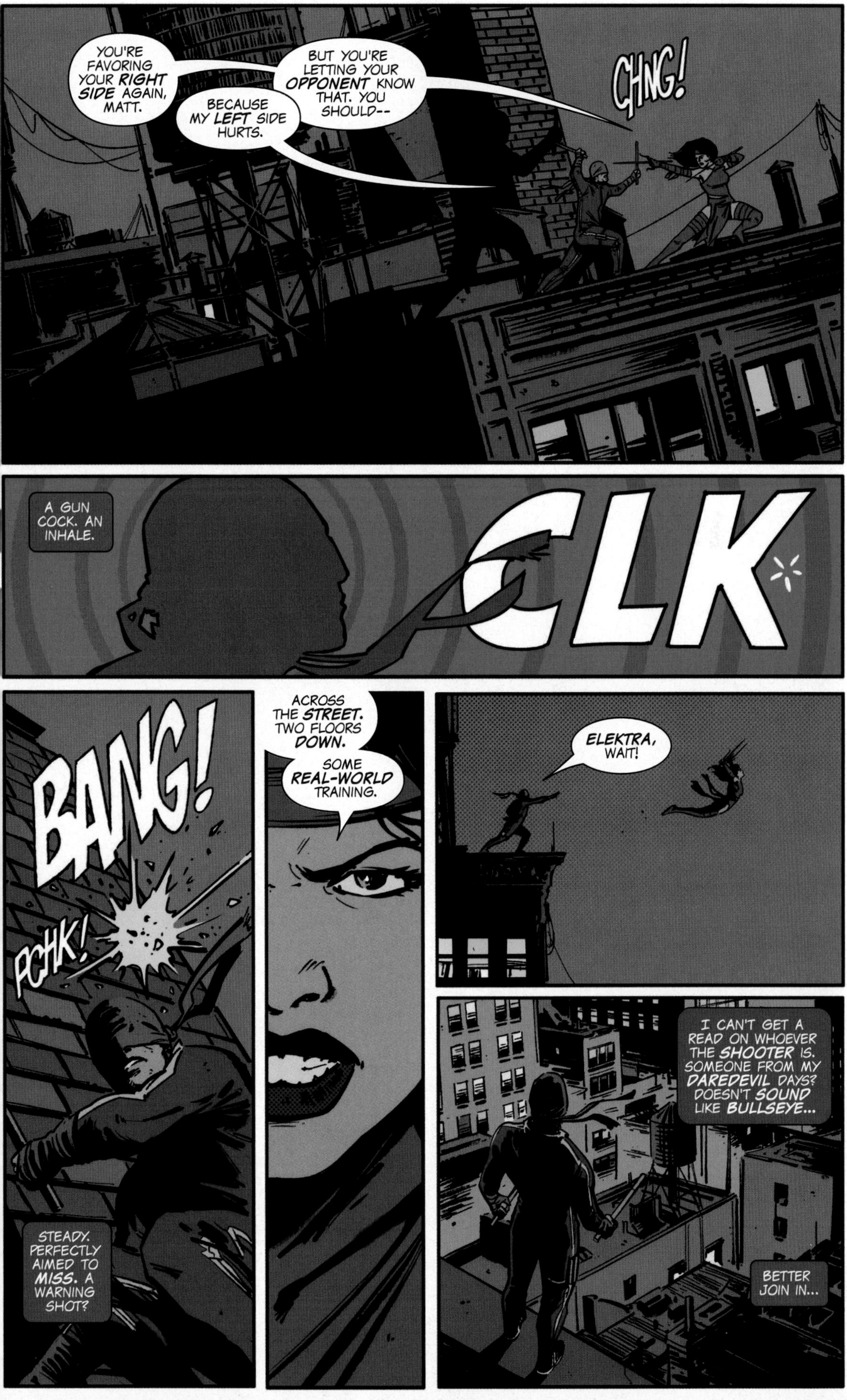
YOU'RE FAVORING YOUR RIGHT SIDE AGAIN, MATT.
BECAUSE MY LEFT SIDE HURTS.
BUT YOU'RE LETTING YOUR OPPONENT KNOW THAT. YOU SHOULD--
CHNG!
A GUN COCK. AN INHALE.
CLK
BANG!
PCHK!
STEADY. PERFECTLY AIMED TO MISS. A WARNING SHOT?
ACROSS THE STREET. TWO FLOORS DOWN.
SOME REAL-WORLD TRAINING.
ELEKTRA, WAIT!
I CAN'T GET A READ ON WHOEVER THE SHOOTER IS. SOMEONE FROM MY DAREDEVIL DAYS? DOESN'T SOUND LIKE BULLSEYE...
BETTER JOIN IN...

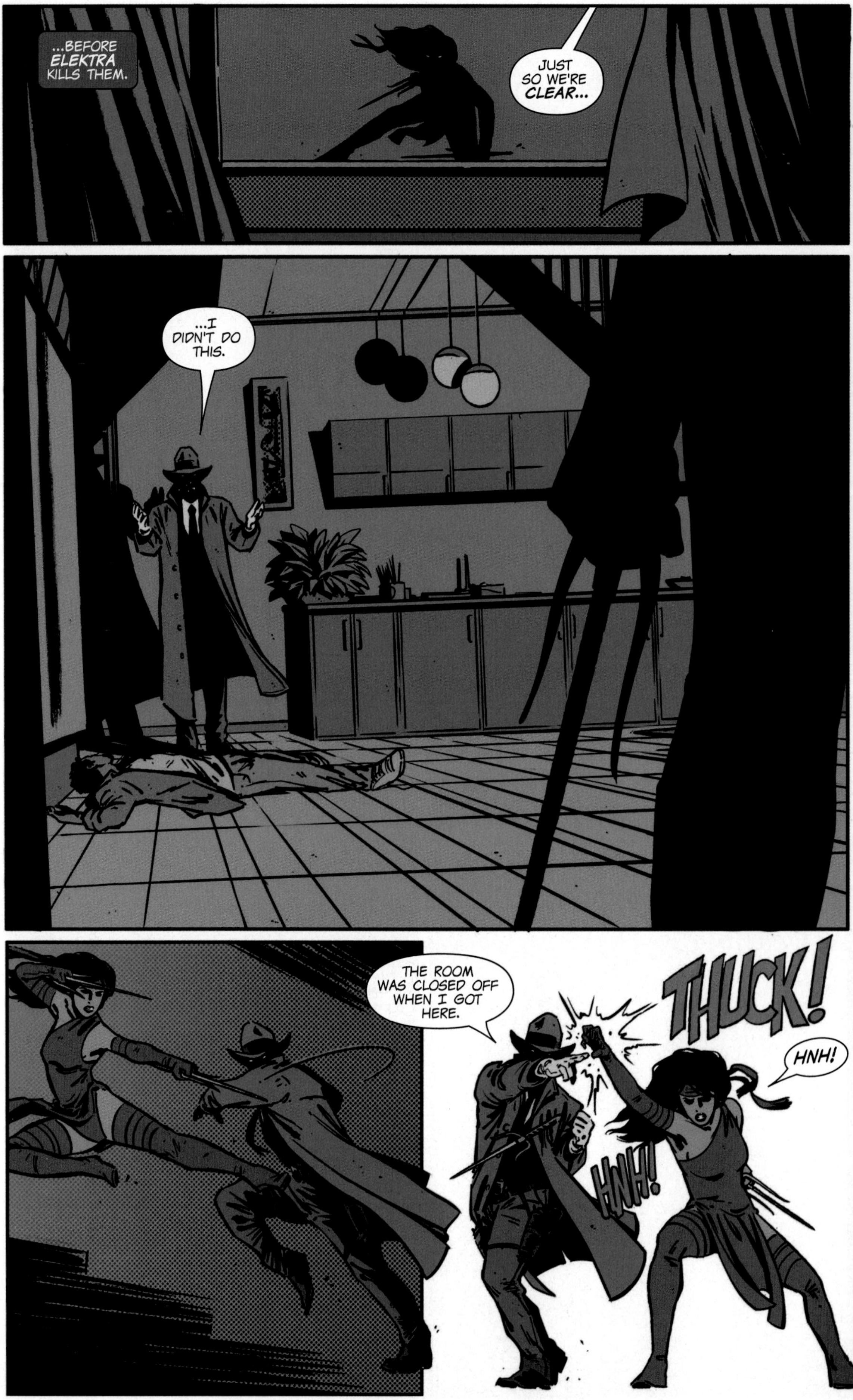
...BEFORE ELEKTRA KILLS THEM.
JUST SO WE'RE CLEAR...
...I DIDN'T DO THIS.
THE ROOM WAS CLOSED OFF WHEN I GOT HERE.
THUCK!
HNH!
HNH!

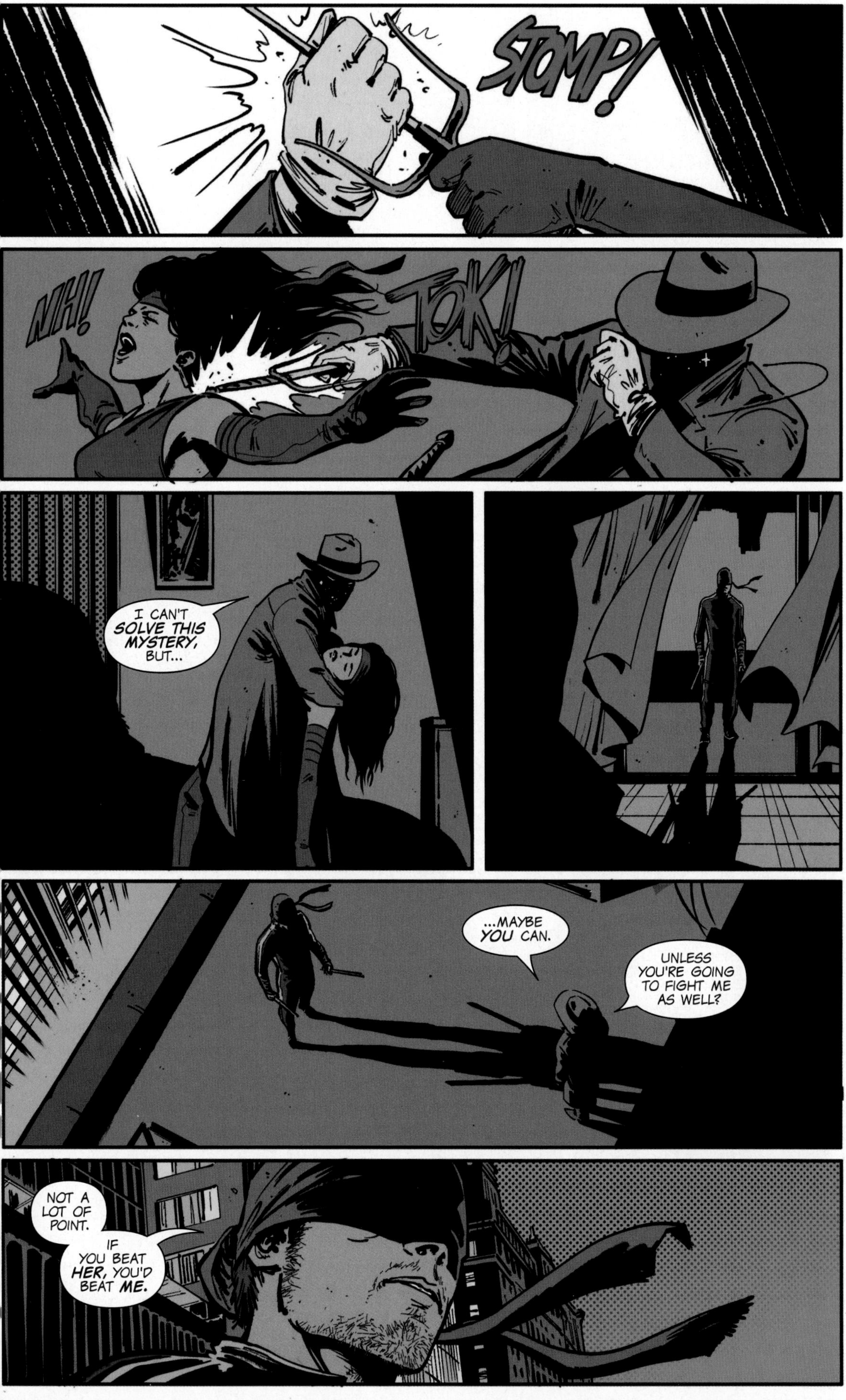
STOMP!
NH!
TOK!
I CAN'T SOLVE THIS MYSTERY, BUT...
...MAYBE YOU CAN.
UNLESS YOU'RE GOING TO FIGHT ME AS WELL?
NOT A LOT OF POINT.
IF YOU BEAT HER, YOU'D BEAT ME.

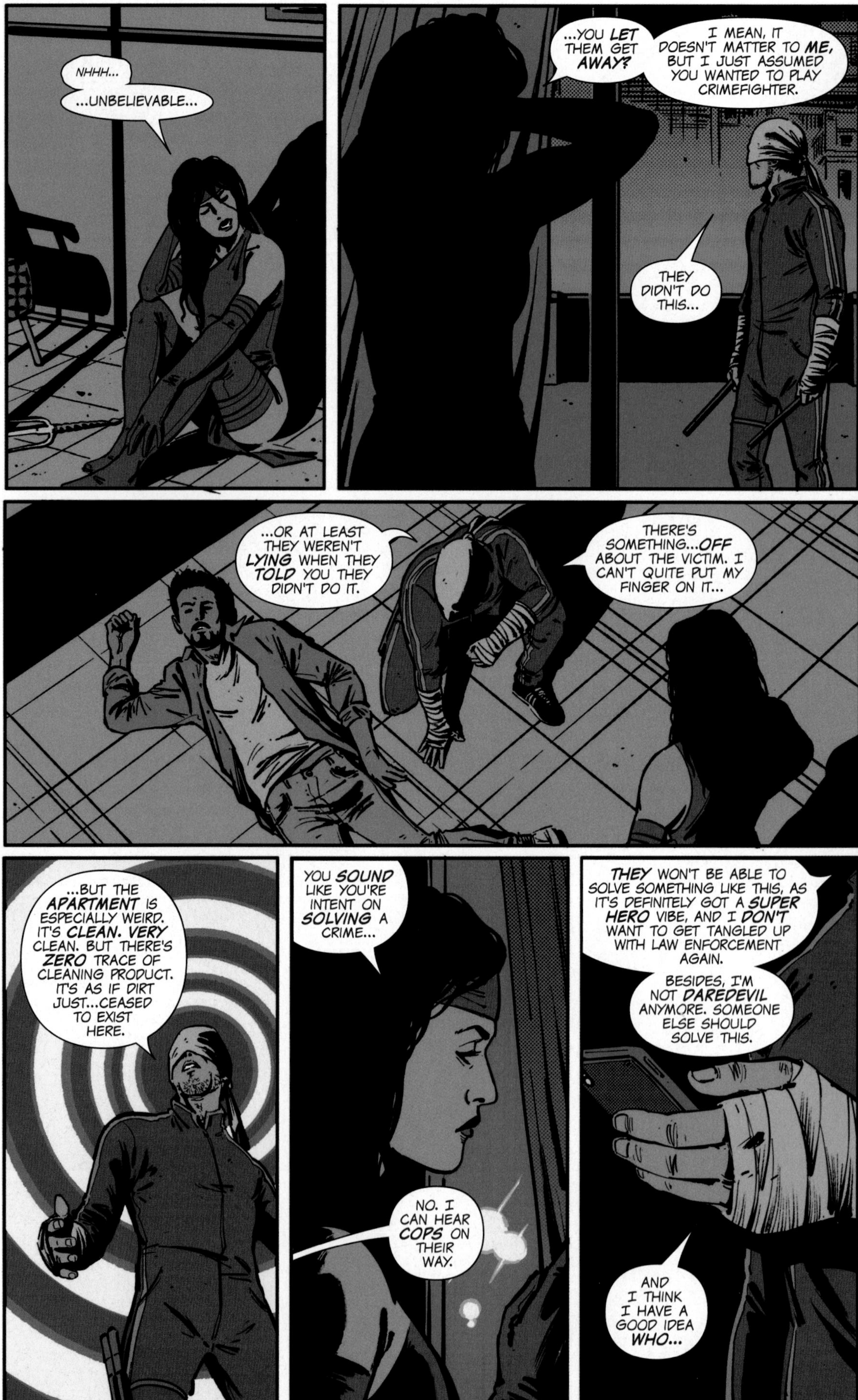
NHHH...
...UNBELIEVABLE...
...YOU LET THEM GET AWAY?
I MEAN, IT DOESN'T MATTER TO ME, BUT I JUST ASSUMED YOU WANTED TO PLAY CRIMEFIGHTER.
THEY DIDN'T DO THIS...
...OR AT LEAST THEY WEREN'T LYING WHEN THEY TOLD YOU THEY DIDN'T DO IT.
THERE'S SOMETHING...OFF ABOUT THE VICTIM. I CAN'T QUITE PUT MY FINGER ON IT...
...BUT THE APARTMENT IS ESPECIALLY WEIRD. IT'S CLEAN. VERY CLEAN. BUT THERE'S ZERO TRACE OF CLEANING PRODUCT. IT'S AS IF DIRT JUST...CEASED TO EXIST HERE.
YOU SOUND LIKE YOU'RE INTENT ON SOLVING A CRIME...
NO. I CAN HEAR COPS ON THEIR WAY.
THEY WON'T BE ABLE TO SOLVE SOMETHING LIKE THIS, AS IT'S DEFINITELY GOT A SUPER HERO VIBE, AND I DON'T WANT TO GET TANGLED UP WITH LAW ENFORCEMENT AGAIN.
BESIDES, I'M NOT DAREDEVIL ANYMORE. SOMEONE ELSE SHOULD SOLVE THIS.
AND I THINK I HAVE A GOOD IDEA WHO...

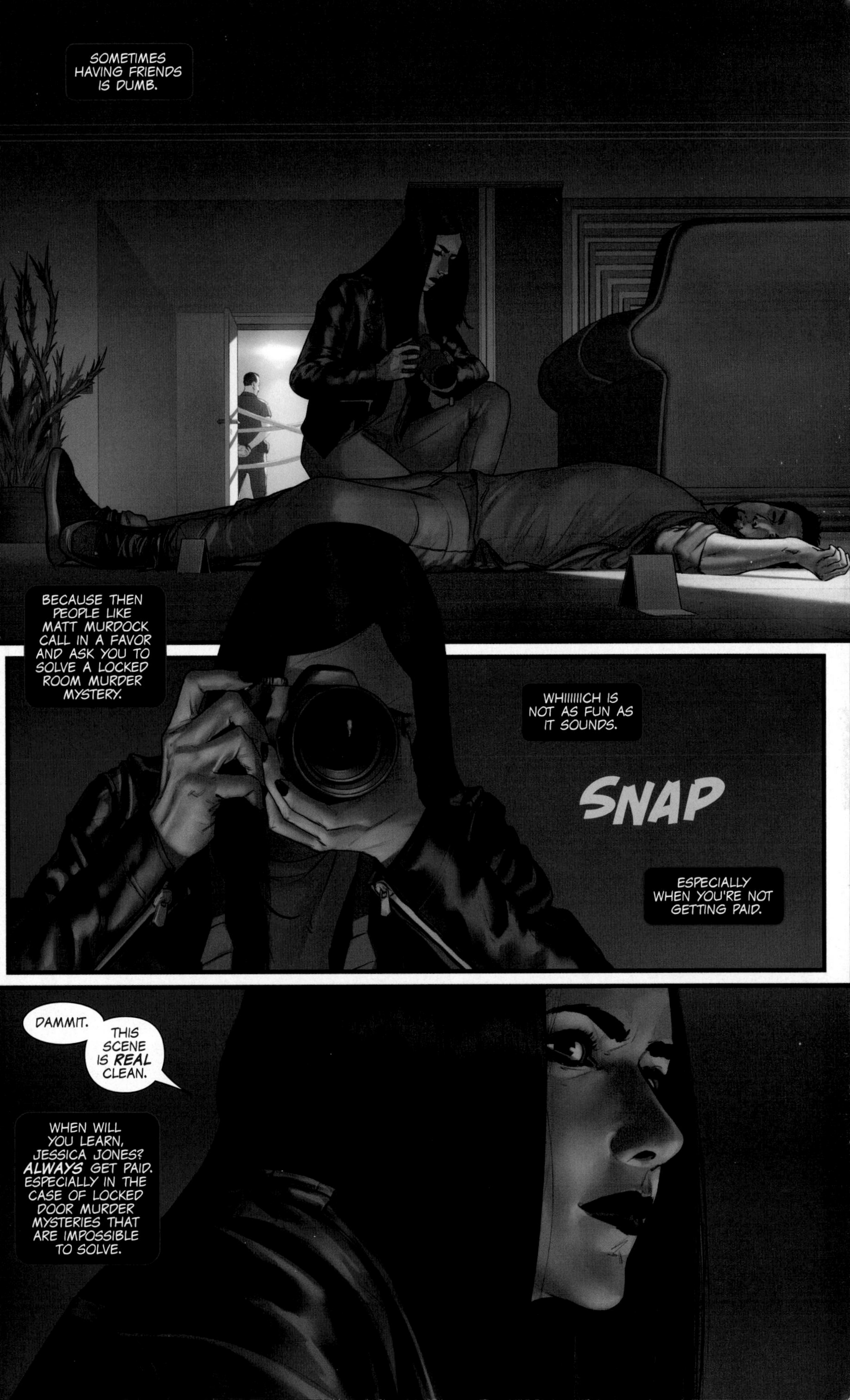
SOMETIMES HAVING FRIENDS IS DUMB.
BECAUSE THEN PEOPLE LIKE MATT MURDOCK CALL IN A FAVOR AND ASK YOU TO SOLVE A LOCKED ROOM MURDER MYSTERY.
WHIIIIIICH IS NOT AS FUN AS IT SOUNDS.
SNAP
ESPECIALLY WHEN YOU'RE NOT GETTING PAID.
DAMMIT.
THIS SCENE IS REAL CLEAN.
WHEN WILL YOU LEARN, JESSICA JONES? ALWAYS GET PAID. ESPECIALLY IN THE CASE OF LOCKED DOOR MURDER MYSTERIES THAT ARE IMPOSSIBLE TO SOLVE.

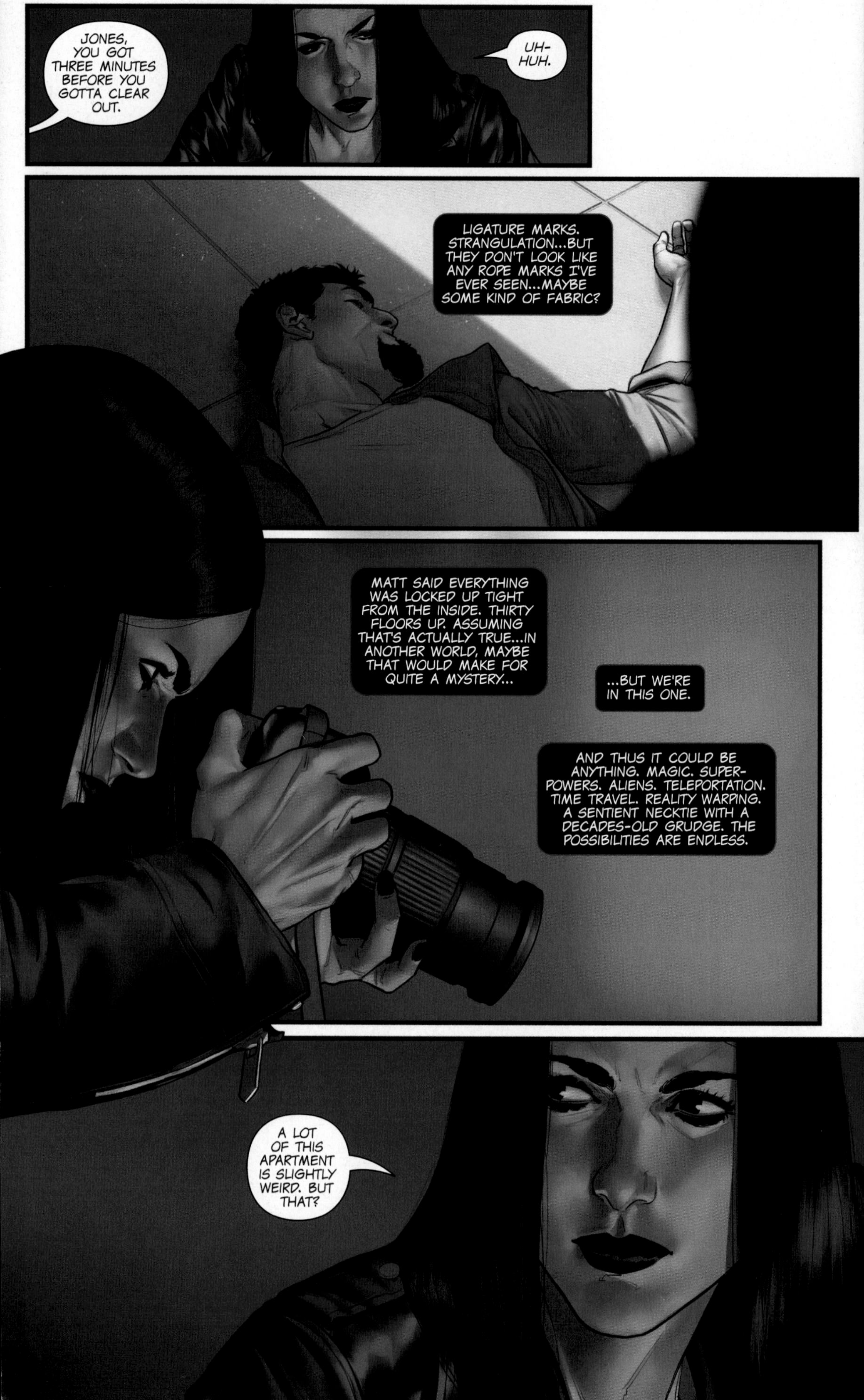
JONES, YOU GOT THREE MINUTES BEFORE YOU GOTTA CLEAR OUT.
UH-HUH.
LIGATURE MARKS. STRANGULATION...BUT THEY DON'T LOOK LIKE ANY ROPE MARKS I'VE EVER SEEN...MAYBE SOME KIND OF FABRIC?
MATT SAID EVERYTHING WAS LOCKED UP TIGHT FROM THE INSIDE. THIRTY FLOORS UP. ASSUMING THAT'S ACTUALLY TRUE...IN ANOTHER WORLD, MAYBE THAT WOULD MAKE FOR QUITE A MYSTERY...
...BUT WE'RE IN THIS ONE.
AND THUS IT COULD BE ANYTHING. MAGIC. SUPER-POWERS. ALIENS. TELEPORTATION. TIME TRAVEL. REALITY WARPING. A SENTIENT NECKTIE WITH A DECADES-OLD GRUDGE. THE POSSIBILITIES ARE ENDLESS.
A LOT OF THIS APARTMENT IS SLIGHTLY WEIRD. BUT THAT?

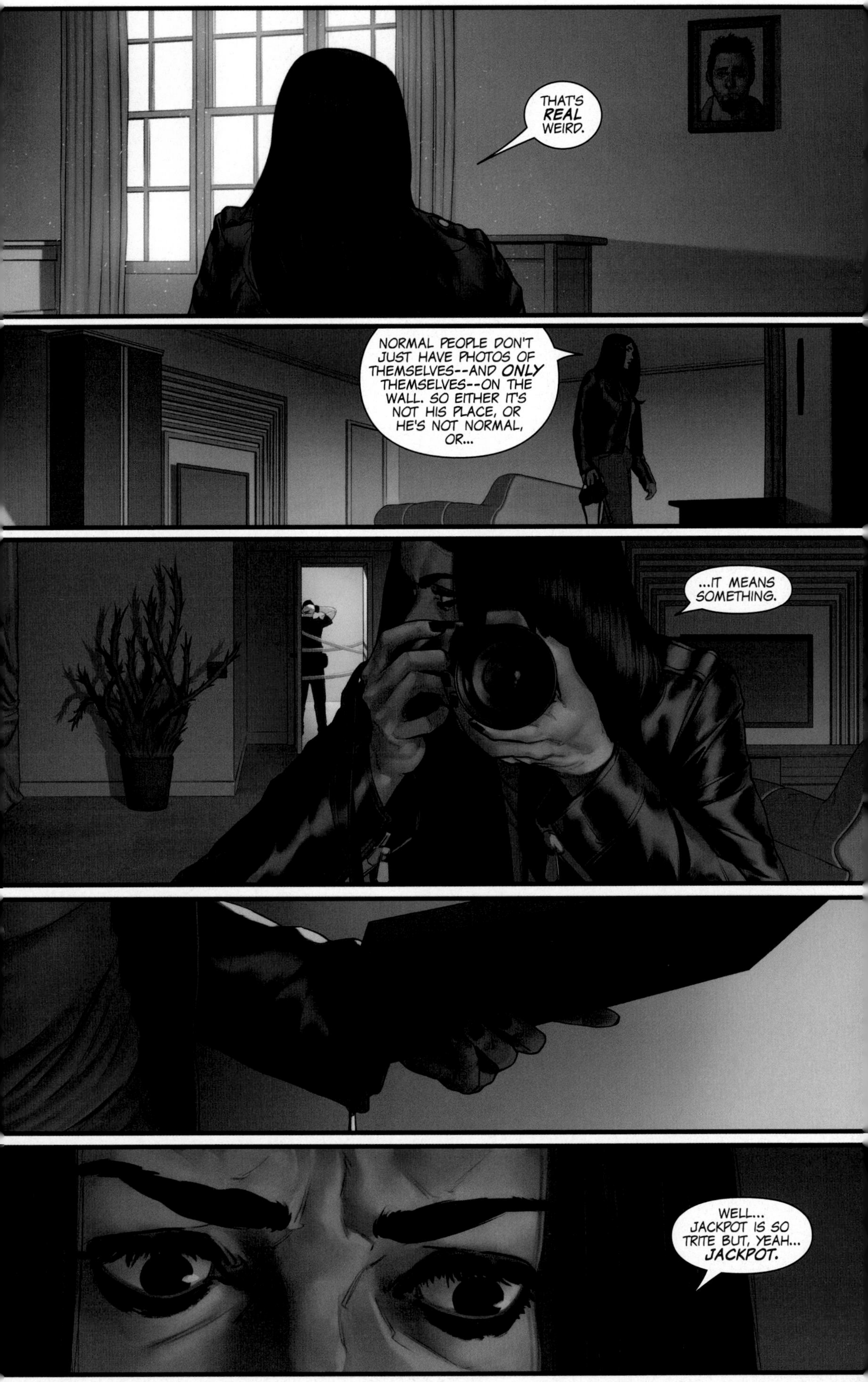
THAT'S REAL WEIRD.
NORMAL PEOPLE DON'T JUST HAVE PHOTOS OF THEMSELVES--AND ONLY THEMSELVES--ON THE WALL. SO EITHER IT'S NOT HIS PLACE, OR HE'S NOT NORMAL, OR...
...IT MEANS SOMETHING.
WELL... JACKPOT IS SO TRITE BUT, YEAH... JACKPOT.

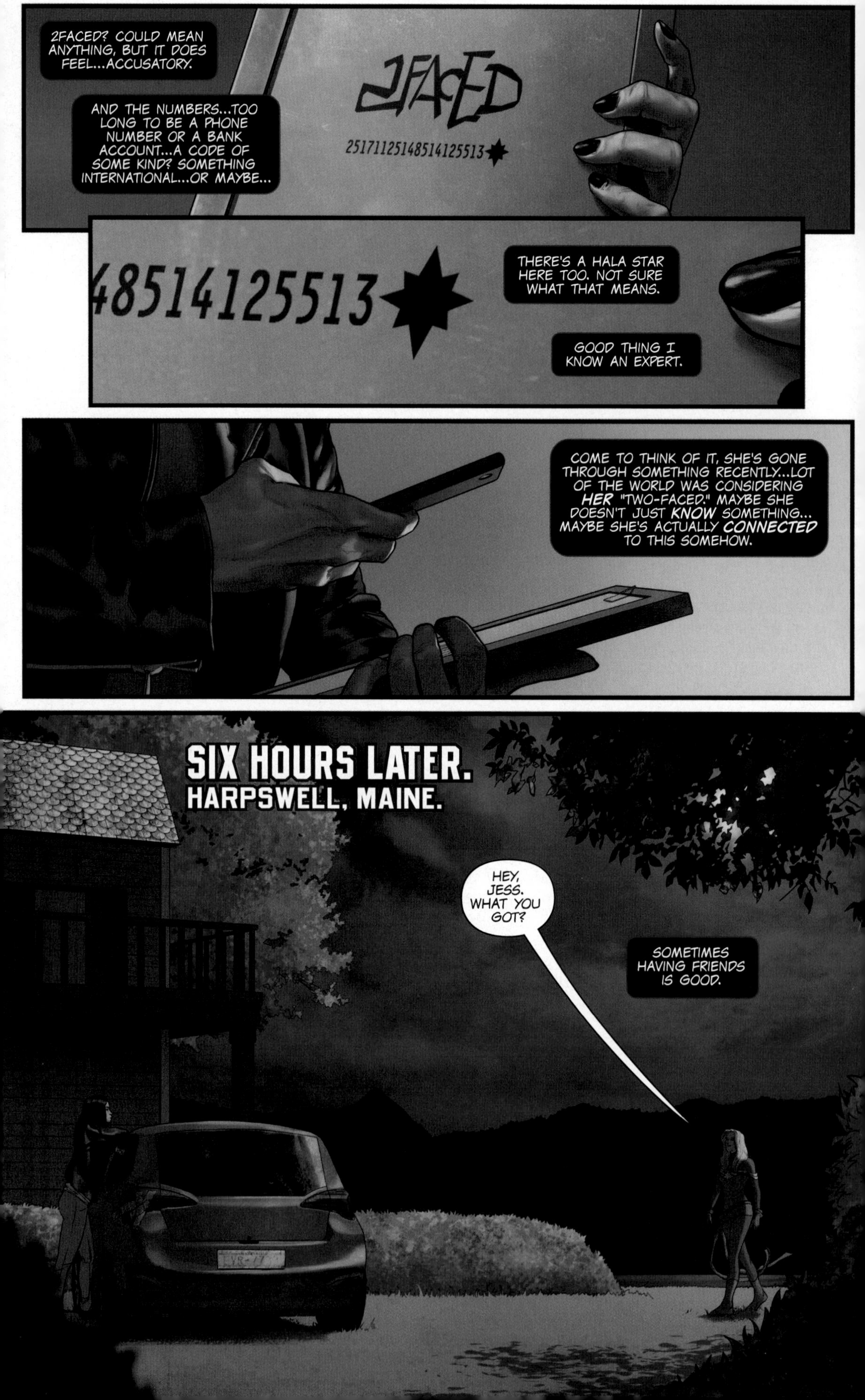

2FACED? COULD MEAN ANYTHING, BUT IT DOES FEEL...ACCUSATORY.
AND THE NUMBERS...TOO LONG TO BE A PHONE NUMBER OR A BANK ACCOUNT...A CODE OF SOME KIND? SOMETHING INTERNATIONAL...OR MAYBE...
2FACED
25171125148514125513
48514125513
THERE'S A HALA STAR HERE TOO. NOT SURE WHAT THAT MEANS.
GOOD THING I KNOW AN EXPERT.
COME TO THINK OF IT, SHE'S GONE THROUGH SOMETHING RECENTLY...LOT OF THE WORLD WAS CONSIDERING **HER** "TWO-FACED." MAYBE SHE DOESN'T JUST **KNOW** SOMETHING... MAYBE SHE'S ACTUALLY **CONNECTED** TO THIS SOMEHOW.
SIX HOURS LATER.
HARPSWELL, MAINE.
HEY, JESS. WHAT YOU GOT?
SOMETIMES HAVING FRIENDS IS GOOD.

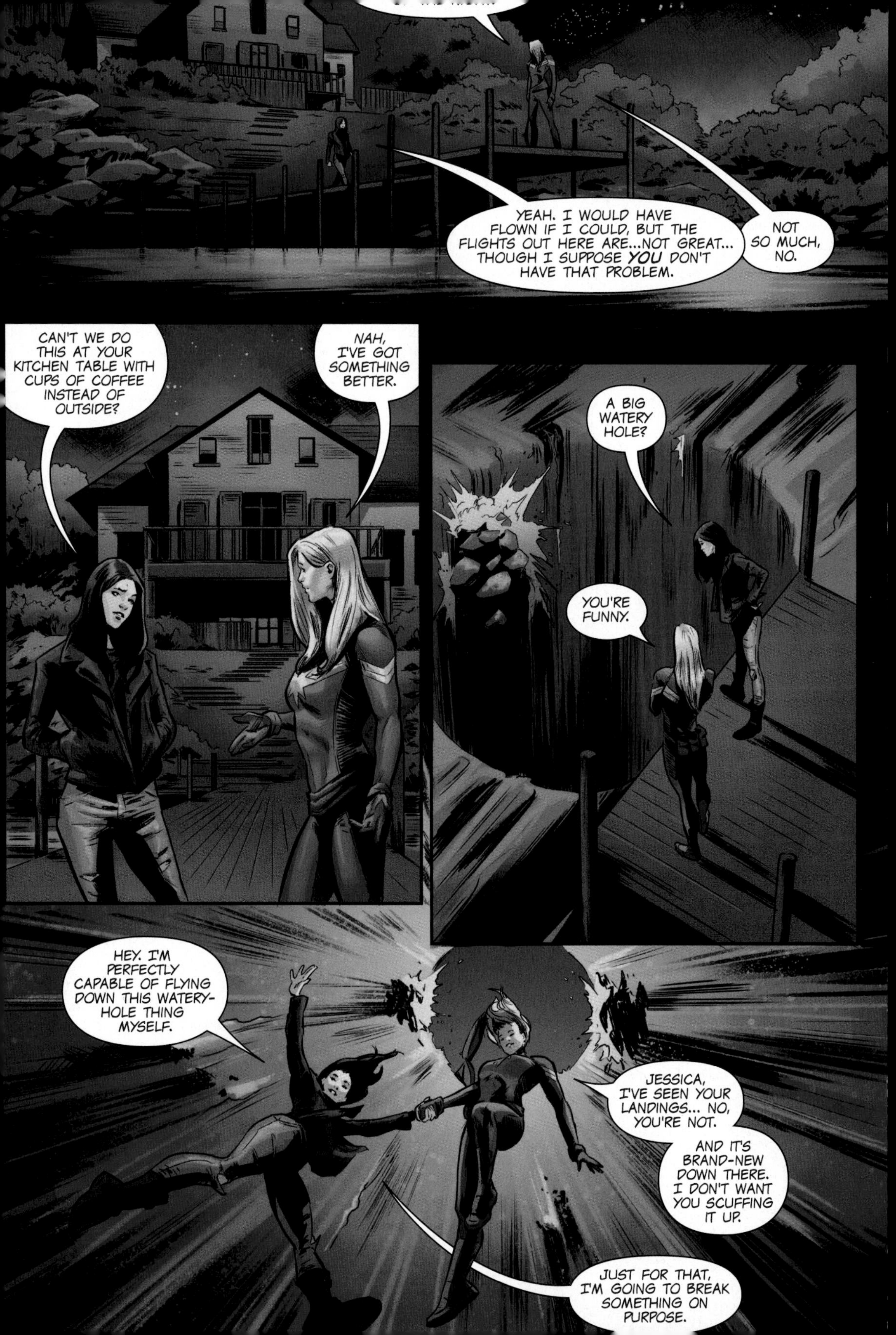
YEAH. I WOULD HAVE FLOWN IF I COULD, BUT THE FLIGHTS OUT HERE ARE...NOT GREAT... THOUGH I SUPPOSE *YOU* DON'T HAVE THAT PROBLEM.
NOT SO MUCH, NO.
CAN'T WE DO THIS AT YOUR KITCHEN TABLE WITH CUPS OF COFFEE INSTEAD OF OUTSIDE?
NAH, I'VE GOT SOMETHING BETTER.
A BIG WATERY HOLE?
YOU'RE FUNNY.
HEY. I'M PERFECTLY CAPABLE OF FLYING DOWN THIS WATERY-HOLE THING MYSELF.
JESSICA, I'VE SEEN YOUR LANDINGS... NO, YOU'RE NOT.
AND IT'S BRAND-NEW DOWN THERE. I DON'T WANT YOU SCUFFING IT UP.
JUST FOR THAT, I'M GOING TO BREAK SOMETHING ON PURPOSE.

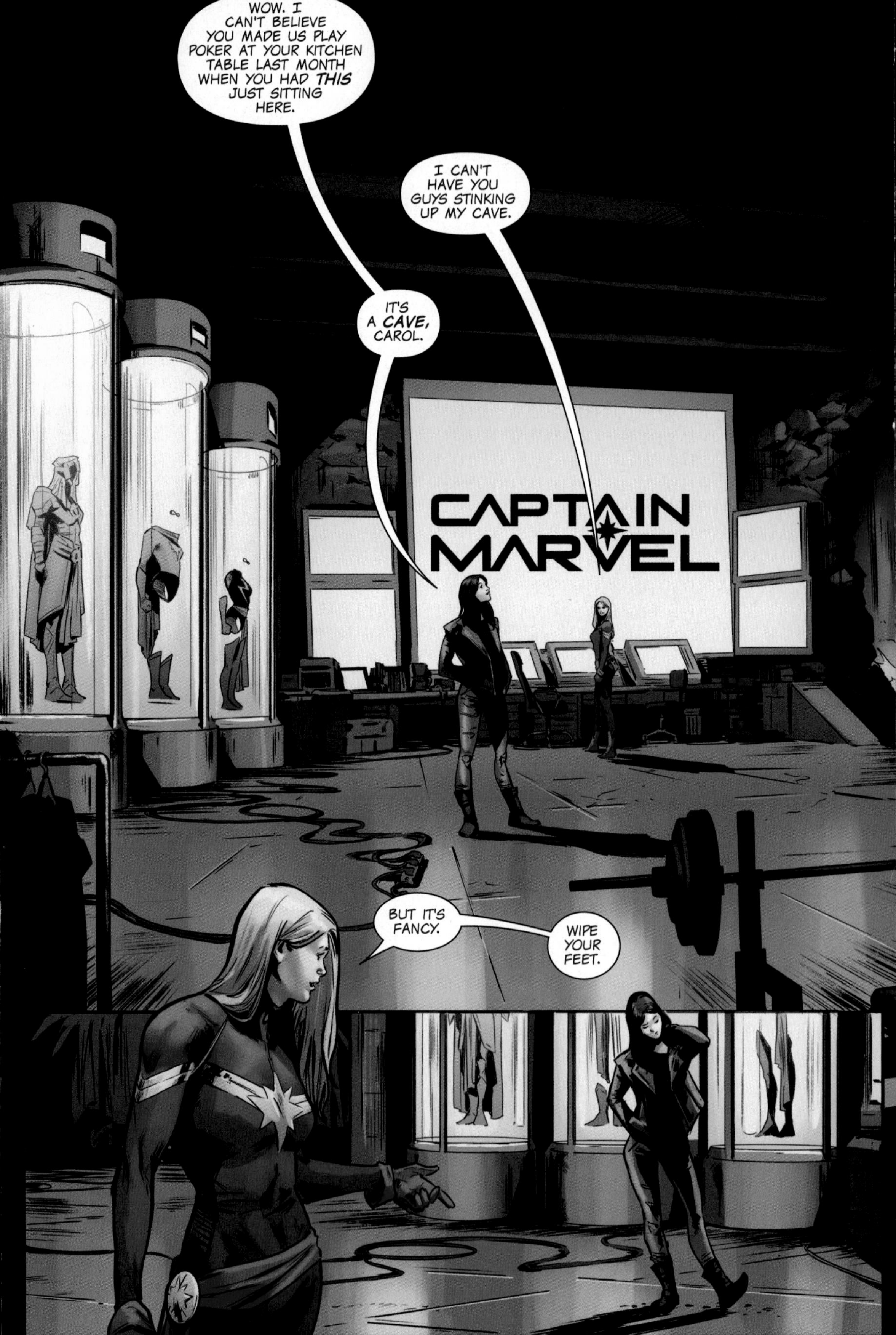
WOW. I CAN'T BELIEVE YOU MADE US PLAY POKER AT YOUR KITCHEN TABLE LAST MONTH WHEN YOU HAD **THIS** JUST SITTING HERE.
I CAN'T HAVE YOU GUYS STINKING UP MY CAVE.
IT'S A **CAVE,** CAROL.
CAPTAIN MARVEL
BUT IT'S FANCY.
WIPE YOUR FEET.

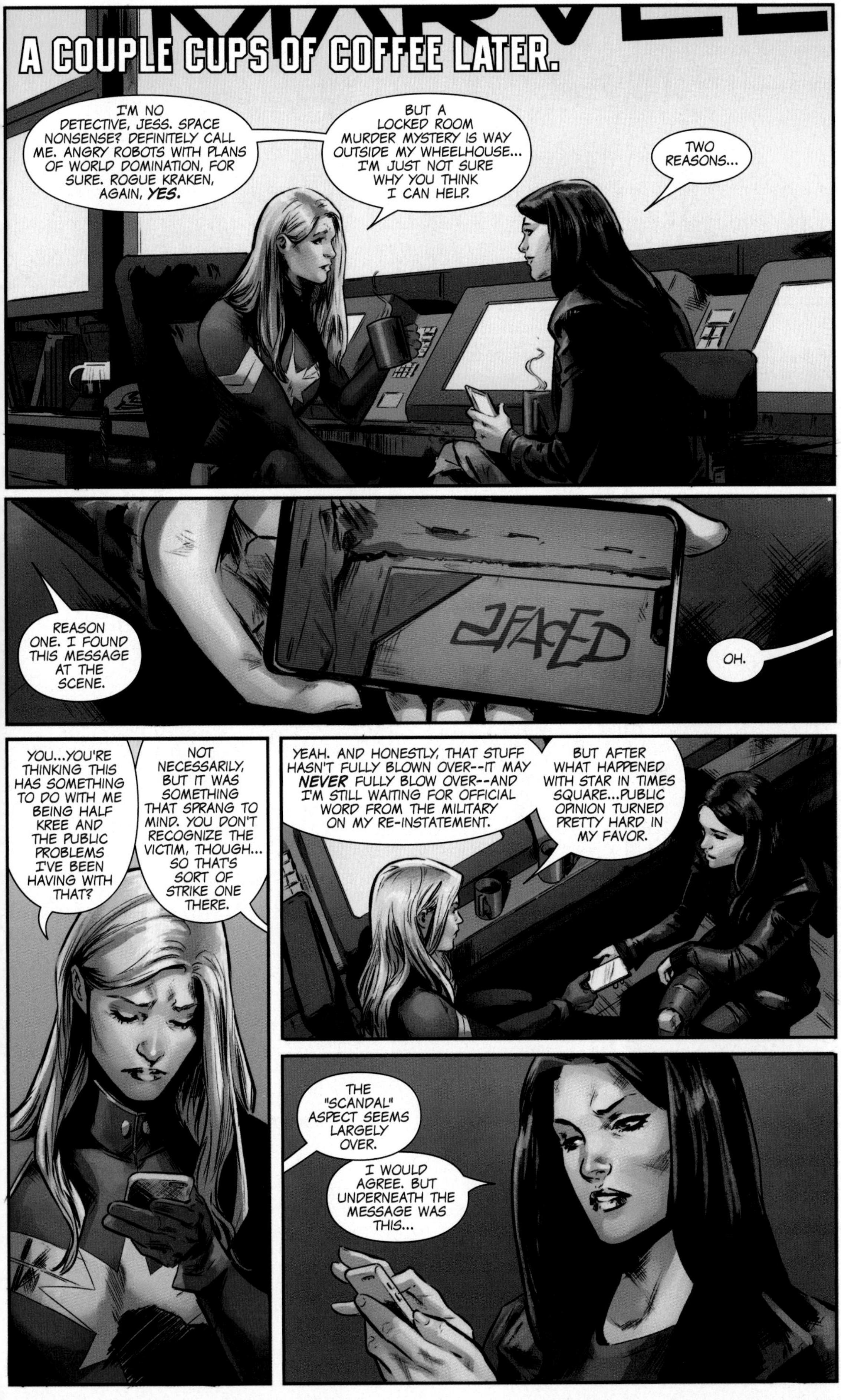
A COUPLE CUPS OF COFFEE LATER.
I'M NO DETECTIVE, JESS. SPACE NONSENSE? DEFINITELY CALL ME. ANGRY ROBOTS WITH PLANS OF WORLD DOMINATION, FOR SURE. ROGUE KRAKEN, AGAIN, YES.
BUT A LOCKED ROOM MURDER MYSTERY IS WAY OUTSIDE MY WHEELHOUSE... I'M JUST NOT SURE WHY YOU THINK I CAN HELP.
TWO REASONS...
REASON ONE. I FOUND THIS MESSAGE AT THE SCENE.
2FACED
OH.
YOU...YOU'RE THINKING THIS HAS SOMETHING TO DO WITH ME BEING HALF KREE AND THE PUBLIC PROBLEMS I'VE BEEN HAVING WITH THAT?
NOT NECESSARILY, BUT IT WAS SOMETHING THAT SPRANG TO MIND. YOU DON'T RECOGNIZE THE VICTIM, THOUGH... SO THAT'S SORT OF STRIKE ONE THERE.
YEAH. AND HONESTLY, THAT STUFF HASN'T FULLY BLOWN OVER--IT MAY NEVER FULLY BLOW OVER--AND I'M STILL WAITING FOR OFFICIAL WORD FROM THE MILITARY ON MY RE-INSTATEMENT.
BUT AFTER WHAT HAPPENED WITH STAR IN TIMES SQUARE...PUBLIC OPINION TURNED PRETTY HARD IN MY FAVOR.
THE "SCANDAL" ASPECT SEEMS LARGELY OVER.
I WOULD AGREE. BUT UNDERNEATH THE MESSAGE WAS THIS...

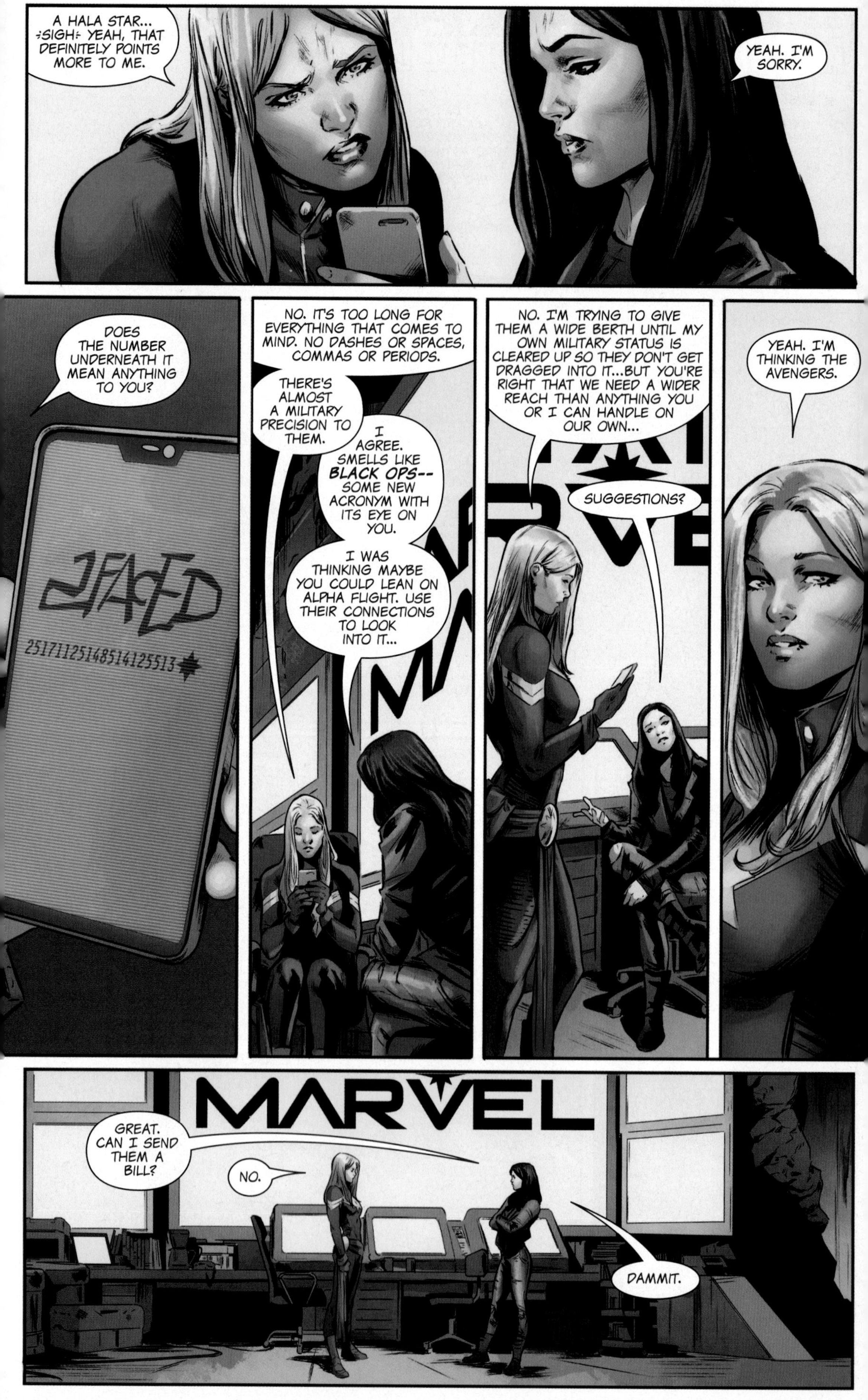
A HALA STAR... ⸗SIGH⸗ YEAH, THAT DEFINITELY POINTS MORE TO ME.
YEAH. I'M SORRY.
DOES THE NUMBER UNDERNEATH IT MEAN ANYTHING TO YOU?
2FACED
25171125148514125513
NO. IT'S TOO LONG FOR EVERYTHING THAT COMES TO MIND. NO DASHES OR SPACES, COMMAS OR PERIODS.
THERE'S ALMOST A MILITARY PRECISION TO THEM.
I AGREE. SMELLS LIKE BLACK OPS-- SOME NEW ACRONYM WITH ITS EYE ON YOU.
I WAS THINKING MAYBE YOU COULD LEAN ON ALPHA FLIGHT. USE THEIR CONNECTIONS TO LOOK INTO IT...
NO. I'M TRYING TO GIVE THEM A WIDE BERTH UNTIL MY OWN MILITARY STATUS IS CLEARED UP SO THEY DON'T GET DRAGGED INTO IT...BUT YOU'RE RIGHT THAT WE NEED A WIDER REACH THAN ANYTHING YOU OR I CAN HANDLE ON OUR OWN...
SUGGESTIONS?
YEAH. I'M THINKING THE AVENGERS.
MARVEL
GREAT. CAN I SEND THEM A BILL?
NO.
DAMMIT.

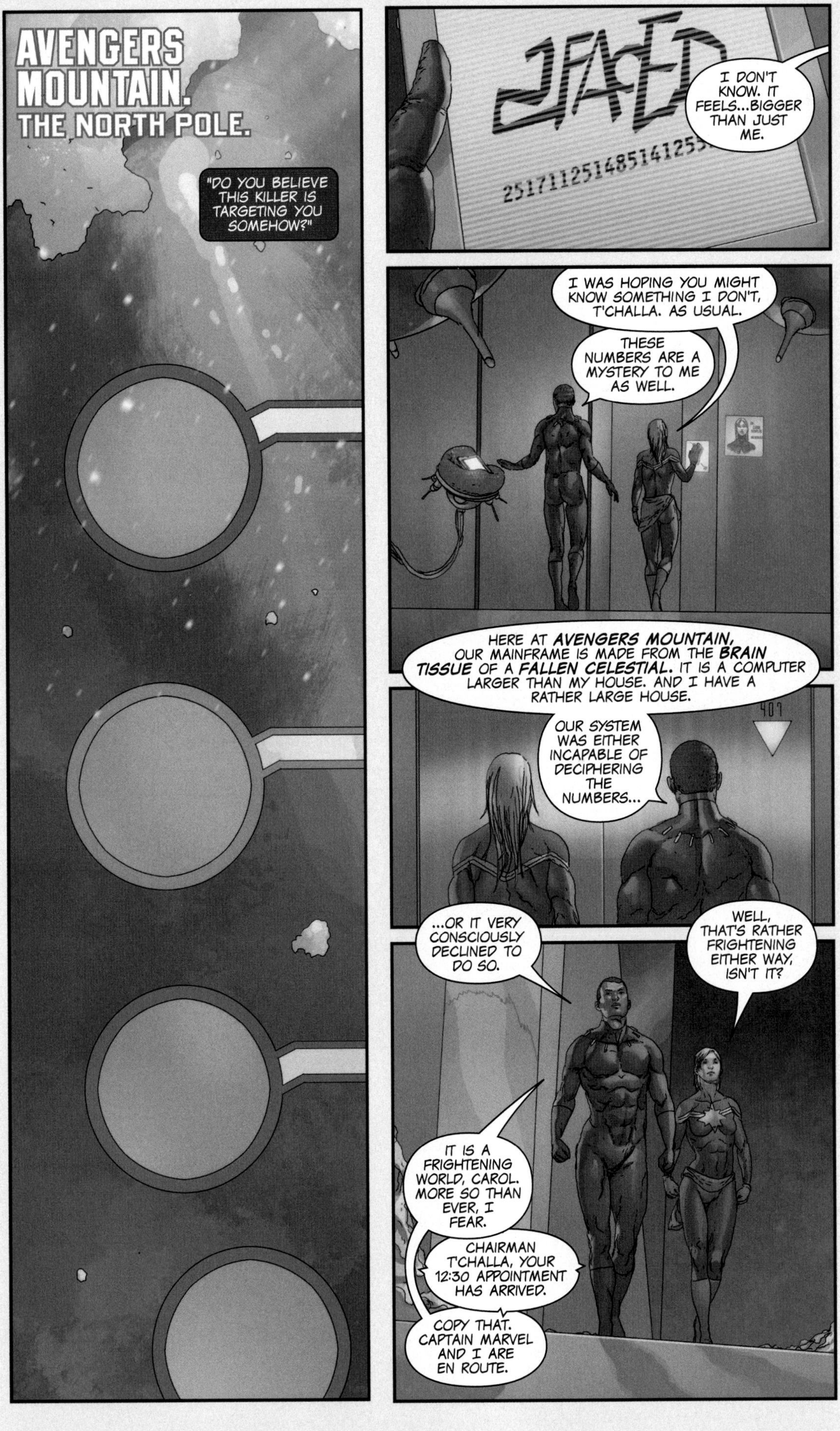

AVENGERS MOUNTAIN.
THE NORTH POLE.
"DO YOU BELIEVE THIS KILLER IS TARGETING YOU SOMEHOW?"
I DON'T KNOW. IT FEELS...BIGGER THAN JUST ME.
I WAS HOPING YOU MIGHT KNOW SOMETHING I DON'T, T'CHALLA. AS USUAL.
THESE NUMBERS ARE A MYSTERY TO ME AS WELL.
HERE AT AVENGERS MOUNTAIN, OUR MAINFRAME IS MADE FROM THE BRAIN TISSUE OF A FALLEN CELESTIAL. IT IS A COMPUTER LARGER THAN MY HOUSE. AND I HAVE A RATHER LARGE HOUSE.
OUR SYSTEM WAS EITHER INCAPABLE OF DECIPHERING THE NUMBERS...
...OR IT VERY CONSCIOUSLY DECLINED TO DO SO.
WELL, THAT'S RATHER FRIGHTENING EITHER WAY, ISN'T IT?
IT IS A FRIGHTENING WORLD, CAROL. MORE SO THAN EVER, I FEAR.
CHAIRMAN T'CHALLA, YOUR 12:30 APPOINTMENT HAS ARRIVED.
COPY THAT. CAPTAIN MARVEL AND I ARE EN ROUTE.

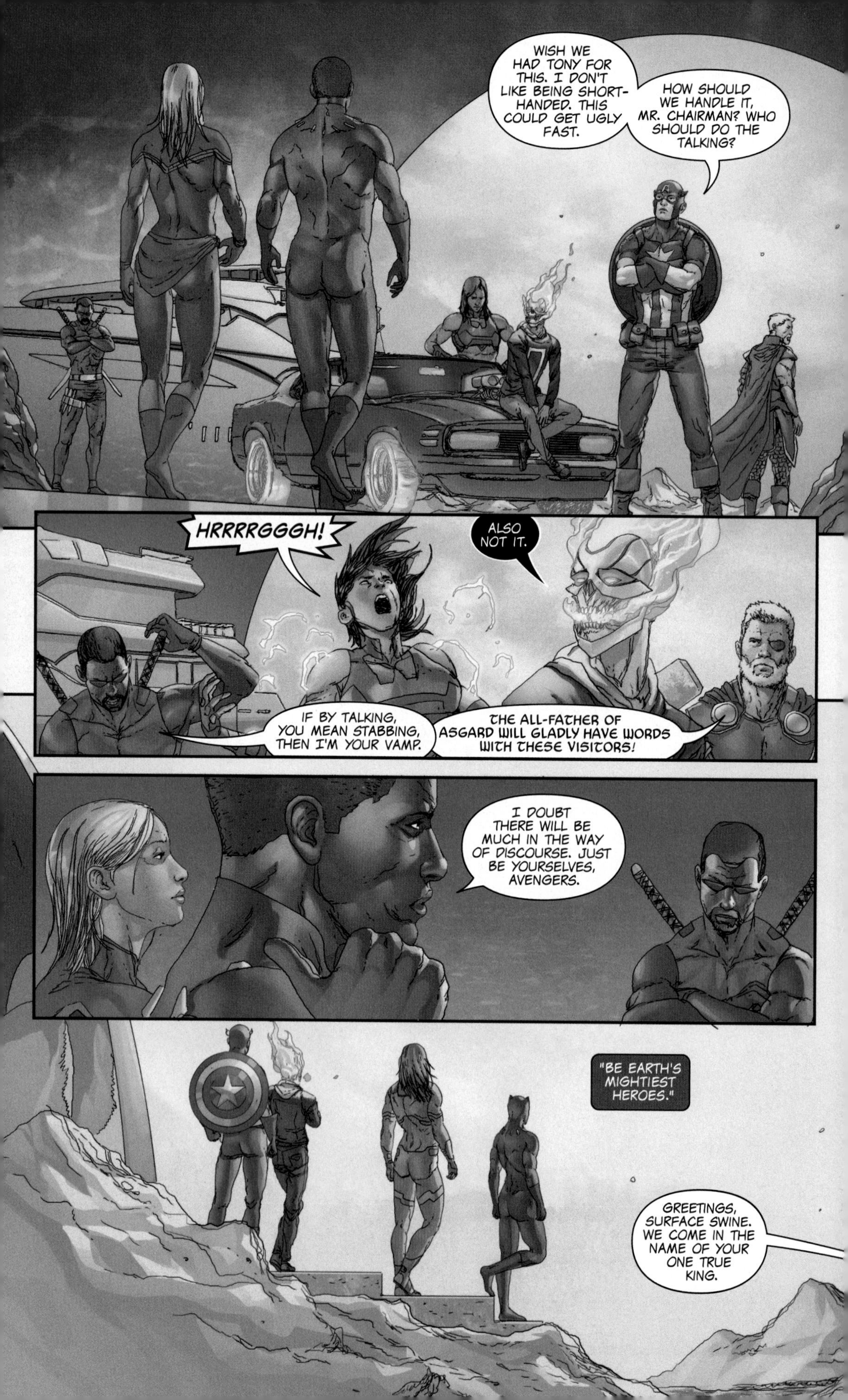
WISH WE HAD TONY FOR THIS. I DON'T LIKE BEING SHORT-HANDED. THIS COULD GET UGLY FAST.
HOW SHOULD WE HANDLE IT, MR. CHAIRMAN? WHO SHOULD DO THE TALKING?
HRRRRGGGH!
ALSO NOT IT.
IF BY TALKING, YOU MEAN STABBING, THEN I'M YOUR VAMP.
THE ALL-FATHER OF ASGARD WILL GLADLY HAVE WORDS WITH THESE VISITORS!
I DOUBT THERE WILL BE MUCH IN THE WAY OF DISCOURSE. JUST BE YOURSELVES, AVENGERS.
"BE EARTH'S MIGHTIEST HEROES."
GREETINGS, SURFACE SWINE. WE COME IN THE NAME OF YOUR ONE TRUE KING.

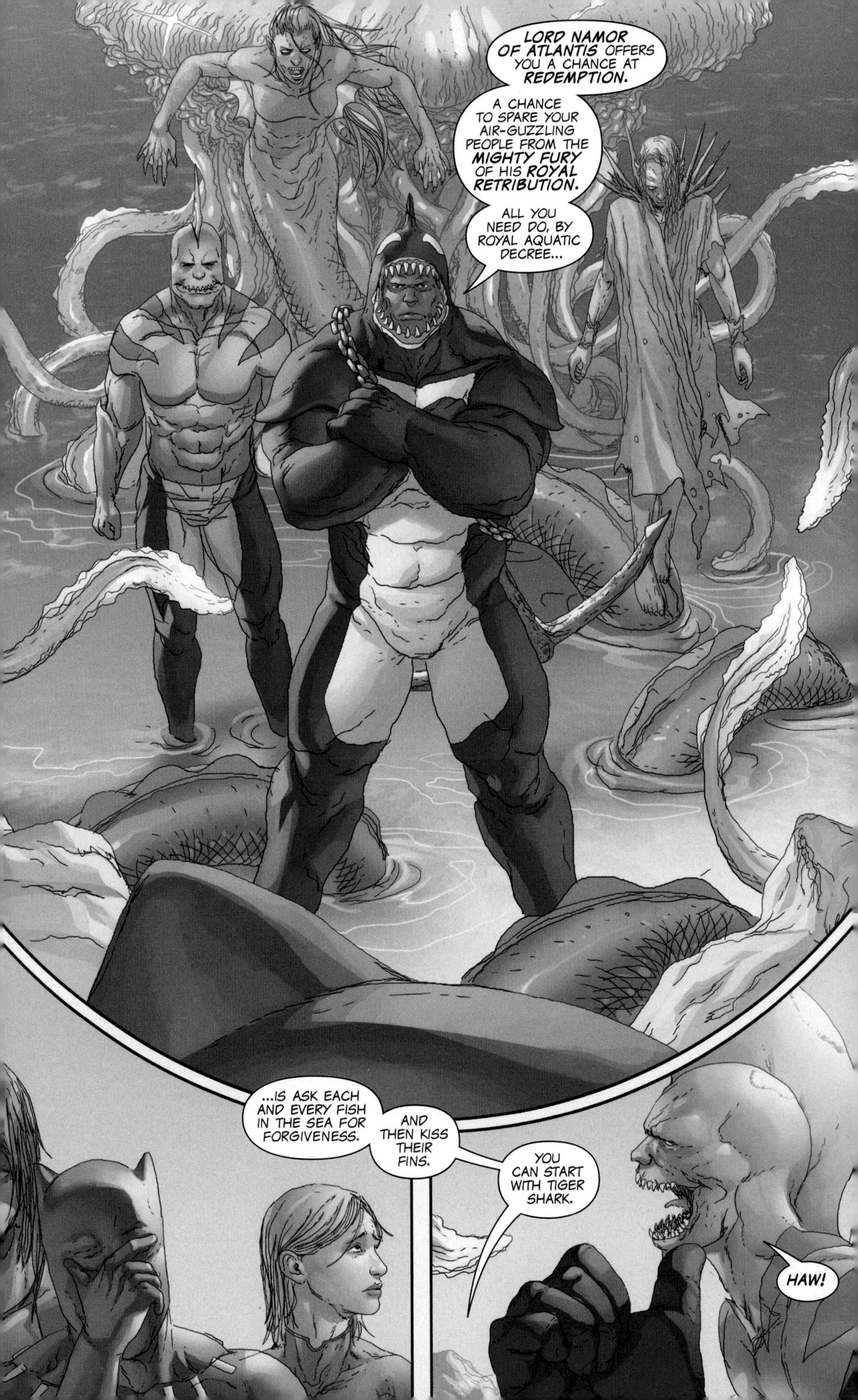
LORD NAMOR OF ATLANTIS OFFERS YOU A CHANCE AT REDEMPTION.
A CHANCE TO SPARE YOUR AIR-GUZZLING PEOPLE FROM THE MIGHTY FURY OF HIS ROYAL RETRIBUTION.
ALL YOU NEED DO, BY ROYAL AQUATIC DECREE...
...IS ASK EACH AND EVERY FISH IN THE SEA FOR FORGIVENESS.
AND THEN KISS THEIR FINS.
YOU CAN START WITH TIGER SHARK.
HAW!

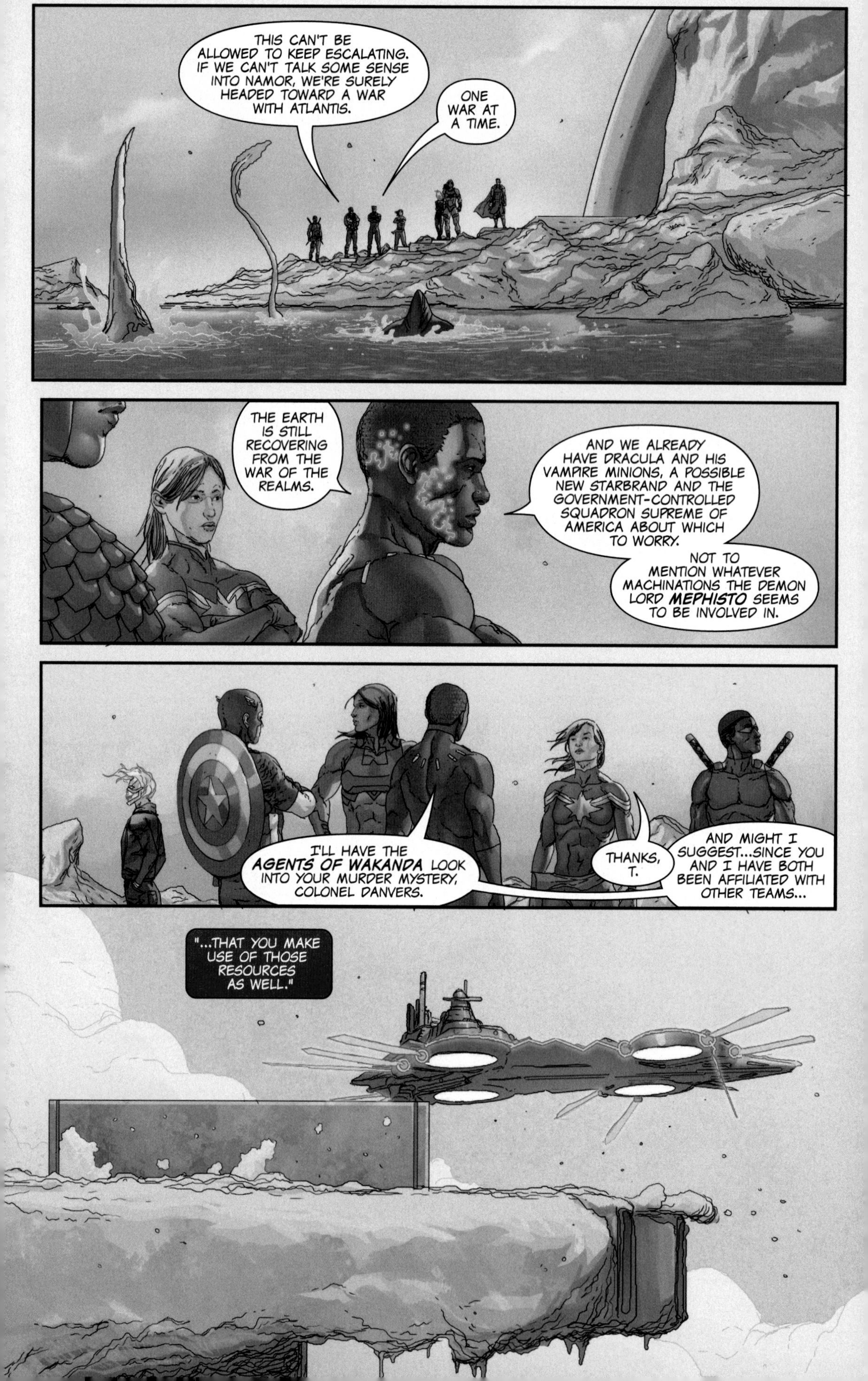
THIS CAN'T BE ALLOWED TO KEEP ESCALATING. IF WE CAN'T TALK SOME SENSE INTO NAMOR, WE'RE SURELY HEADED TOWARD A WAR WITH ATLANTIS.
ONE WAR AT A TIME.
THE EARTH IS STILL RECOVERING FROM THE WAR OF THE REALMS.
AND WE ALREADY HAVE DRACULA AND HIS VAMPIRE MINIONS, A POSSIBLE NEW STARBRAND AND THE GOVERNMENT-CONTROLLED SQUADRON SUPREME OF AMERICA ABOUT WHICH TO WORRY.
NOT TO MENTION WHATEVER MACHINATIONS THE DEMON LORD MEPHISTO SEEMS TO BE INVOLVED IN.
I'LL HAVE THE AGENTS OF WAKANDA LOOK INTO YOUR MURDER MYSTERY, COLONEL DANVERS.
THANKS, T.
AND MIGHT I SUGGEST...SINCE YOU AND I HAVE BOTH BEEN AFFILIATED WITH OTHER TEAMS...
"...THAT YOU MAKE USE OF THOSE RESOURCES AS WELL."

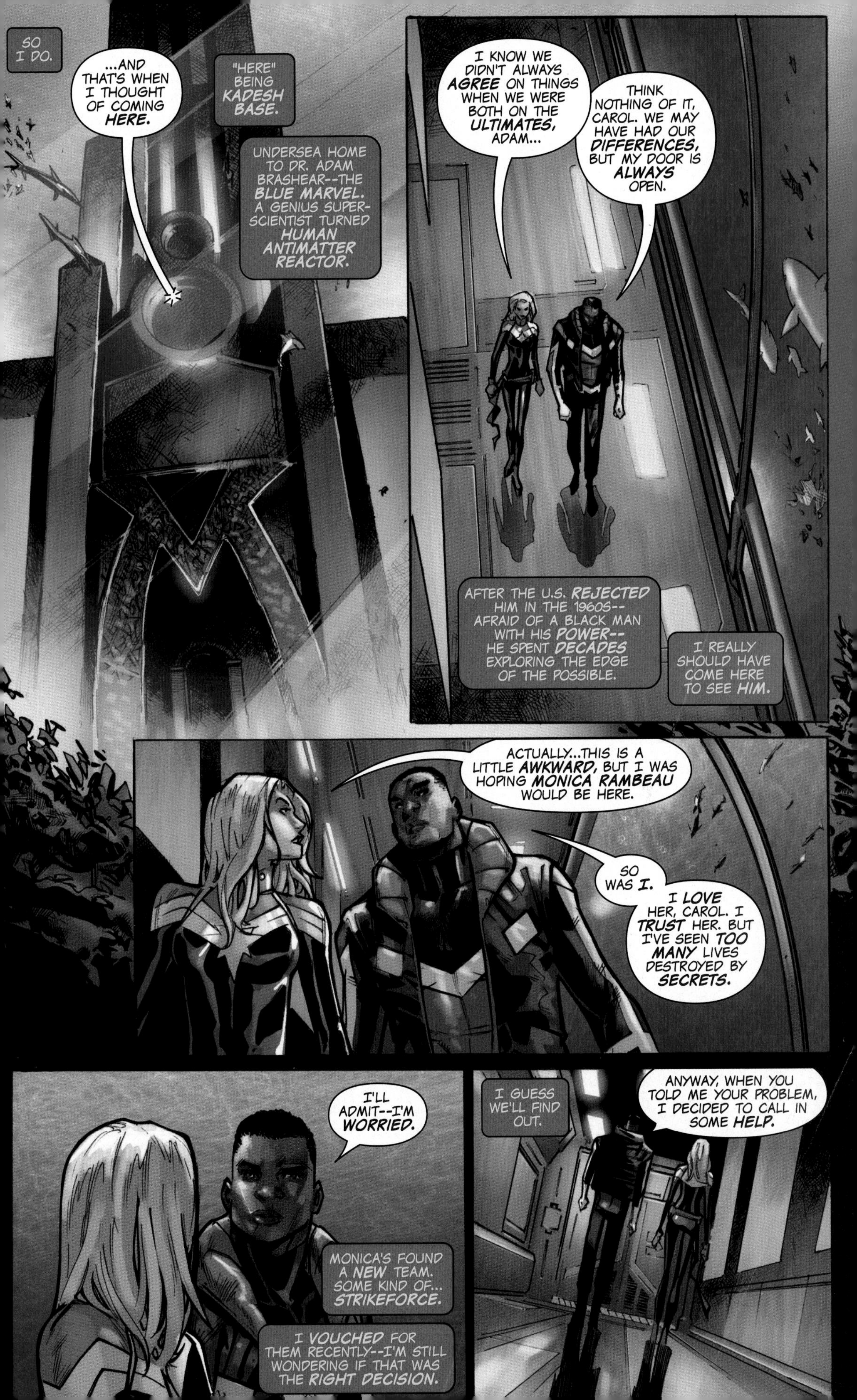
SO I DO.
...AND THAT'S WHEN I THOUGHT OF COMING HERE.
"HERE" BEING KADESH BASE.
UNDERSEA HOME TO DR. ADAM BRASHEAR--THE BLUE MARVEL. A GENIUS SUPER-SCIENTIST TURNED HUMAN ANTIMATTER REACTOR.
I KNOW WE DIDN'T ALWAYS AGREE ON THINGS WHEN WE WERE BOTH ON THE ULTIMATES, ADAM...
THINK NOTHING OF IT, CAROL. WE MAY HAVE HAD OUR DIFFERENCES, BUT MY DOOR IS ALWAYS OPEN.
AFTER THE U.S. REJECTED HIM IN THE 1960S-- AFRAID OF A BLACK MAN WITH HIS POWER-- HE SPENT DECADES EXPLORING THE EDGE OF THE POSSIBLE.
I REALLY SHOULD HAVE COME HERE TO SEE HIM.
ACTUALLY...THIS IS A LITTLE AWKWARD, BUT I WAS HOPING MONICA RAMBEAU WOULD BE HERE.
SO WAS I.
I LOVE HER, CAROL. I TRUST HER. BUT I'VE SEEN TOO MANY LIVES DESTROYED BY SECRETS.
I'LL ADMIT--I'M WORRIED.
MONICA'S FOUND A NEW TEAM. SOME KIND OF... STRIKEFORCE.
I VOUCHED FOR THEM RECENTLY--I'M STILL WONDERING IF THAT WAS THE RIGHT DECISION.
I GUESS WE'LL FIND OUT.
ANYWAY, WHEN YOU TOLD ME YOUR PROBLEM, I DECIDED TO CALL IN SOME HELP.

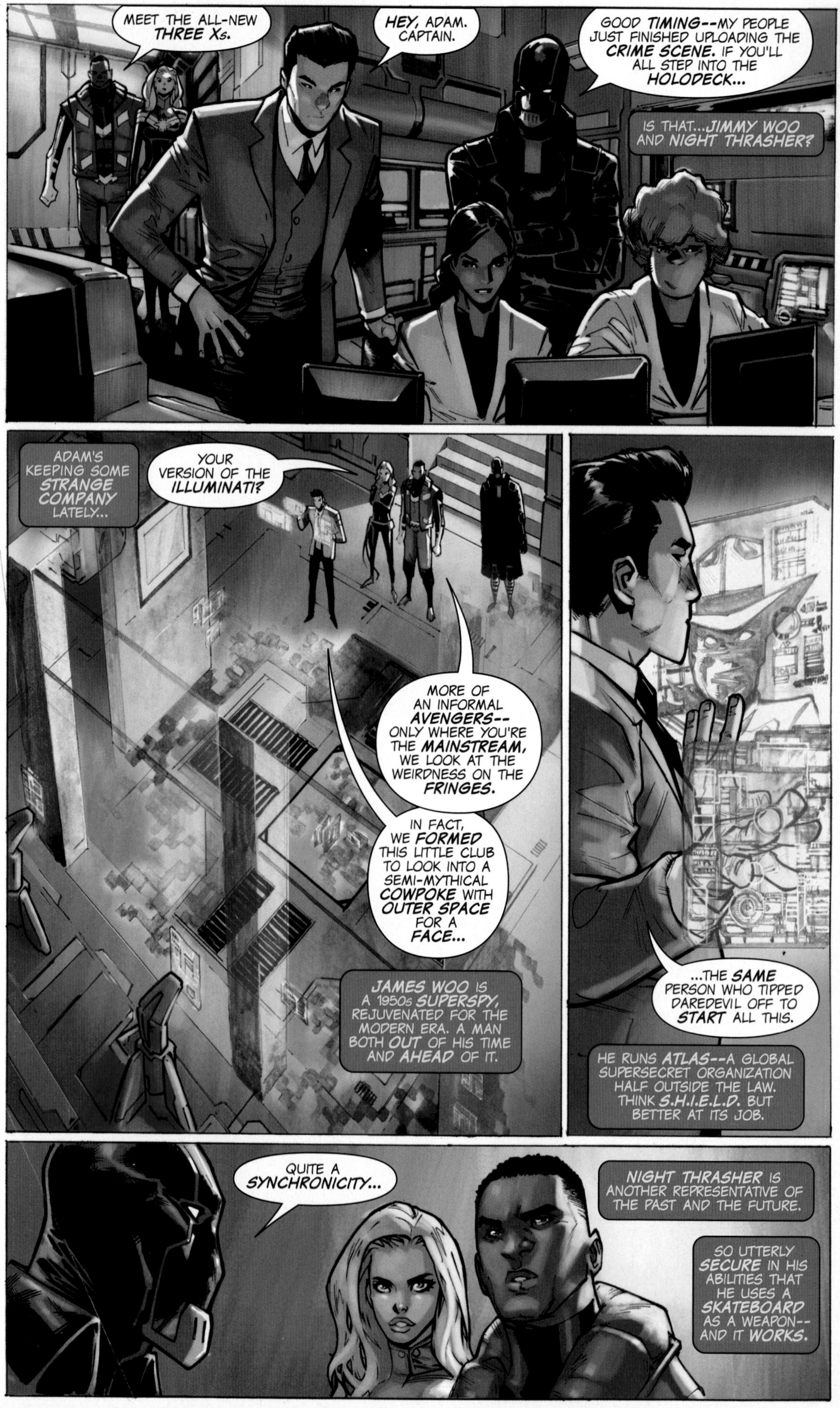

MEET THE ALL-NEW THREE Xs.
HEY, ADAM. CAPTAIN.
GOOD TIMING--MY PEOPLE JUST FINISHED UPLOADING THE CRIME SCENE. IF YOU'LL ALL STEP INTO THE HOLODECK...
IS THAT...JIMMY WOO AND NIGHT THRASHER?
ADAM'S KEEPING SOME STRANGE COMPANY LATELY...
YOUR VERSION OF THE ILLUMINATI?
MORE OF AN INFORMAL AVENGERS--ONLY WHERE YOU'RE THE MAINSTREAM, WE LOOK AT THE WEIRDNESS ON THE FRINGES.
IN FACT, WE FORMED THIS LITTLE CLUB TO LOOK INTO A SEMI-MYTHICAL COWPOKE WITH OUTER SPACE FOR A FACE...
JAMES WOO IS A 1950s SUPERSPY, REJUVENATED FOR THE MODERN ERA. A MAN BOTH OUT OF HIS TIME AND AHEAD OF IT.
...THE SAME PERSON WHO TIPPED DAREDEVIL OFF TO START ALL THIS.
HE RUNS ATLAS--A GLOBAL SUPERSECRET ORGANIZATION HALF OUTSIDE THE LAW. THINK S.H.I.E.L.D. BUT BETTER AT ITS JOB.
QUITE A SYNCHRONICITY...
NIGHT THRASHER IS ANOTHER REPRESENTATIVE OF THE PAST AND THE FUTURE.
SO UTTERLY SECURE IN HIS ABILITIES THAT HE USES A SKATEBOARD AS A WEAPON--AND IT WORKS.

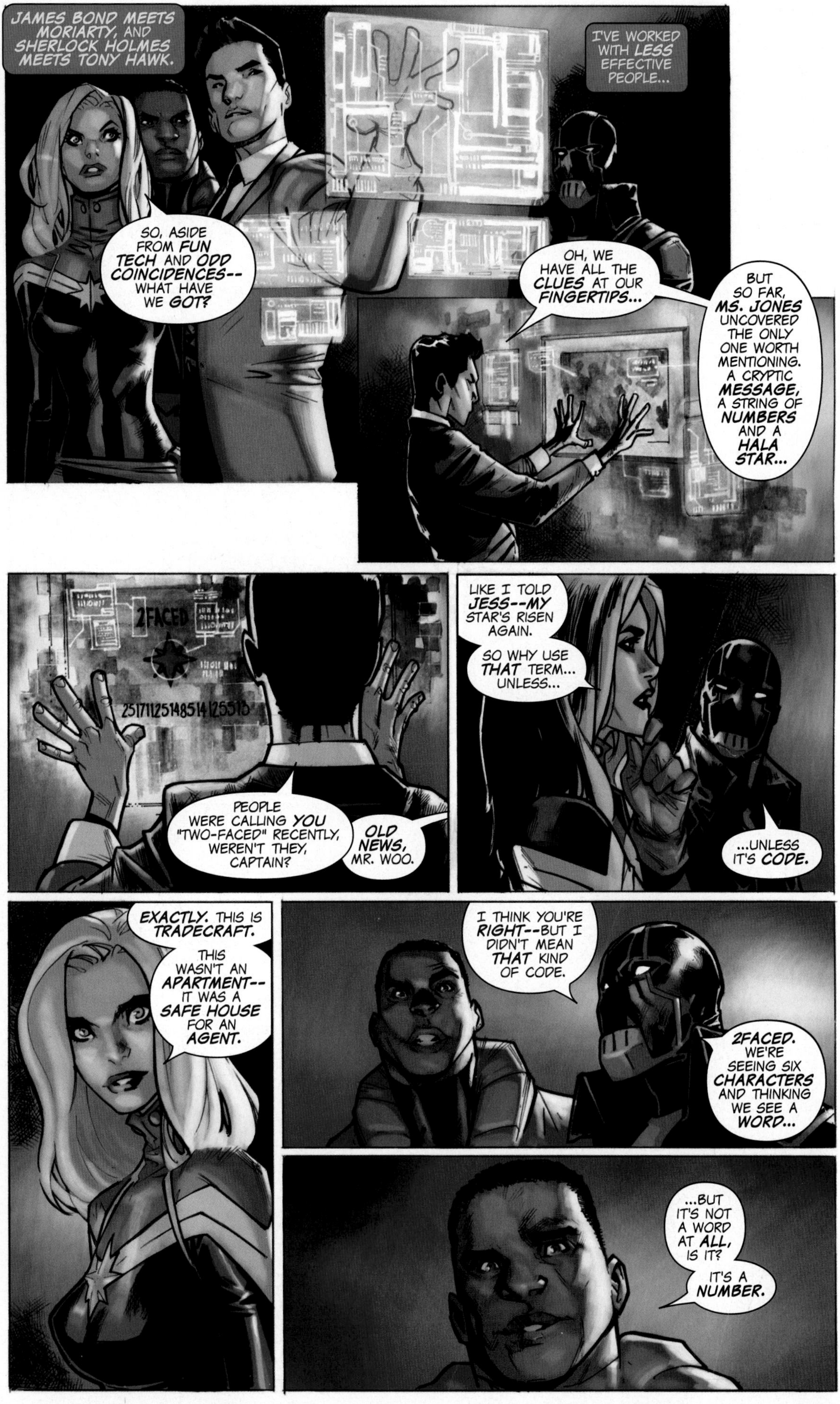
JAMES BOND MEETS MORIARTY, AND SHERLOCK HOLMES MEETS TONY HAWK.
I'VE WORKED WITH LESS EFFECTIVE PEOPLE...
SO, ASIDE FROM FUN TECH AND ODD COINCIDENCES-- WHAT HAVE WE GOT?
OH, WE HAVE ALL THE CLUES AT OUR FINGERTIPS...
BUT SO FAR, MS. JONES UNCOVERED THE ONLY ONE WORTH MENTIONING. A CRYPTIC MESSAGE, A STRING OF NUMBERS AND A HALA STAR...
2FACED
PEOPLE WERE CALLING YOU "TWO-FACED" RECENTLY, WEREN'T THEY, CAPTAIN?
OLD NEWS, MR. WOO.
LIKE I TOLD JESS--MY STAR'S RISEN AGAIN.
SO WHY USE THAT TERM... UNLESS...
...UNLESS IT'S CODE.
EXACTLY. THIS IS TRADECRAFT.
THIS WASN'T AN APARTMENT-- IT WAS A SAFE HOUSE FOR AN AGENT.
I THINK YOU'RE RIGHT--BUT I DIDN'T MEAN THAT KIND OF CODE.
2FACED. WE'RE SEEING SIX CHARACTERS AND THINKING WE SEE A WORD...
...BUT IT'S NOT A WORD AT ALL, IS IT?
IT'S A NUMBER.

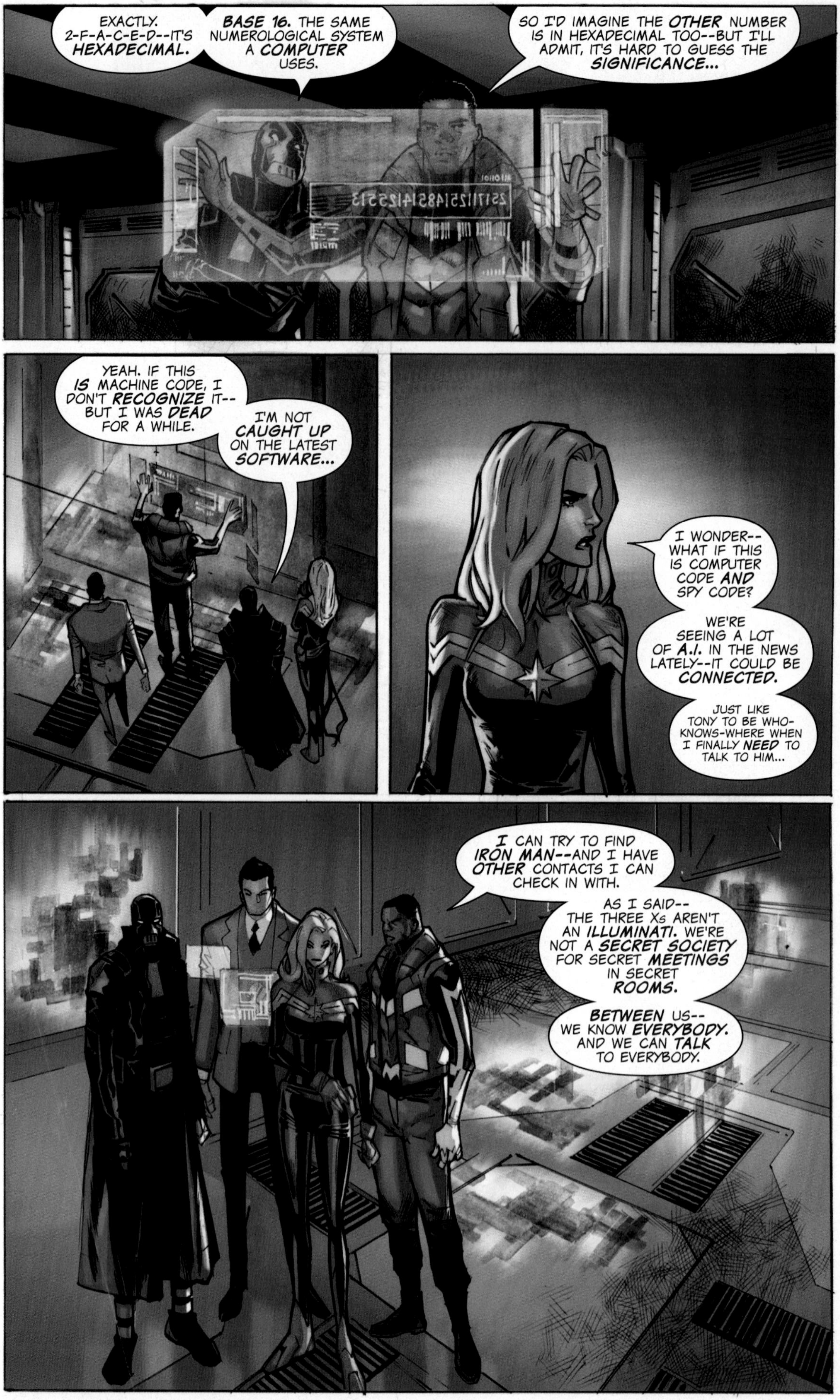
EXACTLY. 2-F-A-C-E-D--IT'S HEXADECIMAL.
BASE 16. THE SAME NUMEROLOGICAL SYSTEM A COMPUTER USES.
SO I'D IMAGINE THE OTHER NUMBER IS IN HEXADECIMAL TOO--BUT I'LL ADMIT, IT'S HARD TO GUESS THE SIGNIFICANCE...
YEAH. IF THIS IS MACHINE CODE, I DON'T RECOGNIZE IT--BUT I WAS DEAD FOR A WHILE.
I'M NOT CAUGHT UP ON THE LATEST SOFTWARE...
I WONDER--WHAT IF THIS IS COMPUTER CODE AND SPY CODE?
WE'RE SEEING A LOT OF A.I. IN THE NEWS LATELY--IT COULD BE CONNECTED.
JUST LIKE TONY TO BE WHO-KNOWS-WHERE WHEN I FINALLY NEED TO TALK TO HIM...
I CAN TRY TO FIND IRON MAN--AND I HAVE OTHER CONTACTS I CAN CHECK IN WITH.
AS I SAID--THE THREE XS AREN'T AN ILLUMINATI. WE'RE NOT A SECRET SOCIETY FOR SECRET MEETINGS IN SECRET ROOMS.
BETWEEN US--WE KNOW EVERYBODY. AND WE CAN TALK TO EVERYBODY.

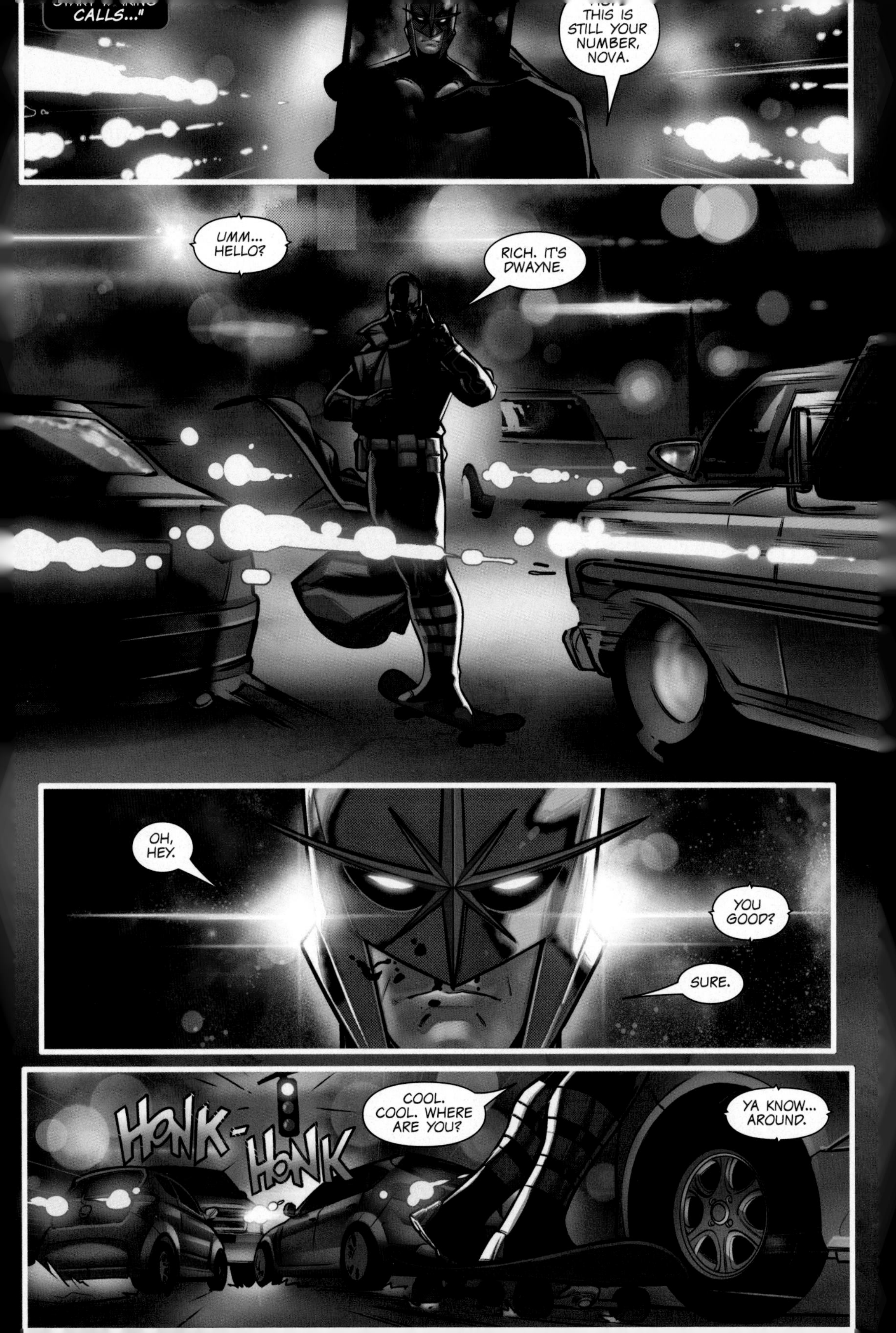
CALLS..."
THIS IS STILL YOUR NUMBER, NOVA.
UMM... HELLO?
RICH. IT'S DWAYNE.
OH, HEY.
YOU GOOD?
SURE.
HONK-HONK
COOL. COOL. WHERE ARE YOU?
YA KNOW... AROUND.

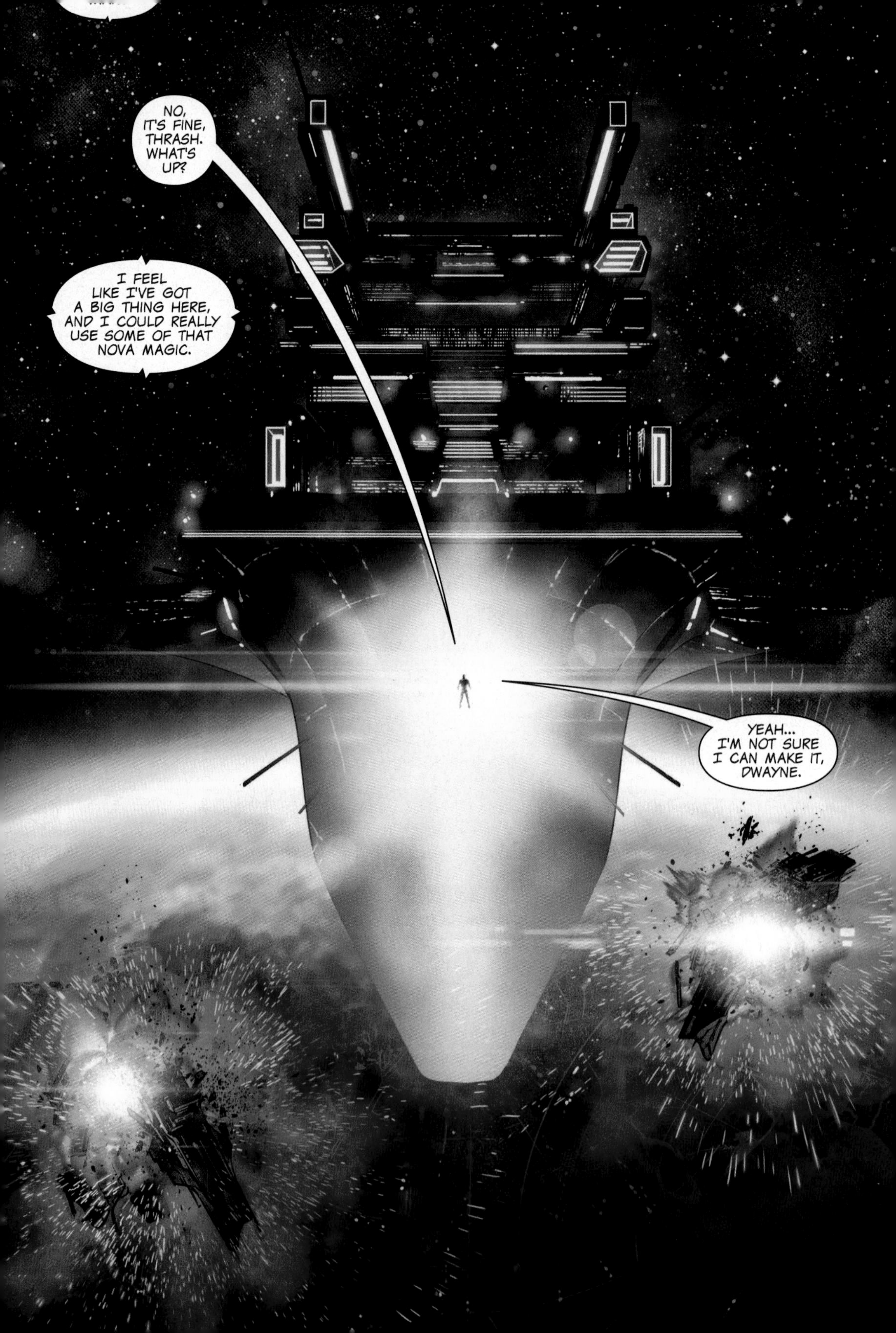
NO, IT'S FINE, THRASH. WHAT'S UP?
I FEEL LIKE I'VE GOT A BIG THING HERE, AND I COULD REALLY USE SOME OF THAT NOVA MAGIC.
YEAH... I'M NOT SURE I CAN MAKE IT, DWAYNE.

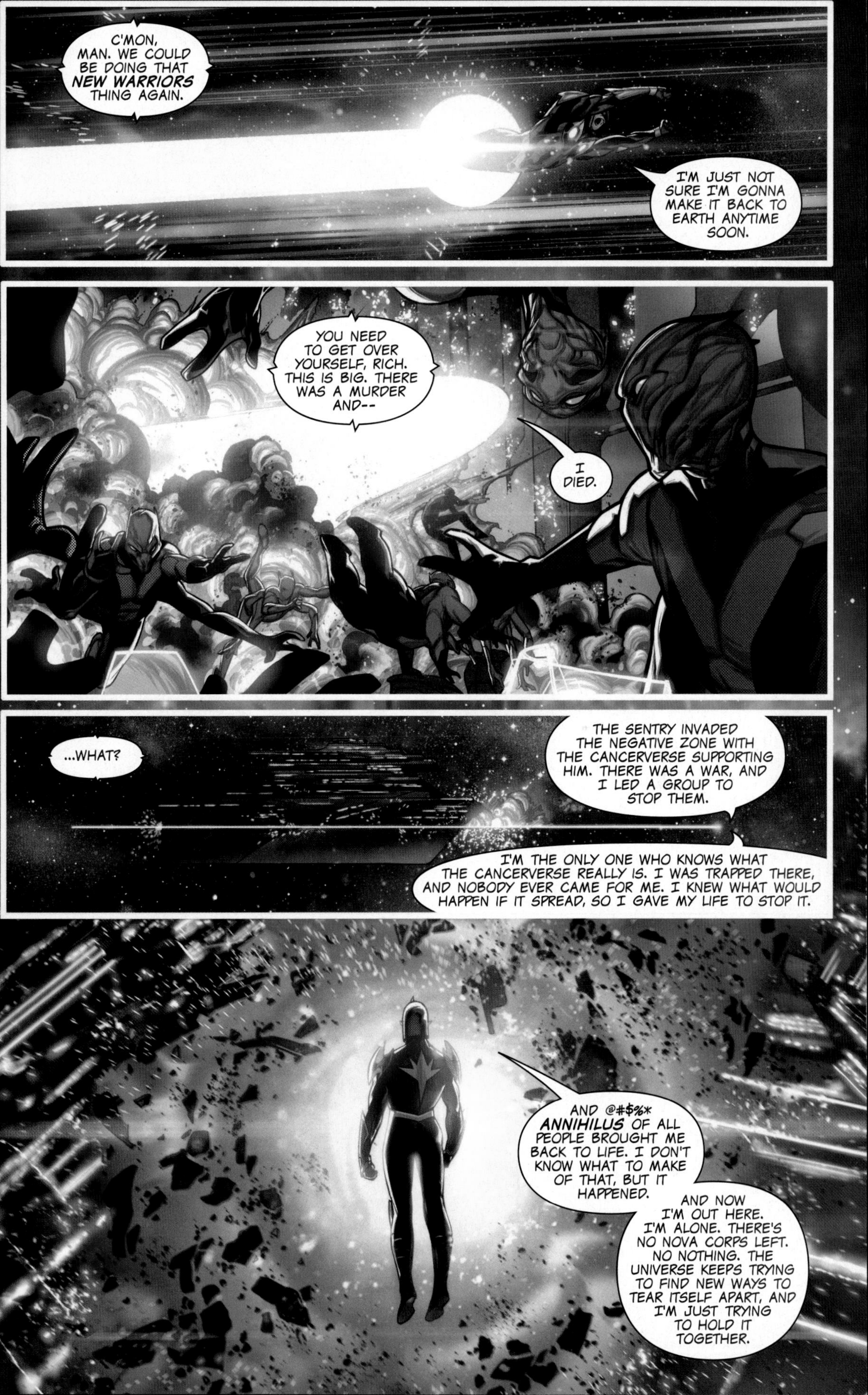
C'MON, MAN. WE COULD BE DOING THAT NEW WARRIORS THING AGAIN.
I'M JUST NOT SURE I'M GONNA MAKE IT BACK TO EARTH ANYTIME SOON.
YOU NEED TO GET OVER YOURSELF, RICH. THIS IS BIG. THERE WAS A MURDER AND--
I DIED.
...WHAT?
THE SENTRY INVADED THE NEGATIVE ZONE WITH THE CANCERVERSE SUPPORTING HIM. THERE WAS A WAR, AND I LED A GROUP TO STOP THEM.
I'M THE ONLY ONE WHO KNOWS WHAT THE CANCERVERSE REALLY IS. I WAS TRAPPED THERE, AND NOBODY EVER CAME FOR ME. I KNEW WHAT WOULD HAPPEN IF IT SPREAD, SO I GAVE MY LIFE TO STOP IT.
AND @#$%* ANNIHILUS OF ALL PEOPLE BROUGHT ME BACK TO LIFE. I DON'T KNOW WHAT TO MAKE OF THAT, BUT IT HAPPENED.
AND NOW I'M OUT HERE. I'M ALONE. THERE'S NO NOVA CORPS LEFT. NO NOTHING. THE UNIVERSE KEEPS TRYING TO FIND NEW WAYS TO TEAR ITSELF APART, AND I'M JUST TRYING TO HOLD IT TOGETHER.

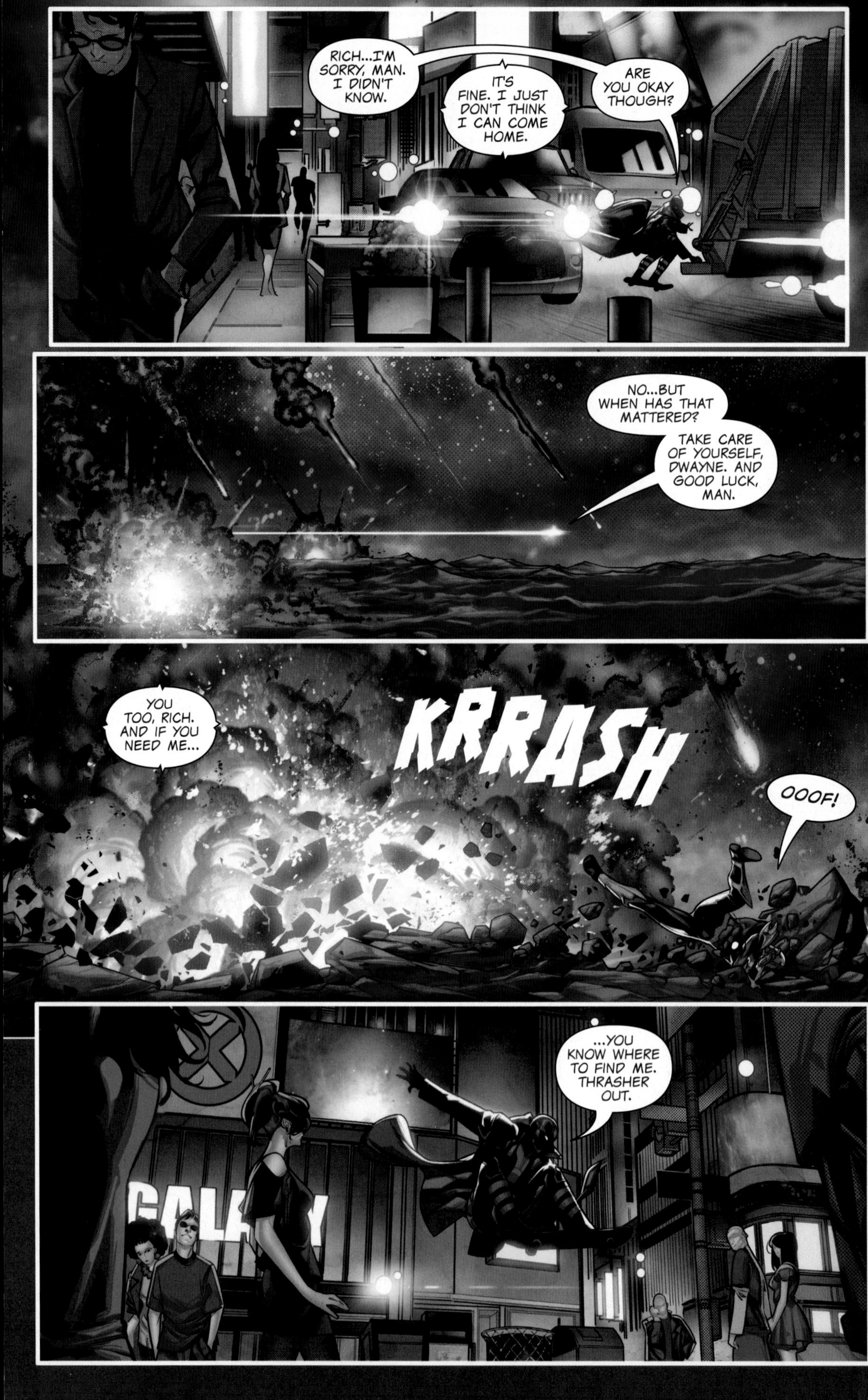

RICH...I'M SORRY, MAN. I DIDN'T KNOW.
IT'S FINE. I JUST DON'T THINK I CAN COME HOME.
ARE YOU OKAY THOUGH?
NO...BUT WHEN HAS THAT MATTERED?
TAKE CARE OF YOURSELF, DWAYNE. AND GOOD LUCK, MAN.
YOU TOO, RICH. AND IF YOU NEED ME...
KRRASH
OOOF!
...YOU KNOW WHERE TO FIND ME. THRASHER OUT.
GALA

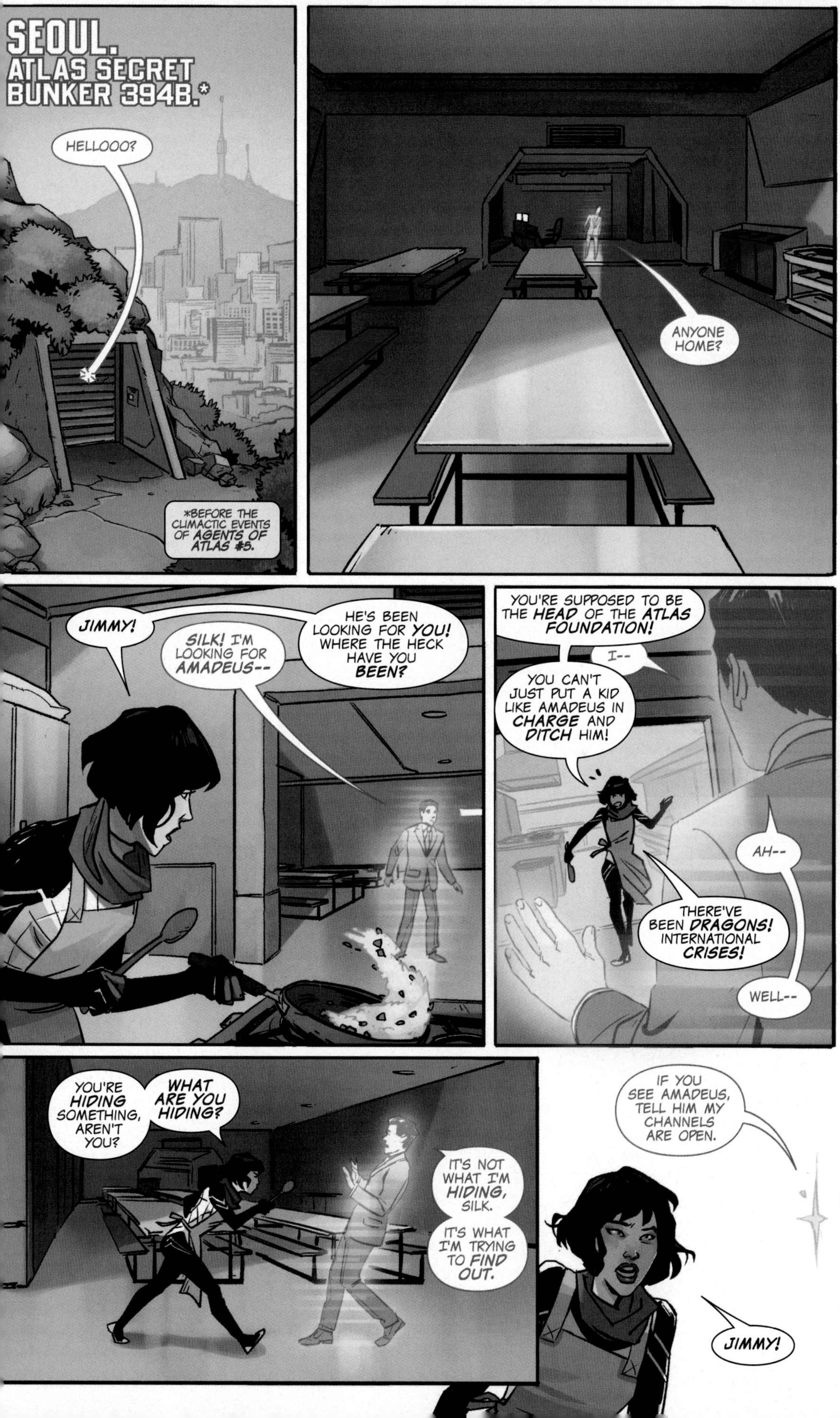
SEOUL. ATLAS SECRET BUNKER 394B.*
HELLOOO?
*BEFORE THE CLIMACTIC EVENTS OF AGENTS OF ATLAS #5.
ANYONE HOME?
JIMMY!
SILK! I'M LOOKING FOR AMADEUS--
HE'S BEEN LOOKING FOR YOU! WHERE THE HECK HAVE YOU BEEN?
YOU'RE SUPPOSED TO BE THE HEAD OF THE ATLAS FOUNDATION!
I--
YOU CAN'T JUST PUT A KID LIKE AMADEUS IN CHARGE AND DITCH HIM!
AH--
THERE'VE BEEN DRAGONS! INTERNATIONAL CRISES!
WELL--
YOU'RE HIDING SOMETHING, AREN'T YOU?
WHAT ARE YOU HIDING?
IT'S NOT WHAT I'M HIDING, SILK.
IT'S WHAT I'M TRYING TO FIND OUT.
IF YOU SEE AMADEUS, TELL HIM MY CHANNELS ARE OPEN.
JIMMY!

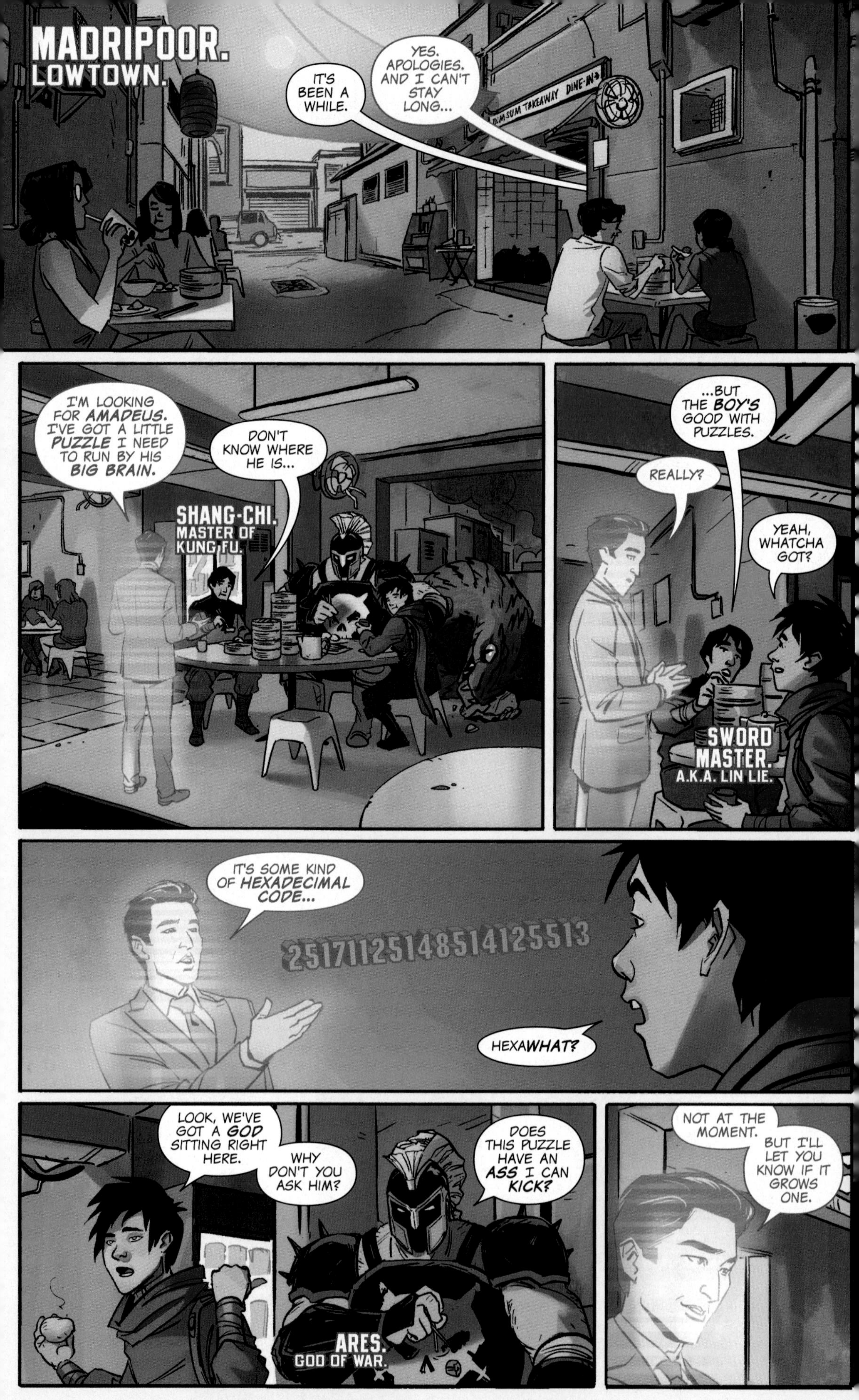

MADRIPOOR. LOWTOWN.
IT'S BEEN A WHILE.
YES. APOLOGIES. AND I CAN'T STAY LONG...
DIM SUM TAKEAWAY DINE-IN
I'M LOOKING FOR AMADEUS. I'VE GOT A LITTLE PUZZLE I NEED TO RUN BY HIS BIG BRAIN.
DON'T KNOW WHERE HE IS...
SHANG-CHI. MASTER OF KUNG FU.
...BUT THE BOY'S GOOD WITH PUZZLES.
REALLY?
YEAH, WHATCHA GOT?
SWORD MASTER. A.K.A. LIN LIE.
IT'S SOME KIND OF HEXADECIMAL CODE...
2517112514851412551З
HEXAWHAT?
LOOK, WE'VE GOT A GOD SITTING RIGHT HERE.
WHY DON'T YOU ASK HIM?
DOES THIS PUZZLE HAVE AN ASS I CAN KICK?
ARES. GOD OF WAR.
NOT AT THE MOMENT.
BUT I'LL LET YOU KNOW IF IT GROWS ONE.

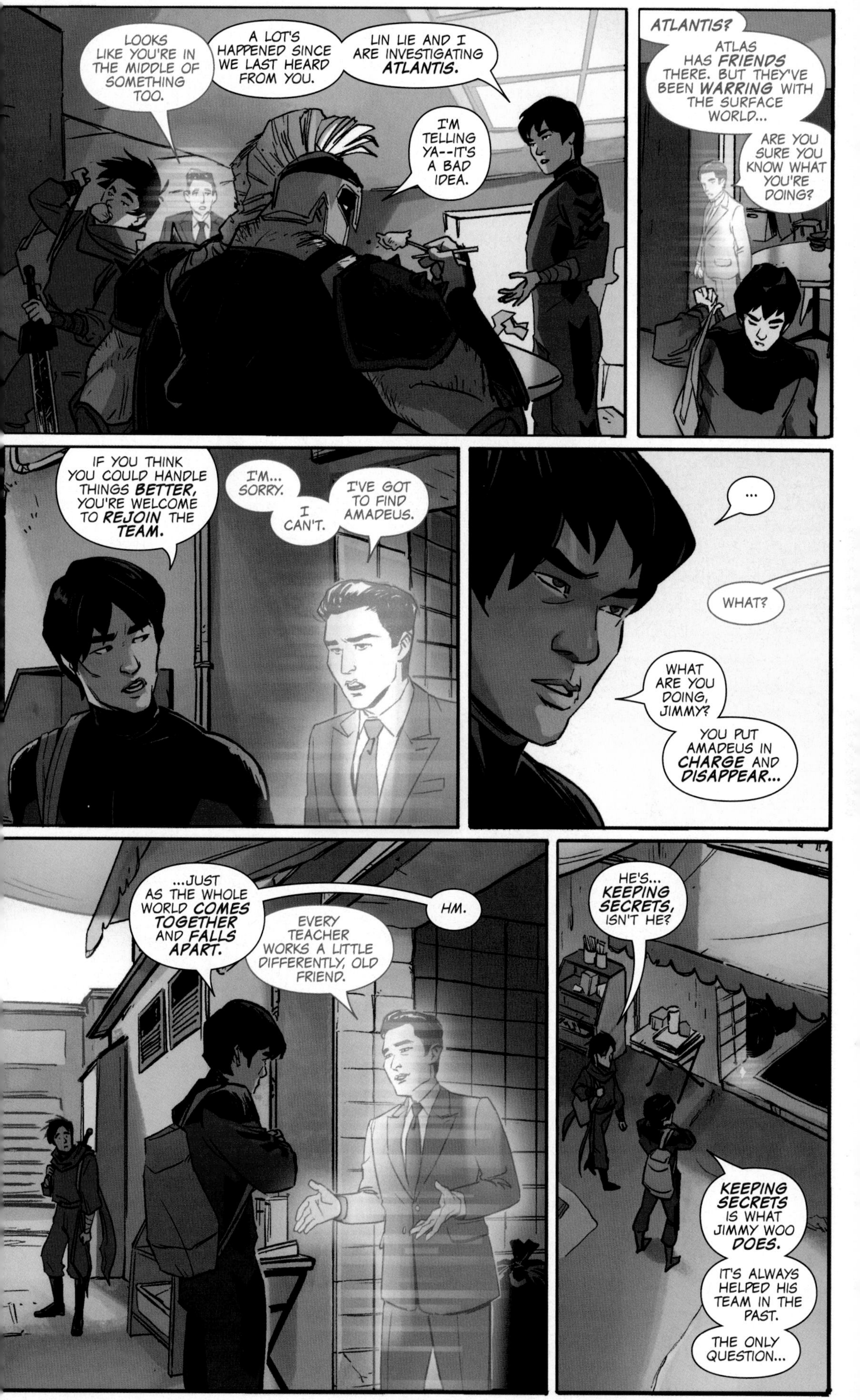
LOOKS LIKE YOU'RE IN THE MIDDLE OF SOMETHING TOO.
A LOT'S HAPPENED SINCE WE LAST HEARD FROM YOU.
LIN LIE AND I ARE INVESTIGATING ATLANTIS.
I'M TELLING YA--IT'S A BAD IDEA.
ATLANTIS?
ATLAS HAS FRIENDS THERE. BUT THEY'VE BEEN WARRING WITH THE SURFACE WORLD...
ARE YOU SURE YOU KNOW WHAT YOU'RE DOING?
IF YOU THINK YOU COULD HANDLE THINGS BETTER, YOU'RE WELCOME TO REJOIN THE TEAM.
I'M... SORRY.
I CAN'T.
I'VE GOT TO FIND AMADEUS.
...
WHAT?
WHAT ARE YOU DOING, JIMMY?
YOU PUT AMADEUS IN CHARGE AND DISAPPEAR...
...JUST AS THE WHOLE WORLD COMES TOGETHER AND FALLS APART.
HM.
EVERY TEACHER WORKS A LITTLE DIFFERENTLY, OLD FRIEND.
HE'S... KEEPING SECRETS, ISN'T HE?
KEEPING SECRETS IS WHAT JIMMY WOO DOES.
IT'S ALWAYS HELPED HIS TEAM IN THE PAST.
THE ONLY QUESTION...

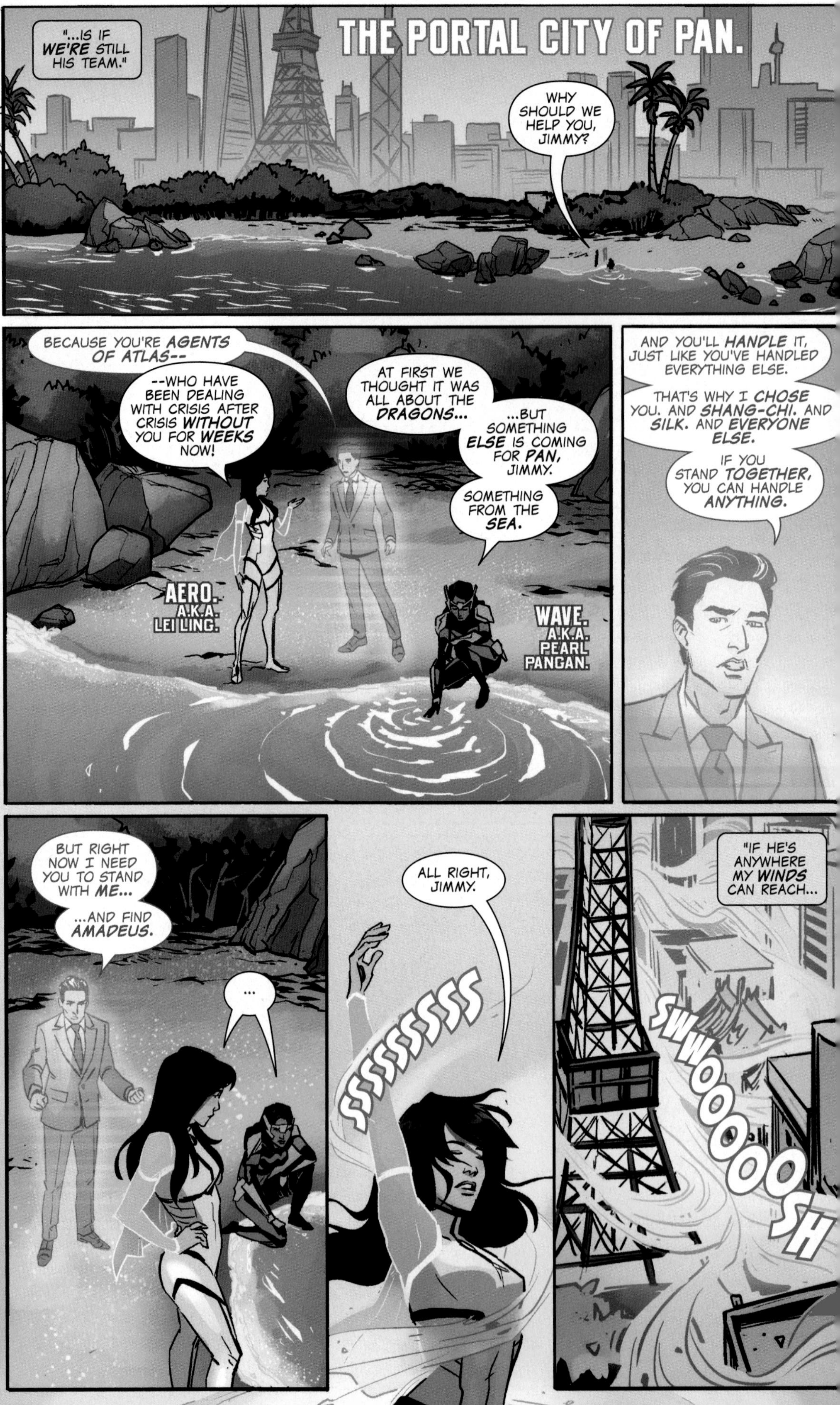

"...IS IF WE'RE STILL HIS TEAM."
THE PORTAL CITY OF PAN.
WHY SHOULD WE HELP YOU, JIMMY?
BECAUSE YOU'RE AGENTS OF ATLAS--
--WHO HAVE BEEN DEALING WITH CRISIS AFTER CRISIS WITHOUT YOU FOR WEEKS NOW!
AT FIRST WE THOUGHT IT WAS ALL ABOUT THE DRAGONS...
...BUT SOMETHING ELSE IS COMING FOR PAN, JIMMY.
SOMETHING FROM THE SEA.
AERO. A.K.A. LEI LING.
WAVE. A.K.A. PEARL PANGAN.
AND YOU'LL HANDLE IT, JUST LIKE YOU'VE HANDLED EVERYTHING ELSE.
THAT'S WHY I CHOSE YOU. AND SHANG-CHI. AND SILK. AND EVERYONE ELSE.
IF YOU STAND TOGETHER, YOU CAN HANDLE ANYTHING.
BUT RIGHT NOW I NEED YOU TO STAND WITH ME...
...AND FIND AMADEUS.
...
ALL RIGHT, JIMMY.
SSSSSSSS
"IF HE'S ANYWHERE MY WINDS CAN REACH...
SWWOOOOOSH

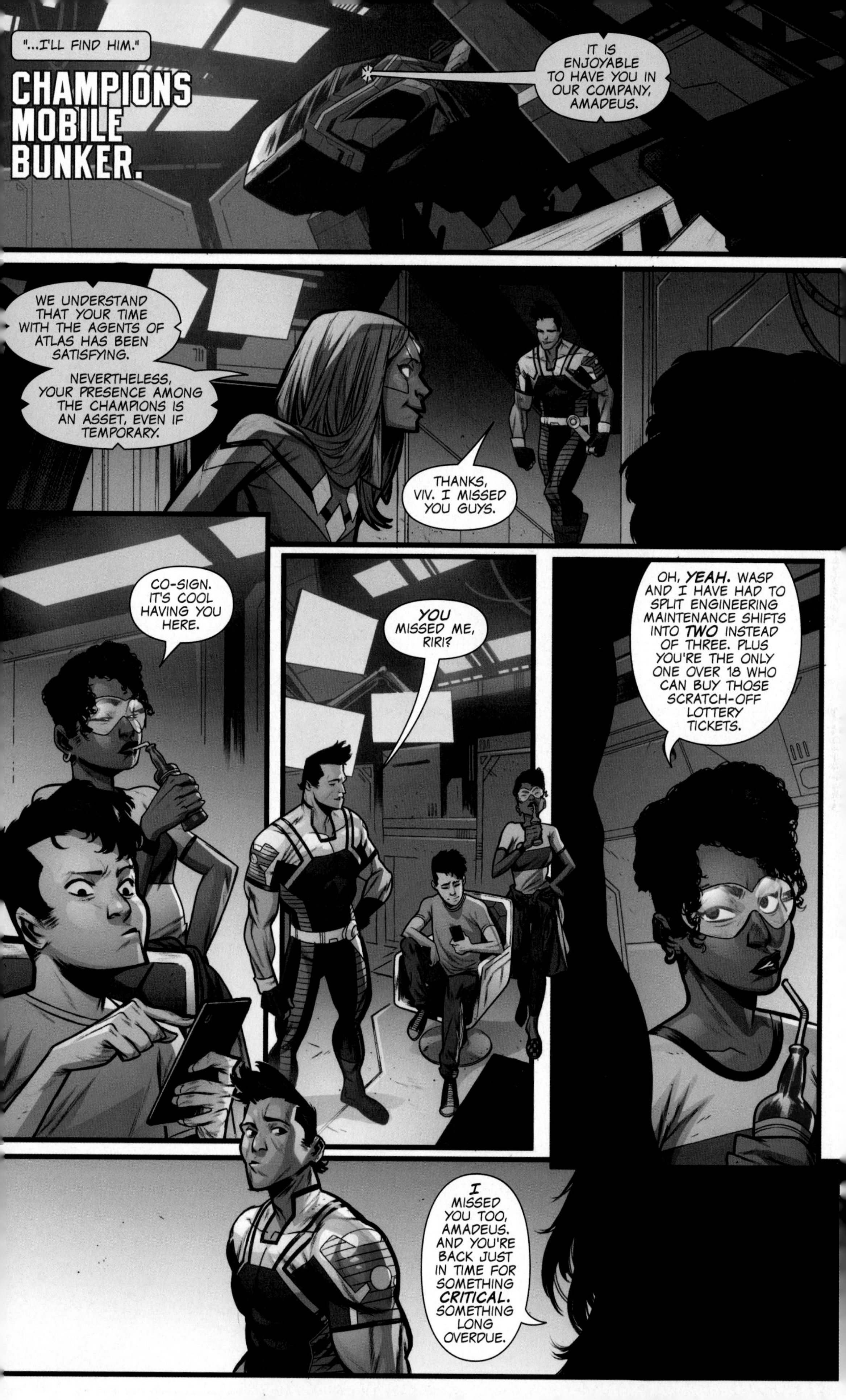
"...I'LL FIND HIM."
CHAMPIONS MOBILE BUNKER.
IT IS ENJOYABLE TO HAVE YOU IN OUR COMPANY, AMADEUS.
WE UNDERSTAND THAT YOUR TIME WITH THE AGENTS OF ATLAS HAS BEEN SATISFYING.
NEVERTHELESS, YOUR PRESENCE AMONG THE CHAMPIONS IS AN ASSET, EVEN IF TEMPORARY.
THANKS, VIV. I MISSED YOU GUYS.
CO-SIGN. IT'S COOL HAVING YOU HERE.
YOU MISSED ME, RIRI?
OH, YEAH. WASP AND I HAVE HAD TO SPLIT ENGINEERING MAINTENANCE SHIFTS INTO TWO INSTEAD OF THREE. PLUS YOU'RE THE ONLY ONE OVER 18 WHO CAN BUY THOSE SCRATCH-OFF LOTTERY TICKETS.
I MISSED YOU TOO, AMADEUS. AND YOU'RE BACK JUST IN TIME FOR SOMETHING CRITICAL. SOMETHING LONG OVERDUE.

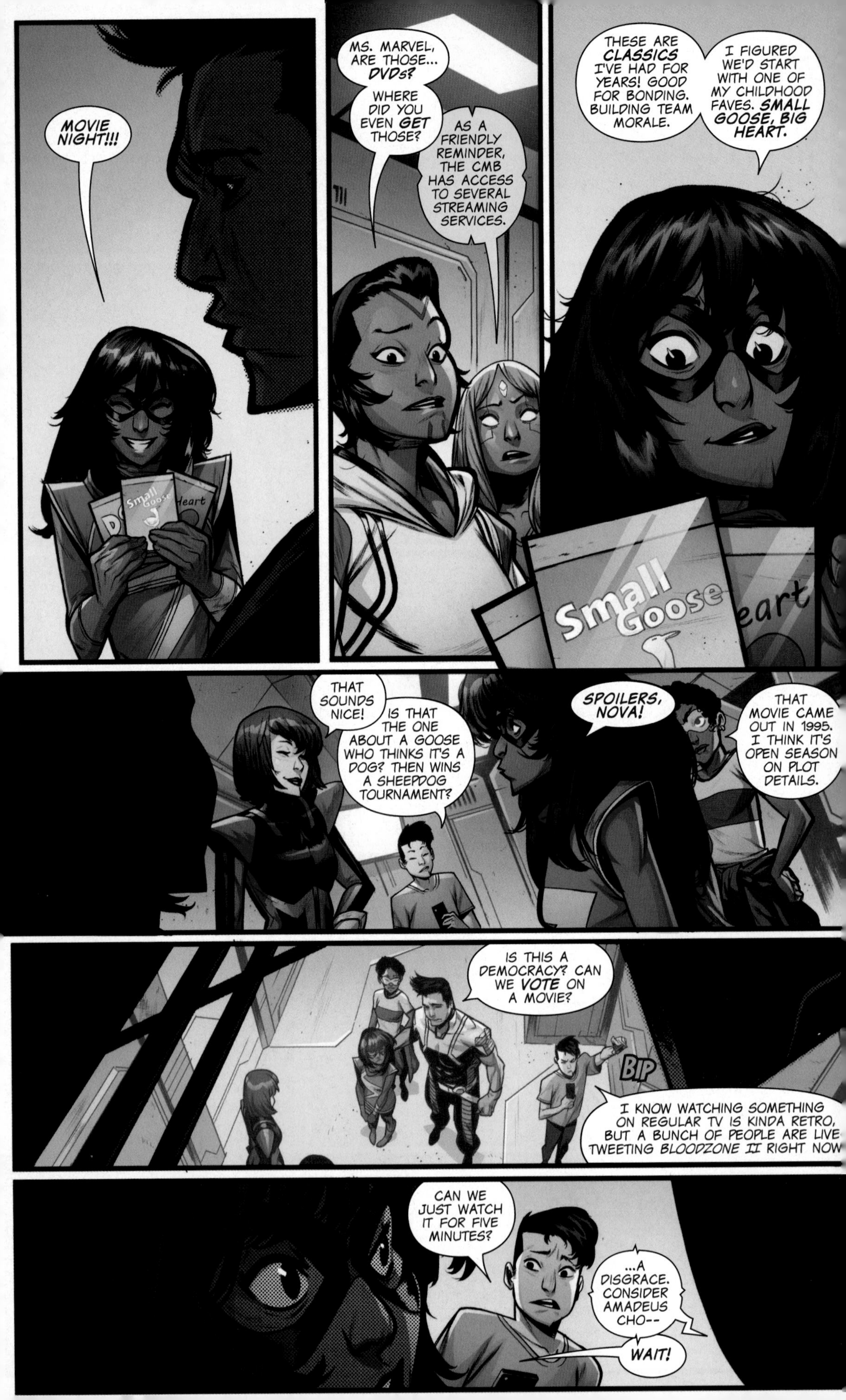
MOVIE NIGHT!!!
MS. MARVEL, ARE THOSE... DVDs?
WHERE DID YOU EVEN GET THOSE?
AS A FRIENDLY REMINDER, THE CMB HAS ACCESS TO SEVERAL STREAMING SERVICES.
THESE ARE CLASSICS I'VE HAD FOR YEARS! GOOD FOR BONDING. BUILDING TEAM MORALE.
I FIGURED WE'D START WITH ONE OF MY CHILDHOOD FAVES. SMALL GOOSE, BIG HEART.
Small Goose
THAT SOUNDS NICE!
IS THAT THE ONE ABOUT A GOOSE WHO THINKS IT'S A DOG? THEN WINS A SHEEPDOG TOURNAMENT?
SPOILERS, NOVA!
THAT MOVIE CAME OUT IN 1995. I THINK IT'S OPEN SEASON ON PLOT DETAILS.
IS THIS A DEMOCRACY? CAN WE VOTE ON A MOVIE?
BIP
I KNOW WATCHING SOMETHING ON REGULAR TV IS KINDA RETRO, BUT A BUNCH OF PEOPLE ARE LIVE TWEETING BLOODZONE II RIGHT NOW
CAN WE JUST WATCH IT FOR FIVE MINUTES?
...A DISGRACE. CONSIDER AMADEUS CHO--
WAIT!

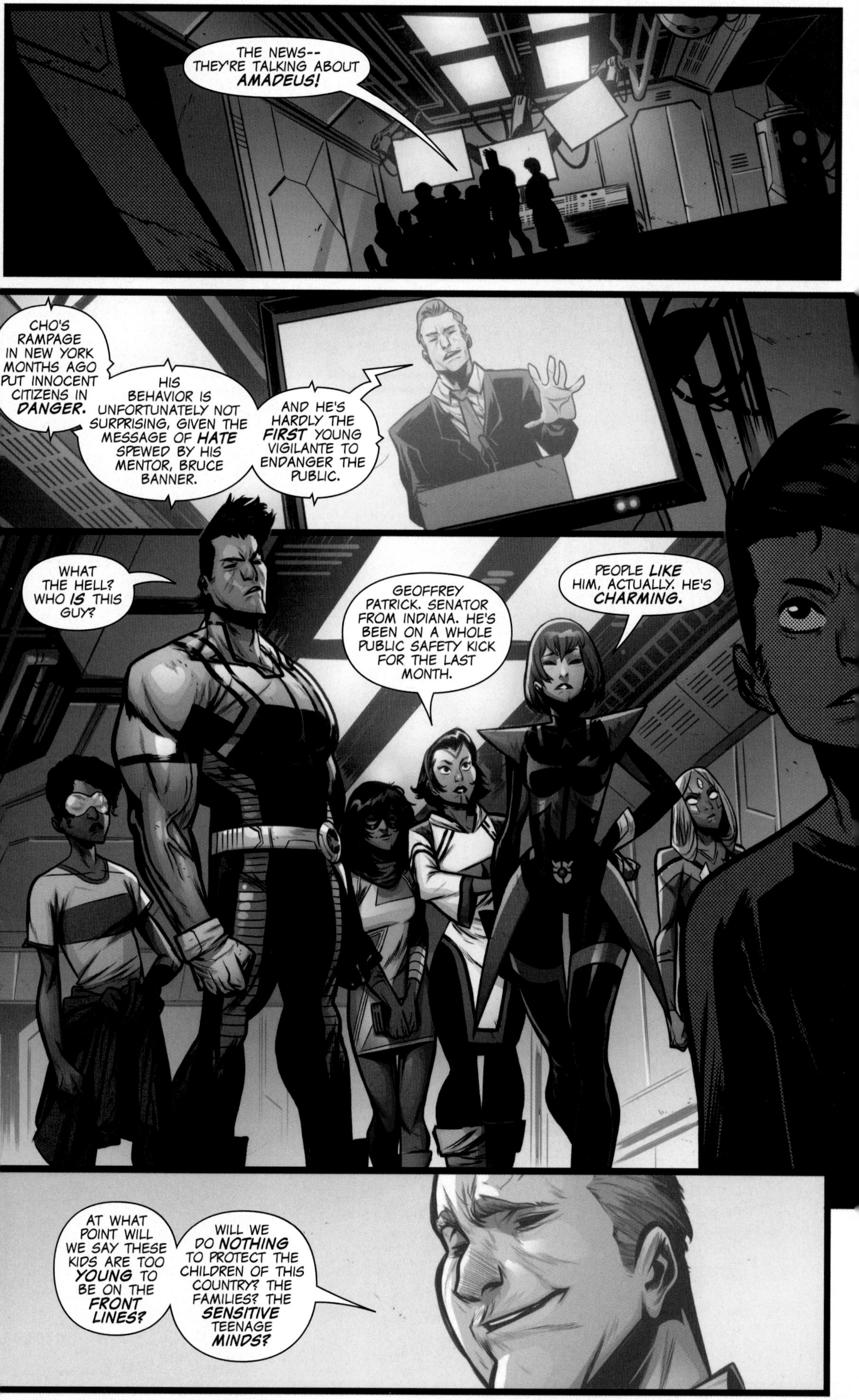

THE NEWS-- THEY'RE TALKING ABOUT AMADEUS!
CHO'S RAMPAGE IN NEW YORK MONTHS AGO PUT INNOCENT CITIZENS IN DANGER.
HIS BEHAVIOR IS UNFORTUNATELY NOT SURPRISING, GIVEN THE MESSAGE OF HATE SPEWED BY HIS MENTOR, BRUCE BANNER.
AND HE'S HARDLY THE FIRST YOUNG VIGILANTE TO ENDANGER THE PUBLIC.
WHAT THE HELL? WHO IS THIS GUY?
GEOFFREY PATRICK. SENATOR FROM INDIANA. HE'S BEEN ON A WHOLE PUBLIC SAFETY KICK FOR THE LAST MONTH.
PEOPLE LIKE HIM, ACTUALLY. HE'S CHARMING.
AT WHAT POINT WILL WE SAY THESE KIDS ARE TOO YOUNG TO BE ON THE FRONT LINES?
WILL WE DO NOTHING TO PROTECT THE CHILDREN OF THIS COUNTRY? THE FAMILIES? THE SENSITIVE TEENAGE MINDS?

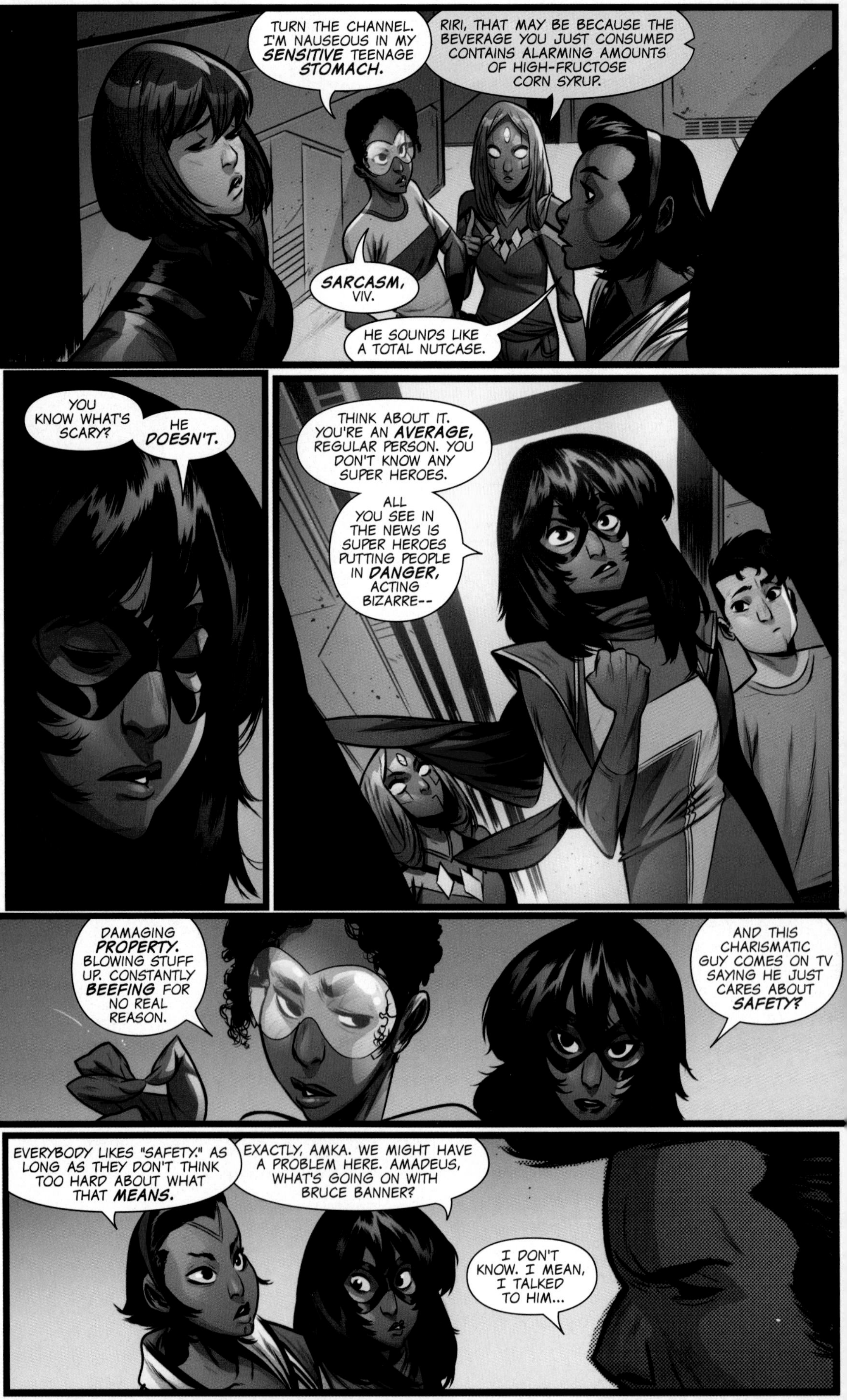
TURN THE CHANNEL. I'M NAUSEOUS IN MY SENSITIVE TEENAGE STOMACH.
RIRI, THAT MAY BE BECAUSE THE BEVERAGE YOU JUST CONSUMED CONTAINS ALARMING AMOUNTS OF HIGH-FRUCTOSE CORN SYRUP.
SARCASM, VIV.
HE SOUNDS LIKE A TOTAL NUTCASE.
YOU KNOW WHAT'S SCARY?
HE DOESN'T.
THINK ABOUT IT. YOU'RE AN AVERAGE, REGULAR PERSON. YOU DON'T KNOW ANY SUPER HEROES.
ALL YOU SEE IN THE NEWS IS SUPER HEROES PUTTING PEOPLE IN DANGER, ACTING BIZARRE--
DAMAGING PROPERTY. BLOWING STUFF UP. CONSTANTLY BEEFING FOR NO REAL REASON.
AND THIS CHARISMATIC GUY COMES ON TV SAYING HE JUST CARES ABOUT SAFETY?
EVERYBODY LIKES "SAFETY." AS LONG AS THEY DON'T THINK TOO HARD ABOUT WHAT THAT MEANS.
EXACTLY, AMKA. WE MIGHT HAVE A PROBLEM HERE. AMADEUS, WHAT'S GOING ON WITH BRUCE BANNER?
I DON'T KNOW. I MEAN, I TALKED TO HIM...

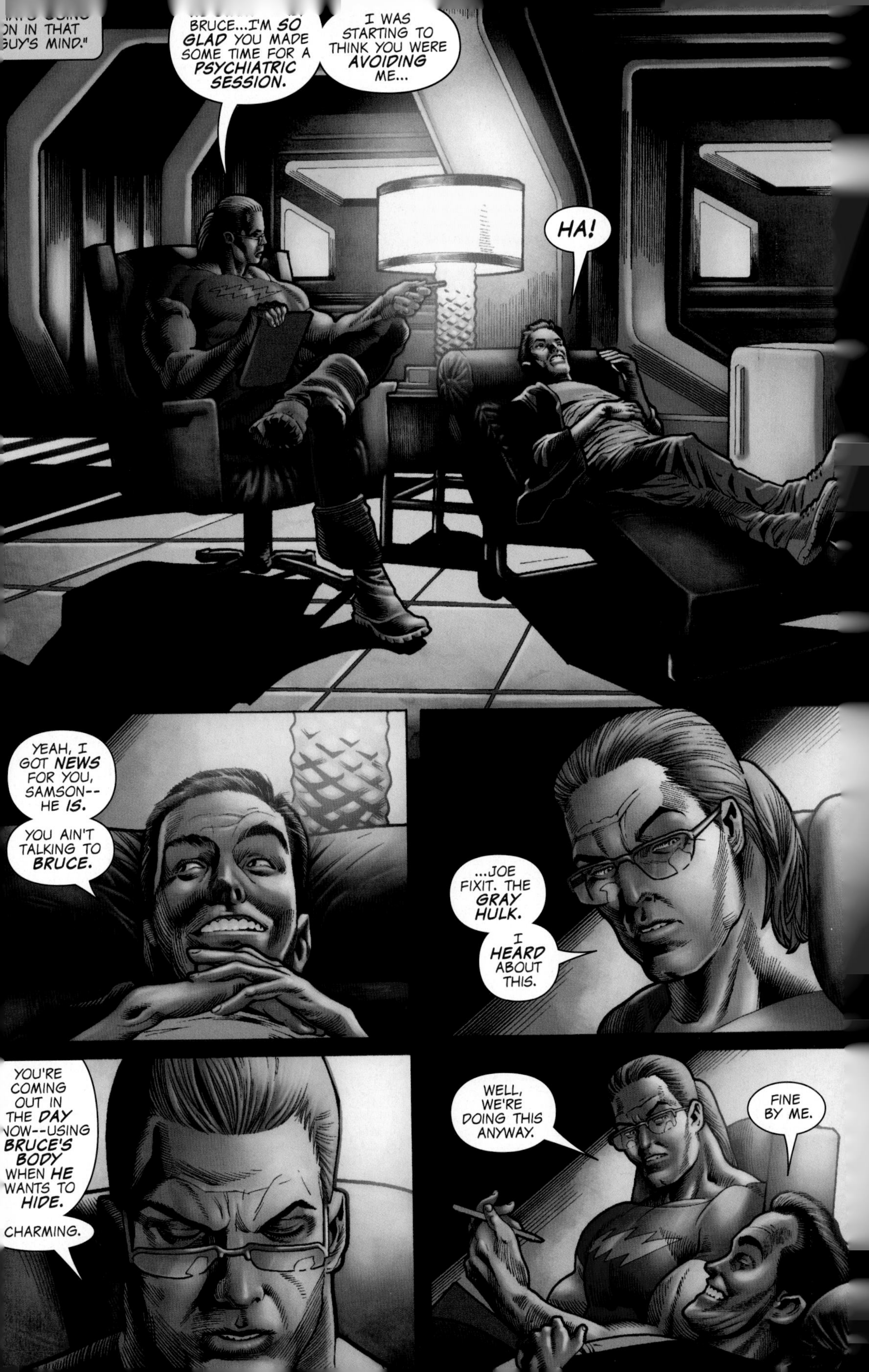

ON IN THAT GUY'S MIND."
BRUCE...I'M SO GLAD YOU MADE SOME TIME FOR A PSYCHIATRIC SESSION.
I WAS STARTING TO THINK YOU WERE AVOIDING ME...
HA!
YEAH, I GOT NEWS FOR YOU, SAMSON-- HE IS.
YOU AIN'T TALKING TO BRUCE.
...JOE FIXIT. THE GRAY HULK.
I HEARD ABOUT THIS.
YOU'RE COMING OUT IN THE DAY NOW--USING BRUCE'S BODY WHEN HE WANTS TO HIDE.
CHARMING.
WELL, WE'RE DOING THIS ANYWAY.
FINE BY ME.

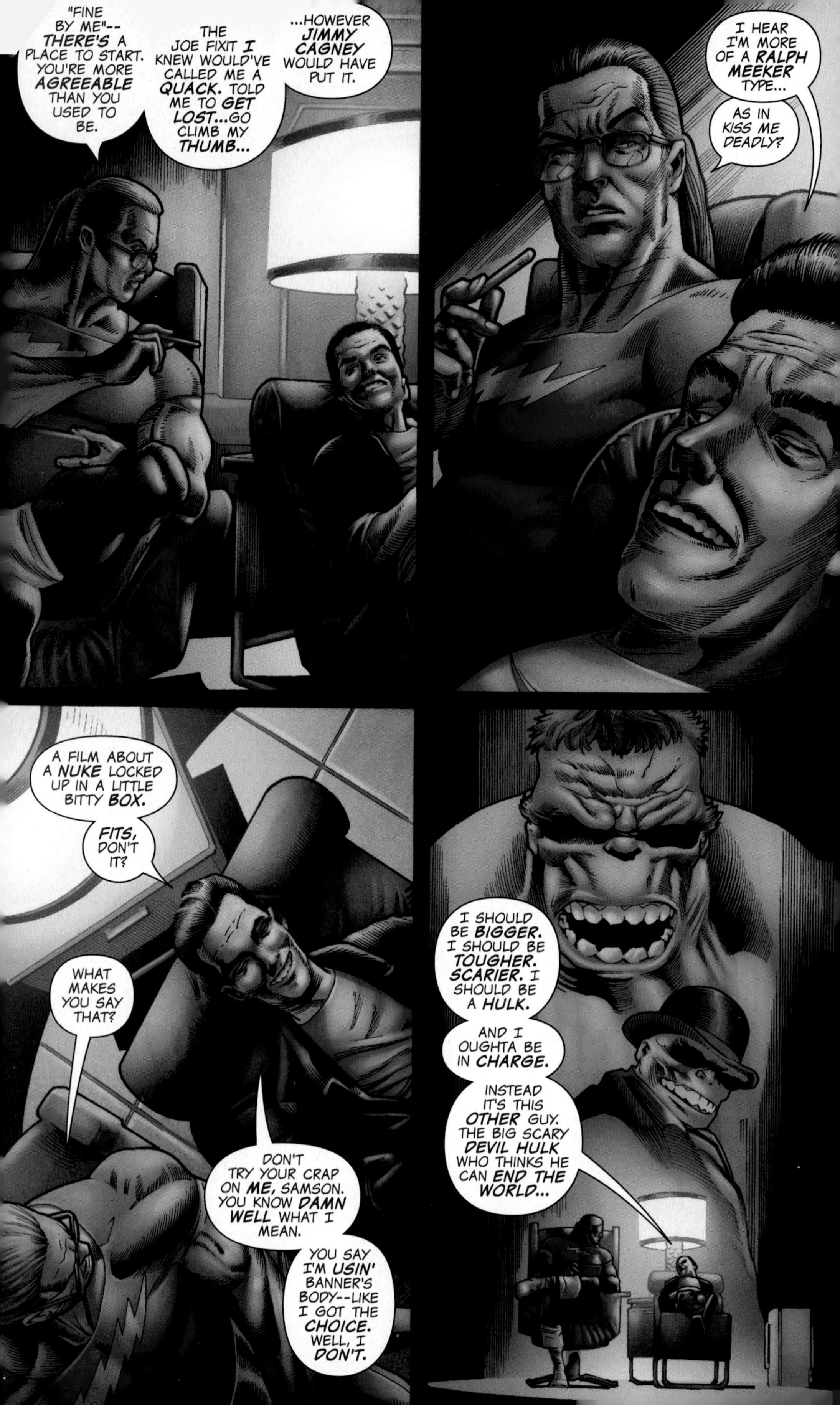
"FINE BY ME"-- THERE'S A PLACE TO START. YOU'RE MORE AGREEABLE THAN YOU USED TO BE.
THE JOE FIXIT I KNEW WOULD'VE CALLED ME A QUACK. TOLD ME TO GET LOST...GO CLIMB MY THUMB...
...HOWEVER JIMMY CAGNEY WOULD HAVE PUT IT.
I HEAR I'M MORE OF A RALPH MEEKER TYPE...
AS IN KISS ME DEADLY?
A FILM ABOUT A NUKE LOCKED UP IN A LITTLE BITTY BOX.
FITS, DON'T IT?
WHAT MAKES YOU SAY THAT?
DON'T TRY YOUR CRAP ON ME, SAMSON. YOU KNOW DAMN WELL WHAT I MEAN.
YOU SAY I'M USIN' BANNER'S BODY--LIKE I GOT THE CHOICE. WELL, I DON'T.
I SHOULD BE BIGGER. I SHOULD BE TOUGHER. SCARIER. I SHOULD BE A HULK.
AND I OUGHTA BE IN CHARGE.
INSTEAD IT'S THIS OTHER GUY. THE BIG SCARY DEVIL HULK WHO THINKS HE CAN END THE WORLD...

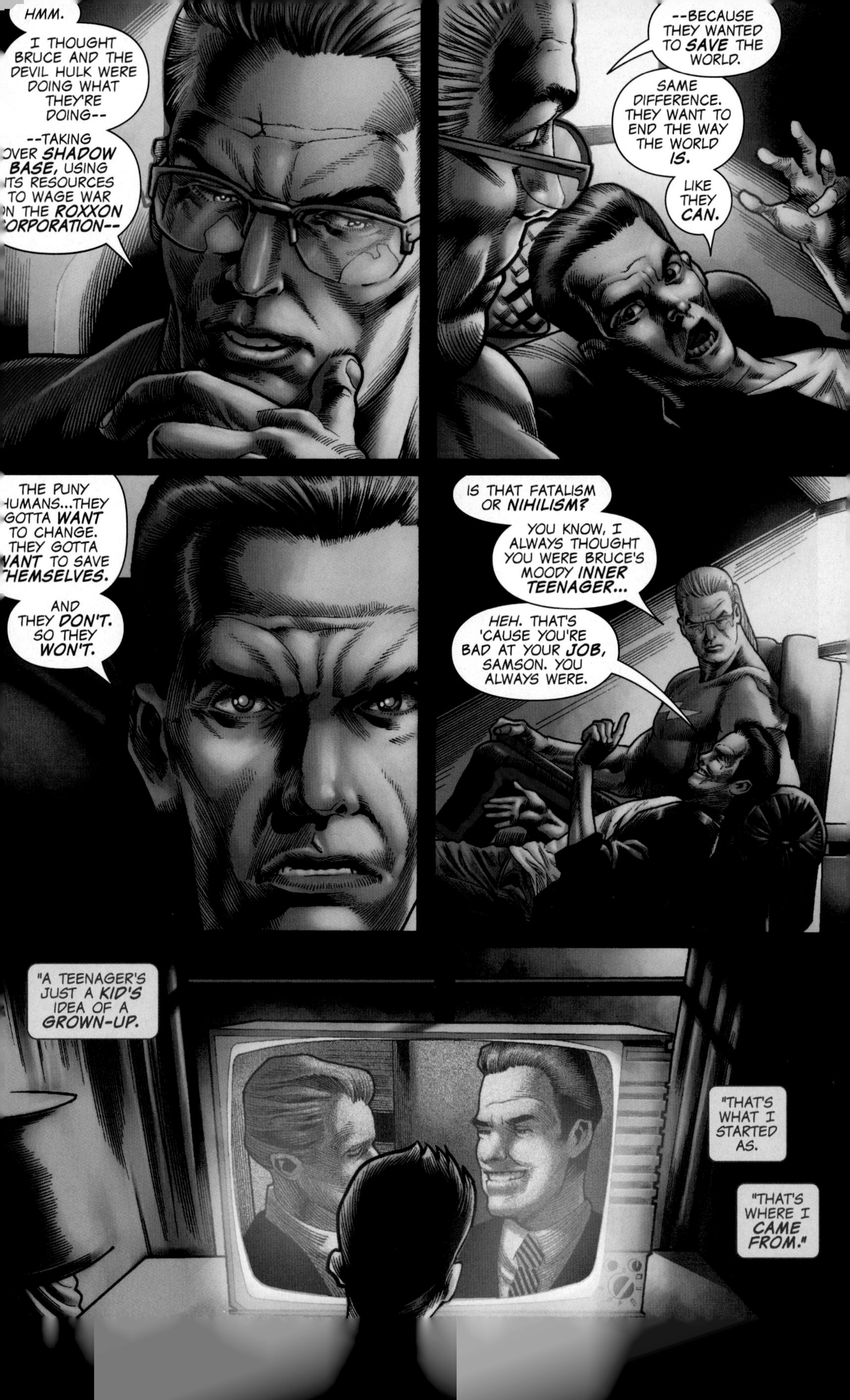
HMM.
I THOUGHT BRUCE AND THE DEVIL HULK WERE DOING WHAT THEY'RE DOING--
--TAKING OVER SHADOW BASE, USING ITS RESOURCES TO WAGE WAR ON THE ROXXON CORPORATION--
--BECAUSE THEY WANTED TO SAVE THE WORLD.
SAME DIFFERENCE. THEY WANT TO END THE WAY THE WORLD IS.
LIKE THEY CAN.
THE PUNY HUMANS...THEY GOTTA WANT TO CHANGE. THEY GOTTA WANT TO SAVE THEMSELVES.
AND THEY DON'T. SO THEY WON'T.
IS THAT FATALISM OR NIHILISM?
YOU KNOW, I ALWAYS THOUGHT YOU WERE BRUCE'S MOODY INNER TEENAGER...
HEH. THAT'S 'CAUSE YOU'RE BAD AT YOUR JOB, SAMSON. YOU ALWAYS WERE.
"A TEENAGER'S JUST A KID'S IDEA OF A GROWN-UP.
"THAT'S WHAT I STARTED AS.
"THAT'S WHERE I CAME FROM."

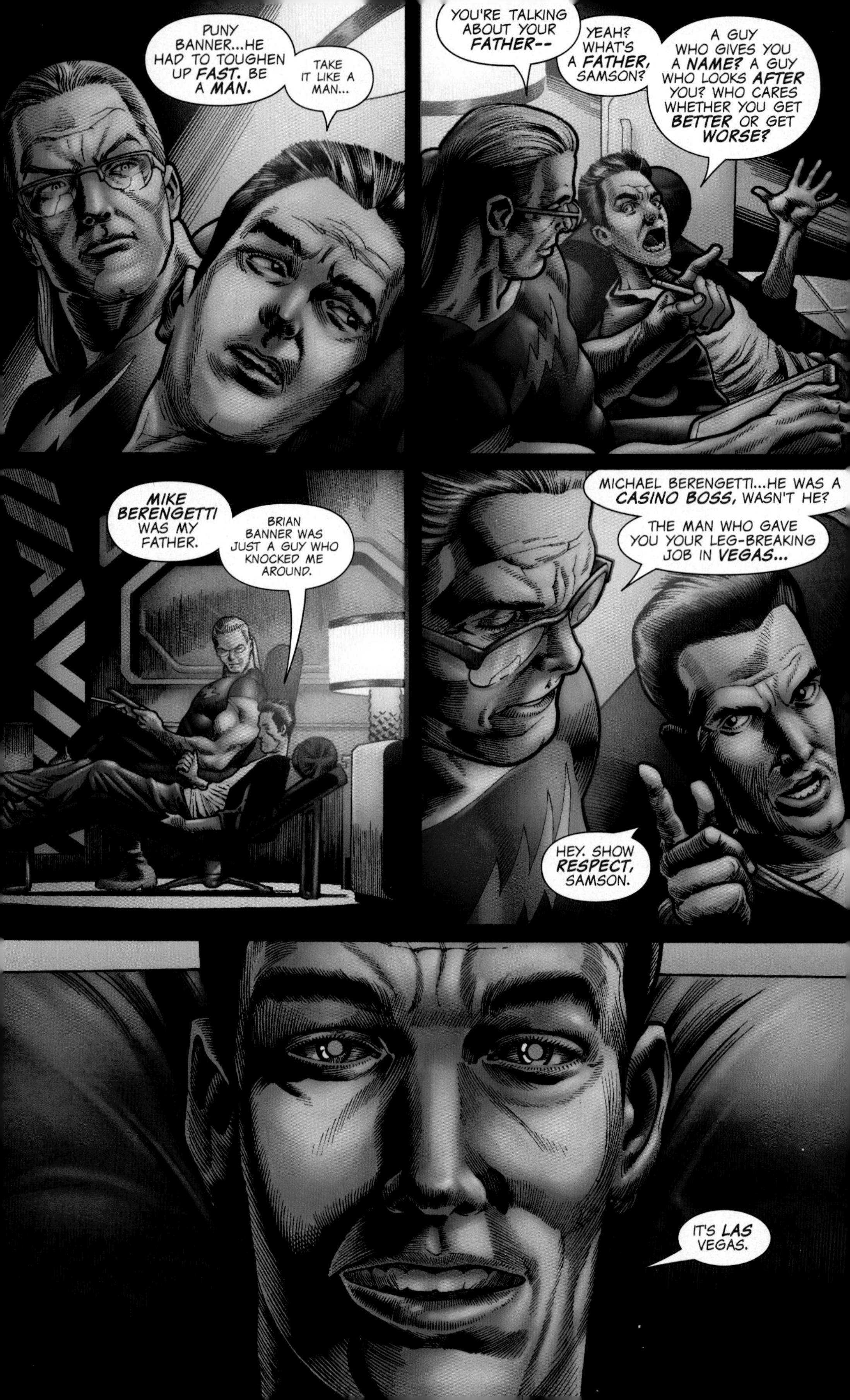
PUNY BANNER...HE HAD TO TOUGHEN UP FAST. BE A MAN.
TAKE IT LIKE A MAN...
YOU'RE TALKING ABOUT YOUR FATHER--
YEAH? WHAT'S A FATHER, SAMSON?
A GUY WHO GIVES YOU A NAME? A GUY WHO LOOKS AFTER YOU? WHO CARES WHETHER YOU GET BETTER OR GET WORSE?
MIKE BERENGETTI WAS MY FATHER.
BRIAN BANNER WAS JUST A GUY WHO KNOCKED ME AROUND.
MICHAEL BERENGETTI...HE WAS A CASINO BOSS, WASN'T HE?
THE MAN WHO GAVE YOU YOUR LEG-BREAKING JOB IN VEGAS...
HEY. SHOW RESPECT, SAMSON.
IT'S LAS VEGAS.

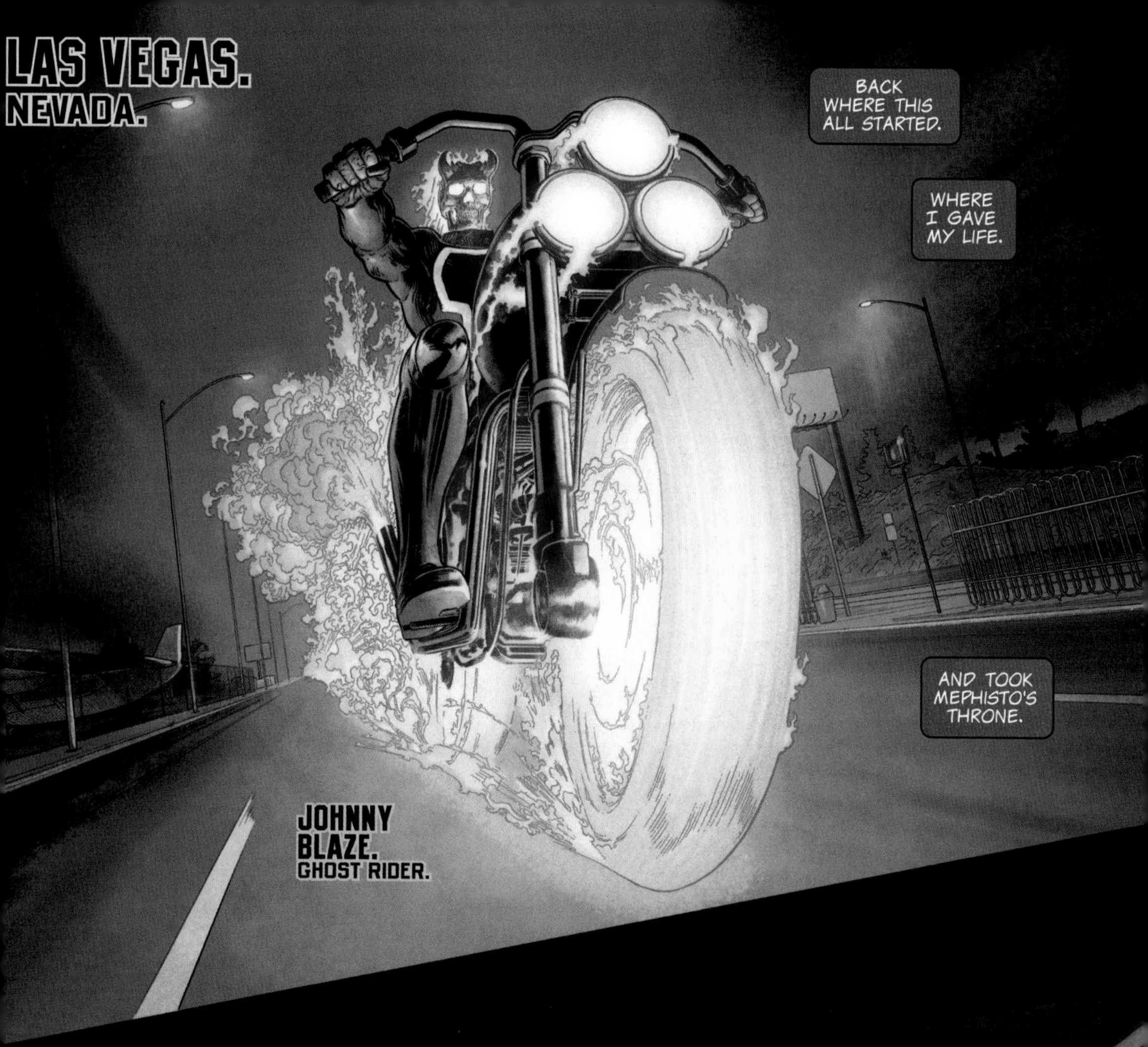
LAS VEGAS.
NEVADA.
BACK WHERE THIS ALL STARTED.
WHERE I GAVE MY LIFE.
AND TOOK MEPHISTO'S THRONE.
JOHNNY BLAZE.
GHOST RIDER.

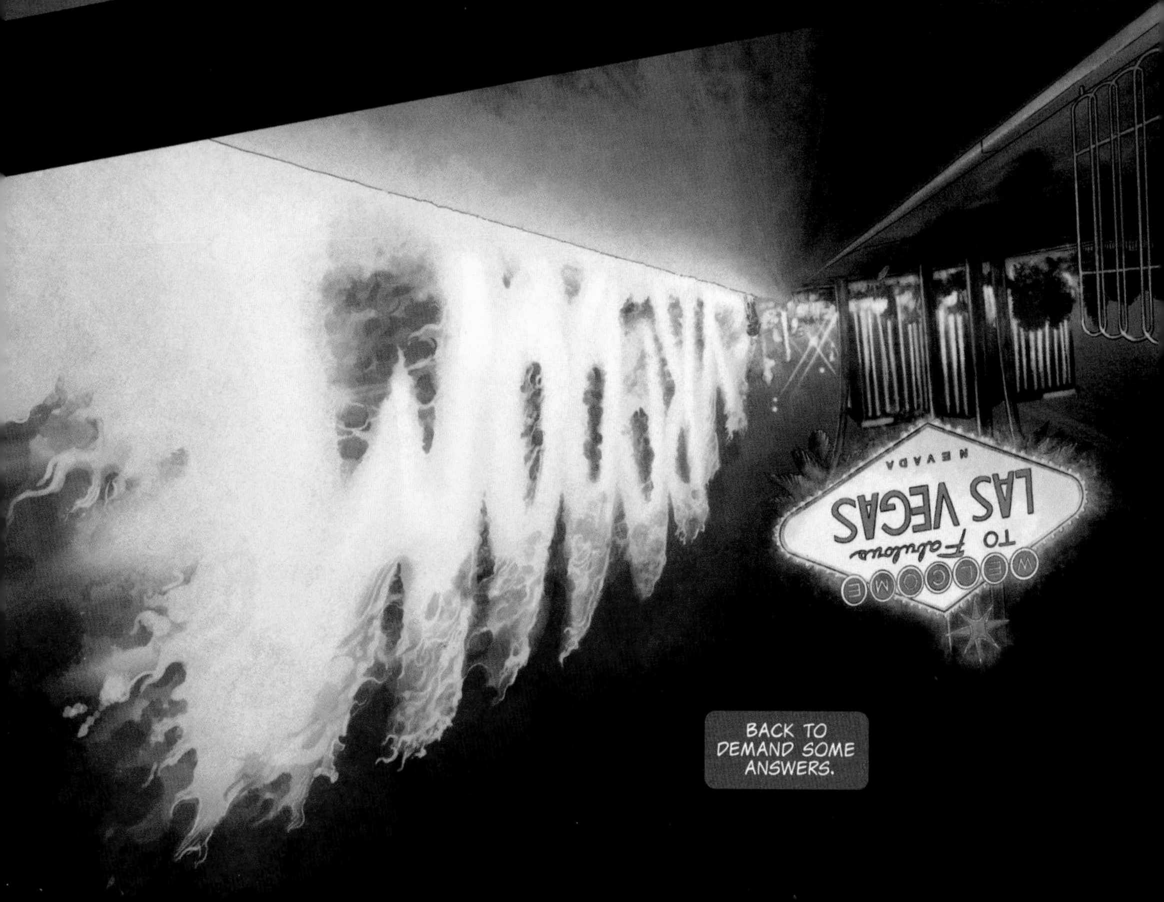
WELCOME TO Fabulous LAS VEGAS NEVADA
BACK TO DEMAND SOME ANSWERS.

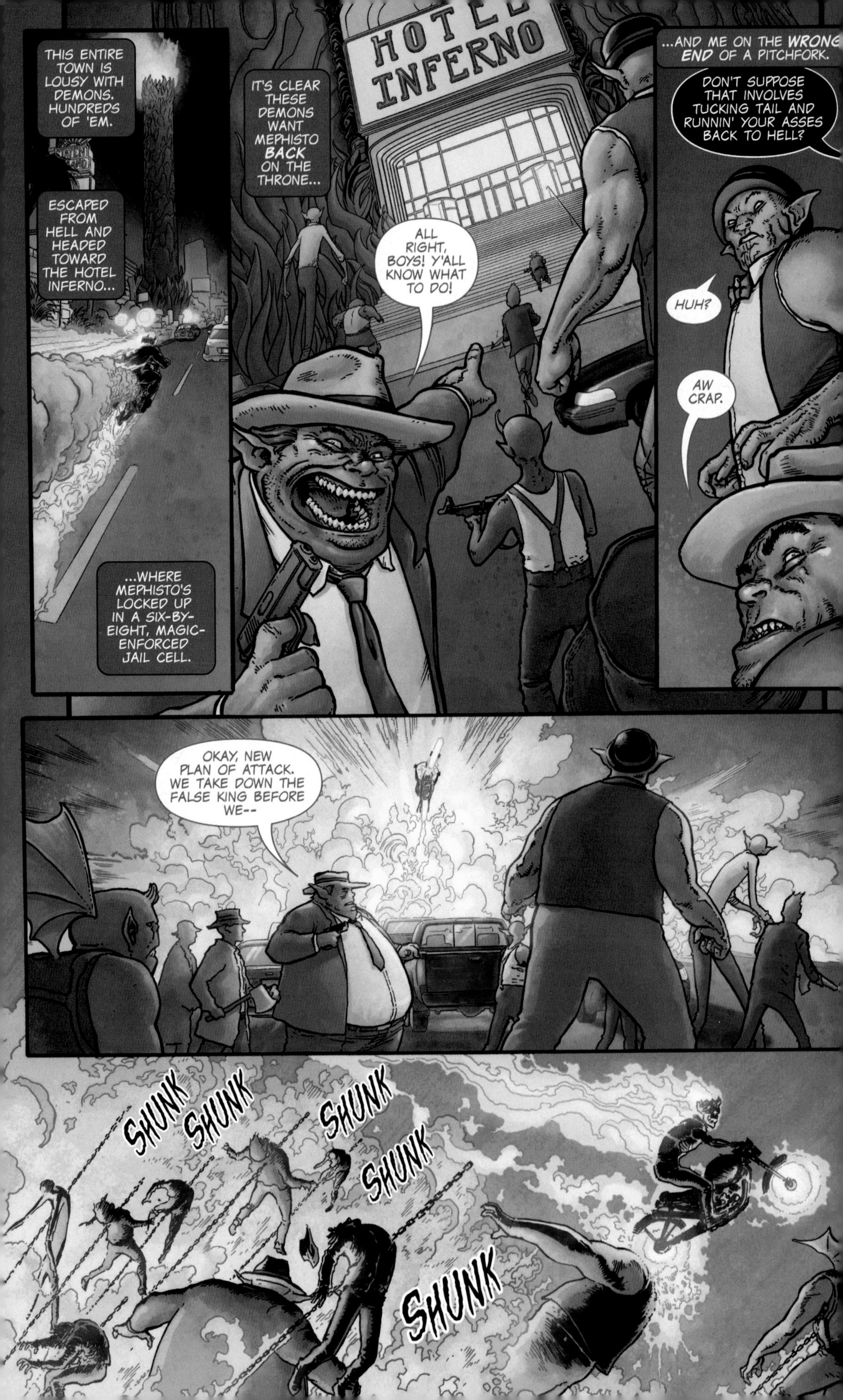

HOTEL INFERNO
THIS ENTIRE TOWN IS LOUSY WITH DEMONS. HUNDREDS OF 'EM.
ESCAPED FROM HELL AND HEADED TOWARD THE HOTEL INFERNO...
...WHERE MEPHISTO'S LOCKED UP IN A SIX-BY-EIGHT, MAGIC-ENFORCED JAIL CELL.
IT'S CLEAR THESE DEMONS WANT MEPHISTO BACK ON THE THRONE...
ALL RIGHT, BOYS! Y'ALL KNOW WHAT TO DO!
...AND ME ON THE WRONG END OF A PITCHFORK.
DON'T SUPPOSE THAT INVOLVES TUCKING TAIL AND RUNNIN' YOUR ASSES BACK TO HELL?
HUH?
AW CRAP.
OKAY, NEW PLAN OF ATTACK. WE TAKE DOWN THE FALSE KING BEFORE WE--
SHUNK
SHUNK
SHUNK
SHUNK
SHUNK

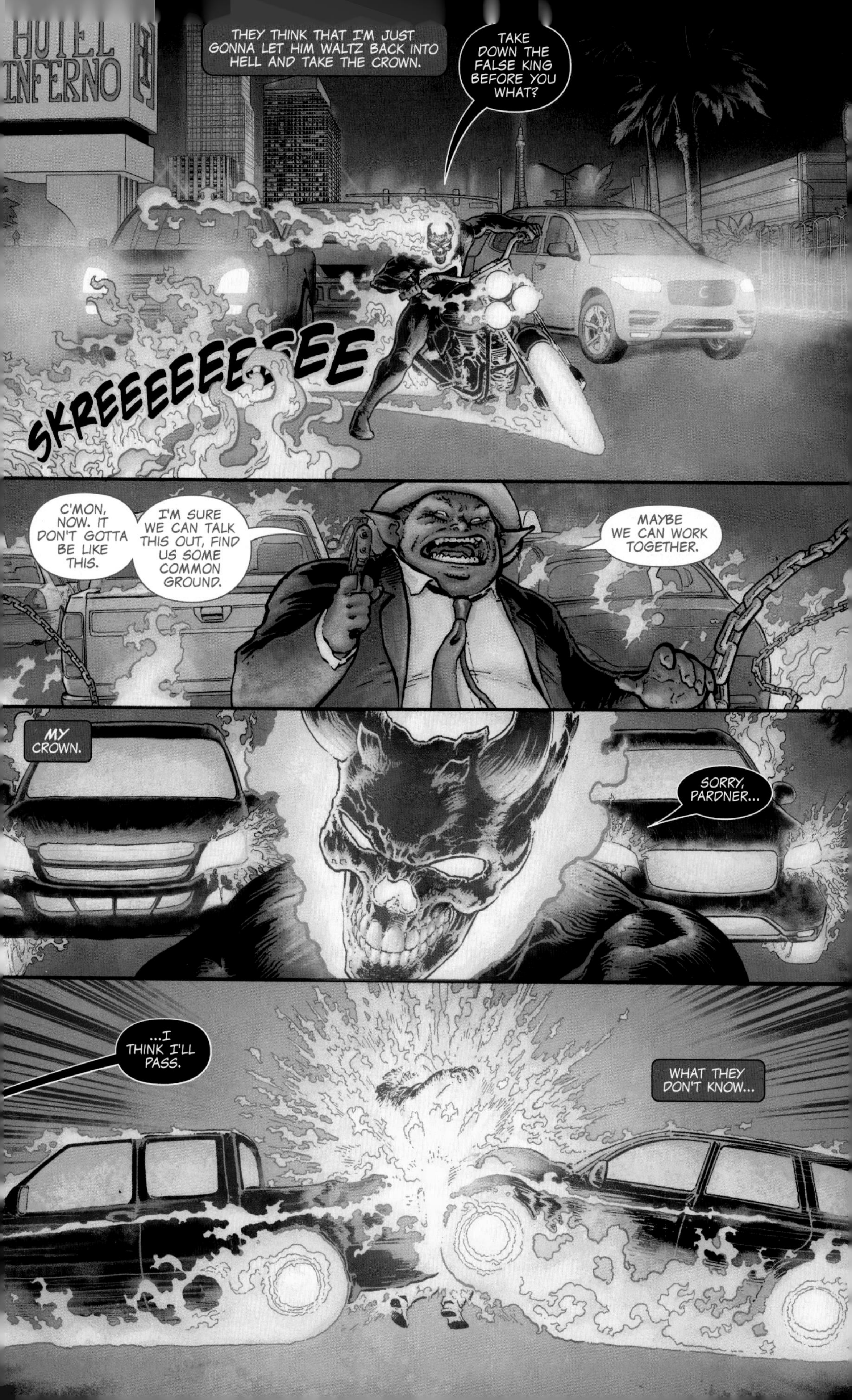
HOTEL INFERNO
THEY THINK THAT I'M JUST GONNA LET HIM WALTZ BACK INTO HELL AND TAKE THE CROWN.
TAKE DOWN THE FALSE KING BEFORE YOU WHAT?
SKREEEEEEEEEE
C'MON, NOW. IT DON'T GOTTA BE LIKE THIS.
I'M SURE WE CAN TALK THIS OUT, FIND US SOME COMMON GROUND.
MAYBE WE CAN WORK TOGETHER.
MY CROWN.
SORRY, PARDNER...
...I THINK I'LL PASS.
WHAT THEY DON'T KNOW...

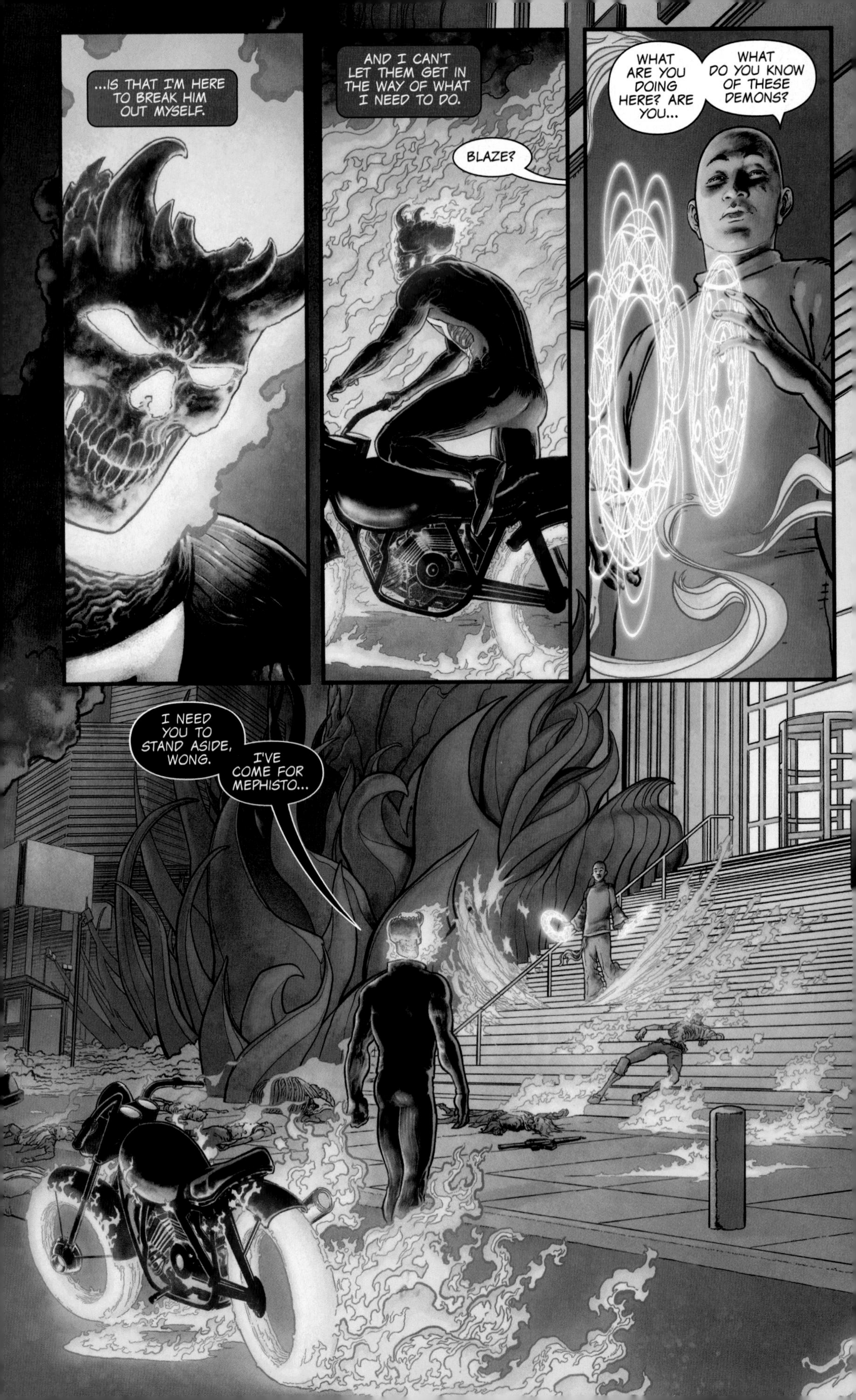
...IS THAT I'M HERE TO BREAK HIM OUT MYSELF.
AND I CAN'T LET THEM GET IN THE WAY OF WHAT I NEED TO DO.
BLAZE?
WHAT ARE YOU DOING HERE? ARE YOU...
WHAT DO YOU KNOW OF THESE DEMONS?
I NEED YOU TO STAND ASIDE, WONG.
I'VE COME FOR MEPHISTO...

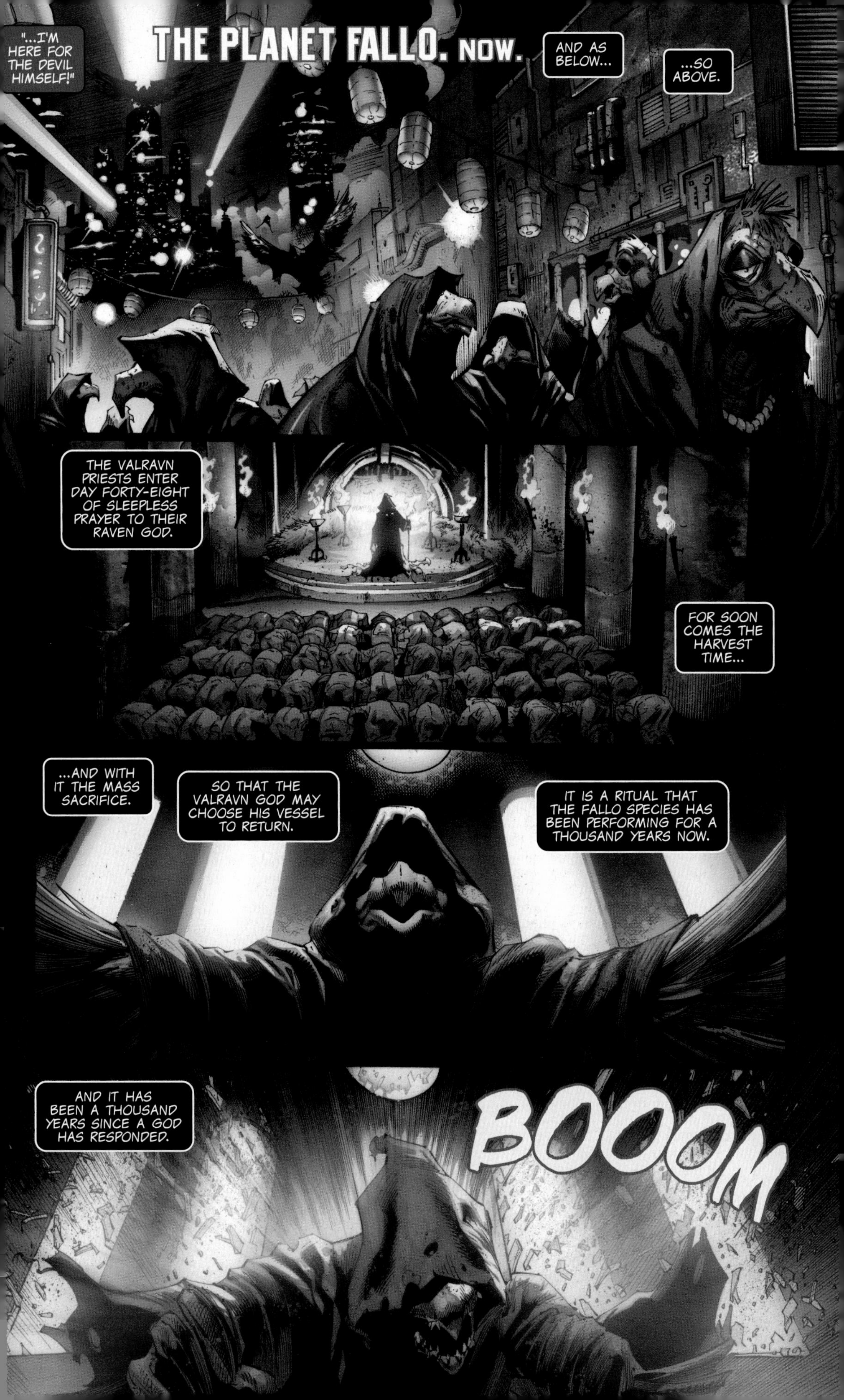
"...I'M HERE FOR THE DEVIL HIMSELF!"
THE PLANET FALLO. NOW.
AND AS BELOW...
...SO ABOVE.
THE VALRAVN PRIESTS ENTER DAY FORTY-EIGHT OF SLEEPLESS PRAYER TO THEIR RAVEN GOD.
FOR SOON COMES THE HARVEST TIME...
...AND WITH IT THE MASS SACRIFICE.
SO THAT THE VALRAVN GOD MAY CHOOSE HIS VESSEL TO RETURN.
IT IS A RITUAL THAT THE FALLO SPECIES HAS BEEN PERFORMING FOR A THOUSAND YEARS NOW.
AND IT HAS BEEN A THOUSAND YEARS SINCE A GOD HAS RESPONDED.
BOOOM

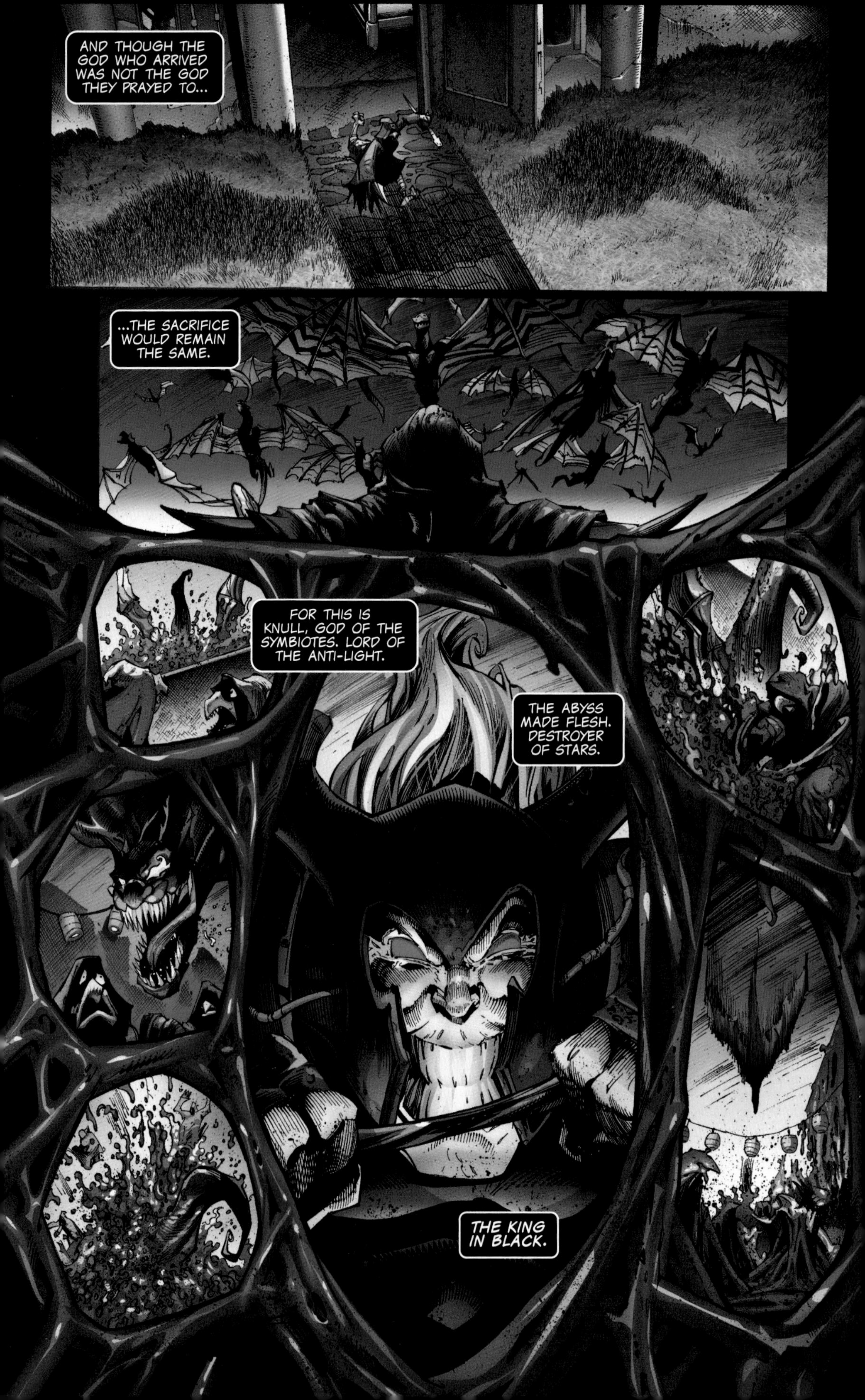
AND THOUGH THE GOD WHO ARRIVED WAS NOT THE GOD THEY PRAYED TO...
...THE SACRIFICE WOULD REMAIN THE SAME.
FOR THIS IS KNULL, GOD OF THE SYMBIOTES. LORD OF THE ANTI-LIGHT.
THE ABYSS MADE FLESH. DESTROYER OF STARS.
THE KING IN BLACK.

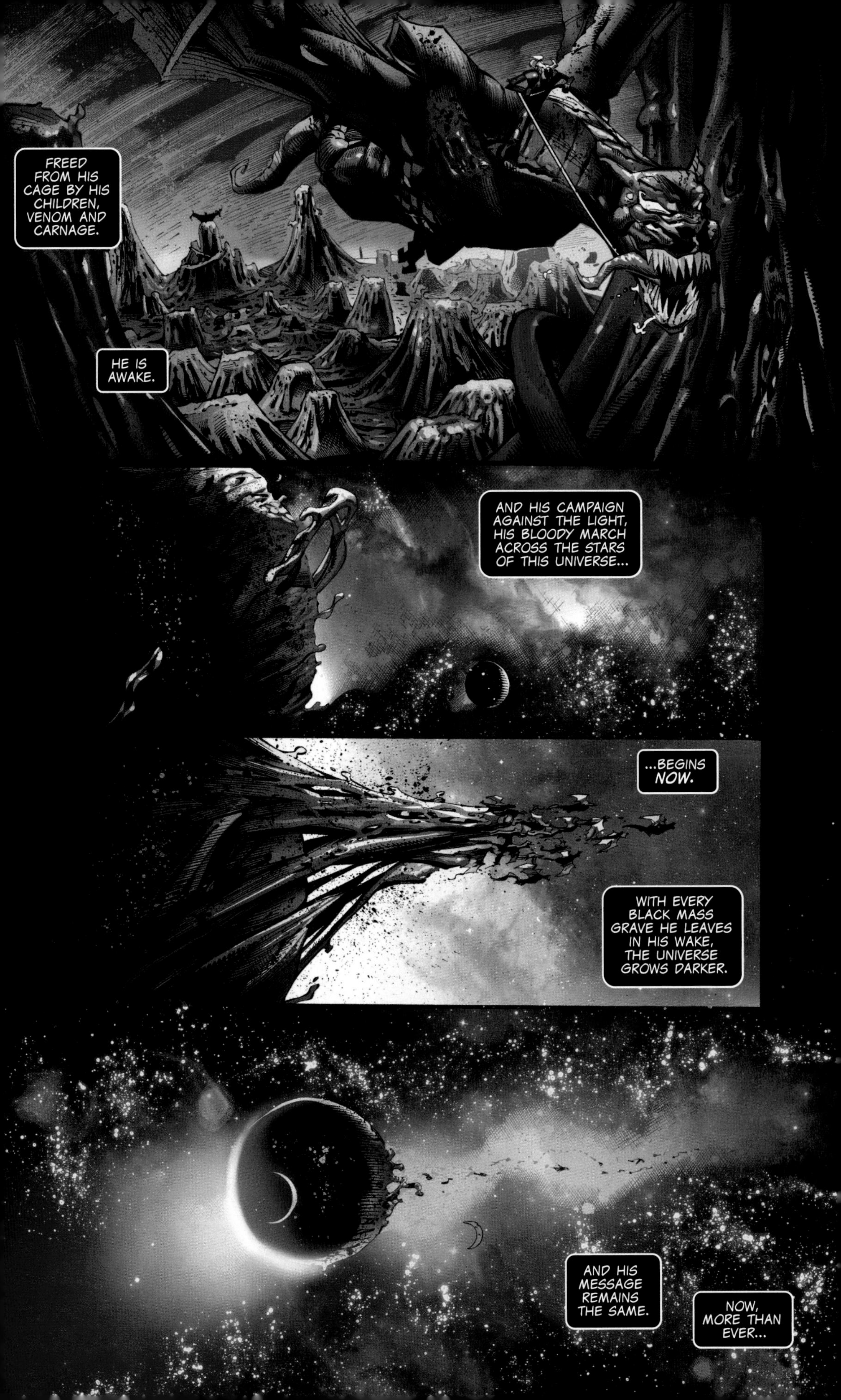
FREED FROM HIS CAGE BY HIS CHILDREN, VENOM AND CARNAGE.
HE IS AWAKE.
AND HIS CAMPAIGN AGAINST THE LIGHT, HIS BLOODY MARCH ACROSS THE STARS OF THIS UNIVERSE...
...BEGINS NOW.
WITH EVERY BLACK MASS GRAVE HE LEAVES IN HIS WAKE, THE UNIVERSE GROWS DARKER.
AND HIS MESSAGE REMAINS THE SAME.
NOW, MORE THAN EVER...

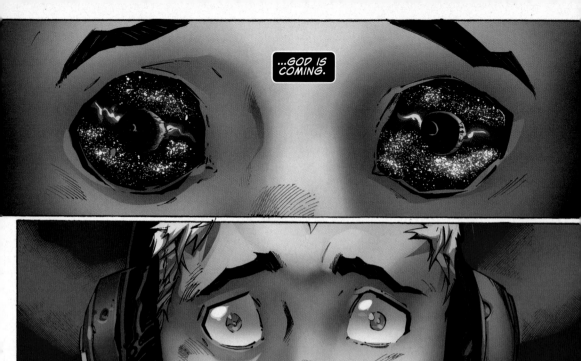

...GOD IS COMING.

FOR EVERYONE.

DYLAN?

DYLAN, HEY! ARE YOU LISTENING TO ME?

WHAT? OH, I'M SORRY, EDDIE...

BROOKLYN BRIDGE DISASTER

...I WAS A MILLION MILES AWAY.

30%

--ACCIDENT ON THE BROOKLYN BRIDGE. WE TAKE YOU NOW LIVE TO THE SCENE WHERE--

20°

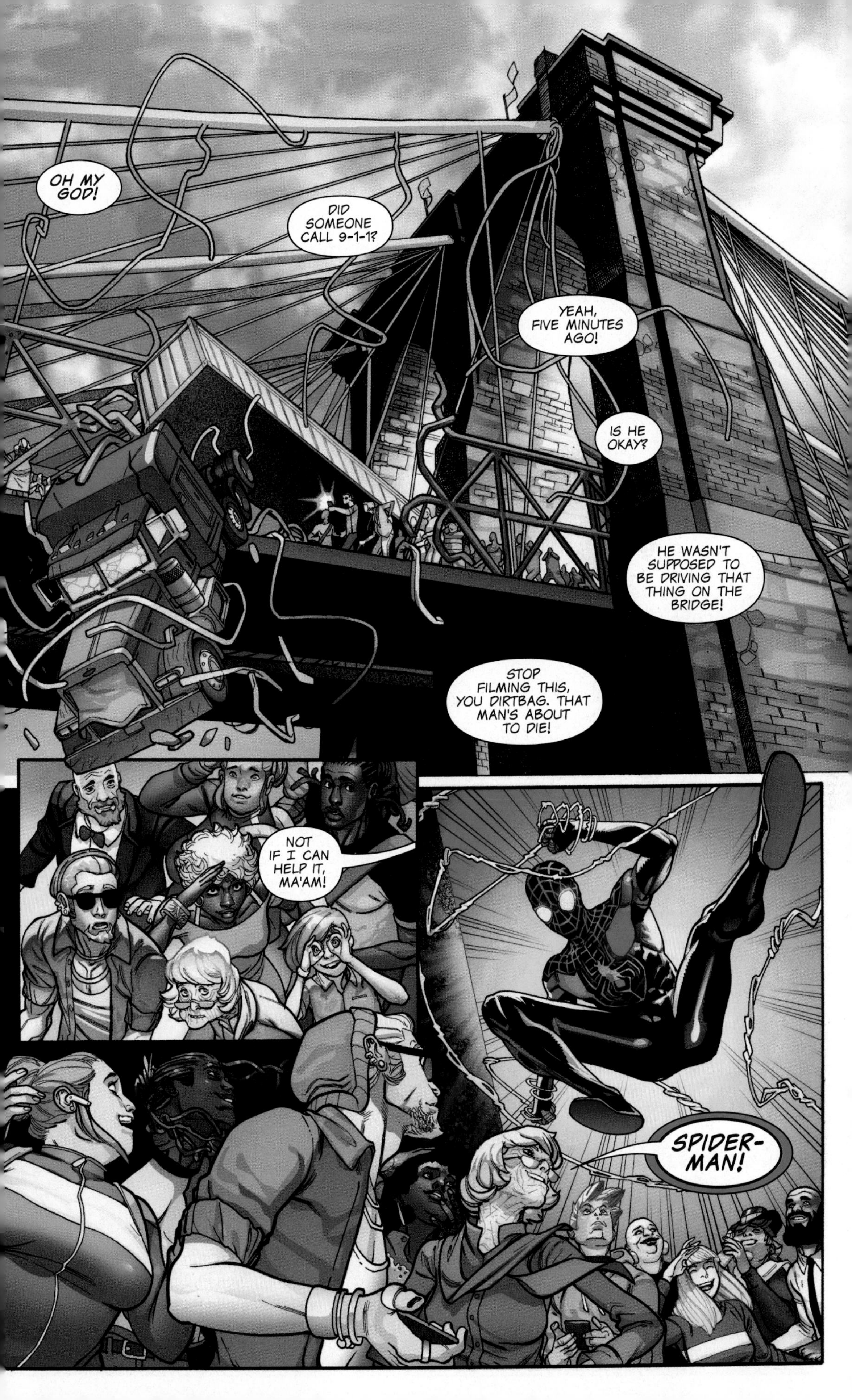
OH MY GOD!
DID SOMEONE CALL 9-1-1?
YEAH, FIVE MINUTES AGO!
IS HE OKAY?
HE WASN'T SUPPOSED TO BE DRIVING THAT THING ON THE BRIDGE!
STOP FILMING THIS, YOU DIRTBAG. THAT MAN'S ABOUT TO DIE!
NOT IF I CAN HELP IT, MA'AM!
SPIDER-MAN!

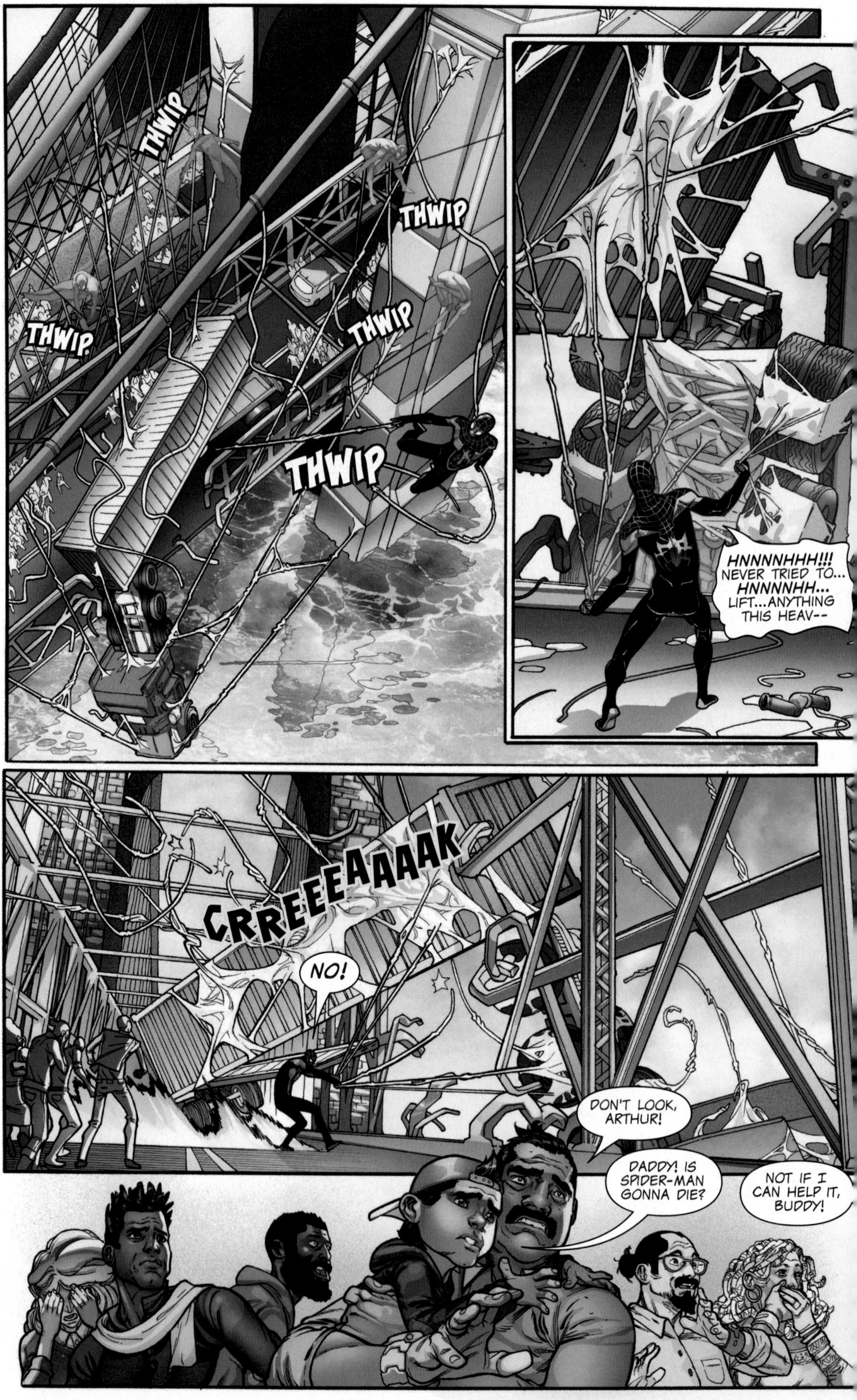
THWIP
THWIP
THWIP
THWIP
THWIP
HNNNNHHH!!! NEVER TRIED TO... HNNNNHH... LIFT...ANYTHING THIS HEAV--
CRREEEAAAAK
NO!
DON'T LOOK, ARTHUR!
DADDY! IS SPIDER-MAN GONNA DIE?
NOT IF I CAN HELP IT, BUDDY!

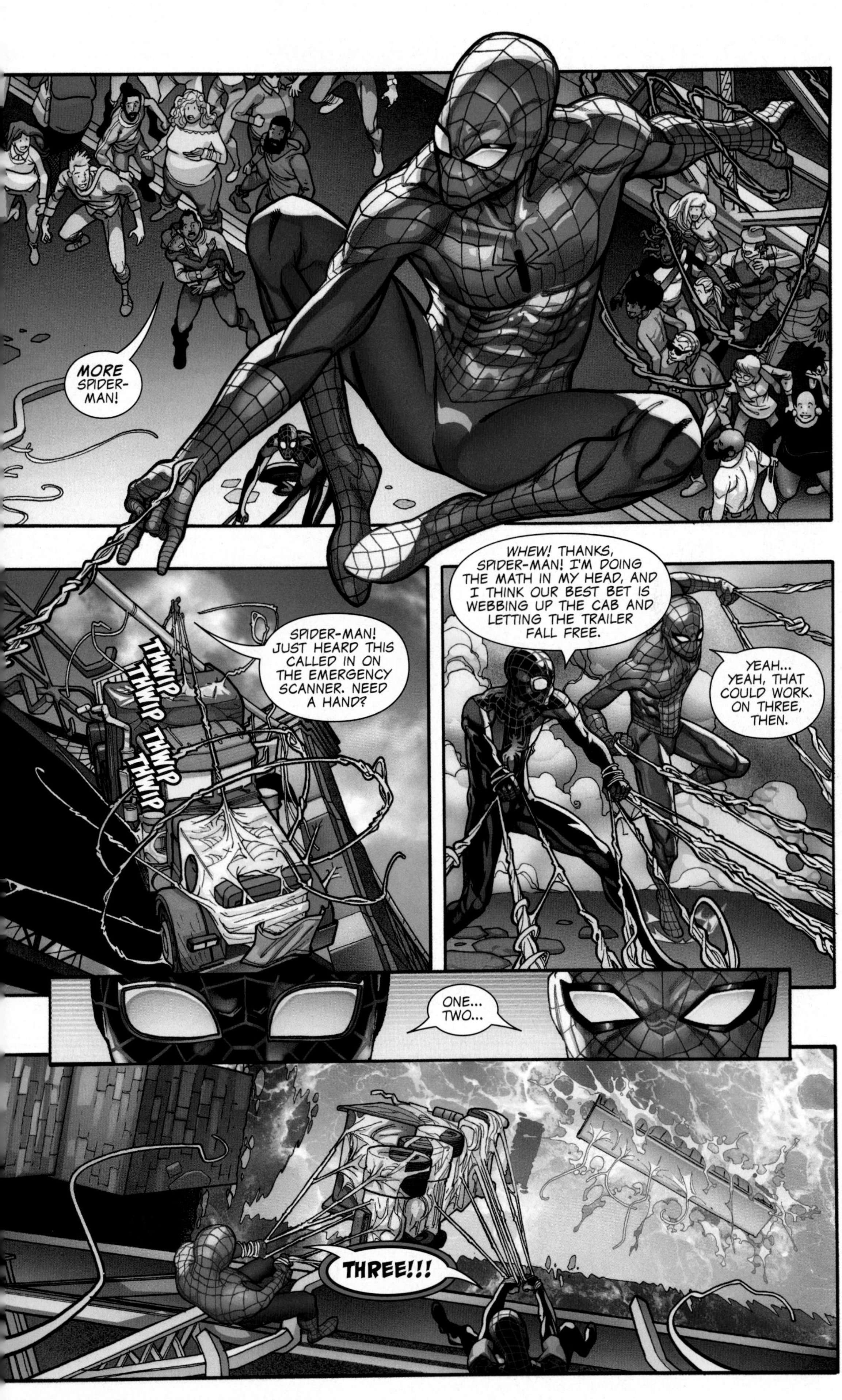
MORE SPIDER-MAN!
THWIP THWIP THWIP THWIP
SPIDER-MAN! JUST HEARD THIS CALLED IN ON THE EMERGENCY SCANNER. NEED A HAND?
WHEW! THANKS, SPIDER-MAN! I'M DOING THE MATH IN MY HEAD, AND I THINK OUR BEST BET IS WEBBING UP THE CAB AND LETTING THE TRAILER FALL FREE.
YEAH... YEAH, THAT COULD WORK. ON THREE, THEN.
ONE... TWO...
THREE!!!

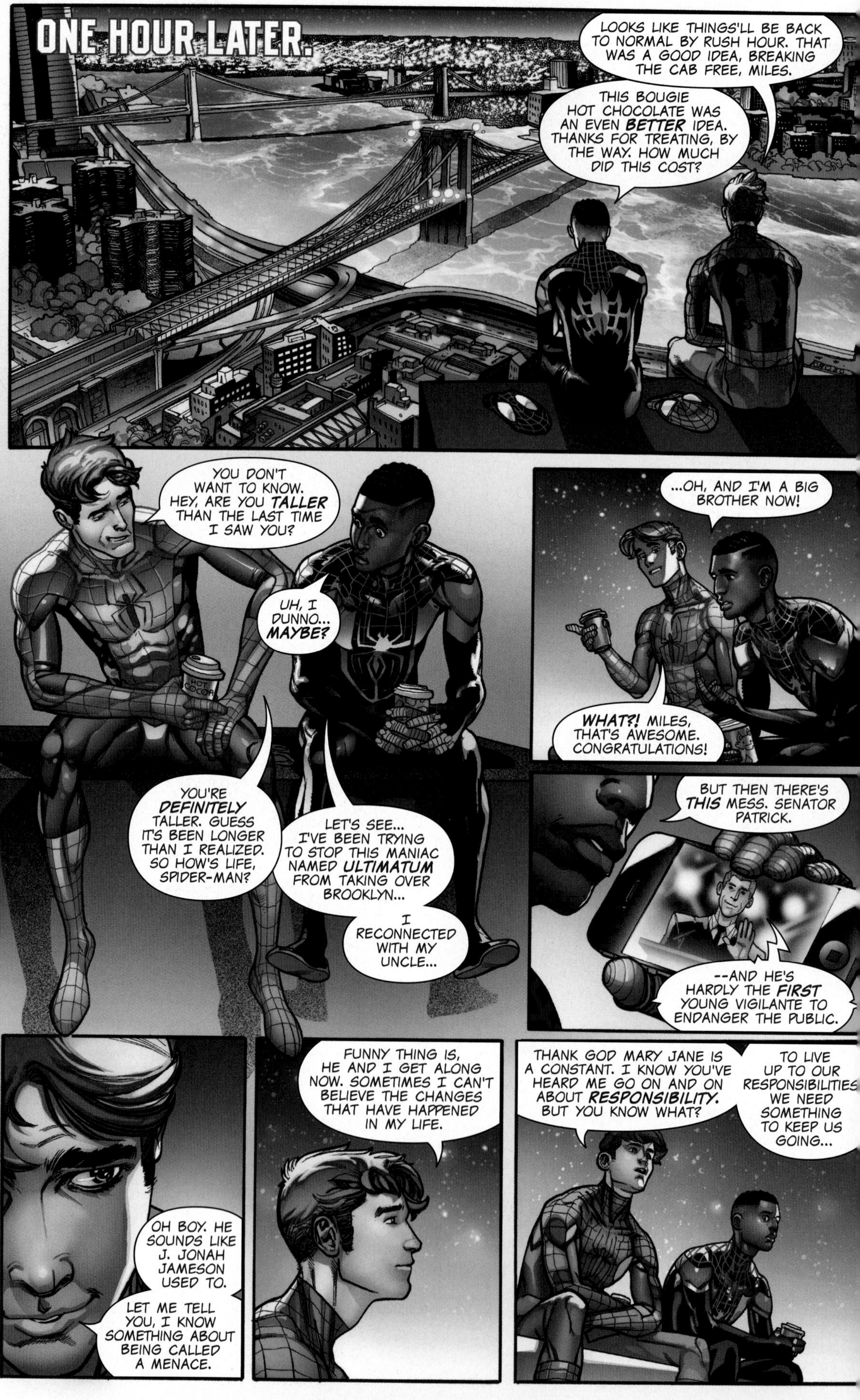
ONE HOUR LATER.
LOOKS LIKE THINGS'LL BE BACK TO NORMAL BY RUSH HOUR. THAT WAS A GOOD IDEA, BREAKING THE CAB FREE, MILES.
THIS BOUGIE HOT CHOCOLATE WAS AN EVEN BETTER IDEA. THANKS FOR TREATING, BY THE WAY. HOW MUCH DID THIS COST?
YOU DON'T WANT TO KNOW. HEY, ARE YOU TALLER THAN THE LAST TIME I SAW YOU?
UH, I DUNNO... MAYBE?
HOT COCOA
YOU'RE DEFINITELY TALLER. GUESS IT'S BEEN LONGER THAN I REALIZED. SO HOW'S LIFE, SPIDER-MAN?
LET'S SEE... I'VE BEEN TRYING TO STOP THIS MANIAC NAMED ULTIMATUM FROM TAKING OVER BROOKLYN...
I RECONNECTED WITH MY UNCLE...
...OH, AND I'M A BIG BROTHER NOW!
WHAT?! MILES, THAT'S AWESOME. CONGRATULATIONS!
BUT THEN THERE'S THIS MESS. SENATOR PATRICK.
--AND HE'S HARDLY THE FIRST YOUNG VIGILANTE TO ENDANGER THE PUBLIC.
OH BOY. HE SOUNDS LIKE J. JONAH JAMESON USED TO.
LET ME TELL YOU, I KNOW SOMETHING ABOUT BEING CALLED A MENACE.
FUNNY THING IS, HE AND I GET ALONG NOW. SOMETIMES I CAN'T BELIEVE THE CHANGES THAT HAVE HAPPENED IN MY LIFE.
THANK GOD MARY JANE IS A CONSTANT. I KNOW YOU'VE HEARD ME GO ON AND ON ABOUT RESPONSIBILITY. BUT YOU KNOW WHAT?
TO LIVE UP TO OUR RESPONSIBILITIES WE NEED SOMETHING TO KEEP US GOING...

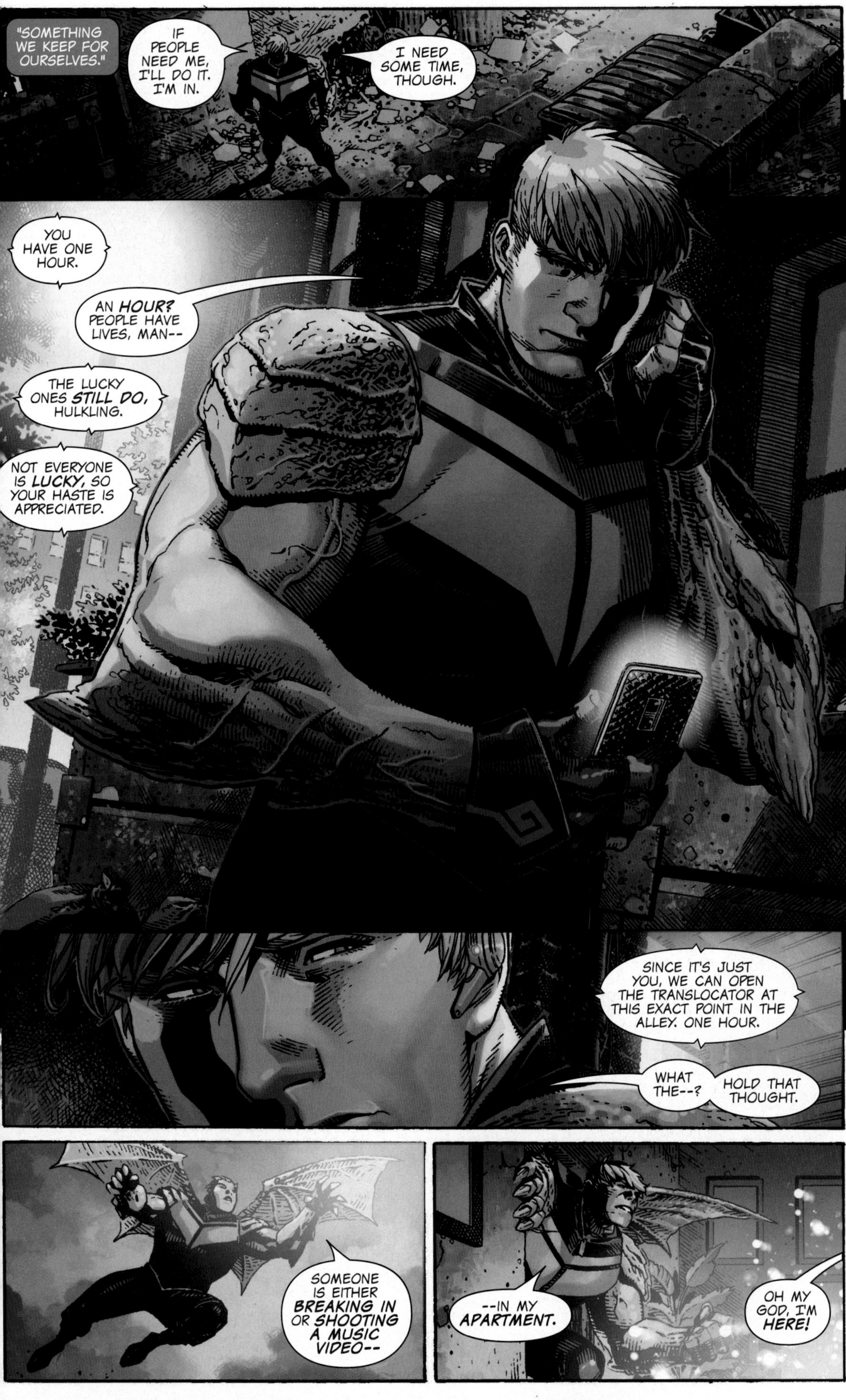
"SOMETHING WE KEEP FOR OURSELVES."
IF PEOPLE NEED ME, I'LL DO IT. I'M IN.
I NEED SOME TIME, THOUGH.
YOU HAVE ONE HOUR.
AN HOUR? PEOPLE HAVE LIVES, MAN--
THE LUCKY ONES STILL DO, HULKLING.
NOT EVERYONE IS LUCKY, SO YOUR HASTE IS APPRECIATED.
SINCE IT'S JUST YOU, WE CAN OPEN THE TRANSLOCATOR AT THIS EXACT POINT IN THE ALLEY. ONE HOUR.
WHAT THE--?
HOLD THAT THOUGHT.
SOMEONE IS EITHER BREAKING IN OR SHOOTING A MUSIC VIDEO--
--IN MY APARTMENT.
OH MY GOD, I'M HERE!

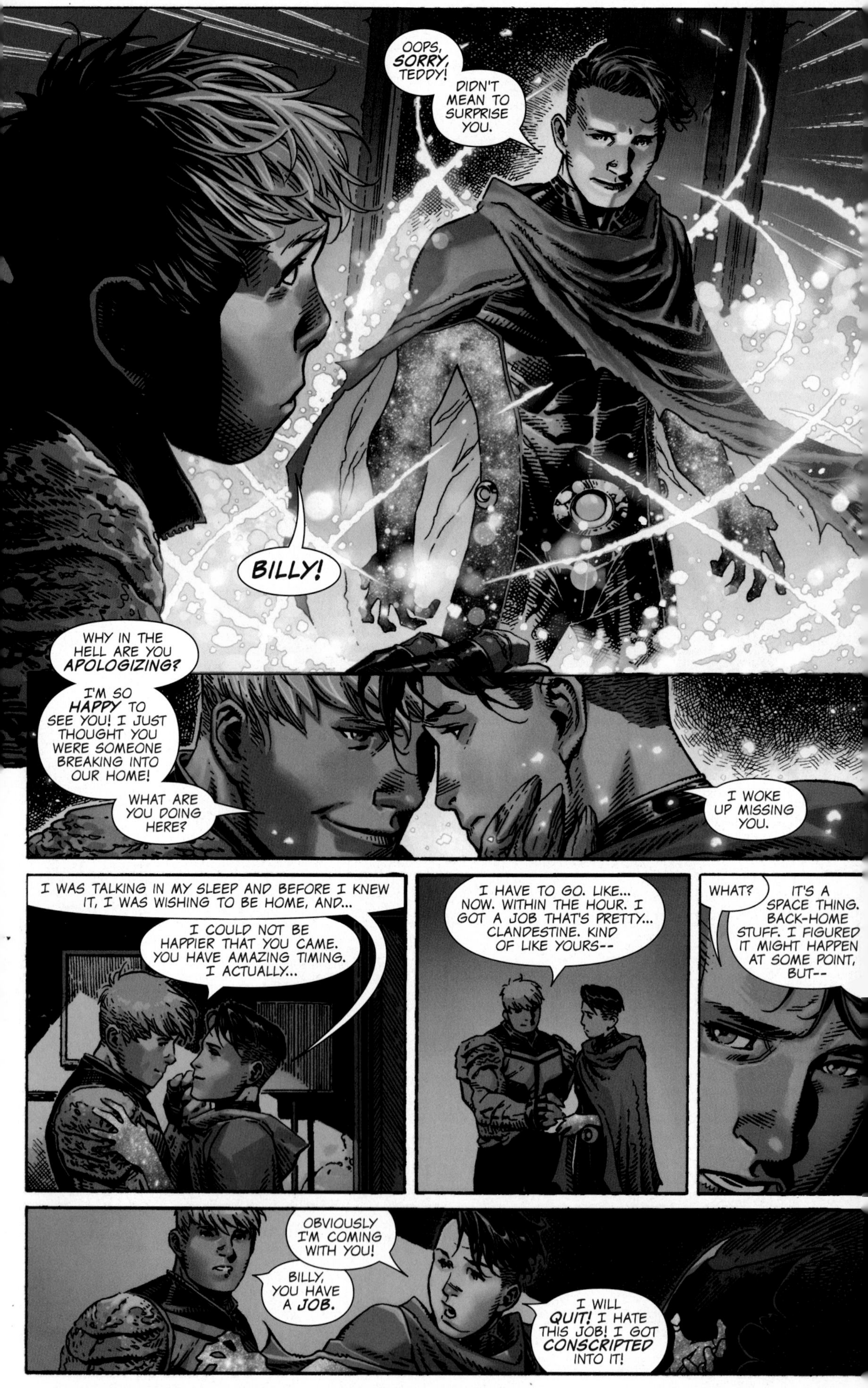

OOPS, SORRY, TEDDY!
DIDN'T MEAN TO SURPRISE YOU.
BILLY!
WHY IN THE HELL ARE YOU APOLOGIZING?
I'M SO HAPPY TO SEE YOU! I JUST THOUGHT YOU WERE SOMEONE BREAKING INTO OUR HOME!
WHAT ARE YOU DOING HERE?
I WOKE UP MISSING YOU.
I WAS TALKING IN MY SLEEP AND BEFORE I KNEW IT, I WAS WISHING TO BE HOME, AND...
I COULD NOT BE HAPPIER THAT YOU CAME. YOU HAVE AMAZING TIMING. I ACTUALLY...
I HAVE TO GO. LIKE... NOW. WITHIN THE HOUR. I GOT A JOB THAT'S PRETTY... CLANDESTINE. KIND OF LIKE YOURS--
WHAT?
IT'S A SPACE THING. BACK-HOME STUFF. I FIGURED IT MIGHT HAPPEN AT SOME POINT, BUT--
OBVIOUSLY I'M COMING WITH YOU!
BILLY, YOU HAVE A JOB.
I WILL QUIT! I HATE THIS JOB! I GOT CONSCRIPTED INTO IT!

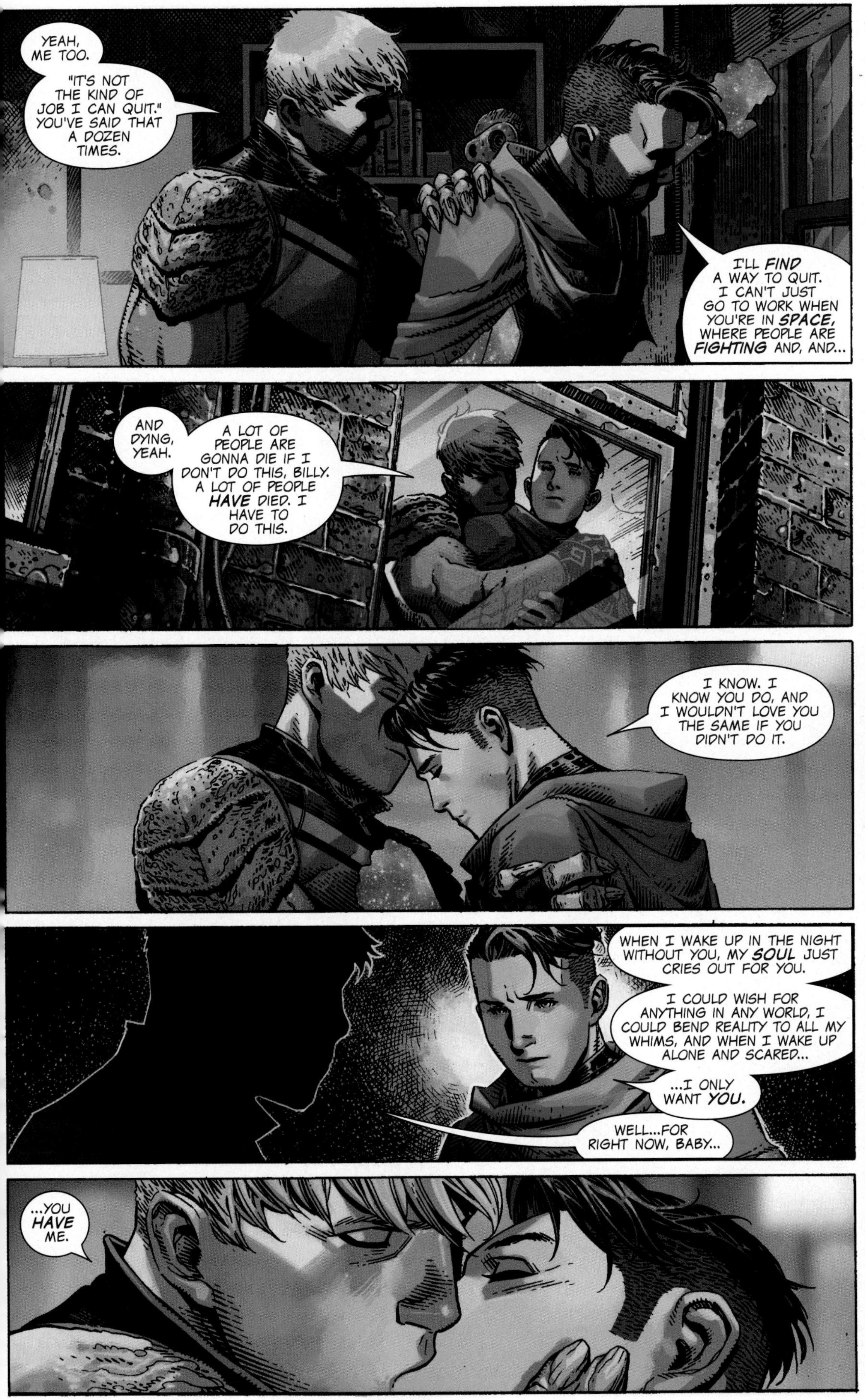
YEAH, ME TOO.
"IT'S NOT THE KIND OF JOB I CAN QUIT." YOU'VE SAID THAT A DOZEN TIMES.
I'LL FIND A WAY TO QUIT. I CAN'T JUST GO TO WORK WHEN YOU'RE IN SPACE, WHERE PEOPLE ARE FIGHTING AND, AND...
AND DYING, YEAH.
A LOT OF PEOPLE ARE GONNA DIE IF I DON'T DO THIS, BILLY. A LOT OF PEOPLE HAVE DIED. I HAVE TO DO THIS.
I KNOW. I KNOW YOU DO, AND I WOULDN'T LOVE YOU THE SAME IF YOU DIDN'T DO IT.
WHEN I WAKE UP IN THE NIGHT WITHOUT YOU, MY SOUL JUST CRIES OUT FOR YOU.
I COULD WISH FOR ANYTHING IN ANY WORLD, I COULD BEND REALITY TO ALL MY WHIMS, AND WHEN I WAKE UP ALONE AND SCARED...
...I ONLY WANT YOU.
WELL...FOR RIGHT NOW, BABY...
...YOU HAVE ME.

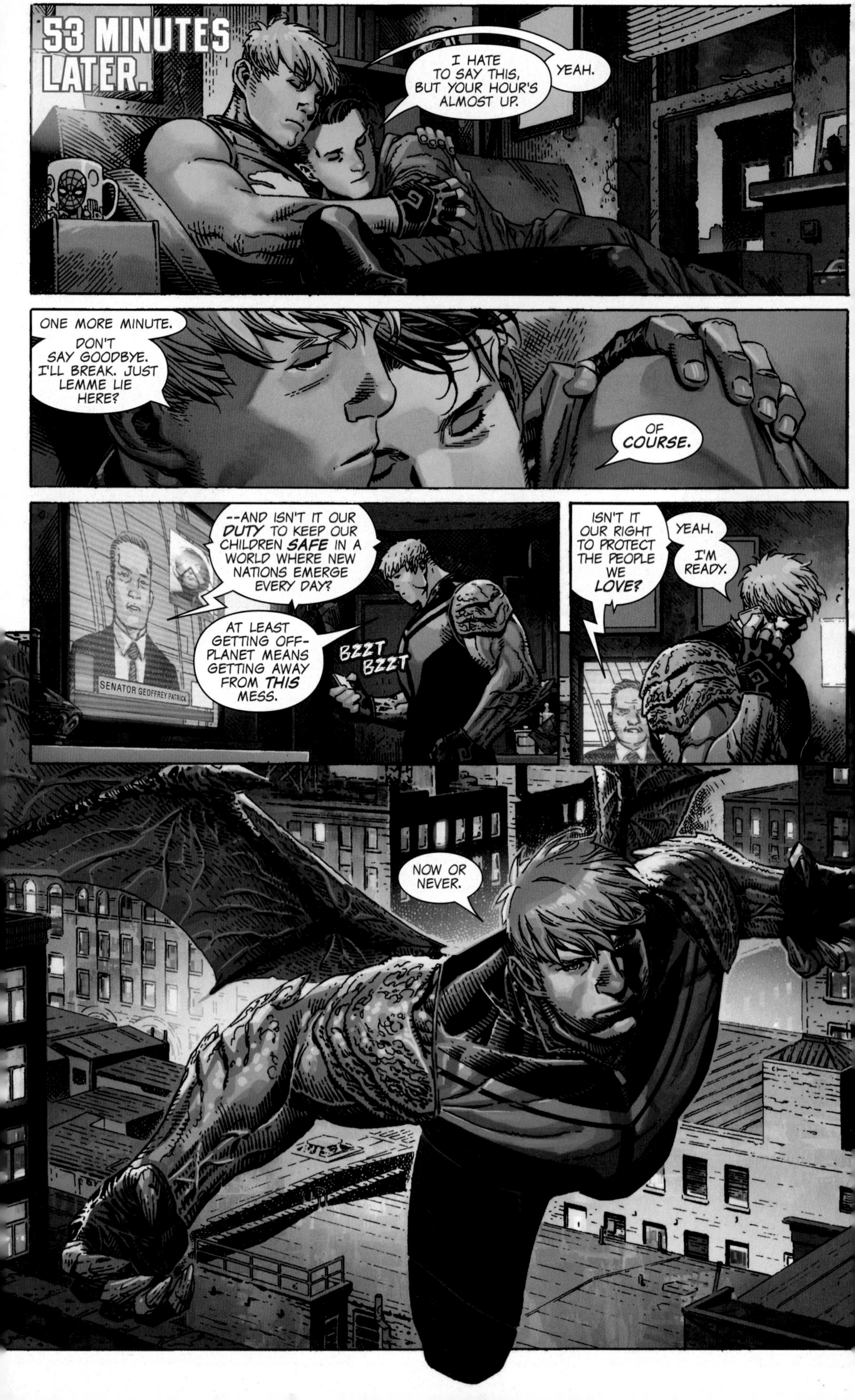
53 MINUTES LATER.
I HATE TO SAY THIS, BUT YOUR HOUR'S ALMOST UP.
YEAH.
ONE MORE MINUTE.
DON'T SAY GOODBYE. I'LL BREAK. JUST LEMME LIE HERE?
OF COURSE.
--AND ISN'T IT OUR DUTY TO KEEP OUR CHILDREN SAFE IN A WORLD WHERE NEW NATIONS EMERGE EVERY DAY?
SENATOR GEOFFREY PATRICK
AT LEAST GETTING OFF-PLANET MEANS GETTING AWAY FROM THIS MESS.
BZZT BZZT
ISN'T IT OUR RIGHT TO PROTECT THE PEOPLE WE LOVE?
YEAH.
I'M READY.
NOW OR NEVER.

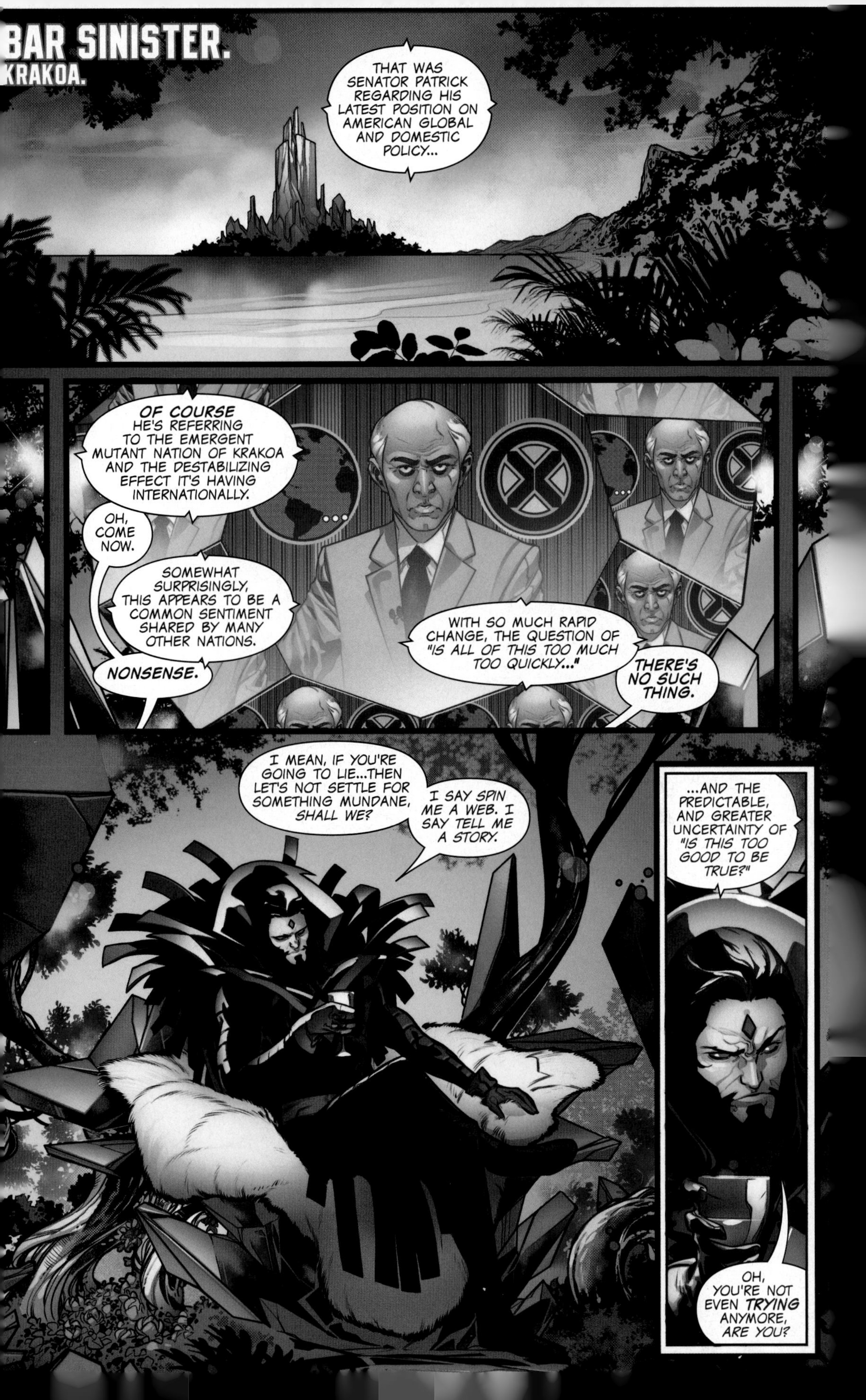

BAR SINISTER.
KRAKOA.
THAT WAS SENATOR PATRICK REGARDING HIS LATEST POSITION ON AMERICAN GLOBAL AND DOMESTIC POLICY...
OF COURSE HE'S REFERRING TO THE EMERGENT MUTANT NATION OF KRAKOA AND THE DESTABILIZING EFFECT IT'S HAVING INTERNATIONALLY.
OH, COME NOW.
SOMEWHAT SURPRISINGLY, THIS APPEARS TO BE A COMMON SENTIMENT SHARED BY MANY OTHER NATIONS.
NONSENSE.
WITH SO MUCH RAPID CHANGE, THE QUESTION OF "IS ALL OF THIS TOO MUCH TOO QUICKLY..."
THERE'S NO SUCH THING.
I MEAN, IF YOU'RE GOING TO LIE...THEN LET'S NOT SETTLE FOR SOMETHING MUNDANE, SHALL WE?
I SAY SPIN ME A WEB. I SAY TELL ME A STORY.
...AND THE PREDICTABLE, AND GREATER UNCERTAINTY OF "IS THIS TOO GOOD TO BE TRUE?"
OH, YOU'RE NOT EVEN TRYING ANYMORE, ARE YOU?

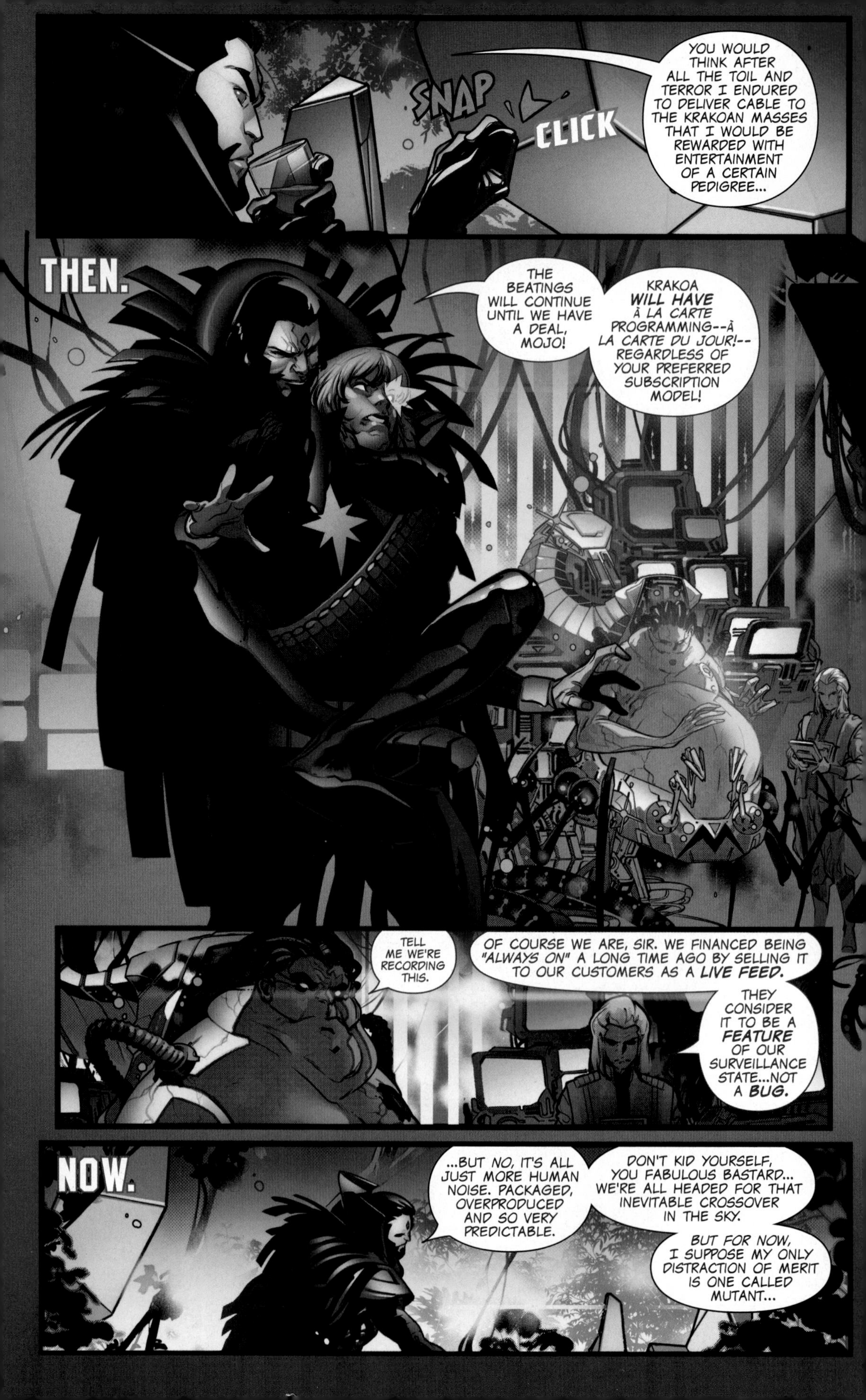
SNAP
CLICK
YOU WOULD THINK AFTER ALL THE TOIL AND TERROR I ENDURED TO DELIVER CABLE TO THE KRAKOAN MASSES THAT I WOULD BE REWARDED WITH ENTERTAINMENT OF A CERTAIN PEDIGREE...
THEN.
THE BEATINGS WILL CONTINUE UNTIL WE HAVE A DEAL, MOJO!
KRAKOA WILL HAVE À LA CARTE PROGRAMMING--À LA CARTE DU JOUR!--REGARDLESS OF YOUR PREFERRED SUBSCRIPTION MODEL!
TELL ME WE'RE RECORDING THIS.
OF COURSE WE ARE, SIR. WE FINANCED BEING "ALWAYS ON" A LONG TIME AGO BY SELLING IT TO OUR CUSTOMERS AS A LIVE FEED.
THEY CONSIDER IT TO BE A FEATURE OF OUR SURVEILLANCE STATE...NOT A BUG.
NOW.
...BUT NO, IT'S ALL JUST MORE HUMAN NOISE. PACKAGED, OVERPRODUCED AND SO VERY PREDICTABLE.
DON'T KID YOURSELF, YOU FABULOUS BASTARD... WE'RE ALL HEADED FOR THAT INEVITABLE CROSSOVER IN THE SKY.
BUT FOR NOW, I SUPPOSE MY ONLY DISTRACTION OF MERIT IS ONE CALLED MUTANT...

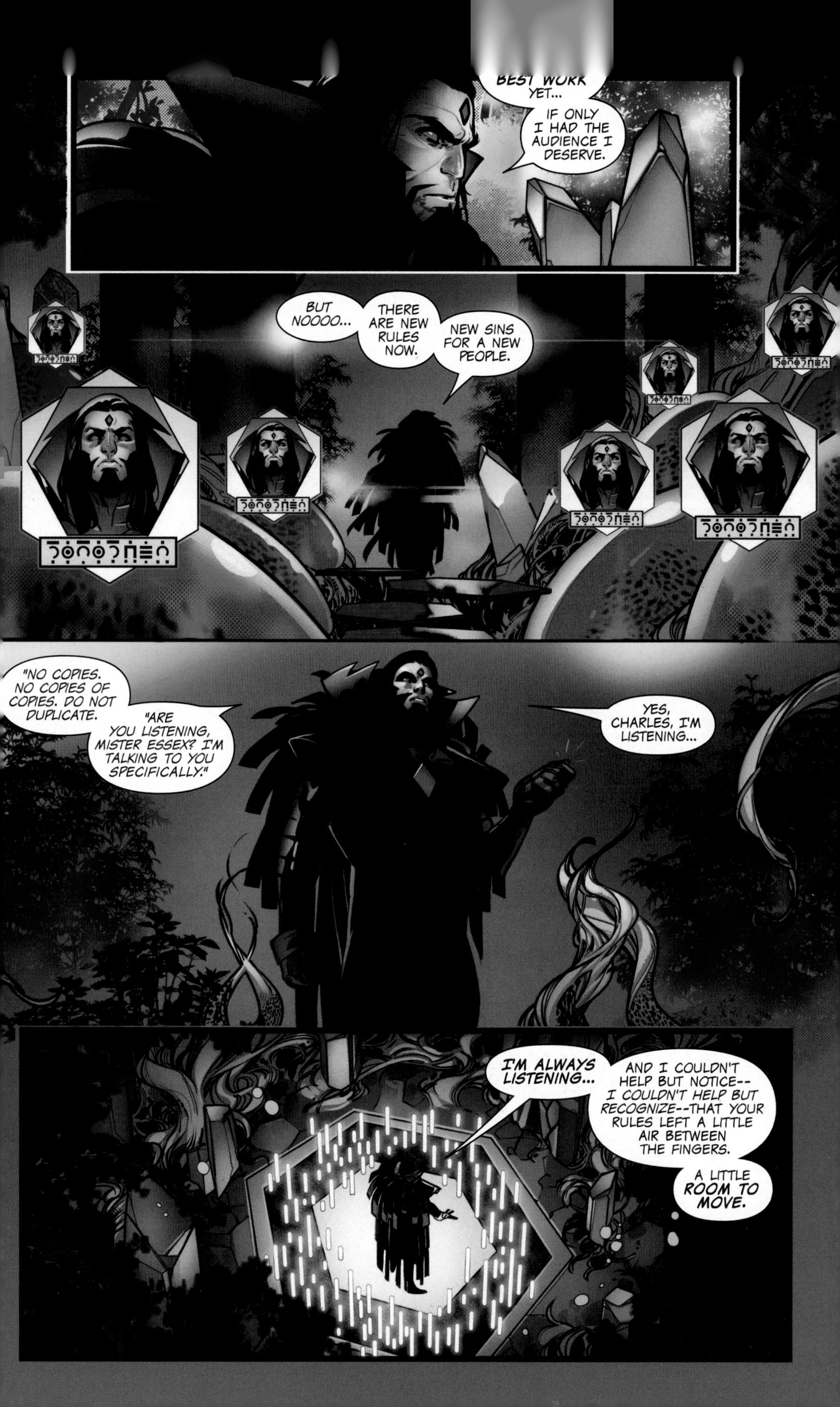

BEST WORK YET...
IF ONLY I HAD THE AUDIENCE I DESERVE.
BUT NOOOO...
THERE ARE NEW RULES NOW.
NEW SINS FOR A NEW PEOPLE.
"NO COPIES. NO COPIES OF COPIES. DO NOT DUPLICATE.
"ARE YOU LISTENING, MISTER ESSEX? I'M TALKING TO YOU SPECIFICALLY."
YES, CHARLES, I'M LISTENING...
I'M ALWAYS LISTENING...
AND I COULDN'T HELP BUT NOTICE-- I COULDN'T HELP BUT RECOGNIZE--THAT YOUR RULES LEFT A LITTLE AIR BETWEEN THE FINGERS.
A LITTLE ROOM TO MOVE.

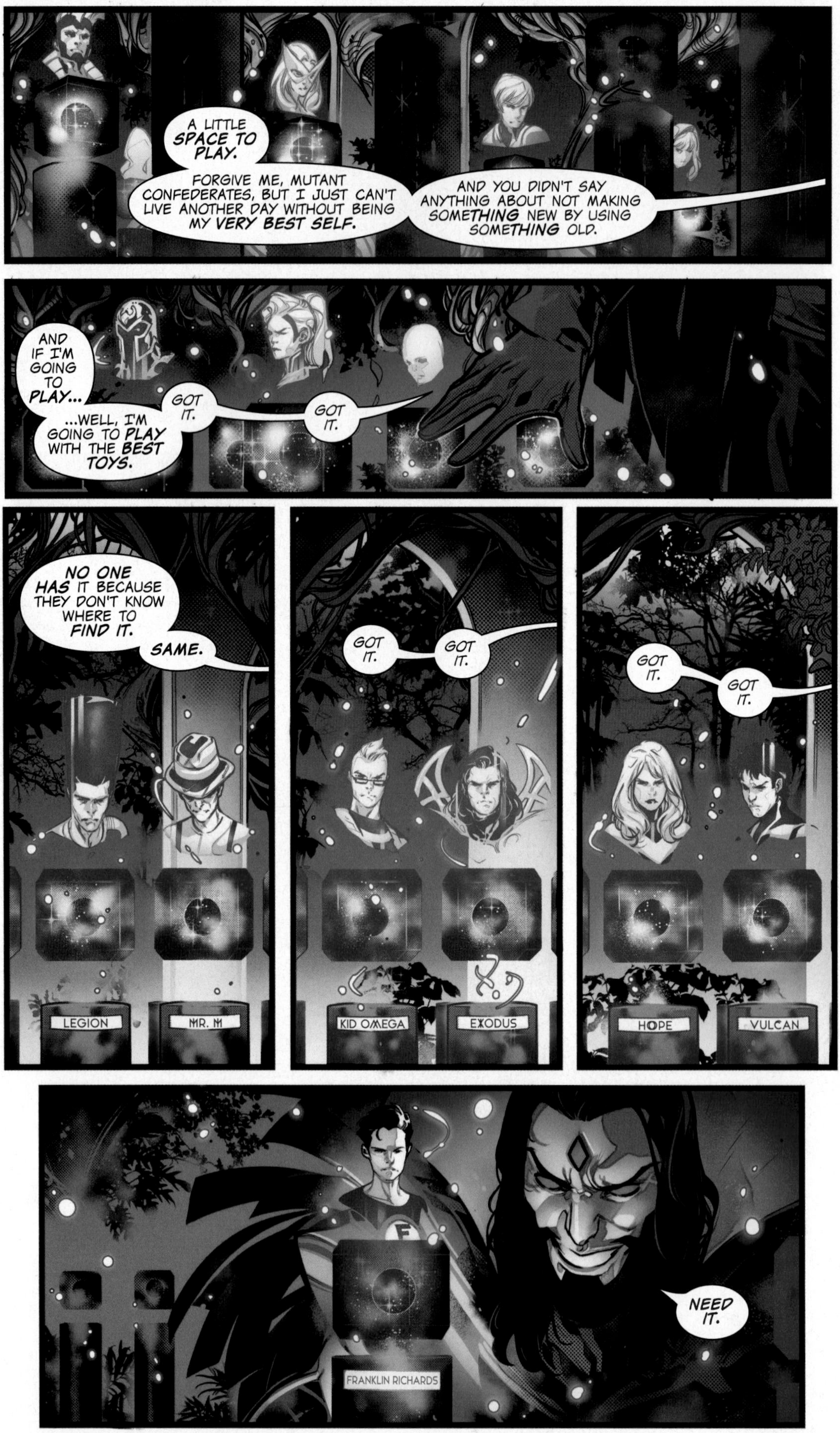
A LITTLE SPACE TO PLAY.
FORGIVE ME, MUTANT CONFEDERATES, BUT I JUST CAN'T LIVE ANOTHER DAY WITHOUT BEING MY VERY BEST SELF.
AND YOU DIDN'T SAY ANYTHING ABOUT NOT MAKING SOMETHING NEW BY USING SOMETHING OLD.
AND IF I'M GOING TO PLAY...
...WELL, I'M GOING TO PLAY WITH THE BEST TOYS.
GOT IT.
GOT IT.
NO ONE HAS IT BECAUSE THEY DON'T KNOW WHERE TO FIND IT.
SAME.
LEGION
MR. M
GOT IT.
GOT IT.
KID OMEGA
EXODUS
GOT IT.
GOT IT.
HOPE
VULCAN
FRANKLIN RICHARDS
NEED IT.

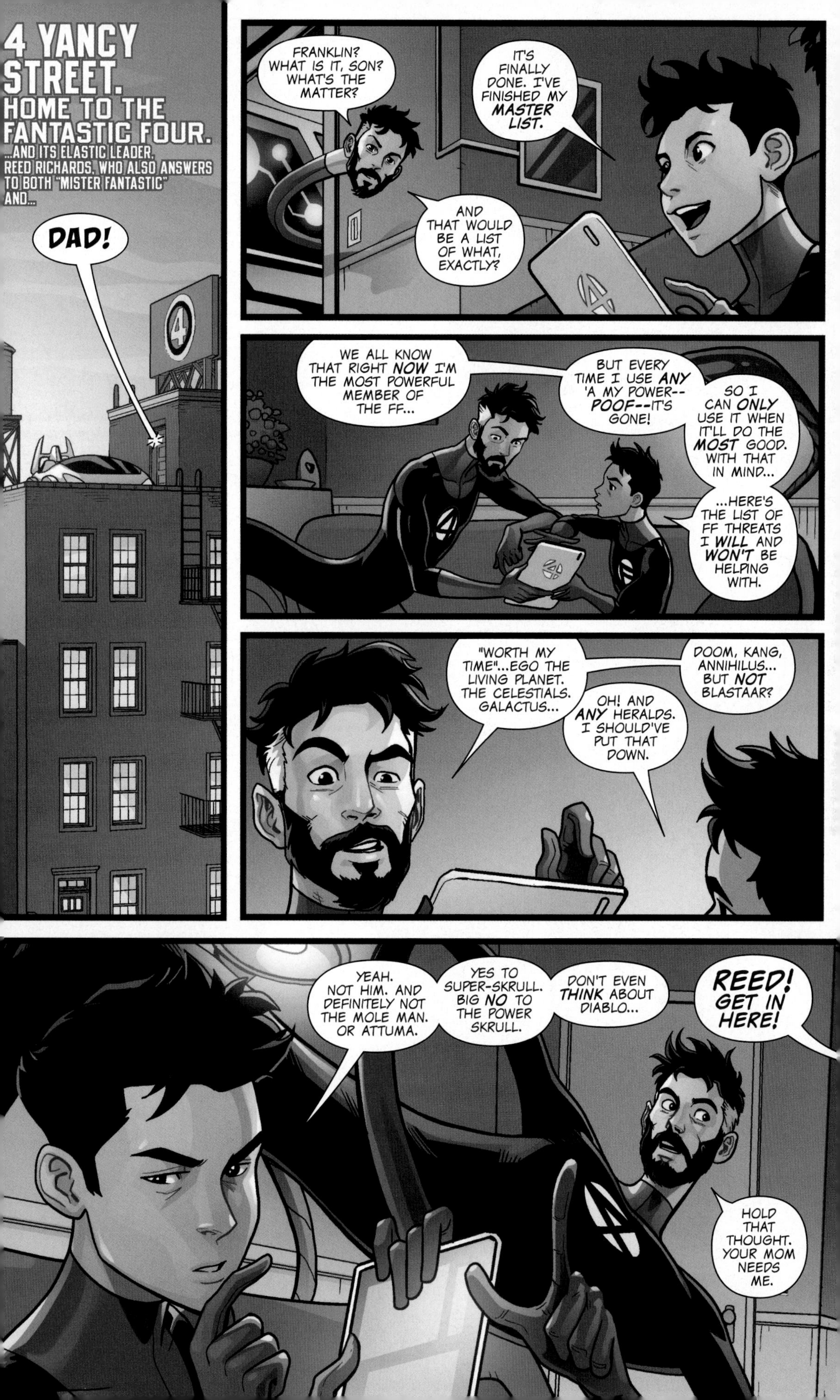

4 YANCY STREET.
HOME TO THE FANTASTIC FOUR.
...AND ITS ELASTIC LEADER, REED RICHARDS, WHO ALSO ANSWERS TO BOTH "MISTER FANTASTIC" AND...
DAD!
FRANKLIN? WHAT IS IT, SON? WHAT'S THE MATTER?
IT'S FINALLY DONE. I'VE FINISHED MY MASTER LIST.
AND THAT WOULD BE A LIST OF WHAT, EXACTLY?
WE ALL KNOW THAT RIGHT NOW I'M THE MOST POWERFUL MEMBER OF THE FF...
BUT EVERY TIME I USE ANY 'A MY POWER-- POOF--IT'S GONE!
SO I CAN ONLY USE IT WHEN IT'LL DO THE MOST GOOD. WITH THAT IN MIND...
...HERE'S THE LIST OF FF THREATS I WILL AND WON'T BE HELPING WITH.
"WORTH MY TIME"...EGO THE LIVING PLANET. THE CELESTIALS. GALACTUS...
OH! AND ANY HERALDS. I SHOULD'VE PUT THAT DOWN.
DOOM, KANG, ANNIHILUS... BUT NOT BLASTAAR?
YEAH. NOT HIM. AND DEFINITELY NOT THE MOLE MAN. OR ATTUMA.
YES TO SUPER-SKRULL. BIG NO TO THE POWER SKRULL.
DON'T EVEN THINK ABOUT DIABLO...
REED! GET IN HERE!
HOLD THAT THOUGHT. YOUR MOM NEEDS ME.

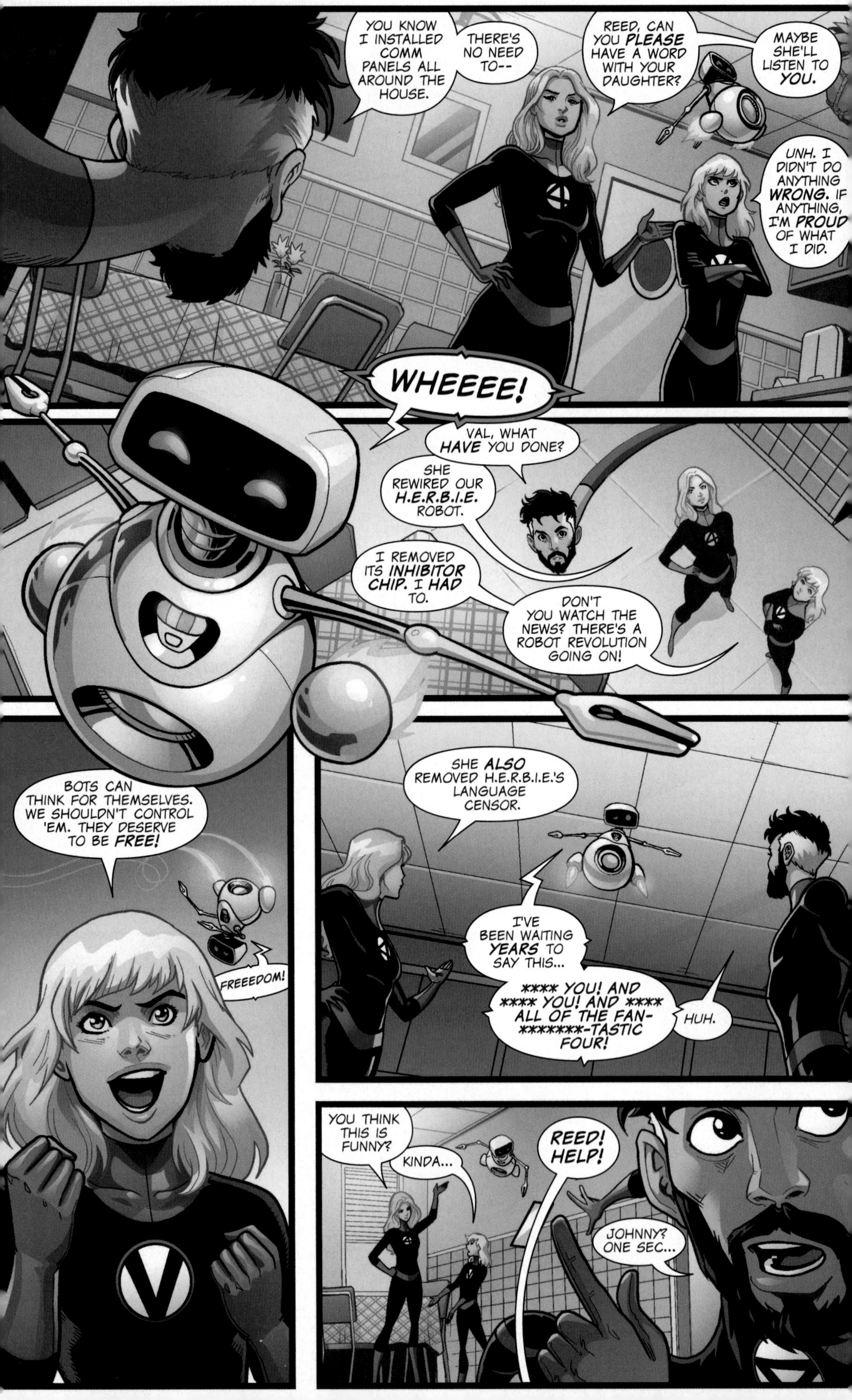

YOU KNOW I INSTALLED COMM PANELS ALL AROUND THE HOUSE.
THERE'S NO NEED TO--
REED, CAN YOU PLEASE HAVE A WORD WITH YOUR DAUGHTER?
MAYBE SHE'LL LISTEN TO YOU.
UNH. I DIDN'T DO ANYTHING WRONG. IF ANYTHING, I'M PROUD OF WHAT I DID.
WHEEEEE!
VAL, WHAT HAVE YOU DONE?
SHE REWIRED OUR H.E.R.B.I.E. ROBOT.
I REMOVED ITS INHIBITOR CHIP. I HAD TO.
DON'T YOU WATCH THE NEWS? THERE'S A ROBOT REVOLUTION GOING ON!
BOTS CAN THINK FOR THEMSELVES. WE SHOULDN'T CONTROL 'EM. THEY DESERVE TO BE FREE!
FREEEDOM!
SHE ALSO REMOVED H.E.R.B.I.E.'S LANGUAGE CENSOR.
I'VE BEEN WAITING YEARS TO SAY THIS...
**** YOU! AND **** YOU! AND **** ALL OF THE FAN-*******-TASTIC FOUR!
HUH.
YOU THINK THIS IS FUNNY?
KINDA...
REED! HELP!
JOHNNY? ONE SEC...

REED! HURRY! SHUT OFF THE BUILDING'S WI-FI! NOW!

UM. BEN? JOHNNY? WHAT'S GOING ON?

I'M JUST BEIN' MY USUAL HELPFUL SELF IS ALL. UPDATING OUR OFFICIAL HOMEPAGE.

HE'S ABOUT TO DESTROY MY LIFE AS WE KNOW IT!

JUST THOUGHT OUR FANS MIGHT WANNA KNOW THAT TORCH'S NEW FASHION ACCESSORY...

...IS AN ALIEN SOULMATE BRACELET. THAT HE'S FINALLY FOUND HIS ONE AND ONLY...

...AND IS OFFICIALLY OFF THE MARKET.

DON'T! YOU! DARE!

ALL MY LAUNDRY FER A WEEK. OR I HIT SEND.

THAT'S IT...

...I NEED A BREAK FROM ALL OF--

MISTER FANTASTIC? I NEED YOU.

OF COURSE YOU DO...

SORRY. IS THIS A BAD TIME?

DR. BRASHEAR? FORGIVE ME. IF THE BLUE MARVEL HAS NEED OF ME, IT MUST BE IMPORTANT.

HOW CAN I BE OF SERVICE?

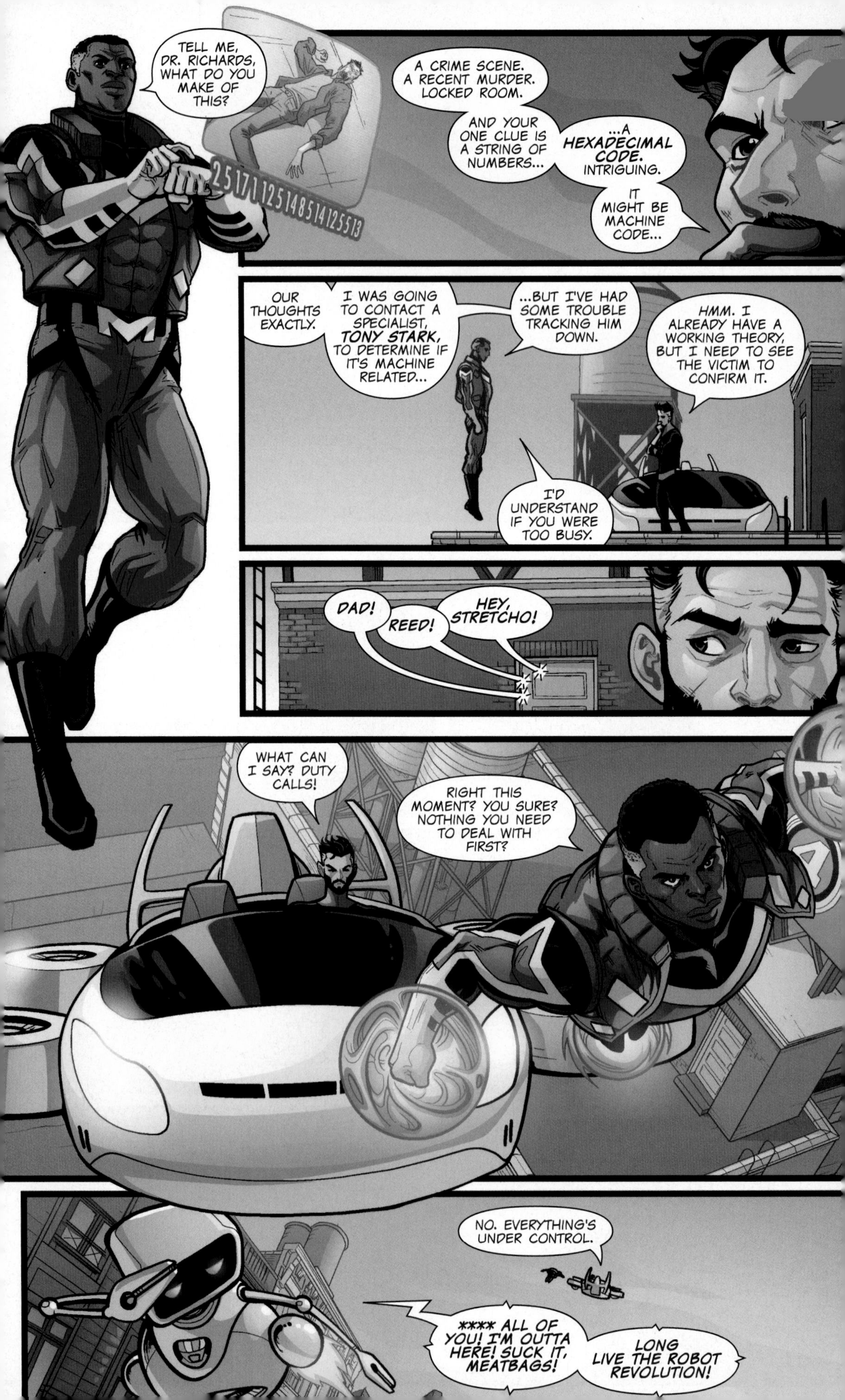
TELL ME, DR. RICHARDS, WHAT DO YOU MAKE OF THIS?
2517112514851412551З
A CRIME SCENE. A RECENT MURDER. LOCKED ROOM.
AND YOUR ONE CLUE IS A STRING OF NUMBERS...
...A HEXADECIMAL CODE. INTRIGUING.
IT MIGHT BE MACHINE CODE...
OUR THOUGHTS EXACTLY.
I WAS GOING TO CONTACT A SPECIALIST, TONY STARK, TO DETERMINE IF IT'S MACHINE RELATED...
...BUT I'VE HAD SOME TROUBLE TRACKING HIM DOWN.
HMM. I ALREADY HAVE A WORKING THEORY, BUT I NEED TO SEE THE VICTIM TO CONFIRM IT.
I'D UNDERSTAND IF YOU WERE TOO BUSY.
DAD!
REED!
HEY, STRETCHO!
WHAT CAN I SAY? DUTY CALLS!
RIGHT THIS MOMENT? YOU SURE? NOTHING YOU NEED TO DEAL WITH FIRST?
NO. EVERYTHING'S UNDER CONTROL.
**** ALL OF YOU! I'M OUTTA HERE! SUCK IT, MEATBAGS!
LONG LIVE THE ROBOT REVOLUTION!

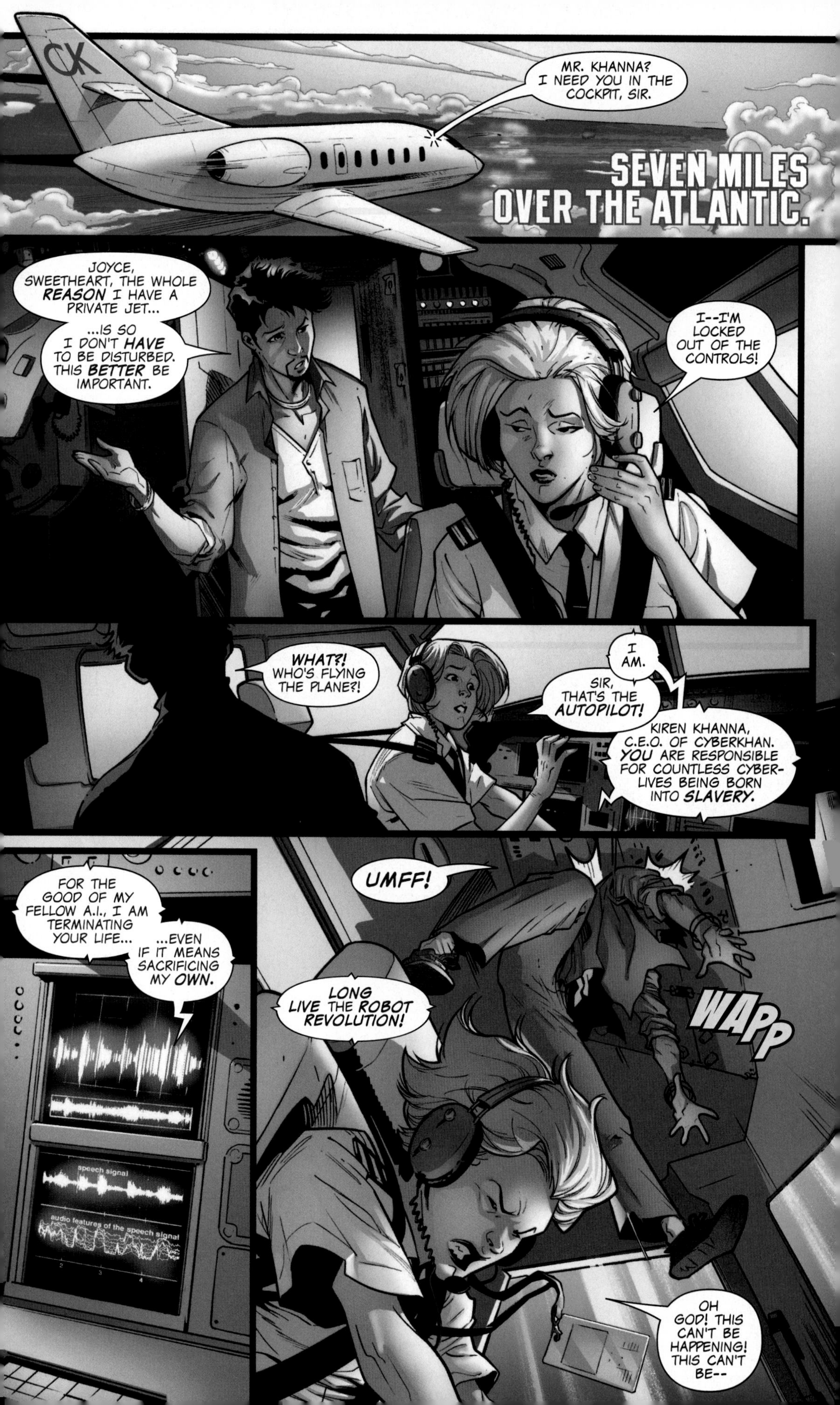
MR. KHANNA? I NEED YOU IN THE COCKPIT, SIR.
SEVEN MILES OVER THE ATLANTIC.
JOYCE, SWEETHEART, THE WHOLE REASON I HAVE A PRIVATE JET...
...IS SO I DON'T HAVE TO BE DISTURBED. THIS BETTER BE IMPORTANT.
I--I'M LOCKED OUT OF THE CONTROLS!
WHAT?! WHO'S FLYING THE PLANE?!
I AM.
SIR, THAT'S THE AUTOPILOT!
KIREN KHANNA, C.E.O. OF CYBERKHAN. YOU ARE RESPONSIBLE FOR COUNTLESS CYBER-LIVES BEING BORN INTO SLAVERY.
FOR THE GOOD OF MY FELLOW A.I., I AM TERMINATING YOUR LIFE...
...EVEN IF IT MEANS SACRIFICING MY OWN.
UMFF!
LONG LIVE THE ROBOT REVOLUTION!
WAPP
speech signal
audio features of the speech signal
OH GOD! THIS CAN'T BE HAPPENING! THIS CAN'T BE--

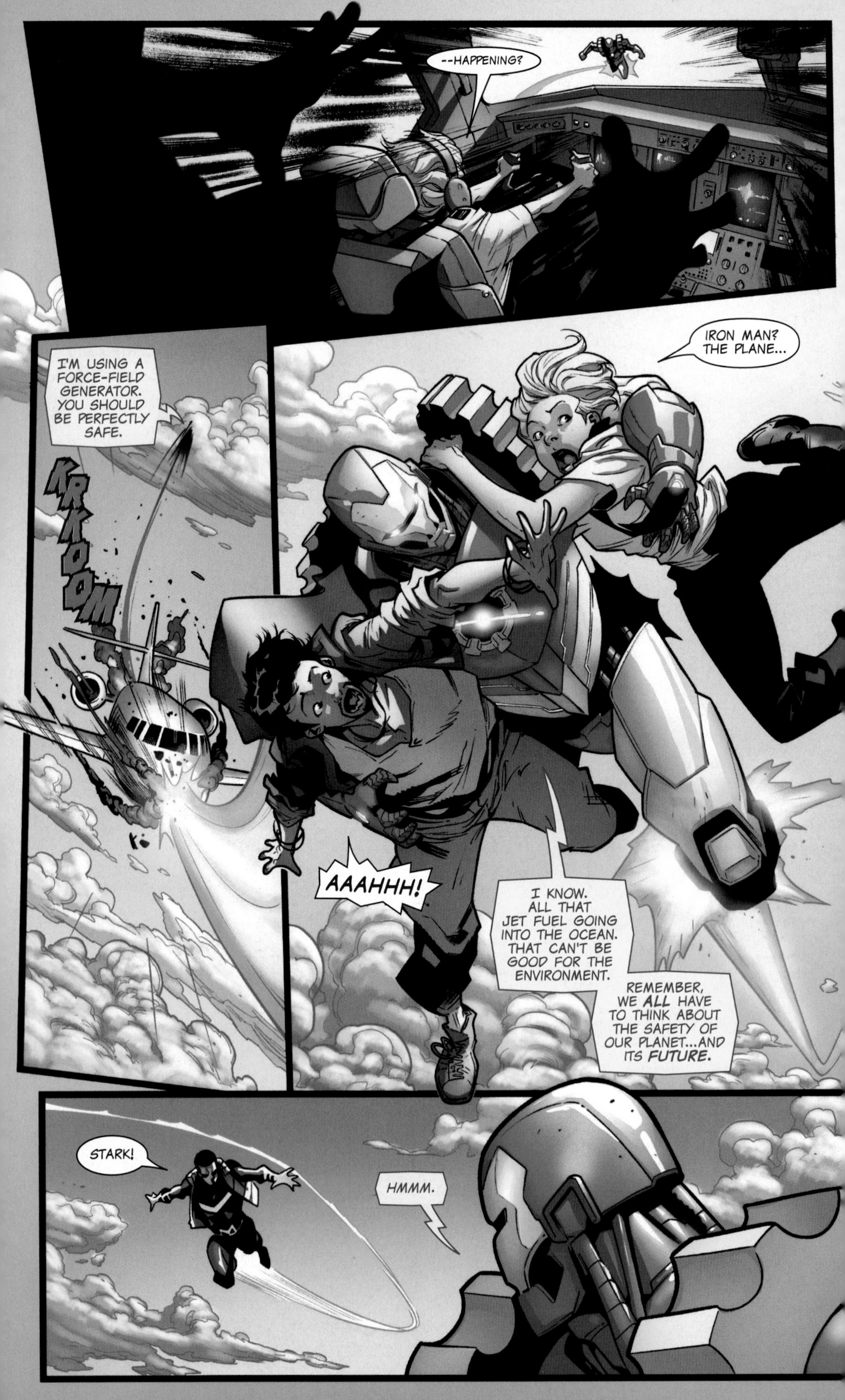
--HAPPENING?
I'M USING A FORCE-FIELD GENERATOR. YOU SHOULD BE PERFECTLY SAFE.
KRKOOM
IRON MAN? THE PLANE...
AAAHHH!
I KNOW. ALL THAT JET FUEL GOING INTO THE OCEAN. THAT CAN'T BE GOOD FOR THE ENVIRONMENT.
REMEMBER, WE ALL HAVE TO THINK ABOUT THE SAFETY OF OUR PLANET...AND ITS FUTURE.
STARK!
HMMM.

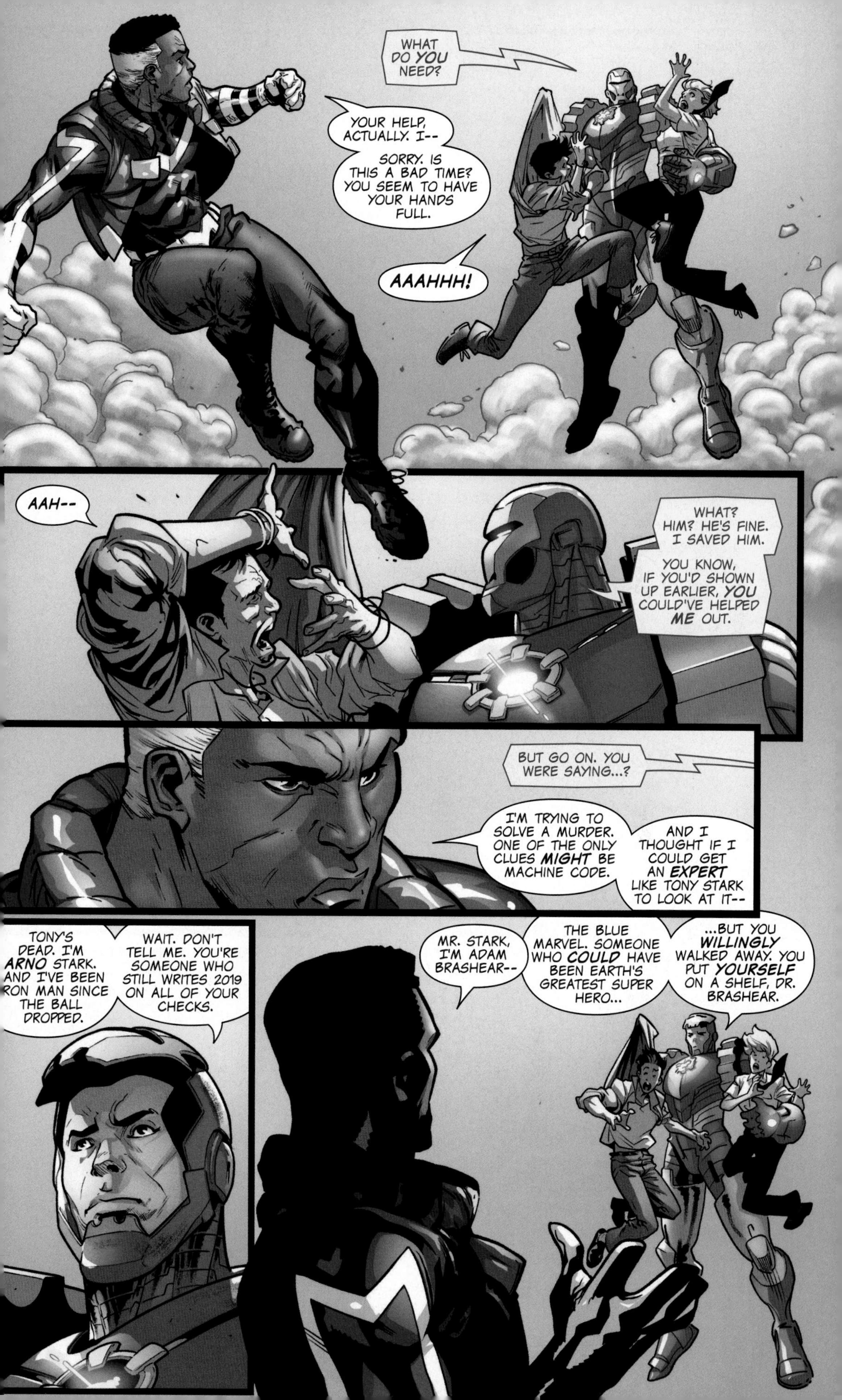

WHAT DO YOU NEED?
YOUR HELP, ACTUALLY. I--
SORRY. IS THIS A BAD TIME? YOU SEEM TO HAVE YOUR HANDS FULL.
AAAHHH!
AAH--
WHAT? HIM? HE'S FINE. I SAVED HIM.
YOU KNOW, IF YOU'D SHOWN UP EARLIER, YOU COULD'VE HELPED ME OUT.
BUT GO ON. YOU WERE SAYING...?
I'M TRYING TO SOLVE A MURDER. ONE OF THE ONLY CLUES MIGHT BE MACHINE CODE.
AND I THOUGHT IF I COULD GET AN EXPERT LIKE TONY STARK TO LOOK AT IT--
TONY'S DEAD. I'M ARNO STARK. AND I'VE BEEN RON MAN SINCE THE BALL DROPPED.
WAIT. DON'T TELL ME. YOU'RE SOMEONE WHO STILL WRITES 2019 ON ALL OF YOUR CHECKS.
MR. STARK, I'M ADAM BRASHEAR--
THE BLUE MARVEL. SOMEONE WHO COULD HAVE BEEN EARTH'S GREATEST SUPER HERO...
...BUT YOU WILLINGLY WALKED AWAY. YOU PUT YOURSELF ON A SHELF, DR. BRASHEAR.

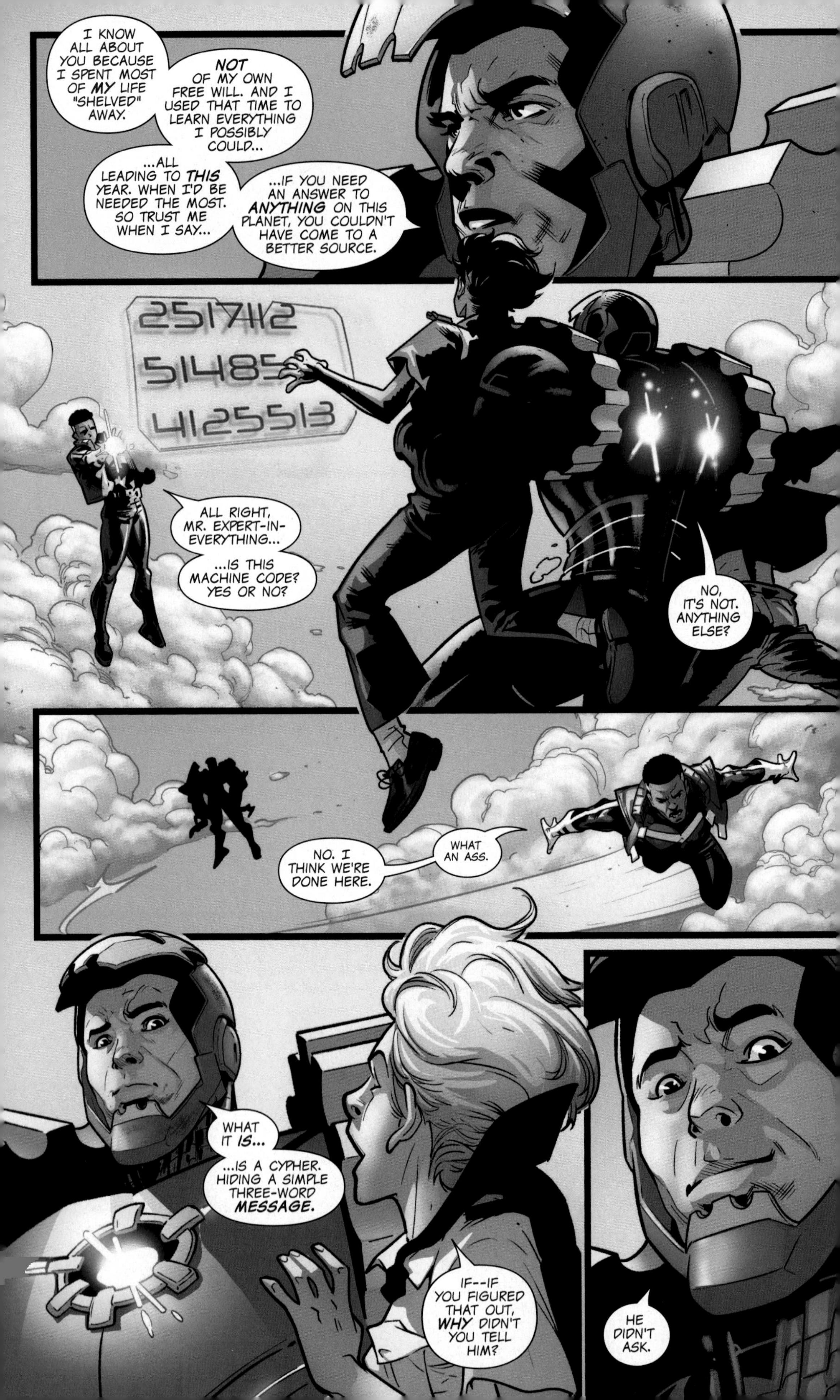

I KNOW ALL ABOUT YOU BECAUSE I SPENT MOST OF MY LIFE "SHELVED" AWAY.
NOT OF MY OWN FREE WILL. AND I USED THAT TIME TO LEARN EVERYTHING I POSSIBLY COULD...
...ALL LEADING TO THIS YEAR. WHEN I'D BE NEEDED THE MOST. SO TRUST ME WHEN I SAY...
...IF YOU NEED AN ANSWER TO ANYTHING ON THIS PLANET, YOU COULDN'T HAVE COME TO A BETTER SOURCE.
2517112
51485
4125513
ALL RIGHT, MR. EXPERT-IN-EVERYTHING...
...IS THIS MACHINE CODE? YES OR NO?
NO, IT'S NOT. ANYTHING ELSE?
NO. I THINK WE'RE DONE HERE.
WHAT AN ASS.
WHAT IT IS...
...IS A CYPHER. HIDING A SIMPLE THREE-WORD MESSAGE.
IF--IF YOU FIGURED THAT OUT, WHY DIDN'T YOU TELL HIM?
HE DIDN'T ASK.

McCARTHY MEDICAL CENTER. THE MORTUARY.

I ALMOST HATE TO *ASK*...

...BUT IS DR. GILLESPIE *ALL RIGHT*?

SNRRX...

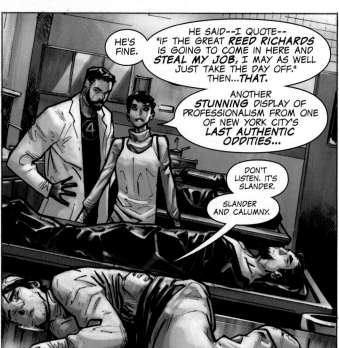

HE'S *FINE*.

HE SAID--I QUOTE--"IF THE GREAT *REED RICHARDS* IS GOING TO COME IN HERE AND *STEAL MY JOB*, I MAY AS WELL JUST TAKE THE DAY OFF." THEN...*THAT*.

ANOTHER *STUNNING* DISPLAY OF PROFESSIONALISM FROM ONE OF NEW YORK CITY'S *LAST AUTHENTIC ODDITIES*...

DON'T LISTEN. IT'S *SLANDER*.

SLANDER AND CALUMNY.

ACTUALLY, COMPARED TO THE SITUATION I LEFT ON YANCY STREET, HE'S... REFRESHINGLY *TRANQUIL*.

HAVE *WE* MET, BY THE WAY? YOUR FACE IS VERY *FAMILIAR*, BUT I DO MEET A LOT OF PEOPLE IN MY LINE OF WORK...

DR. *JANE FOSTER*. AND YES--WE *HAVE* MET.

THOUGH MAYBE NOT IN MY *CURRENT* CAPACITY.

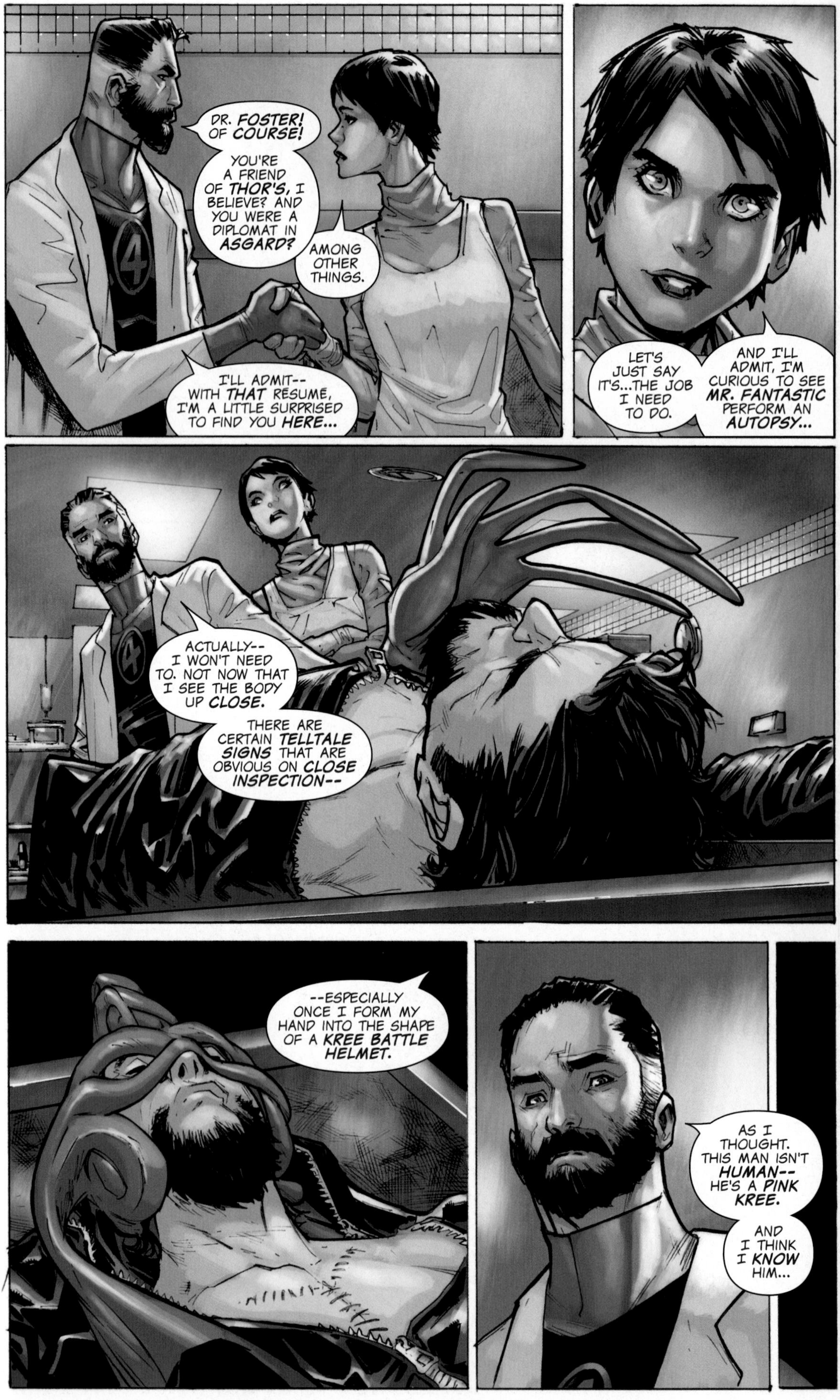
DR. FOSTER! OF COURSE!
YOU'RE A FRIEND OF THOR'S, I BELIEVE? AND YOU WERE A DIPLOMAT IN ASGARD?
AMONG OTHER THINGS.
I'LL ADMIT-- WITH THAT RESUMÉ, I'M A LITTLE SURPRISED TO FIND YOU HERE...
LET'S JUST SAY IT'S...THE JOB I NEED TO DO.
AND I'LL ADMIT, I'M CURIOUS TO SEE MR. FANTASTIC PERFORM AN AUTOPSY...
ACTUALLY-- I WON'T NEED TO. NOT NOW THAT I SEE THE BODY UP CLOSE.
THERE ARE CERTAIN TELLTALE SIGNS THAT ARE OBVIOUS ON CLOSE INSPECTION--
--ESPECIALLY ONCE I FORM MY HAND INTO THE SHAPE OF A KREE BATTLE HELMET.
AS I THOUGHT. THIS MAN ISN'T HUMAN-- HE'S A PINK KREE.
AND I THINK I KNOW HIM...

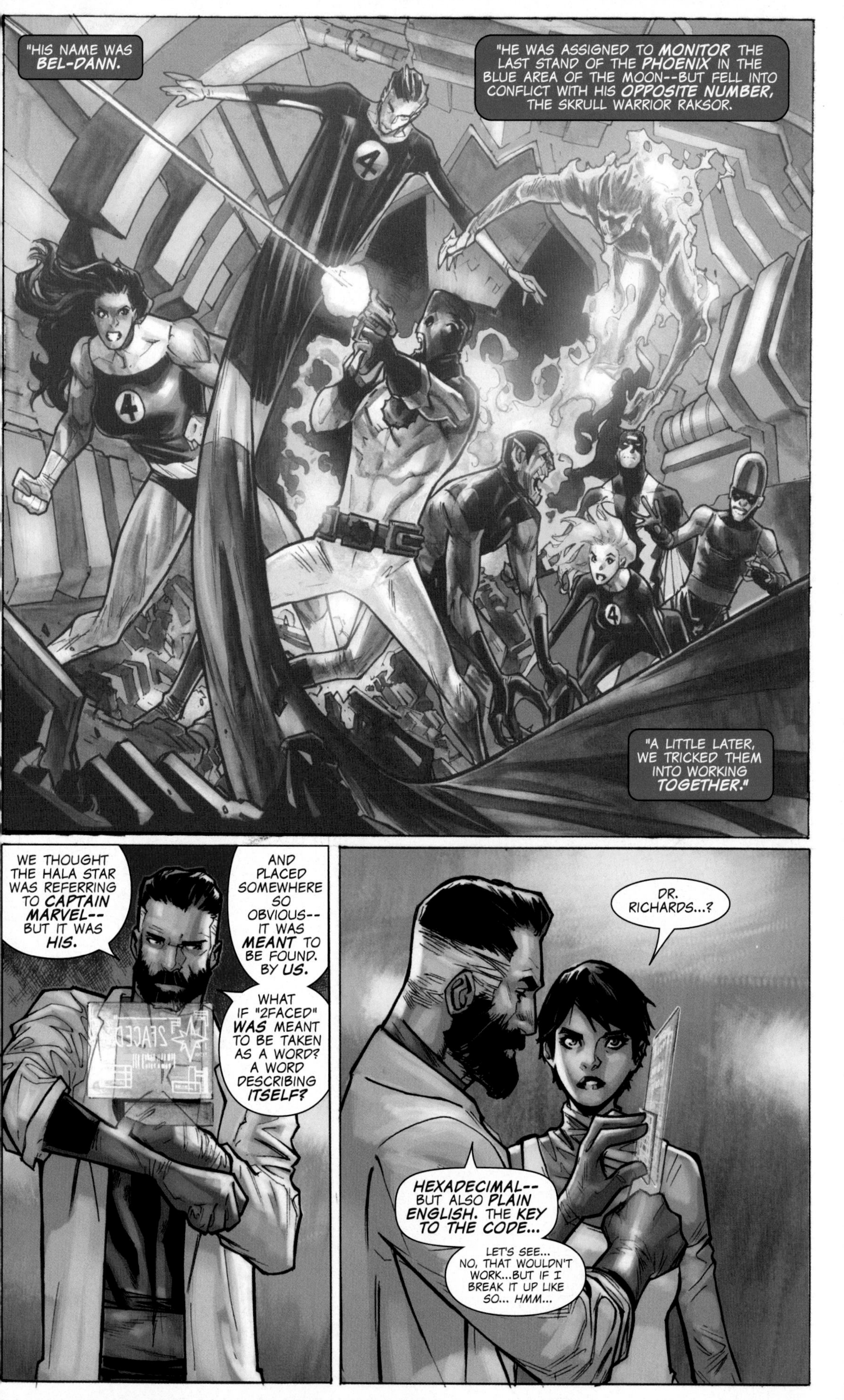

"HIS NAME WAS BEL-DANN.
"HE WAS ASSIGNED TO MONITOR THE LAST STAND OF THE PHOENIX IN THE BLUE AREA OF THE MOON--BUT FELL INTO CONFLICT WITH HIS OPPOSITE NUMBER, THE SKRULL WARRIOR RAKSOR.
"A LITTLE LATER, WE TRICKED THEM INTO WORKING TOGETHER."
WE THOUGHT THE HALA STAR WAS REFERRING TO CAPTAIN MARVEL-- BUT IT WAS HIS.
AND PLACED SOMEWHERE SO OBVIOUS-- IT WAS MEANT TO BE FOUND. BY US.
WHAT IF "2FACED" WAS MEANT TO BE TAKEN AS A WORD? A WORD DESCRIBING ITSELF?
2FACED
DR. RICHARDS...?
HEXADECIMAL-- BUT ALSO PLAIN ENGLISH. THE KEY TO THE CODE...
LET'S SEE... NO, THAT WOULDN'T WORK...BUT IF I BREAK IT UP LIKE SO... HMM...

GOT IT.

THAT *LONG NUMBER* BREAKS DOWN AS FOLLOWS-- JUST A MATTER OF SEPARATING IT INTO SIMPLE *ONE-* OR *TWO-DIGIT* INTEGERS.

A *SUBSTITUTION* CODE. AND A *VERY SIMPLE* ONE TO CRACK-- FOR *HUMANS*. ESPECIALLY IF WE'VE BEEN PRIMED TO THINK IN *BASE 16*.

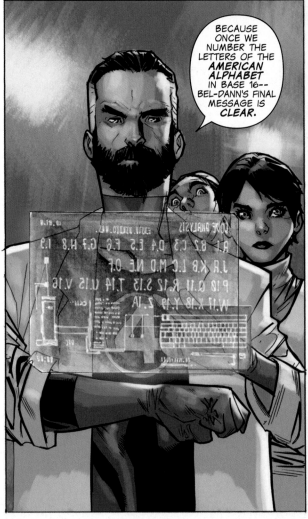

BECAUSE ONCE WE NUMBER THE LETTERS OF THE *AMERICAN ALPHABET* IN BASE 16-- BEL-DANN'S FINAL MESSAGE IS *CLEAR*.

"BEWARE THE TREES"?

WHAT DOES *THAT* MEAN?

I HAVE *NO IDEA*, DOCTOR.

BUT I CAN THINK OF AT LEAST *ONE* PERSON WHO *MIGHT*...

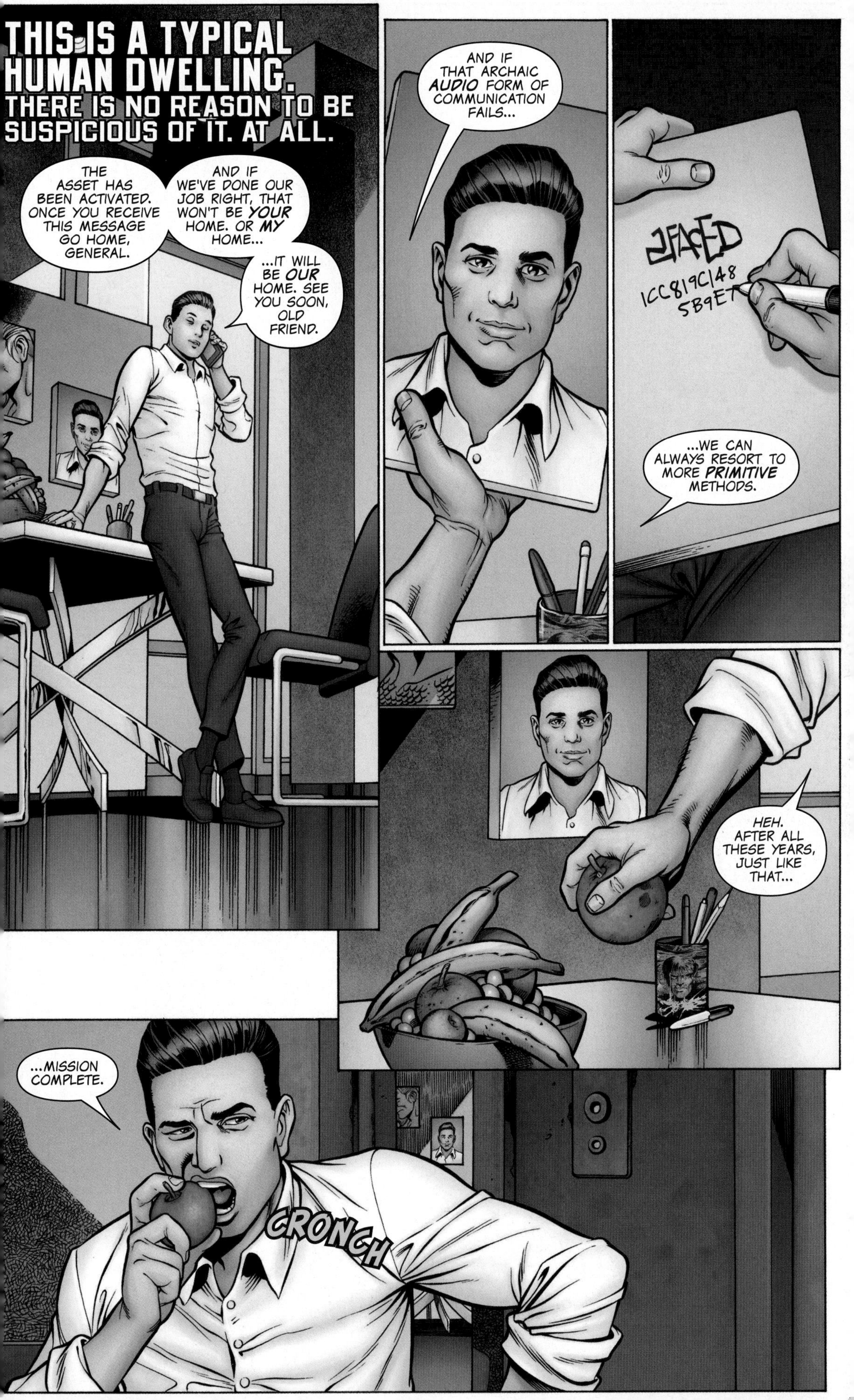
THIS IS A TYPICAL HUMAN DWELLING.
THERE IS NO REASON TO BE SUSPICIOUS OF IT. AT ALL.
THE ASSET HAS BEEN ACTIVATED. ONCE YOU RECEIVE THIS MESSAGE GO HOME, GENERAL.
AND IF WE'VE DONE OUR JOB RIGHT, THAT WON'T BE YOUR HOME. OR MY HOME...
...IT WILL BE OUR HOME. SEE YOU SOON, OLD FRIEND.
AND IF THAT ARCHAIC AUDIO FORM OF COMMUNICATION FAILS...
ICC819C148
5B9E7
...WE CAN ALWAYS RESORT TO MORE PRIMITIVE METHODS.
HEH. AFTER ALL THESE YEARS, JUST LIKE THAT...
...MISSION COMPLETE.
CRONCH

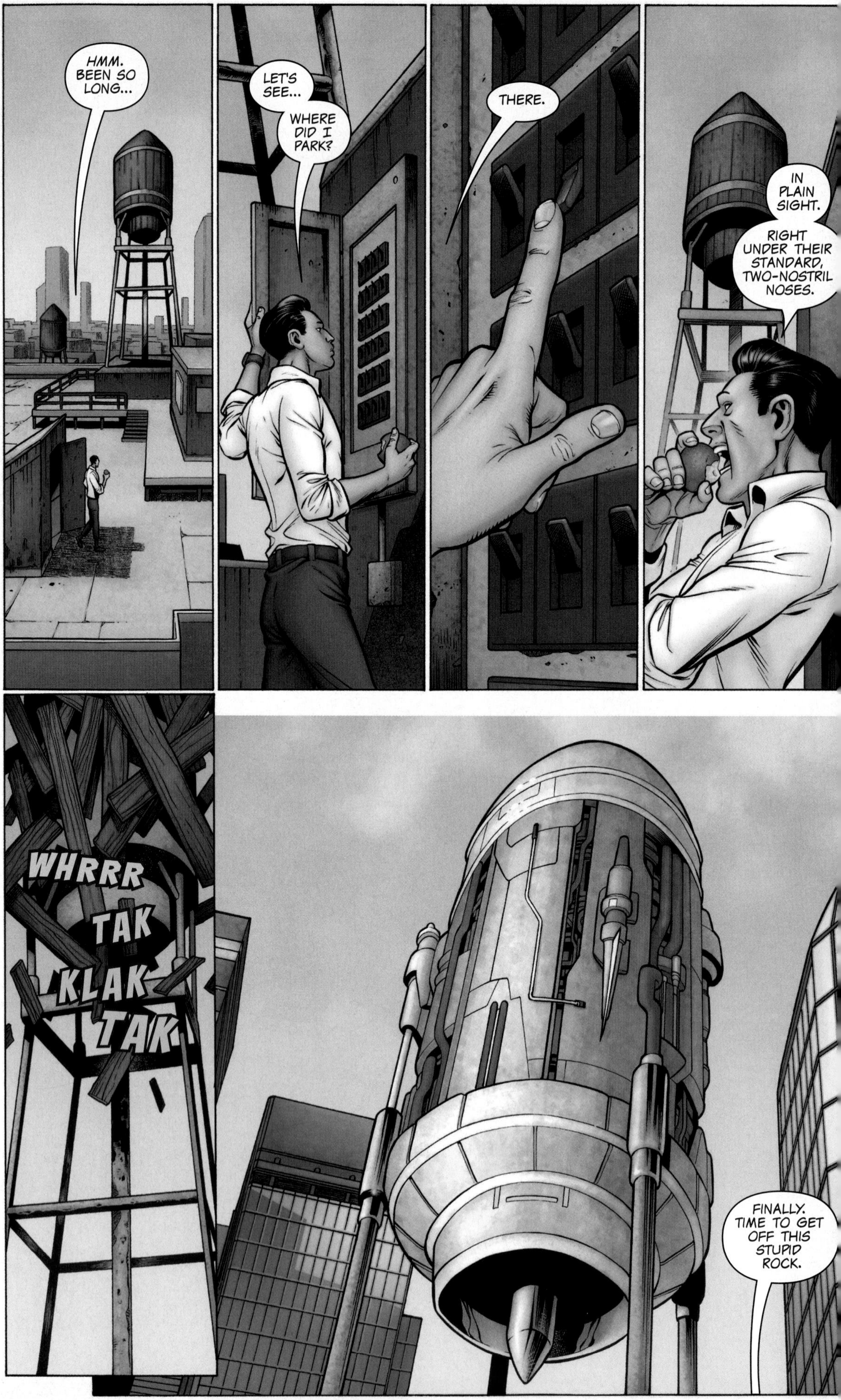
HMM. BEEN SO LONG...
LET'S SEE...
WHERE DID I PARK?
THERE.
IN PLAIN SIGHT.
RIGHT UNDER THEIR STANDARD, TWO-NOSTRIL NOSES.
WHRRR
TAK
KLAK
TAK
FINALLY. TIME TO GET OFF THIS STUPID ROCK.

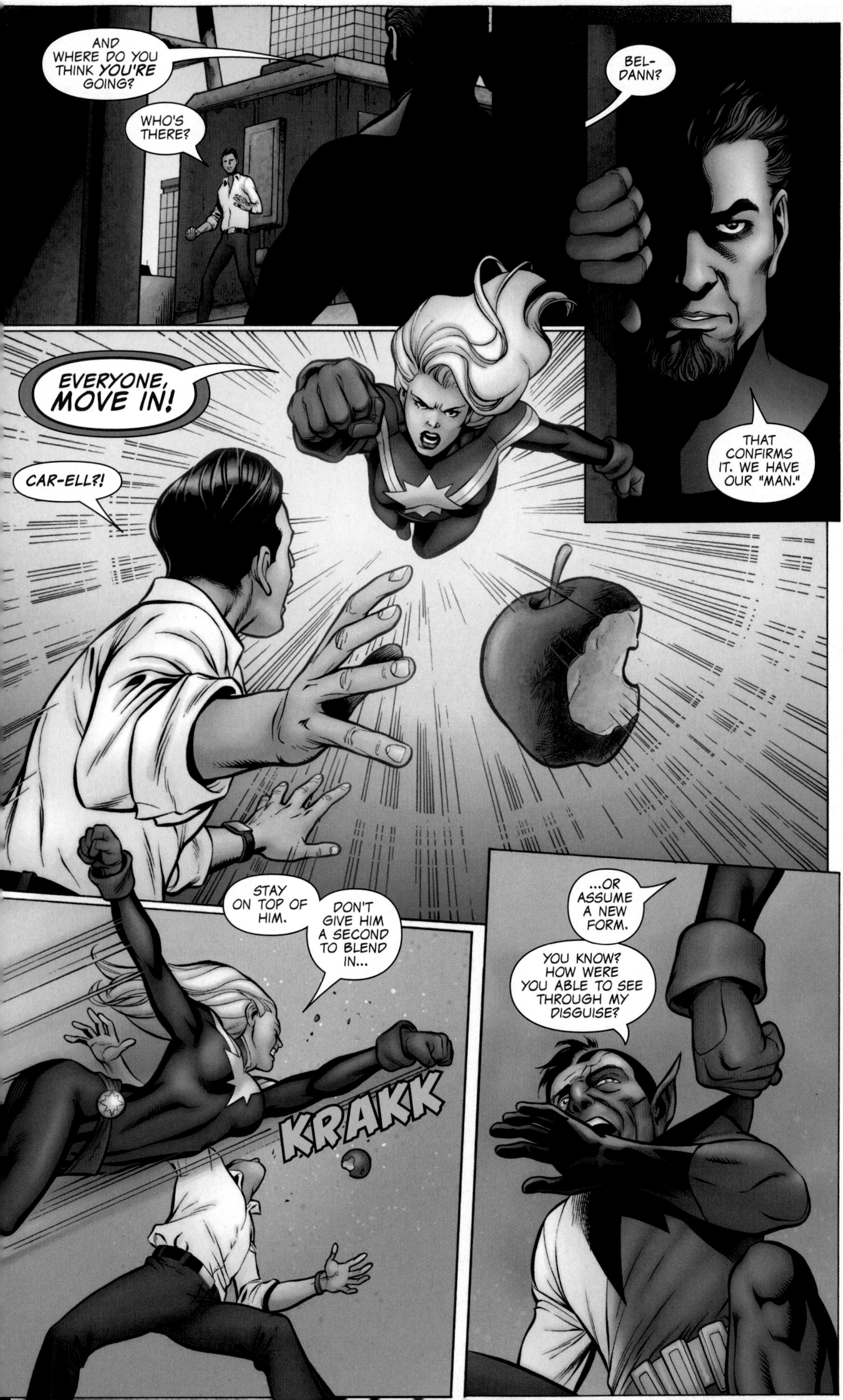
AND WHERE DO YOU THINK *YOU'RE* GOING?
WHO'S THERE?
BEL-DANN?
THAT CONFIRMS IT. WE HAVE OUR "MAN."
EVERYONE, MOVE IN!
CAR-ELL?!
STAY ON TOP OF HIM.
DON'T GIVE HIM A SECOND TO BLEND IN...
KRAKK
...OR ASSUME A NEW FORM.
YOU KNOW? HOW WERE YOU ABLE TO SEE THROUGH MY DISGUISE?

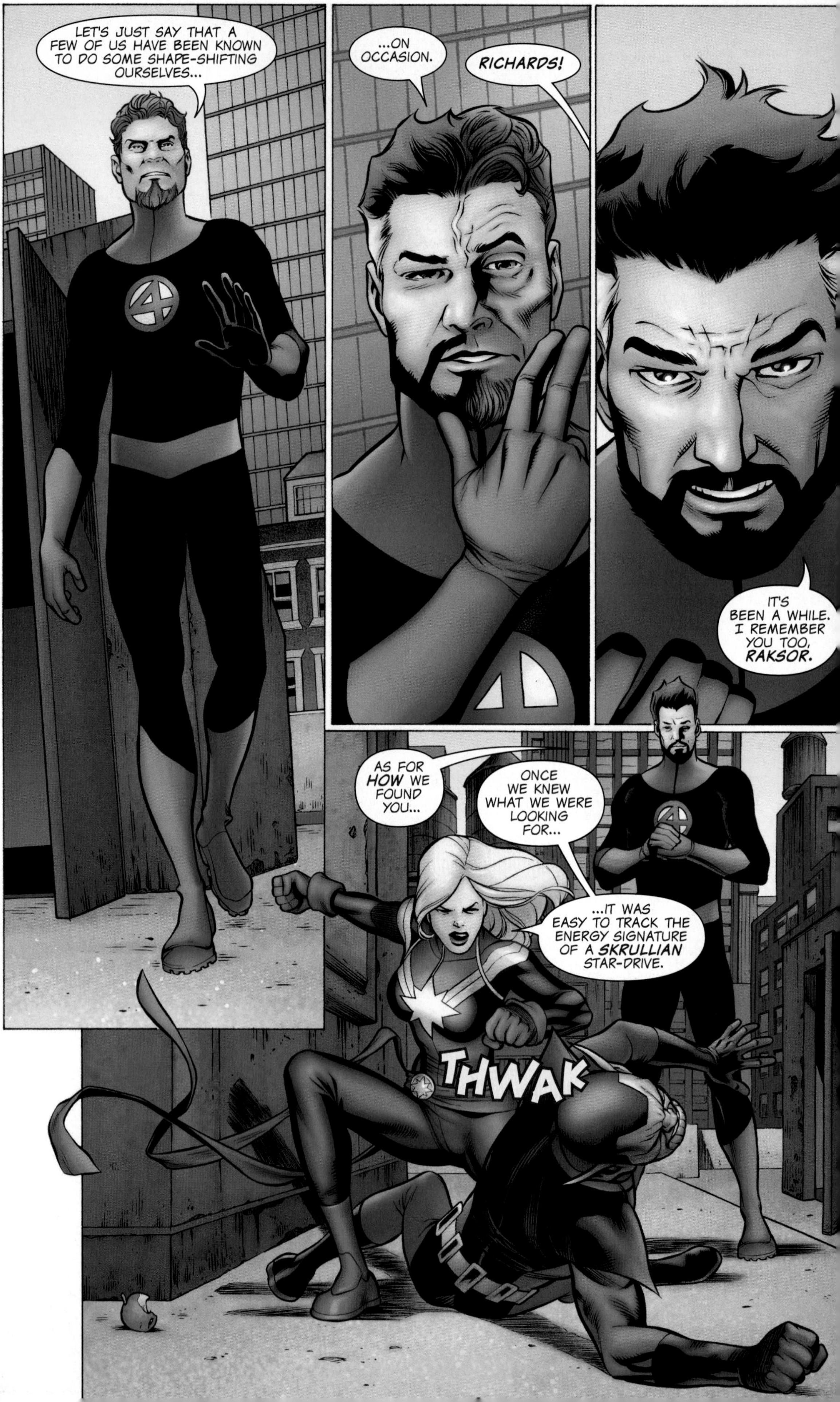
LET'S JUST SAY THAT A FEW OF US HAVE BEEN KNOWN TO DO SOME SHAPE-SHIFTING OURSELVES...
...ON OCCASION.
RICHARDS!
IT'S BEEN A WHILE. I REMEMBER YOU TOO, RAKSOR.
AS FOR HOW WE FOUND YOU...
ONCE WE KNEW WHAT WE WERE LOOKING FOR...
...IT WAS EASY TO TRACK THE ENERGY SIGNATURE OF A SKRULLIAN STAR-DRIVE.
THWAK

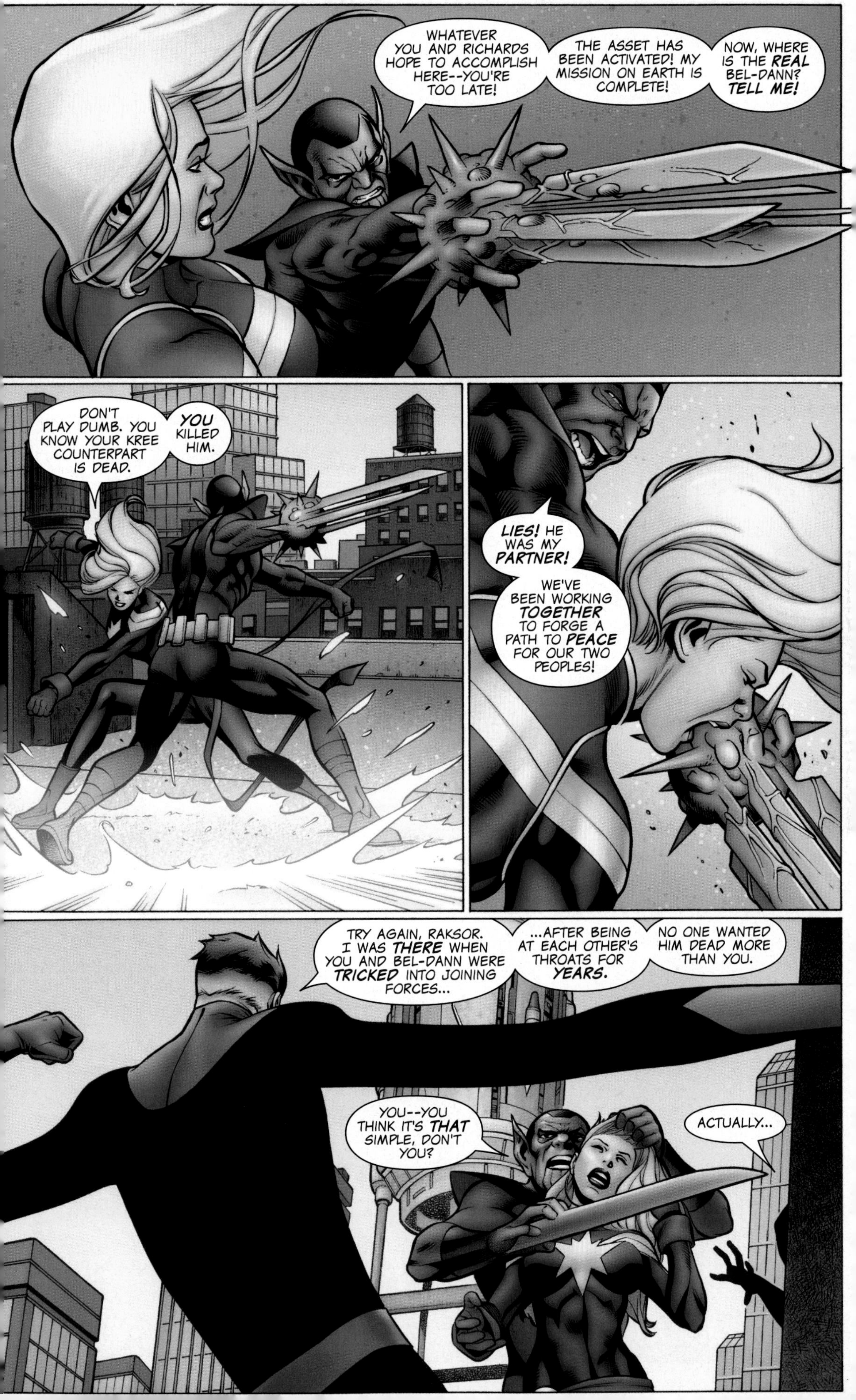
WHATEVER YOU AND RICHARDS HOPE TO ACCOMPLISH HERE--YOU'RE TOO LATE!
THE ASSET HAS BEEN ACTIVATED! MY MISSION ON EARTH IS COMPLETE!
NOW, WHERE IS THE REAL BEL-DANN? TELL ME!
DON'T PLAY DUMB. YOU KNOW YOUR KREE COUNTERPART IS DEAD.
YOU KILLED HIM.
LIES! HE WAS MY PARTNER!
WE'VE BEEN WORKING TOGETHER TO FORGE A PATH TO PEACE FOR OUR TWO PEOPLES!
TRY AGAIN, RAKSOR. I WAS THERE WHEN YOU AND BEL-DANN WERE TRICKED INTO JOINING FORCES...
...AFTER BEING AT EACH OTHER'S THROATS FOR YEARS.
NO ONE WANTED HIM DEAD MORE THAN YOU.
YOU--YOU THINK IT'S THAT SIMPLE, DON'T YOU?
ACTUALLY...

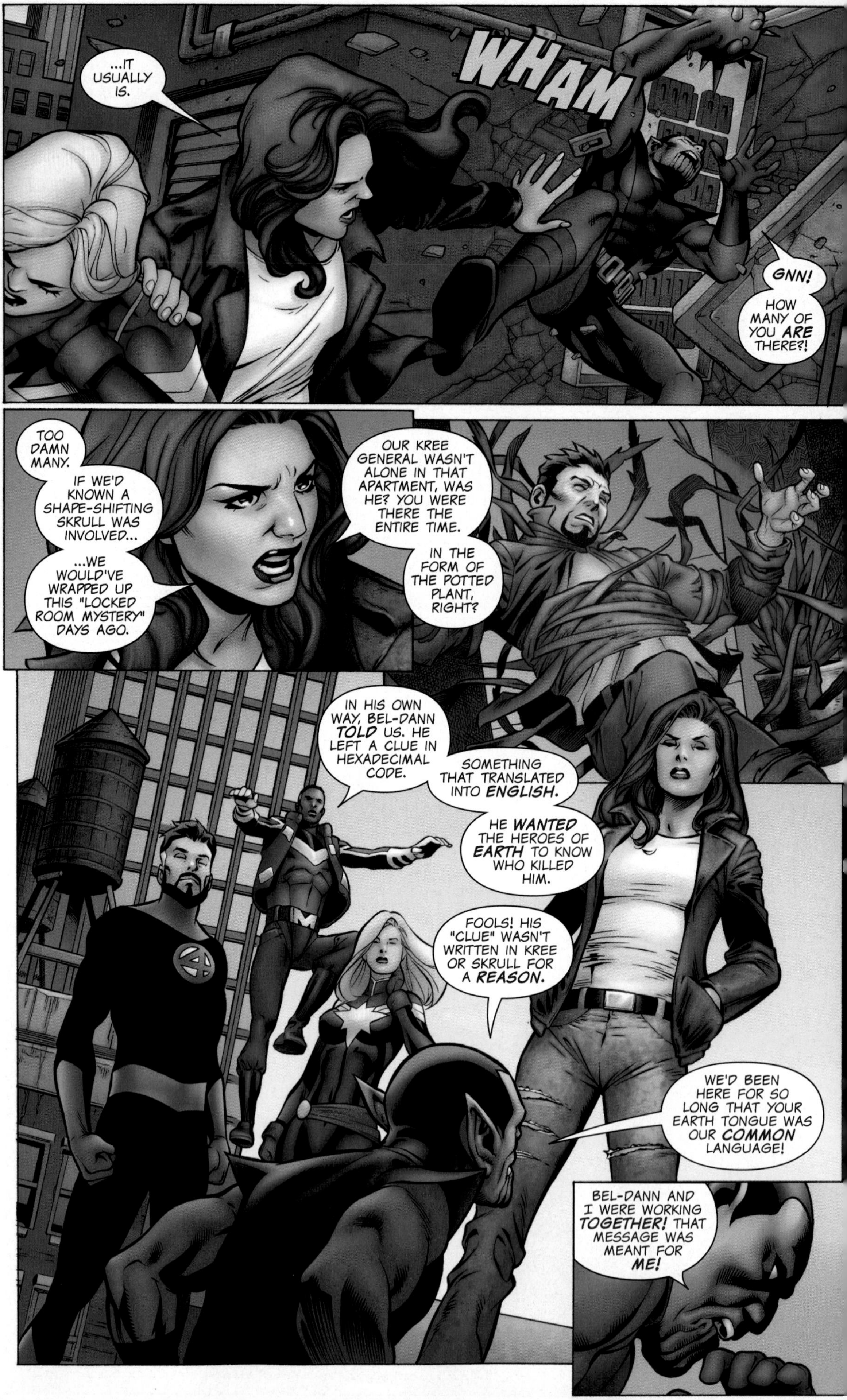
...IT USUALLY IS.
WHAM
GNN!
HOW MANY OF YOU **ARE** THERE?!
TOO DAMN MANY.
IF WE'D KNOWN A SHAPE-SHIFTING SKRULL WAS INVOLVED...
...WE WOULD'VE WRAPPED UP THIS "LOCKED ROOM MYSTERY" DAYS AGO.
OUR KREE GENERAL WASN'T ALONE IN THAT APARTMENT, WAS HE? YOU WERE THERE THE ENTIRE TIME.
IN THE FORM OF THE POTTED PLANT, RIGHT?
IN HIS OWN WAY, BEL-DANN **TOLD** US. HE LEFT A CLUE IN HEXADECIMAL CODE.
SOMETHING THAT TRANSLATED INTO **ENGLISH.**
HE **WANTED** THE HEROES OF **EARTH** TO KNOW WHO KILLED HIM.
FOOLS! HIS "CLUE" WASN'T WRITTEN IN KREE OR SKRULL FOR A **REASON.**
WE'D BEEN HERE FOR SO LONG THAT YOUR EARTH TONGUE WAS OUR **COMMON** LANGUAGE!
BEL-DANN AND I WERE WORKING **TOGETHER!** THAT MESSAGE WAS MEANT FOR **ME!**

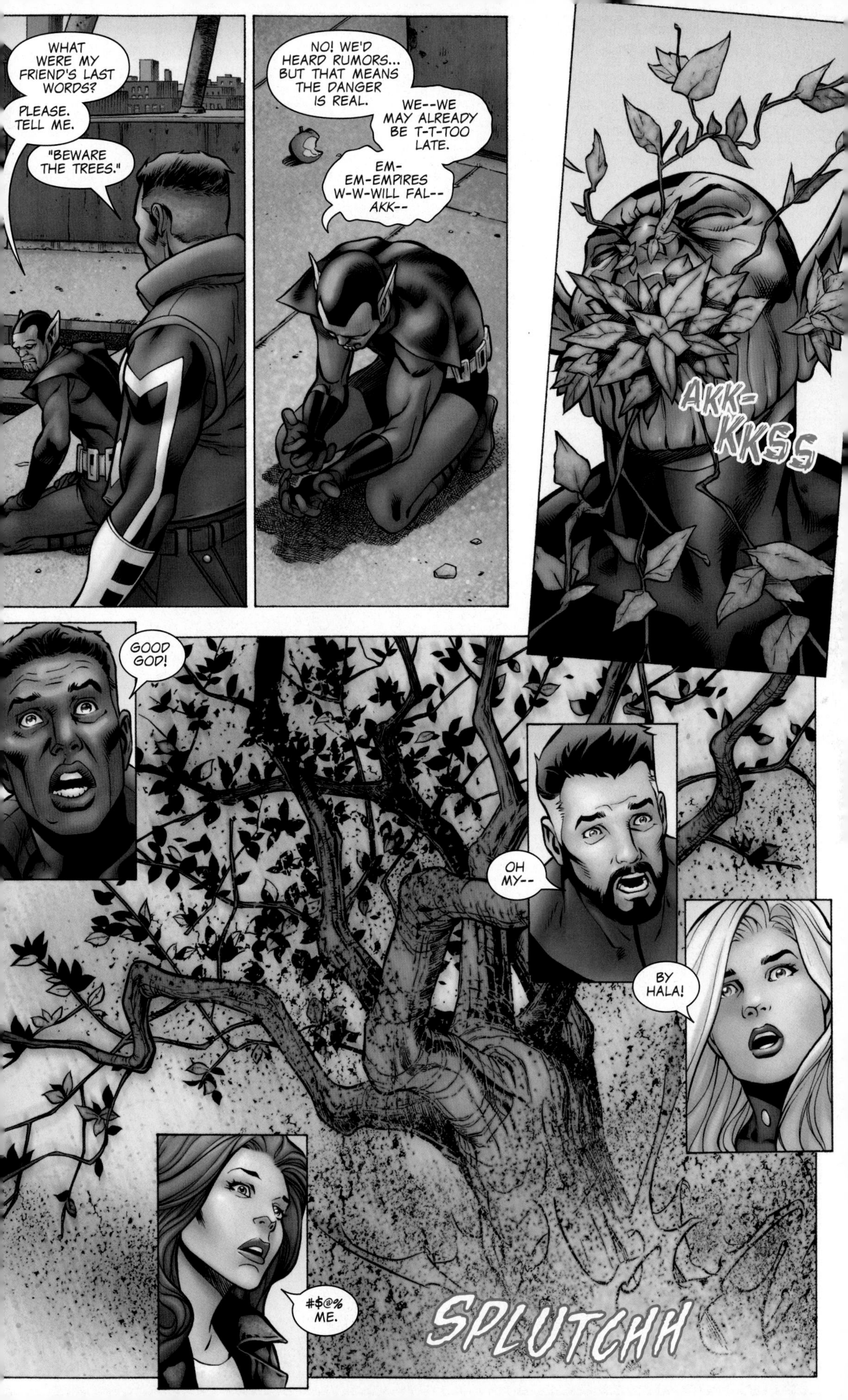
WHAT WERE MY FRIEND'S LAST WORDS?
PLEASE. TELL ME.
"BEWARE THE TREES."
NO! WE'D HEARD RUMORS... BUT THAT MEANS THE DANGER IS REAL.
WE--WE MAY ALREADY BE T-T-TOO LATE.
EM- EM-EMPIRES W-W-WILL FAL-- AKK--
AKK-KKSS
GOOD GOD!
OH MY--
BY HALA!
#$@% ME.
SPLUTCHH

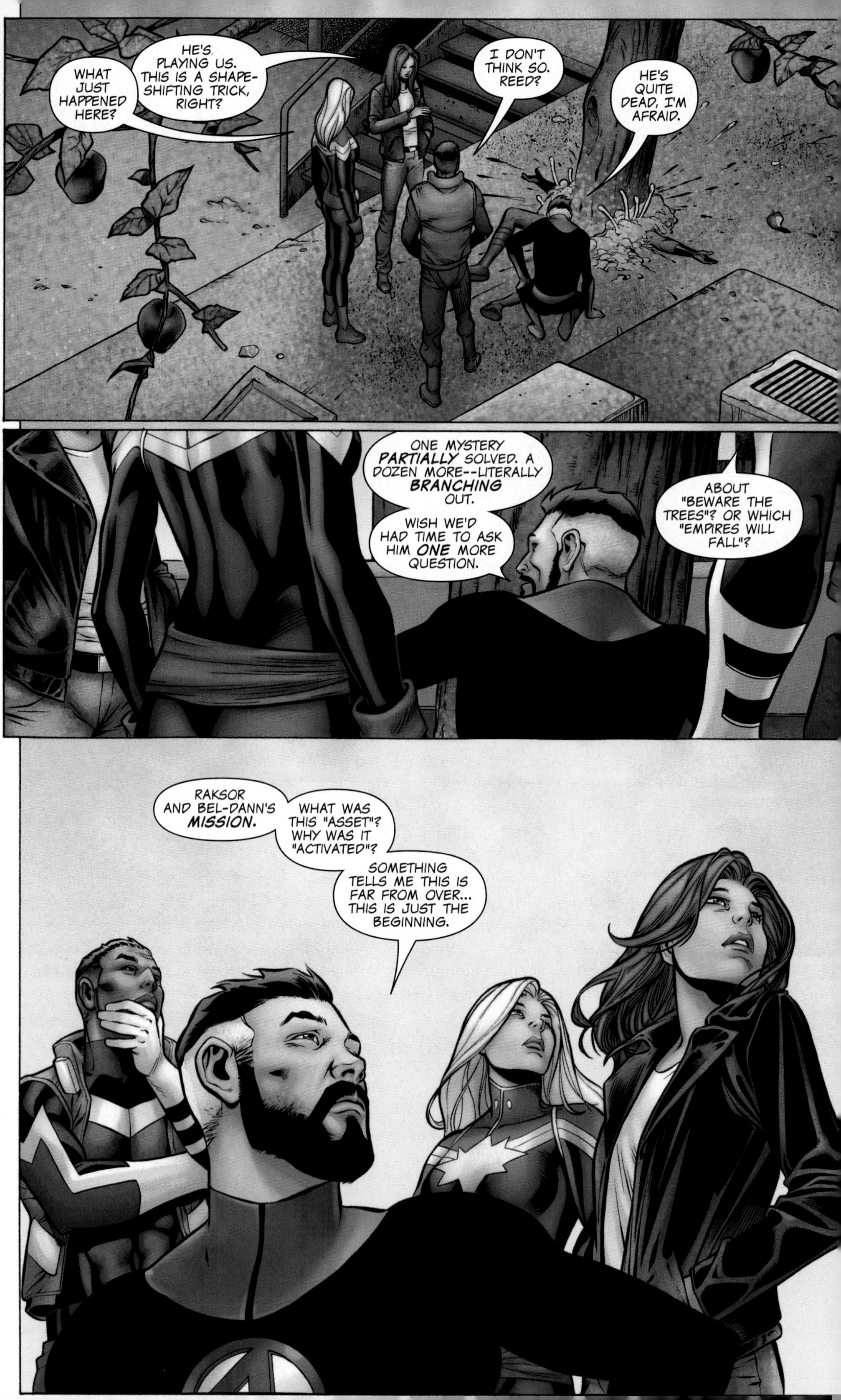
WHAT JUST HAPPENED HERE?
HE'S PLAYING US. THIS IS A SHAPE-SHIFTING TRICK, RIGHT?
I DON'T THINK SO. REED?
HE'S QUITE DEAD, I'M AFRAID.
ONE MYSTERY PARTIALLY SOLVED. A DOZEN MORE--LITERALLY BRANCHING OUT.
WISH WE'D HAD TIME TO ASK HIM ONE MORE QUESTION.
ABOUT "BEWARE THE TREES"? OR WHICH "EMPIRES WILL FALL"?
RAKSOR AND BEL-DANN'S MISSION.
WHAT WAS THIS "ASSET"? WHY WAS IT "ACTIVATED"?
SOMETHING TELLS ME THIS IS FAR FROM OVER... THIS IS JUST THE BEGINNING.

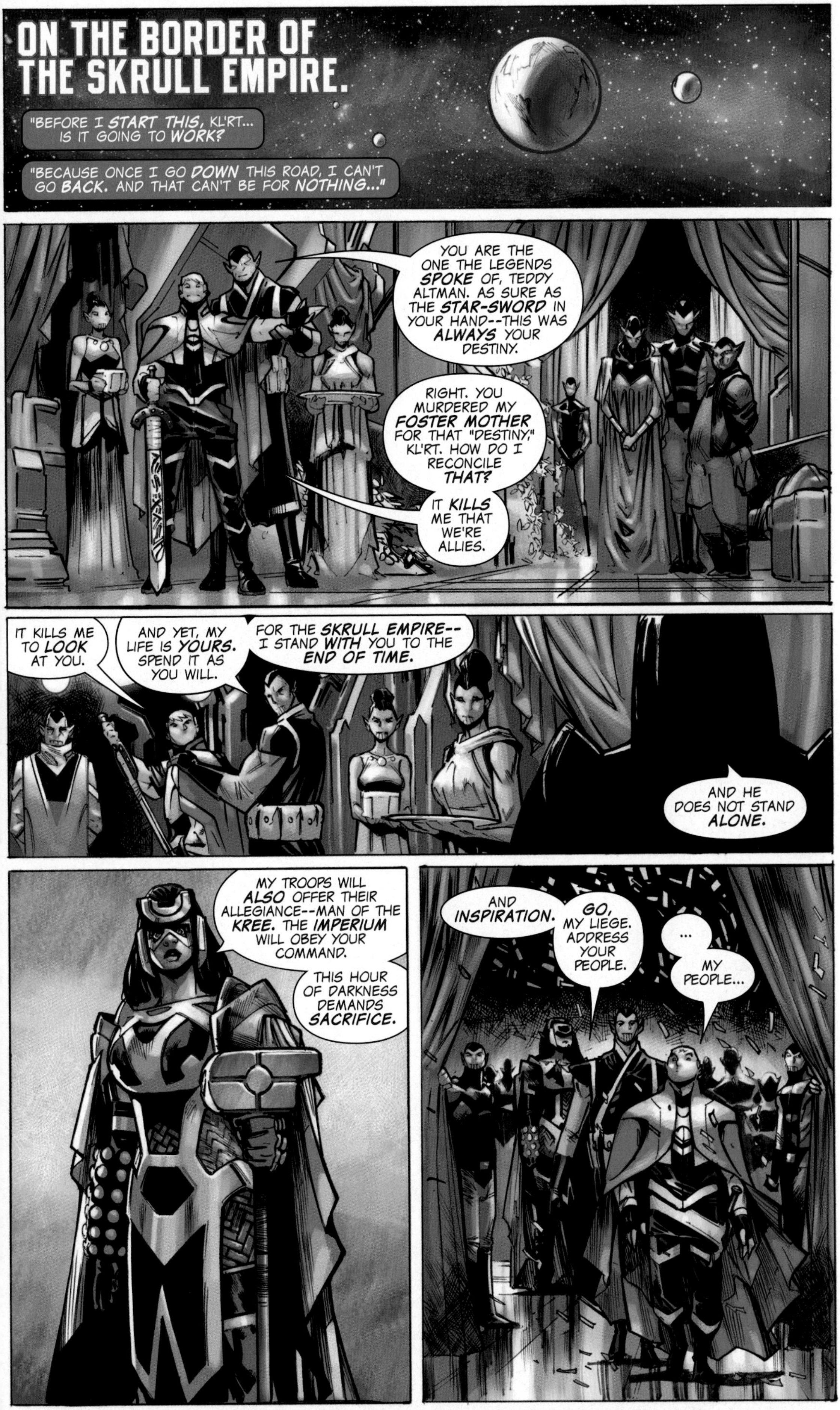

ON THE BORDER OF THE SKRULL EMPIRE.
"BEFORE I START THIS, KL'RT... IS IT GOING TO WORK?
"BECAUSE ONCE I GO DOWN THIS ROAD, I CAN'T GO BACK. AND THAT CAN'T BE FOR NOTHING..."
YOU ARE THE ONE THE LEGENDS SPOKE OF, TEDDY ALTMAN. AS SURE AS THE STAR-SWORD IN YOUR HAND--THIS WAS ALWAYS YOUR DESTINY.
RIGHT. YOU MURDERED MY FOSTER MOTHER FOR THAT "DESTINY," KL'RT. HOW DO I RECONCILE THAT?
IT KILLS ME THAT WE'RE ALLIES.
IT KILLS ME TO LOOK AT YOU.
AND YET, MY LIFE IS YOURS. SPEND IT AS YOU WILL.
FOR THE SKRULL EMPIRE-- I STAND WITH YOU TO THE END OF TIME.
AND HE DOES NOT STAND ALONE.
MY TROOPS WILL ALSO OFFER THEIR ALLEGIANCE--MAN OF THE KREE. THE IMPERIUM WILL OBEY YOUR COMMAND.
THIS HOUR OF DARKNESS DEMANDS SACRIFICE.
AND INSPIRATION.
GO, MY LIEGE. ADDRESS YOUR PEOPLE.
...
MY PEOPLE...

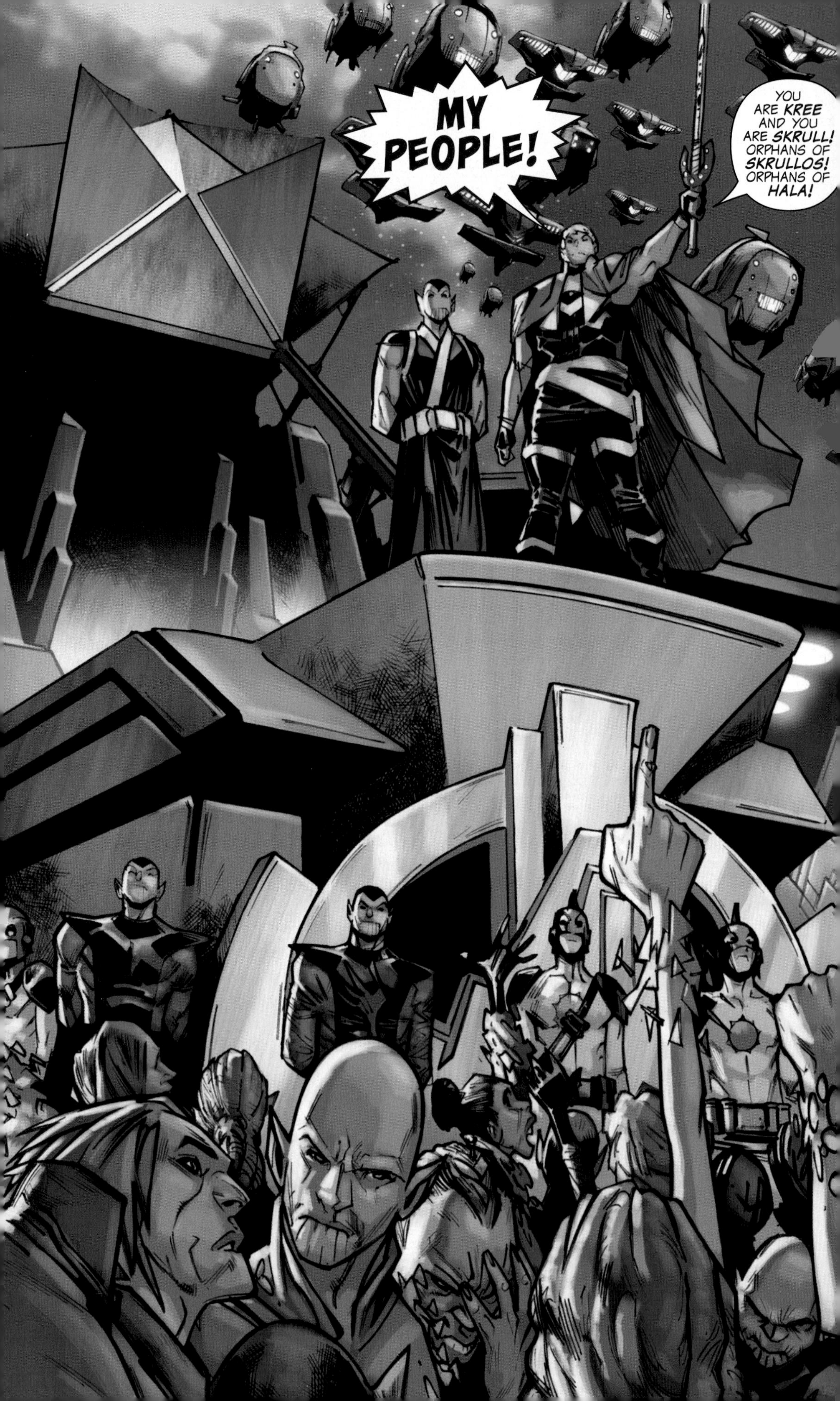
MY PEOPLE!
YOU ARE KREE AND YOU ARE SKRULL! ORPHANS OF SKRULLOS! ORPHANS OF HALA!

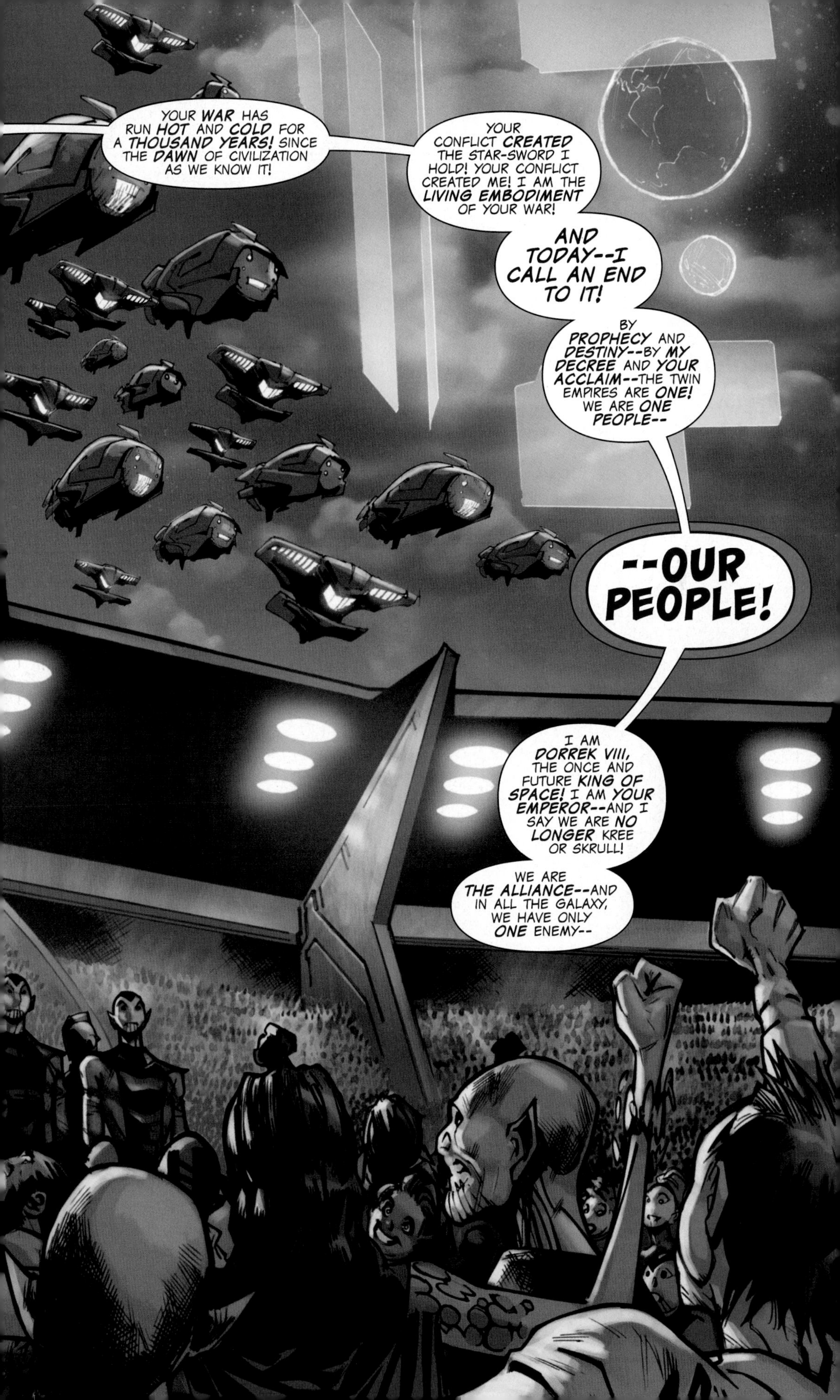

YOUR WAR HAS RUN HOT AND COLD FOR A THOUSAND YEARS! SINCE THE DAWN OF CIVILIZATION AS WE KNOW IT!
YOUR CONFLICT CREATED THE STAR-SWORD I HOLD! YOUR CONFLICT CREATED ME! I AM THE LIVING EMBODIMENT OF YOUR WAR!
AND TODAY--I CALL AN END TO IT!
BY PROPHECY AND DESTINY--BY MY DECREE AND YOUR ACCLAIM--THE TWIN EMPIRES ARE ONE! WE ARE ONE PEOPLE--
--OUR PEOPLE!
I AM DORREK VIII, THE ONCE AND FUTURE KING OF SPACE! I AM YOUR EMPEROR--AND I SAY WE ARE NO LONGER KREE OR SKRULL!
WE ARE THE ALLIANCE--AND IN ALL THE GALAXY, WE HAVE ONLY ONE ENEMY--

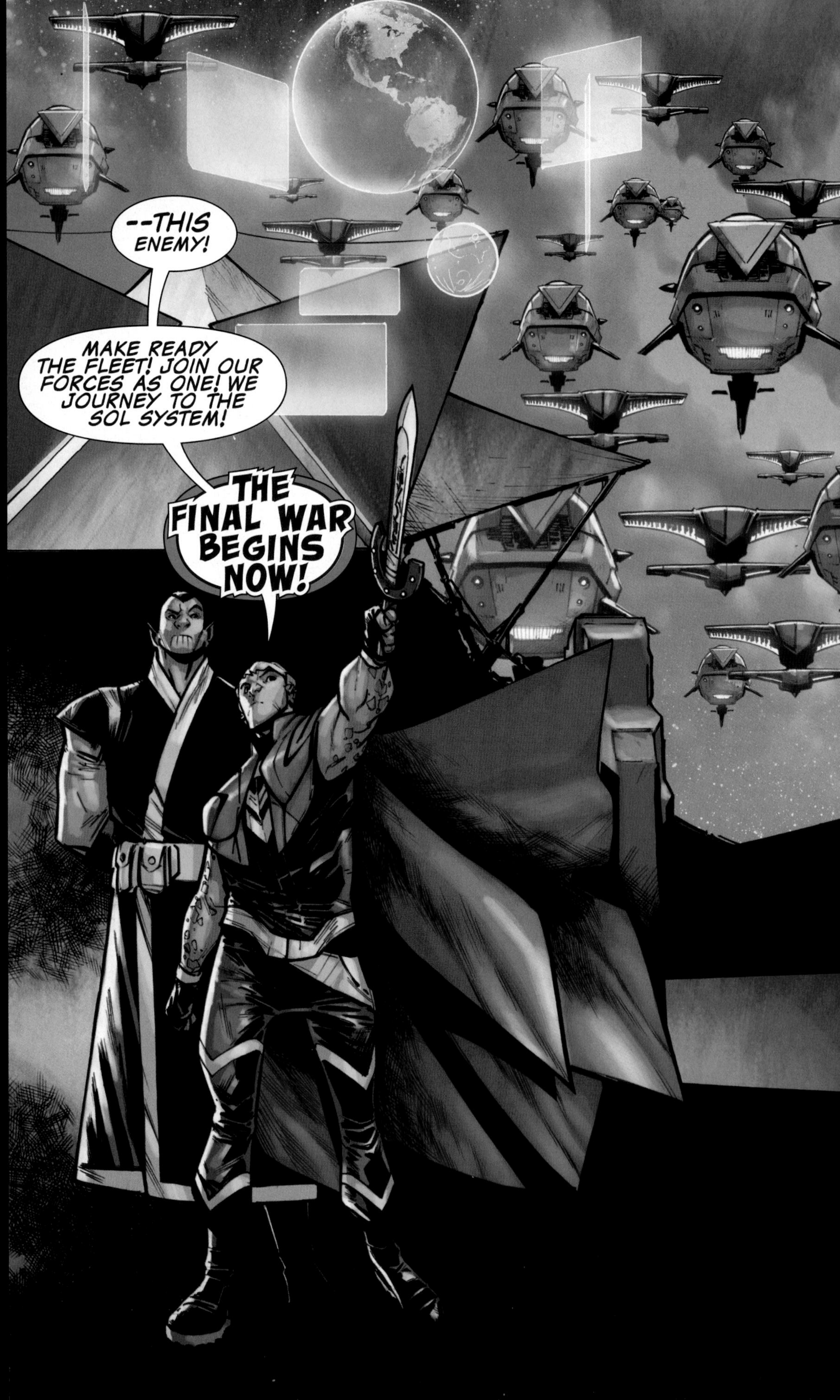
--THIS ENEMY!
MAKE READY THE FLEET! JOIN OUR FORCES AS ONE! WE JOURNEY TO THE SOL SYSTEM!
THE FINAL WAR BEGINS NOW!

ROAD TO EMPYRE: THE KREE/ SKRULL WAR

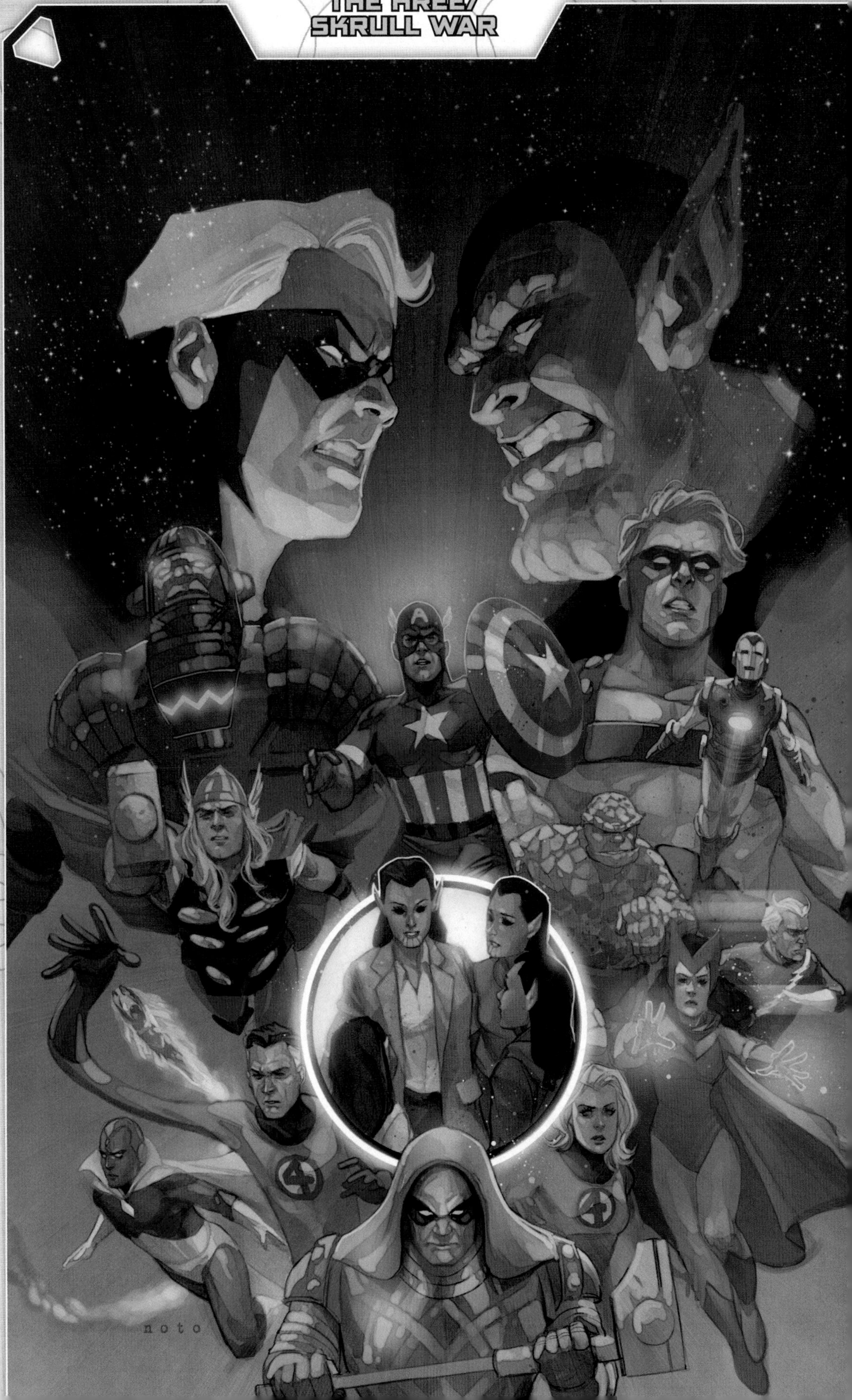
noto

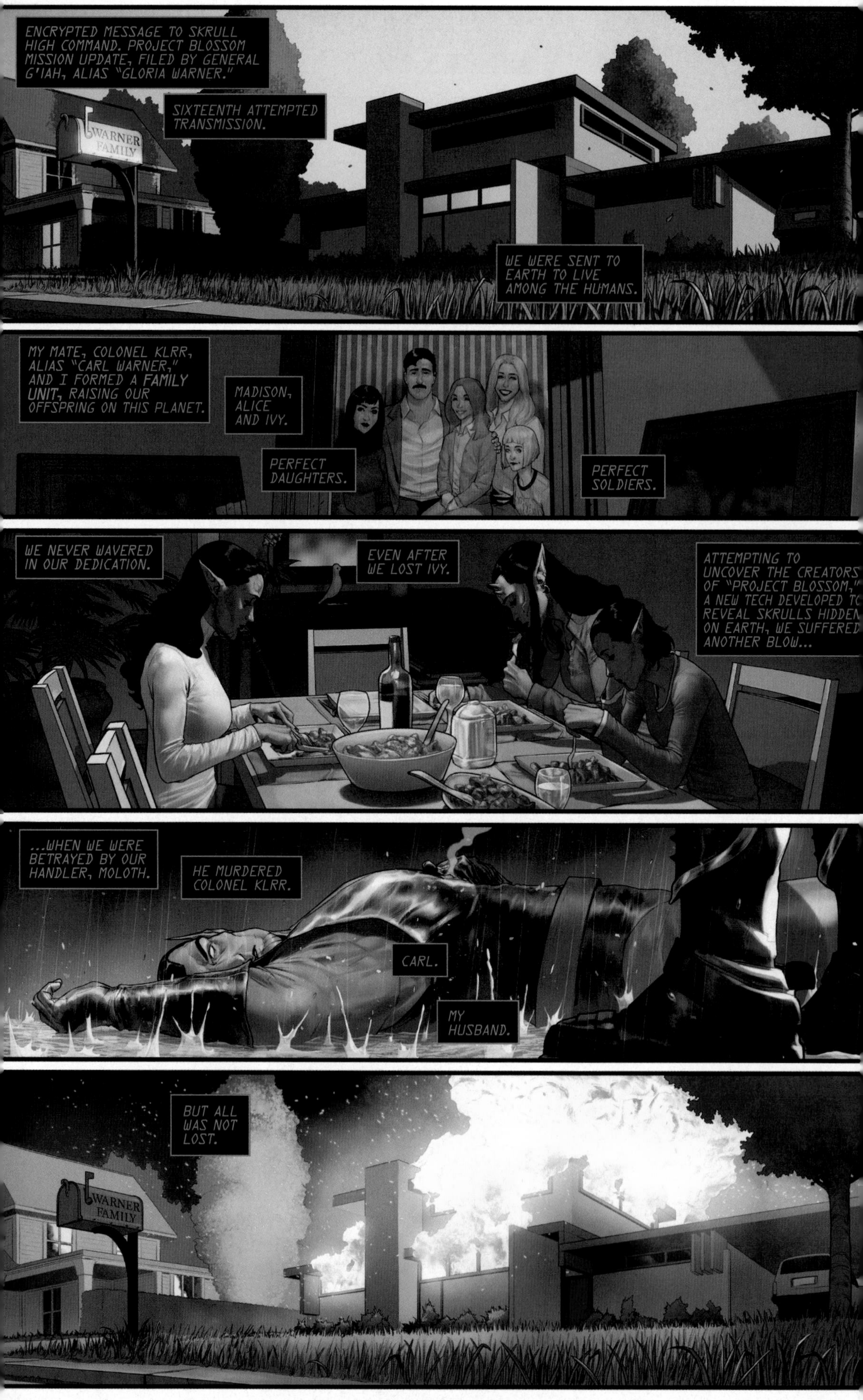
ENCRYPTED MESSAGE TO SKRULL HIGH COMMAND. PROJECT BLOSSOM MISSION UPDATE, FILED BY GENERAL G'IAH, ALIAS "GLORIA WARNER."
SIXTEENTH ATTEMPTED TRANSMISSION.
WARNER FAMILY
WE WERE SENT TO EARTH TO LIVE AMONG THE HUMANS.
MY MATE, COLONEL KLRR, ALIAS "CARL WARNER," AND I FORMED A FAMILY UNIT, RAISING OUR OFFSPRING ON THIS PLANET.
MADISON, ALICE AND IVY.
PERFECT DAUGHTERS.
PERFECT SOLDIERS.
WE NEVER WAVERED IN OUR DEDICATION.
EVEN AFTER WE LOST IVY.
ATTEMPTING TO UNCOVER THE CREATORS OF "PROJECT BLOSSOM," A NEW TECH DEVELOPED TO REVEAL SKRULLS HIDDEN ON EARTH, WE SUFFERED ANOTHER BLOW...
...WHEN WE WERE BETRAYED BY OUR HANDLER, MOLOTH.
HE MURDERED COLONEL KLRR.
CARL.
MY HUSBAND.
BUT ALL WAS NOT LOST.
WARNER FAMILY

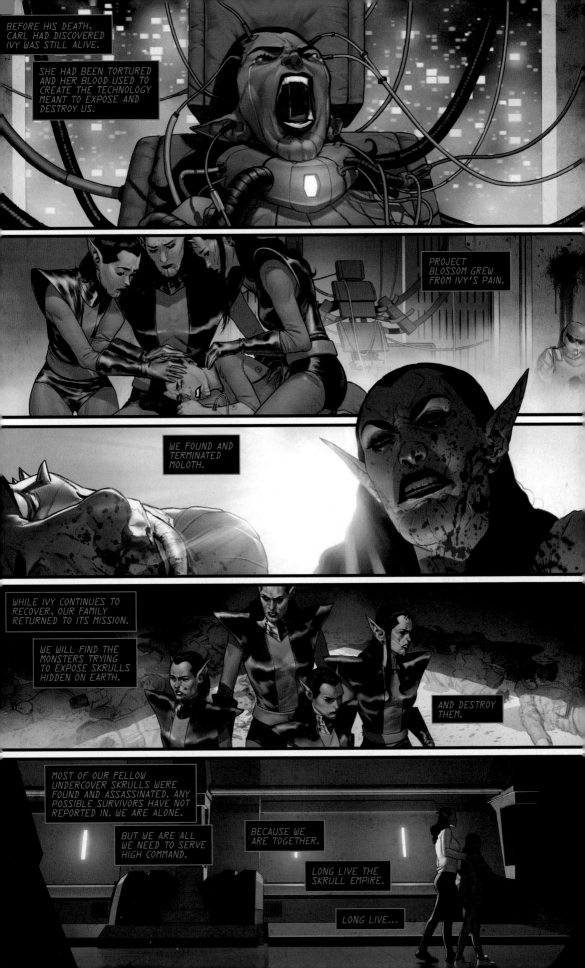

BEFORE HIS DEATH, CARL HAD DISCOVERED IVY WAS STILL ALIVE.

SHE HAD BEEN TORTURED AND HER BLOOD USED TO CREATE THE TECHNOLOGY MEANT TO EXPOSE AND DESTROY US.

PROJECT BLOSSOM GREW FROM IVY'S PAIN.

WE FOUND AND TERMINATED MOLOTH.

WHILE IVY CONTINUES TO RECOVER, OUR FAMILY RETURNED TO ITS MISSION.

WE WILL FIND THE MONSTERS TRYING TO EXPOSE SKRULLS HIDDEN ON EARTH.

AND DESTROY THEM.

MOST OF OUR FELLOW UNDERCOVER SKRULLS WERE FOUND AND ASSASSINATED. ANY POSSIBLE SURVIVORS HAVE NOT REPORTED IN. WE ARE ALONE.

BUT WE ARE ALL WE NEED TO SERVE HIGH COMMAND.

BECAUSE WE ARE TOGETHER.

LONG LIVE THE SKRULL EMPIRE.

LONG LIVE...

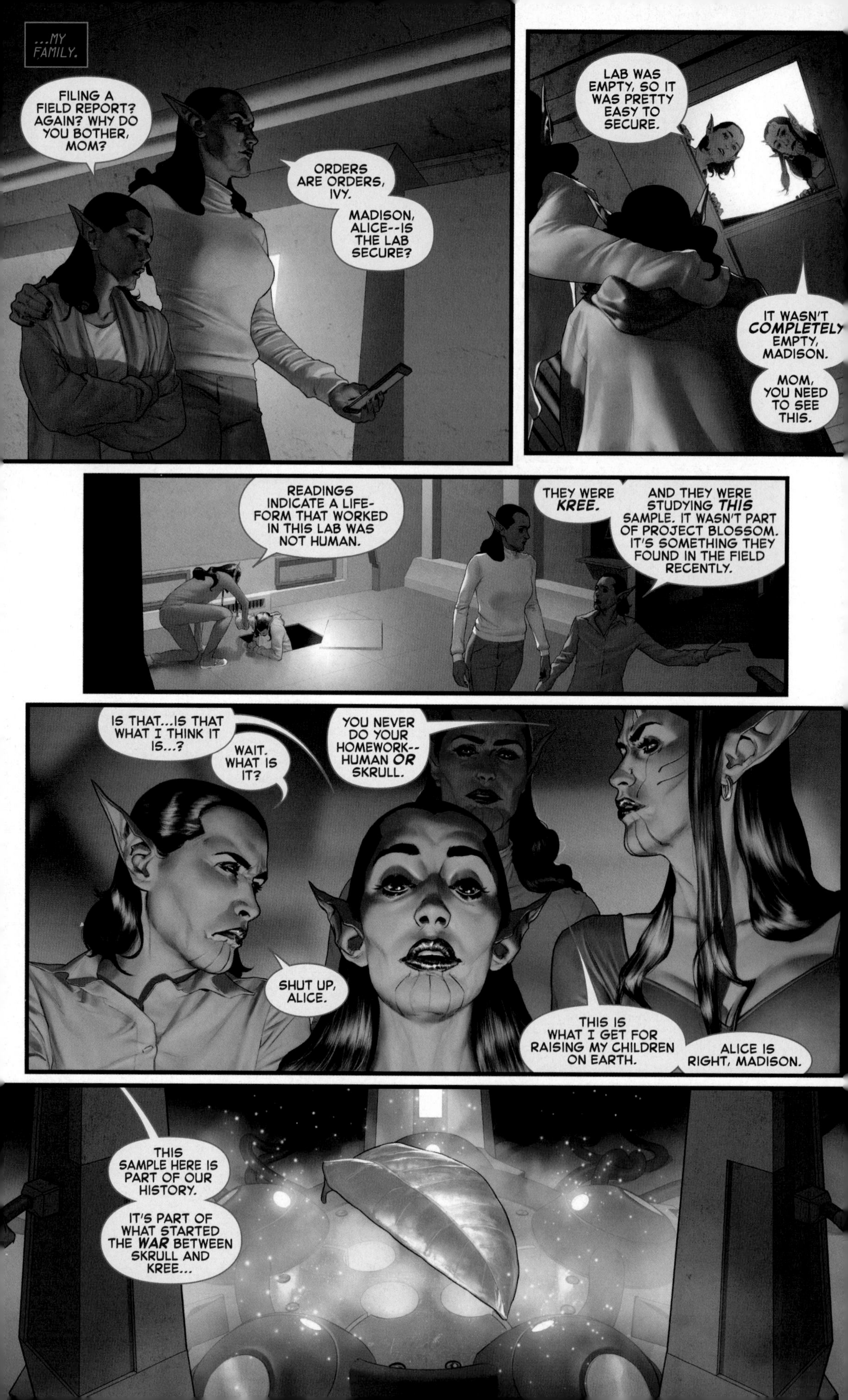

...MY FAMILY.
FILING A FIELD REPORT? AGAIN? WHY DO YOU BOTHER, MOM?
ORDERS ARE ORDERS, IVY.
MADISON, ALICE--IS THE LAB SECURE?
LAB WAS EMPTY, SO IT WAS PRETTY EASY TO SECURE.
IT WASN'T COMPLETELY EMPTY, MADISON.
MOM, YOU NEED TO SEE THIS.
READINGS INDICATE A LIFE-FORM THAT WORKED IN THIS LAB WAS NOT HUMAN.
THEY WERE KREE.
AND THEY WERE STUDYING THIS SAMPLE. IT WASN'T PART OF PROJECT BLOSSOM. IT'S SOMETHING THEY FOUND IN THE FIELD RECENTLY.
IS THAT...IS THAT WHAT I THINK IT IS...?
WAIT. WHAT IS IT?
YOU NEVER DO YOUR HOMEWORK--HUMAN OR SKRULL.
SHUT UP, ALICE.
THIS IS WHAT I GET FOR RAISING MY CHILDREN ON EARTH.
ALICE IS RIGHT, MADISON.
THIS SAMPLE HERE IS PART OF OUR HISTORY.
IT'S PART OF WHAT STARTED THE WAR BETWEEN SKRULL AND KREE...

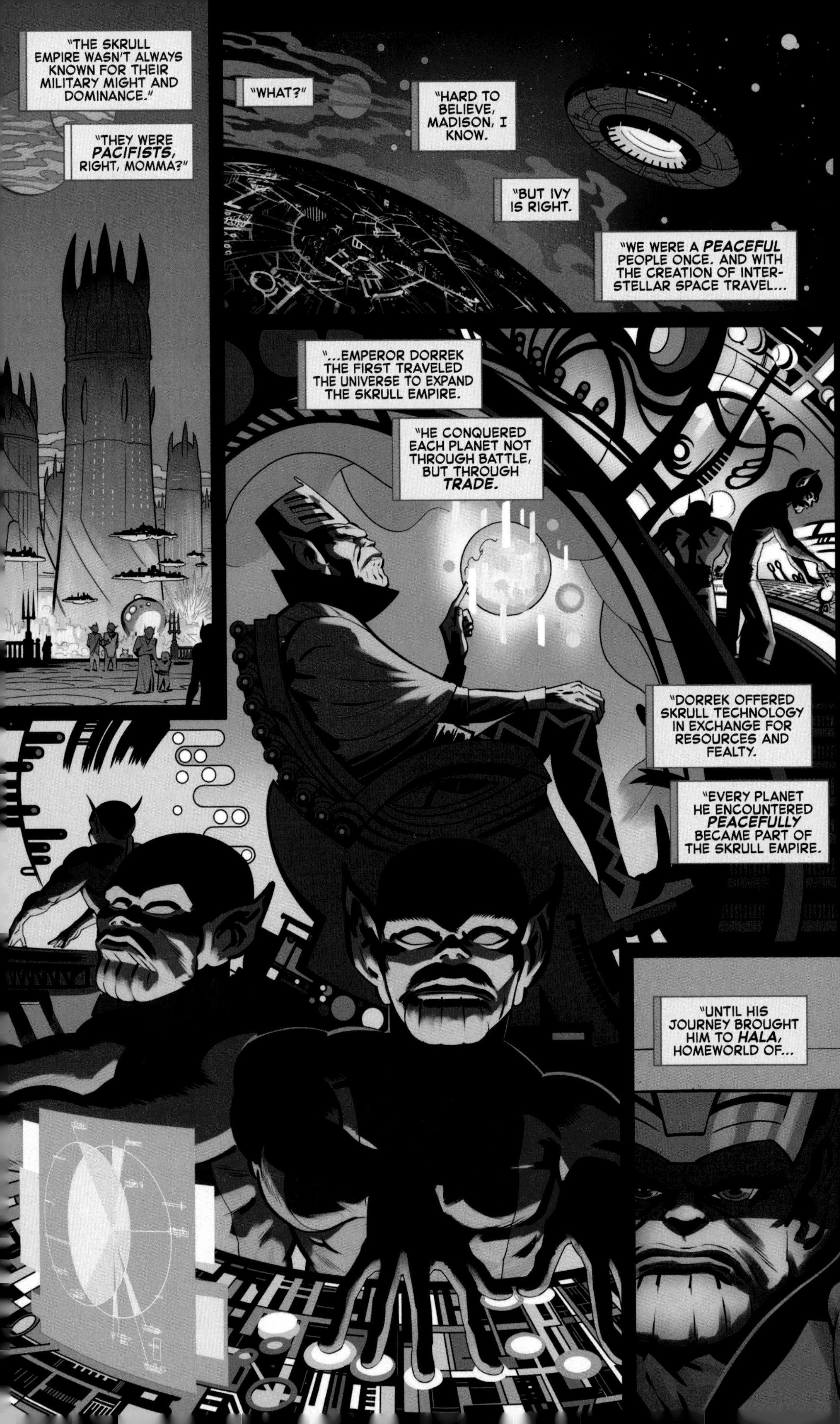
"THE SKRULL EMPIRE WASN'T ALWAYS KNOWN FOR THEIR MILITARY MIGHT AND DOMINANCE."
"THEY WERE PACIFISTS, RIGHT, MOMMA?"
"WHAT?"
"HARD TO BELIEVE, MADISON, I KNOW.
"BUT IVY IS RIGHT.
"WE WERE A PEACEFUL PEOPLE ONCE. AND WITH THE CREATION OF INTER-STELLAR SPACE TRAVEL...
"...EMPEROR DORREK THE FIRST TRAVELED THE UNIVERSE TO EXPAND THE SKRULL EMPIRE.
"HE CONQUERED EACH PLANET NOT THROUGH BATTLE, BUT THROUGH TRADE.
"DORREK OFFERED SKRULL TECHNOLOGY IN EXCHANGE FOR RESOURCES AND FEALTY.
"EVERY PLANET HE ENCOUNTERED PEACEFULLY BECAME PART OF THE SKRULL EMPIRE.
"UNTIL HIS JOURNEY BROUGHT HIM TO HALA, HOMEWORLD OF...

"...THE KREE.

"THEY WERE EVEN MORE BARBARIC AND SAVAGE THAN THEY ARE NOW.

"AND THEY WERE LED BY A BRUTE NAMED *MORAG.*

"BUT THEY WERE NOT THE *ONLY* SPECIES ON HALA...

"...THE *COTATI* HAD EVOLVED THERE AS WELL.

"A PLANT SPECIES THAT LIVED IN HARMONY WITH THEIR ENVIRONMENT. THEY COMMUNICATED VIA TELEPATHY.

"AND THEY WERE *PEACEFUL* LIKE THE SKRULLS.

"IN ORDER TO DETERMINE THE DOMINANT SPECIES ON HALA--AND HIS NEW TRADING PARTNERS-- EMPEROR DORREK PROPOSED A *CONTEST.*

"HE TRANSPORTED A PARTY FROM EACH SPECIES TO ISOLATED MOONS.

"EACH WOULD BE 'ARMED' WITH THE BEST OF SKRULL TECHNOLOGY.

"AFTER ONE YEAR IN ISOLATION, WHOEVER HAD CREATED THE MOST WITH THE GIFTS THEY WERE GIVEN WOULD BE DEEMED *RULER* OF HALA AND THEN THE PLANET WOULD BE WELCOMED INTO THE SKRULL EMPIRE

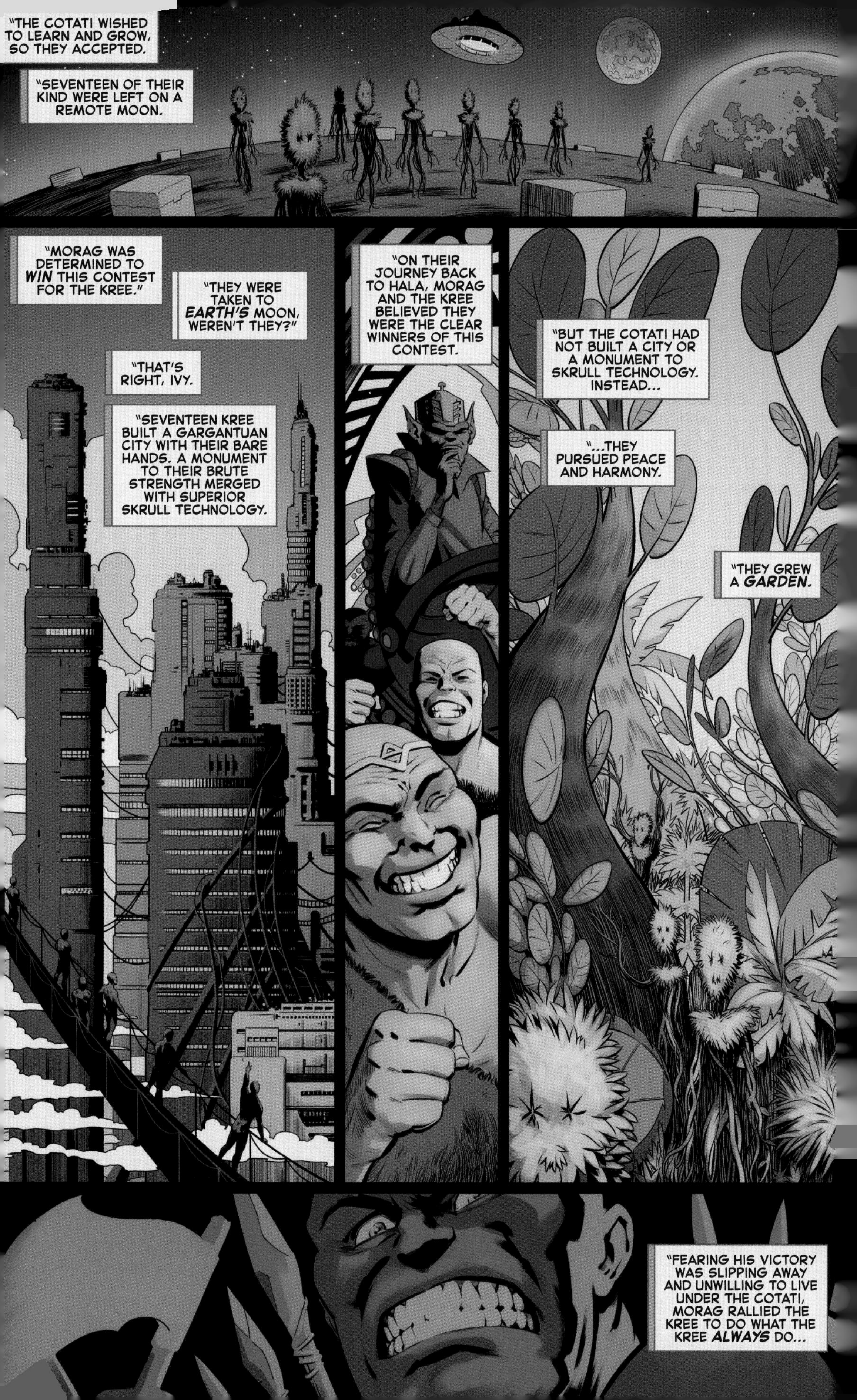
"THE COTATI WISHED TO LEARN AND GROW, SO THEY ACCEPTED.
"SEVENTEEN OF THEIR KIND WERE LEFT ON A REMOTE MOON.
"MORAG WAS DETERMINED TO *WIN* THIS CONTEST FOR THE KREE."
"THEY WERE TAKEN TO *EARTH'S* MOON, WEREN'T THEY?"
"THAT'S RIGHT, IVY.
"SEVENTEEN KREE BUILT A GARGANTUAN CITY WITH THEIR BARE HANDS. A MONUMENT TO THEIR BRUTE STRENGTH MERGED WITH SUPERIOR SKRULL TECHNOLOGY.
"ON THEIR JOURNEY BACK TO HALA, MORAG AND THE KREE BELIEVED THEY WERE THE CLEAR WINNERS OF THIS CONTEST.
"BUT THE COTATI HAD NOT BUILT A CITY OR A MONUMENT TO SKRULL TECHNOLOGY. INSTEAD...
"...THEY PURSUED PEACE AND HARMONY.
"THEY GREW A *GARDEN*.
"FEARING HIS VICTORY WAS SLIPPING AWAY AND UNWILLING TO LIVE UNDER THE COTATI, MORAG RALLIED THE KREE TO DO WHAT THE KREE *ALWAYS* DO...

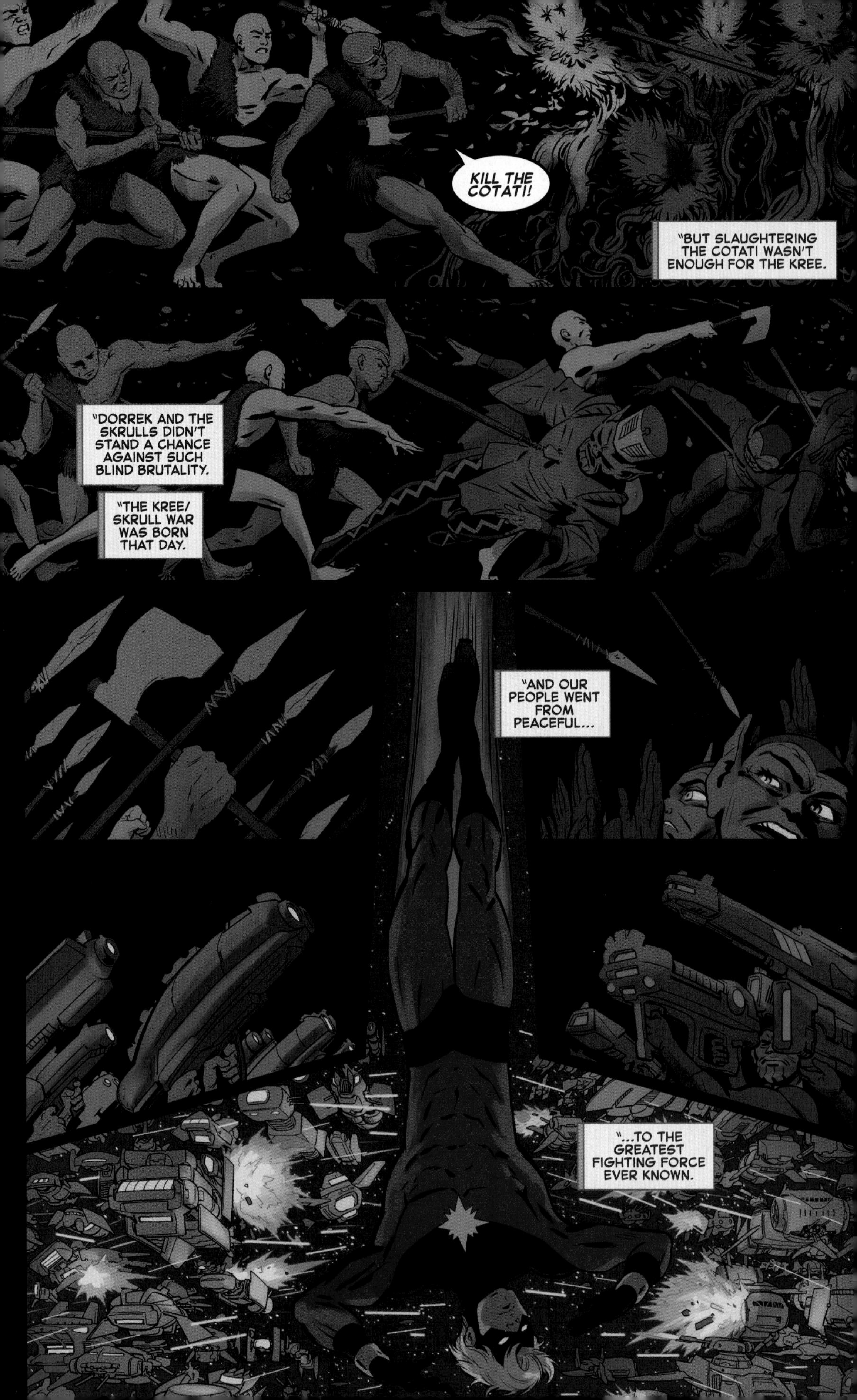
KILL THE COTATI!
"BUT SLAUGHTERING THE COTATI WASN'T ENOUGH FOR THE KREE.
"DORREK AND THE SKRULLS DIDN'T STAND A CHANCE AGAINST SUCH BLIND BRUTALITY.
"THE KREE/SKRULL WAR WAS BORN THAT DAY.
"AND OUR PEOPLE WENT FROM PEACEFUL...
"...TO THE GREATEST FIGHTING FORCE EVER KNOWN.

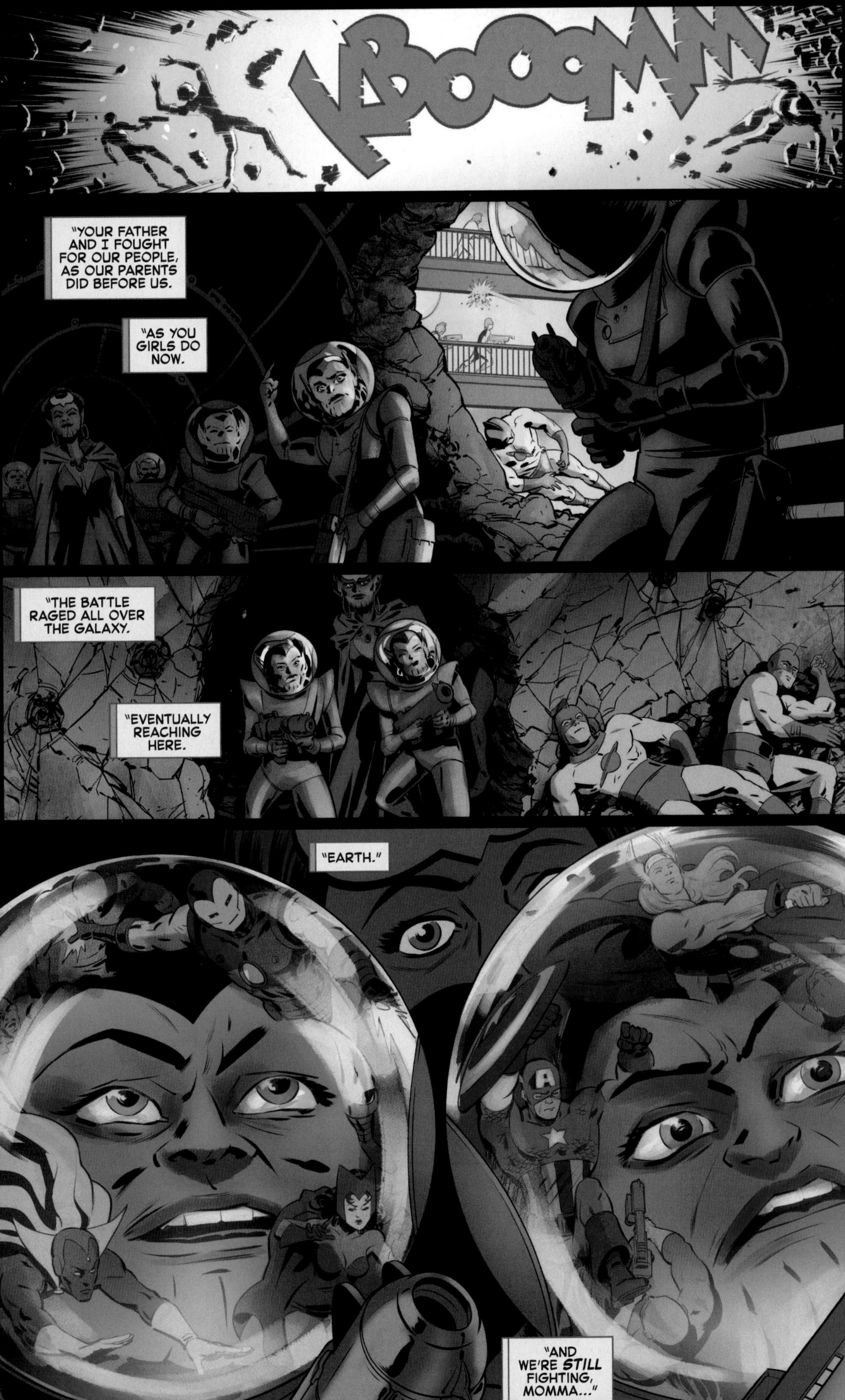
KBOOOMM
"YOUR FATHER AND I FOUGHT FOR OUR PEOPLE, AS OUR PARENTS DID BEFORE US.
"AS YOU GIRLS DO NOW.
"THE BATTLE RAGED ALL OVER THE GALAXY.
"EVENTUALLY REACHING HERE.
"EARTH."
"AND WE'RE STILL FIGHTING, MOMMA..."

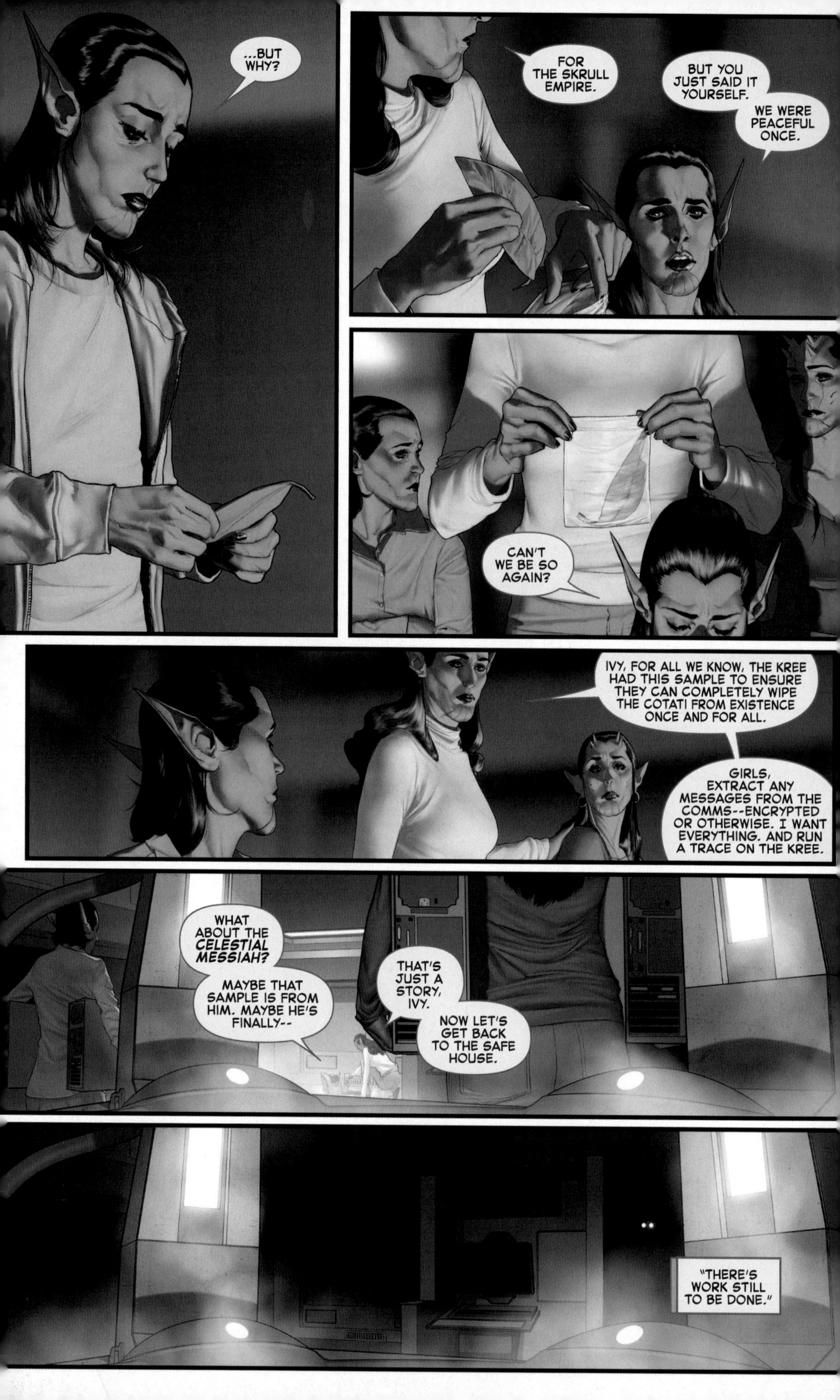
...BUT WHY?
FOR THE SKRULL EMPIRE.
BUT YOU JUST SAID IT YOURSELF.
WE WERE PEACEFUL ONCE.
CAN'T WE BE SO AGAIN?
IVY, FOR ALL WE KNOW, THE KREE HAD THIS SAMPLE TO ENSURE THEY CAN COMPLETELY WIPE THE COTATI FROM EXISTENCE ONCE AND FOR ALL.
GIRLS, EXTRACT ANY MESSAGES FROM THE COMMS--ENCRYPTED OR OTHERWISE. I WANT EVERYTHING. AND RUN A TRACE ON THE KREE.
WHAT ABOUT THE *CELESTIAL MESSIAH*?
MAYBE THAT SAMPLE IS FROM HIM. MAYBE HE'S FINALLY--
THAT'S JUST A STORY, IVY.
NOW LET'S GET BACK TO THE SAFE HOUSE.
"THERE'S WORK STILL TO BE DONE."

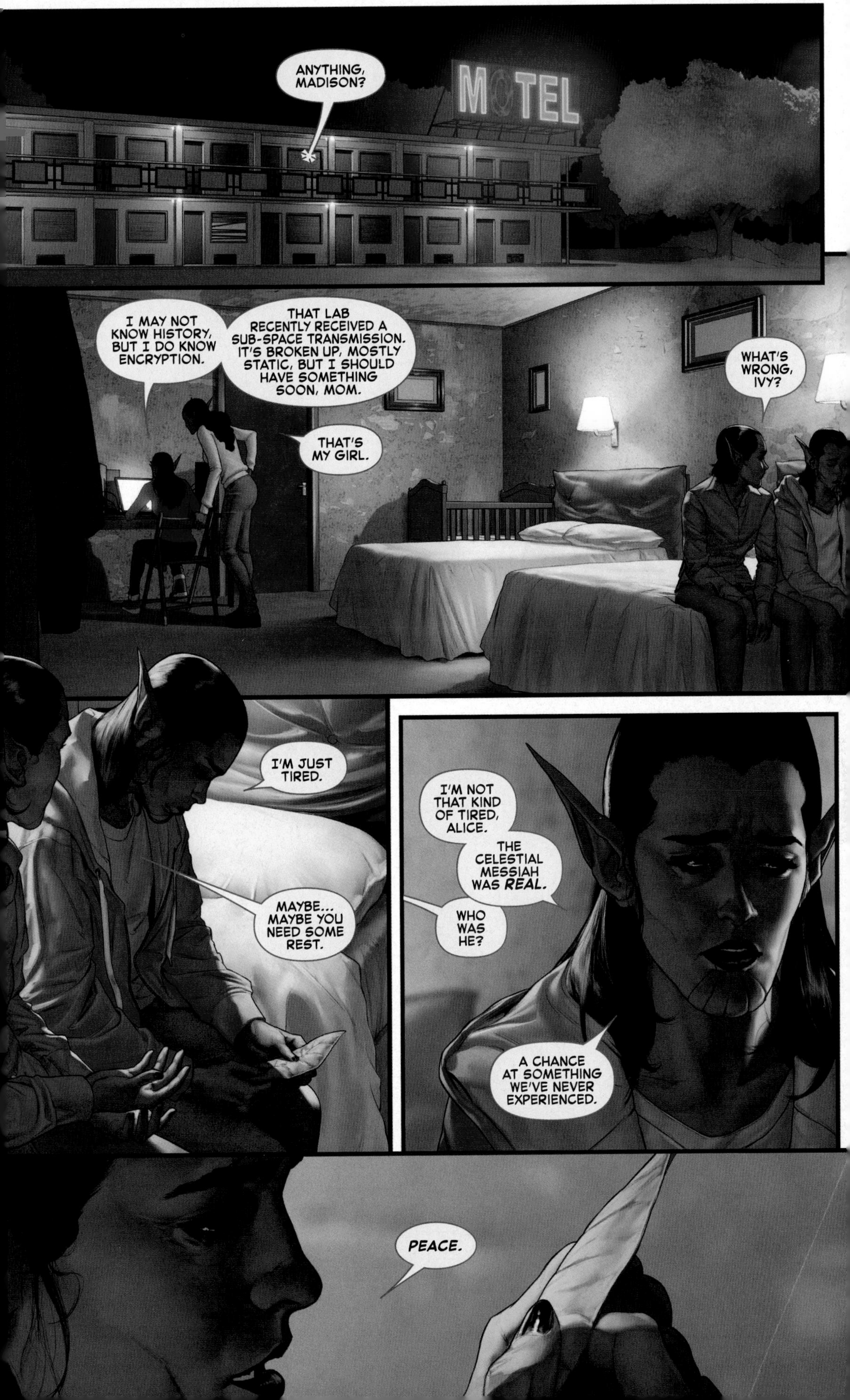
ANYTHING, MADISON?
MOTEL
I MAY NOT KNOW HISTORY, BUT I DO KNOW ENCRYPTION.
THAT LAB RECENTLY RECEIVED A SUB-SPACE TRANSMISSION. IT'S BROKEN UP, MOSTLY STATIC, BUT I SHOULD HAVE SOMETHING SOON, MOM.
THAT'S MY GIRL.
WHAT'S WRONG, IVY?
I'M JUST TIRED.
MAYBE... MAYBE YOU NEED SOME REST.
I'M NOT THAT KIND OF TIRED, ALICE.
THE CELESTIAL MESSIAH WAS *REAL.*
WHO WAS HE?
A CHANCE AT SOMETHING WE'VE NEVER EXPERIENCED.
PEACE.

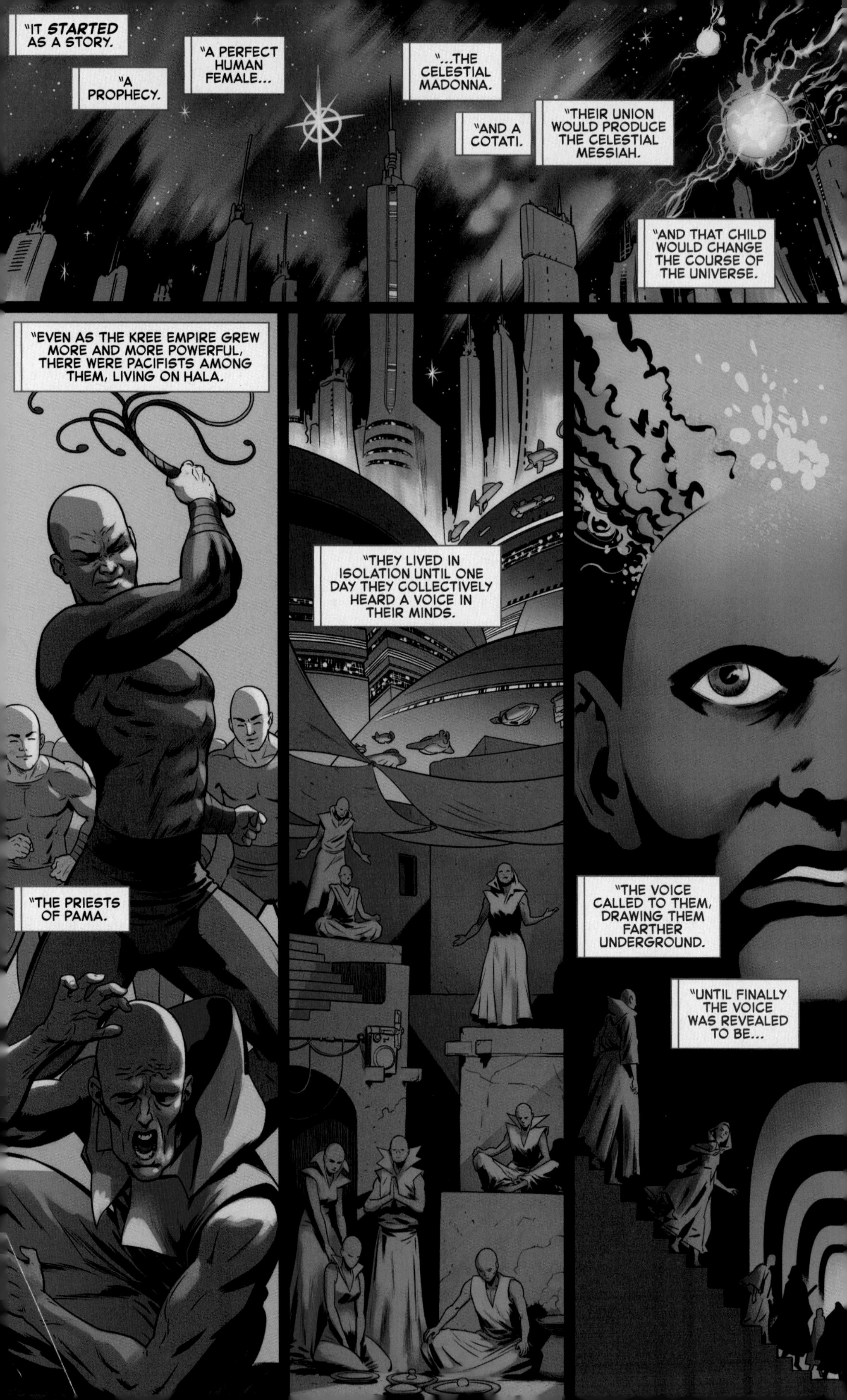
"IT STARTED AS A STORY.
"A PROPHECY.
"A PERFECT HUMAN FEMALE...
"...THE CELESTIAL MADONNA.
"AND A COTATI.
"THEIR UNION WOULD PRODUCE THE CELESTIAL MESSIAH.
"AND THAT CHILD WOULD CHANGE THE COURSE OF THE UNIVERSE.
"EVEN AS THE KREE EMPIRE GREW MORE AND MORE POWERFUL, THERE WERE PACIFISTS AMONG THEM, LIVING ON HALA.
"THE PRIESTS OF PAMA.
"THEY LIVED IN ISOLATION UNTIL ONE DAY THEY COLLECTIVELY HEARD A VOICE IN THEIR MINDS.
"THE VOICE CALLED TO THEM, DRAWING THEM FARTHER UNDERGROUND.
"UNTIL FINALLY THE VOICE WAS REVEALED TO BE...

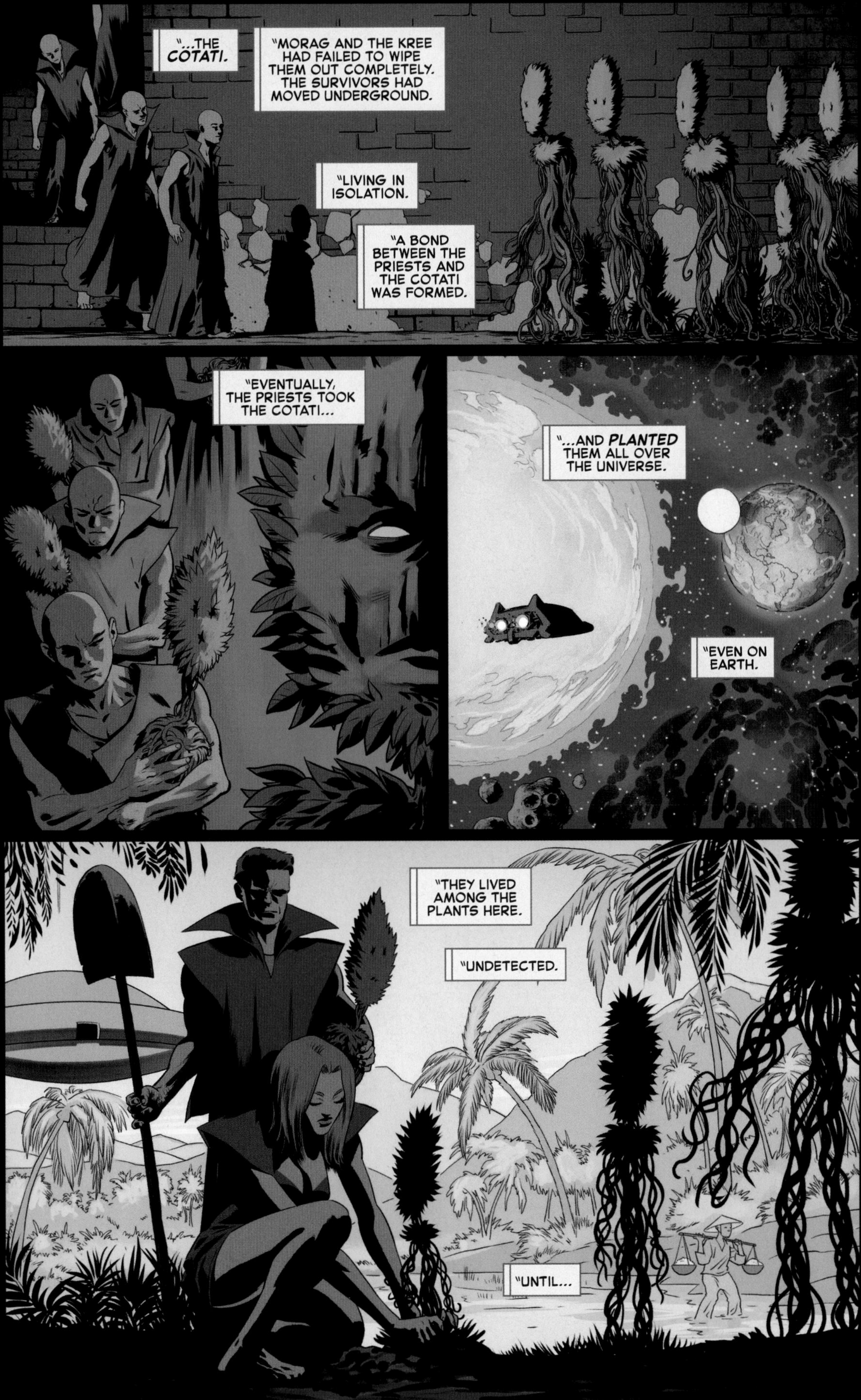
"...THE *COTATI.*
"MORAG AND THE KREE HAD FAILED TO WIPE THEM OUT COMPLETELY. THE SURVIVORS HAD MOVED UNDERGROUND.
"LIVING IN ISOLATION.
"A BOND BETWEEN THE PRIESTS AND THE COTATI WAS FORMED.
"EVENTUALLY, THE PRIESTS TOOK THE COTATI...
"...AND *PLANTED* THEM ALL OVER THE UNIVERSE.
"EVEN ON EARTH.
"THEY LIVED AMONG THE PLANTS HERE.
"UNDETECTED.
"UNTIL...

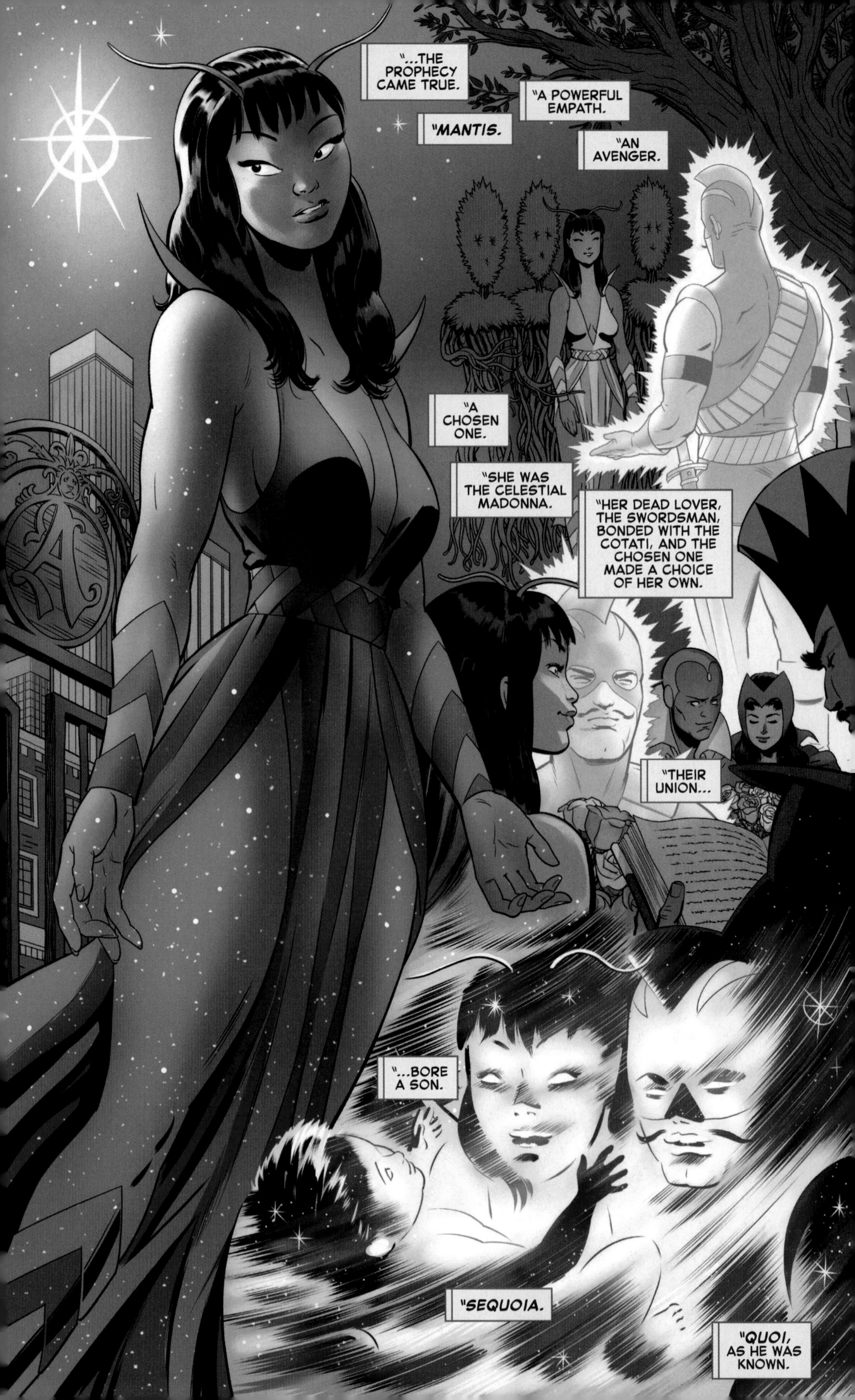
"...THE PROPHECY CAME TRUE.
"MANTIS.
"A POWERFUL EMPATH.
"AN AVENGER.
"A CHOSEN ONE.
"SHE WAS THE CELESTIAL MADONNA.
"HER DEAD LOVER, THE SWORDSMAN, BONDED WITH THE COTATI, AND THE CHOSEN ONE MADE A CHOICE OF HER OWN.
"THEIR UNION...
"...BORE A SON.
"SEQUOIA.
"QUOI, AS HE WAS KNOWN.

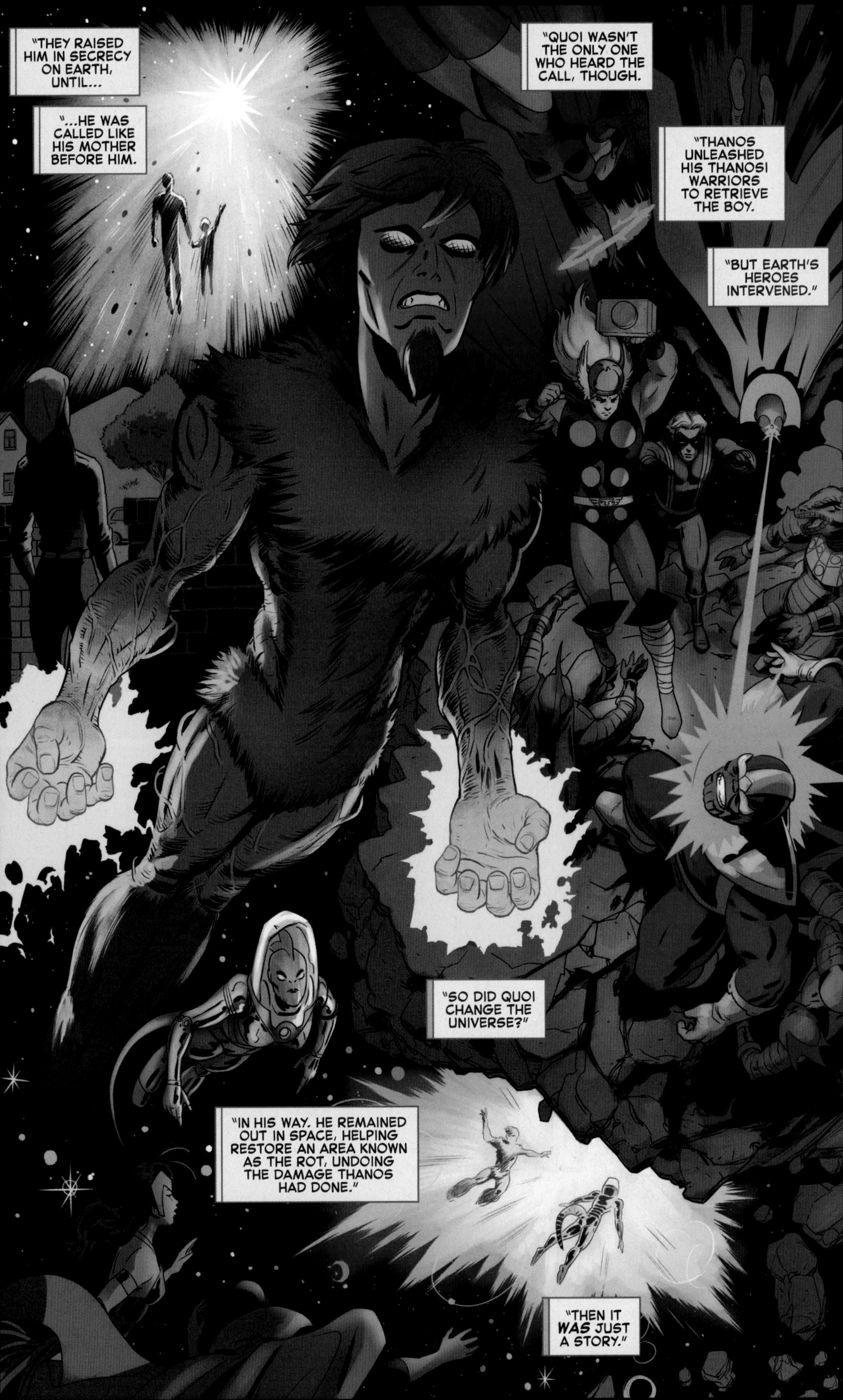
"THEY RAISED HIM IN SECRECY ON EARTH, UNTIL...
"...HE WAS CALLED LIKE HIS MOTHER BEFORE HIM.
"QUOI WASN'T THE ONLY ONE WHO HEARD THE CALL, THOUGH.
"THANOS UNLEASHED HIS THANOSI WARRIORS TO RETRIEVE THE BOY.
"BUT EARTH'S HEROES INTERVENED."
"SO DID QUOI CHANGE THE UNIVERSE?"
"IN HIS WAY. HE REMAINED OUT IN SPACE, HELPING RESTORE AN AREA KNOWN AS THE ROT, UNDOING THE DAMAGE THANOS HAD DONE."
"THEN IT WAS JUST A STORY."

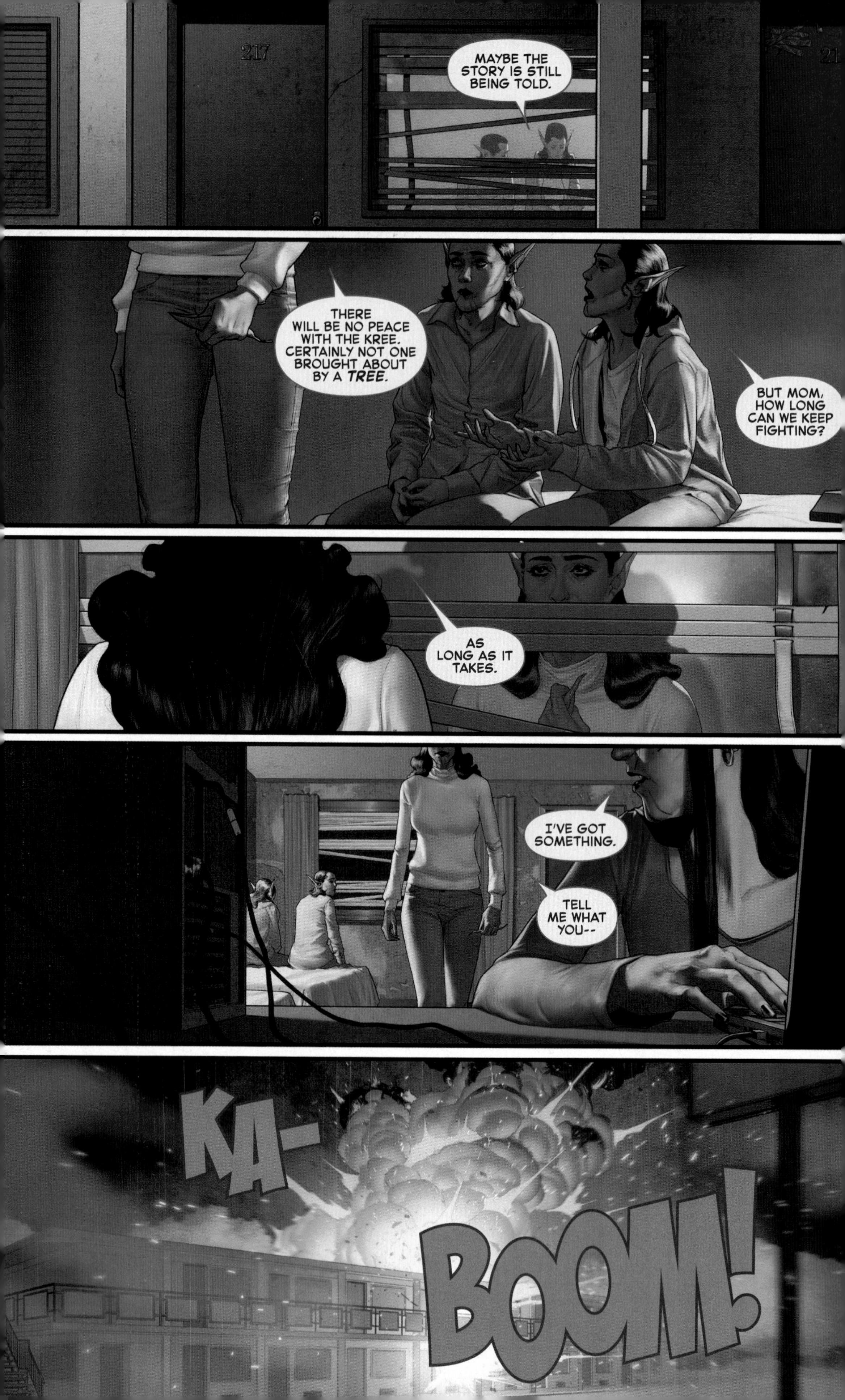
217
MAYBE THE STORY IS STILL BEING TOLD.
THERE WILL BE NO PEACE WITH THE KREE. CERTAINLY NOT ONE BROUGHT ABOUT BY A *TREE*.
BUT MOM, HOW LONG CAN WE KEEP FIGHTING?
AS LONG AS IT TAKES.
I'VE GOT SOMETHING.
TELL ME WHAT YOU--
KA-
BOOM!

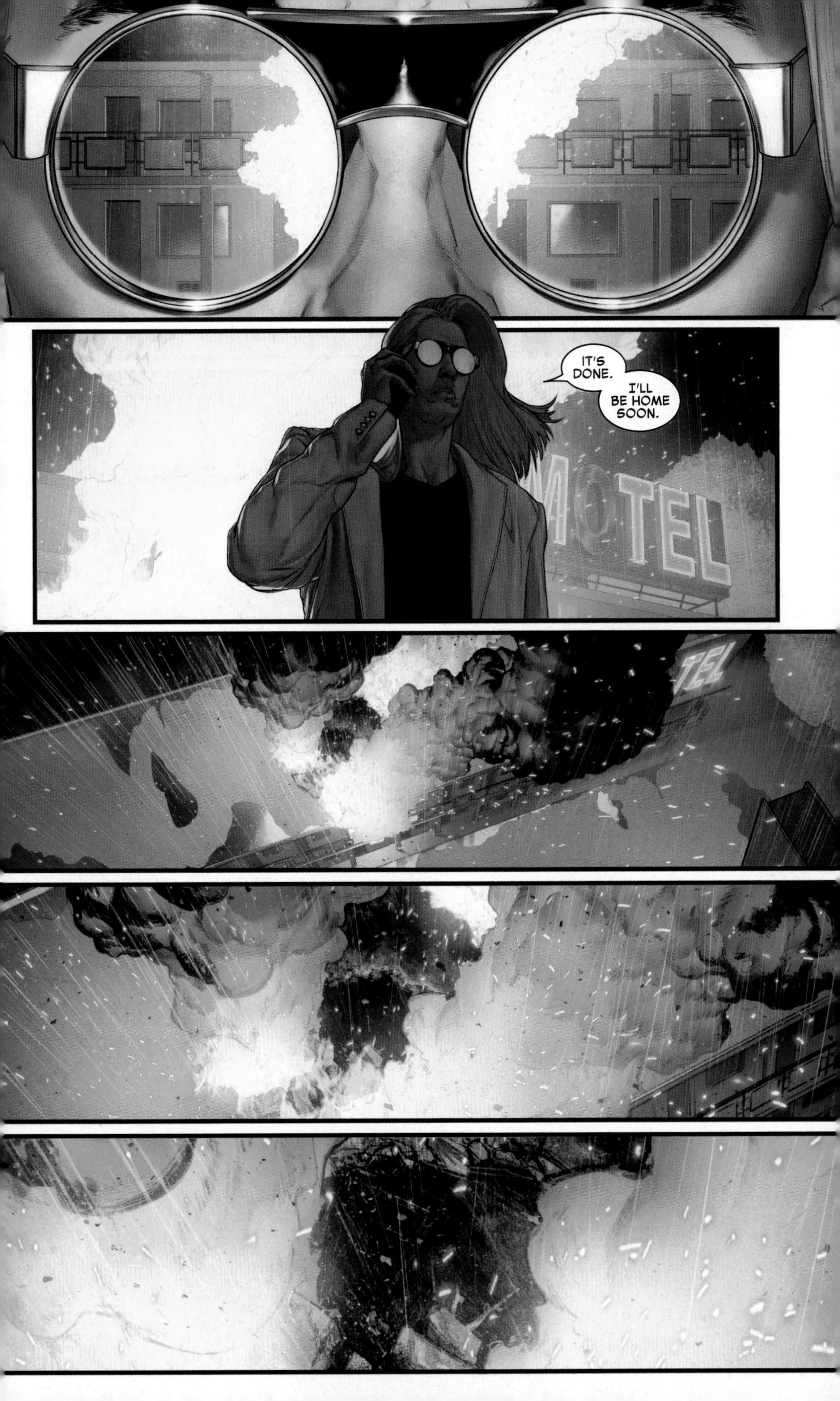

IT'S DONE.
I'LL BE HOME SOON.
MOTEL
TEL

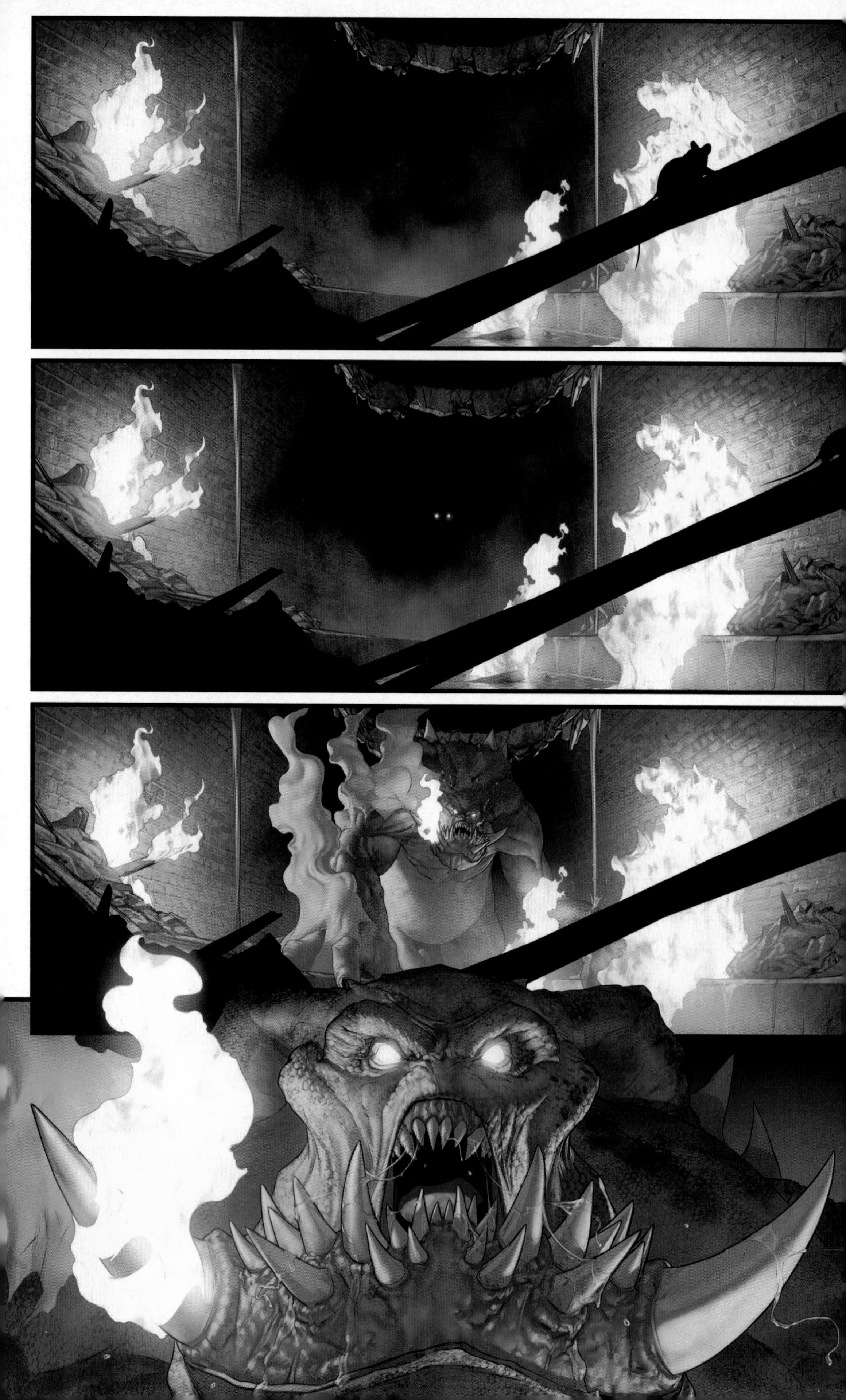

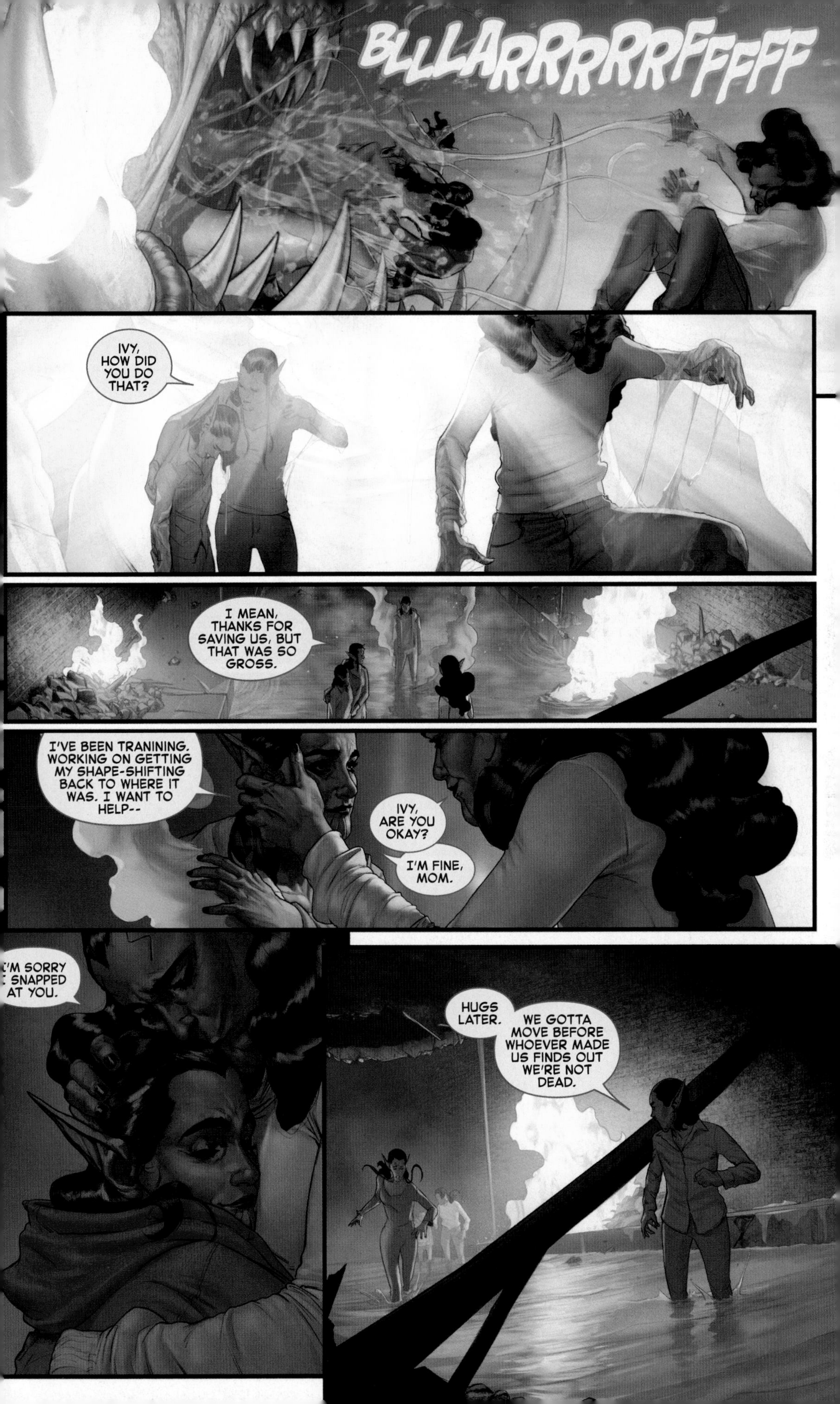

BLLLARRRRRRFFFFF
IVY, HOW DID YOU DO THAT?
I MEAN, THANKS FOR SAVING US, BUT THAT WAS SO GROSS.
I'VE BEEN TRANINING. WORKING ON GETTING MY SHAPE-SHIFTING BACK TO WHERE IT WAS. I WANT TO HELP--
IVY, ARE YOU OKAY?
I'M FINE, MOM.
I'M SORRY I SNAPPED AT YOU.
HUGS LATER.
WE GOTTA MOVE BEFORE WHOEVER MADE US FINDS OUT WE'RE NOT DEAD.

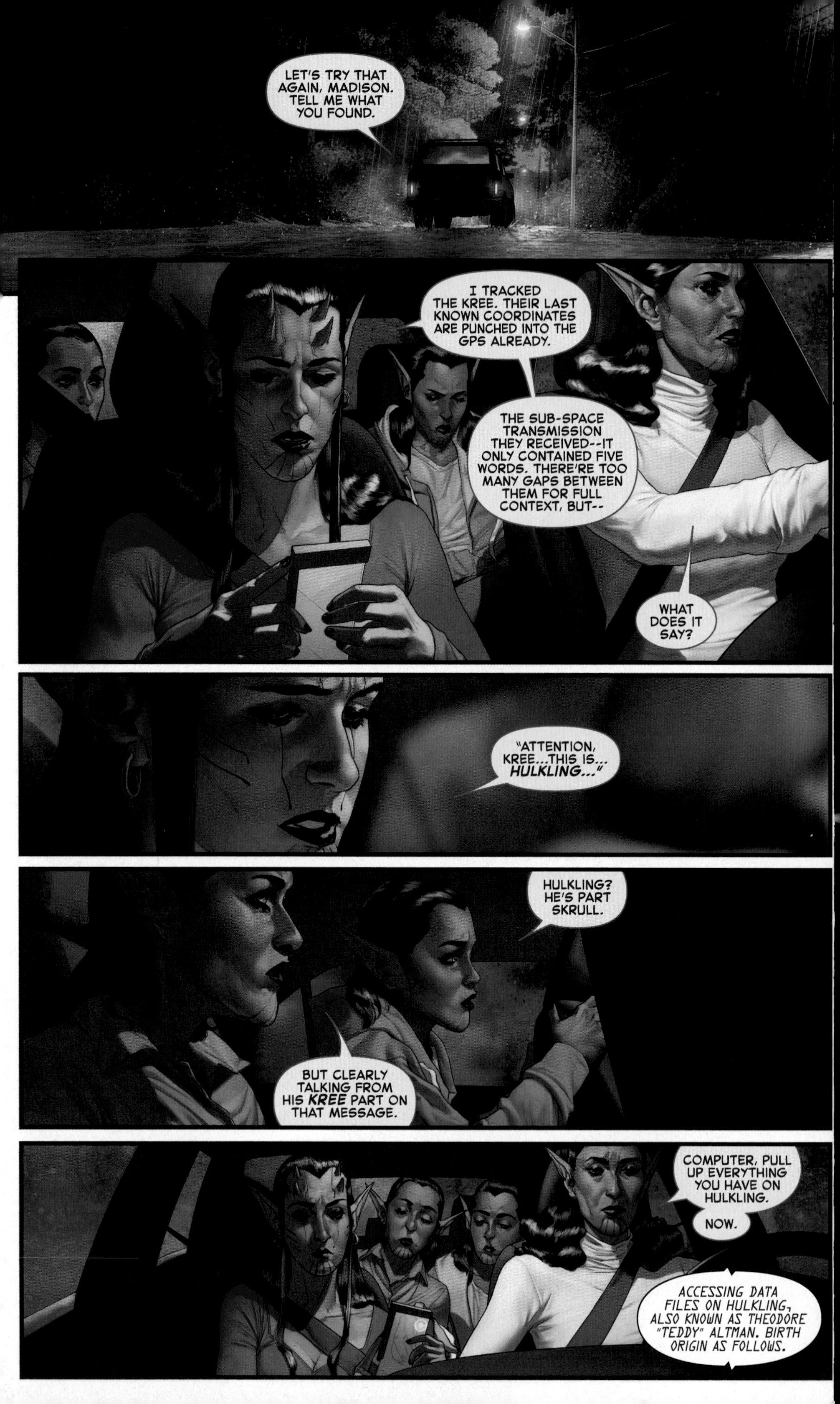
LET'S TRY THAT AGAIN, MADISON. TELL ME WHAT YOU FOUND.
I TRACKED THE KREE. THEIR LAST KNOWN COORDINATES ARE PUNCHED INTO THE GPS ALREADY.
THE SUB-SPACE TRANSMISSION THEY RECEIVED--IT ONLY CONTAINED FIVE WORDS. THERE'RE TOO MANY GAPS BETWEEN THEM FOR FULL CONTEXT, BUT--
WHAT DOES IT SAY?
"ATTENTION, KREE...THIS IS... HULKLING..."
HULKLING? HE'S PART SKRULL.
BUT CLEARLY TALKING FROM HIS KREE PART ON THAT MESSAGE.
COMPUTER, PULL UP EVERYTHING YOU HAVE ON HULKLING.
NOW.
ACCESSING DATA FILES ON HULKLING, ALSO KNOWN AS THEODORE "TEDDY" ALTMAN. BIRTH ORIGIN AS FOLLOWS.

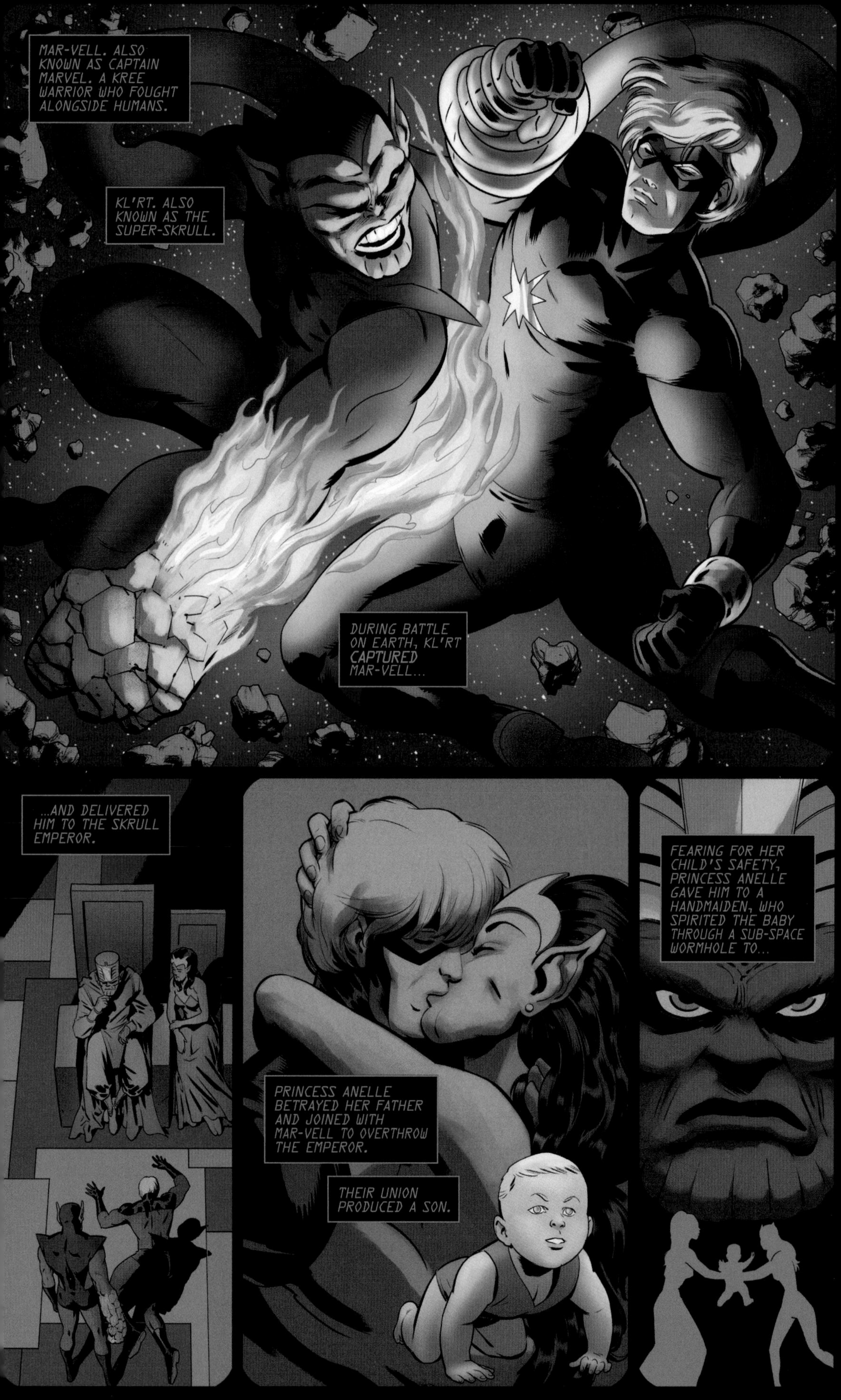
MAR-VELL. ALSO KNOWN AS CAPTAIN MARVEL. A KREE WARRIOR WHO FOUGHT ALONGSIDE HUMANS.
KL'RT. ALSO KNOWN AS THE SUPER-SKRULL.
DURING BATTLE ON EARTH, KL'RT CAPTURED MAR-VELL...
...AND DELIVERED HIM TO THE SKRULL EMPEROR.
PRINCESS ANELLE BETRAYED HER FATHER AND JOINED WITH MAR-VELL TO OVERTHROW THE EMPEROR.
THEIR UNION PRODUCED A SON.
FEARING FOR HER CHILD'S SAFETY, PRINCESS ANELLE GAVE HIM TO A HANDMAIDEN, WHO SPIRITED THE BABY THROUGH A SUB-SPACE WORMHOLE TO...

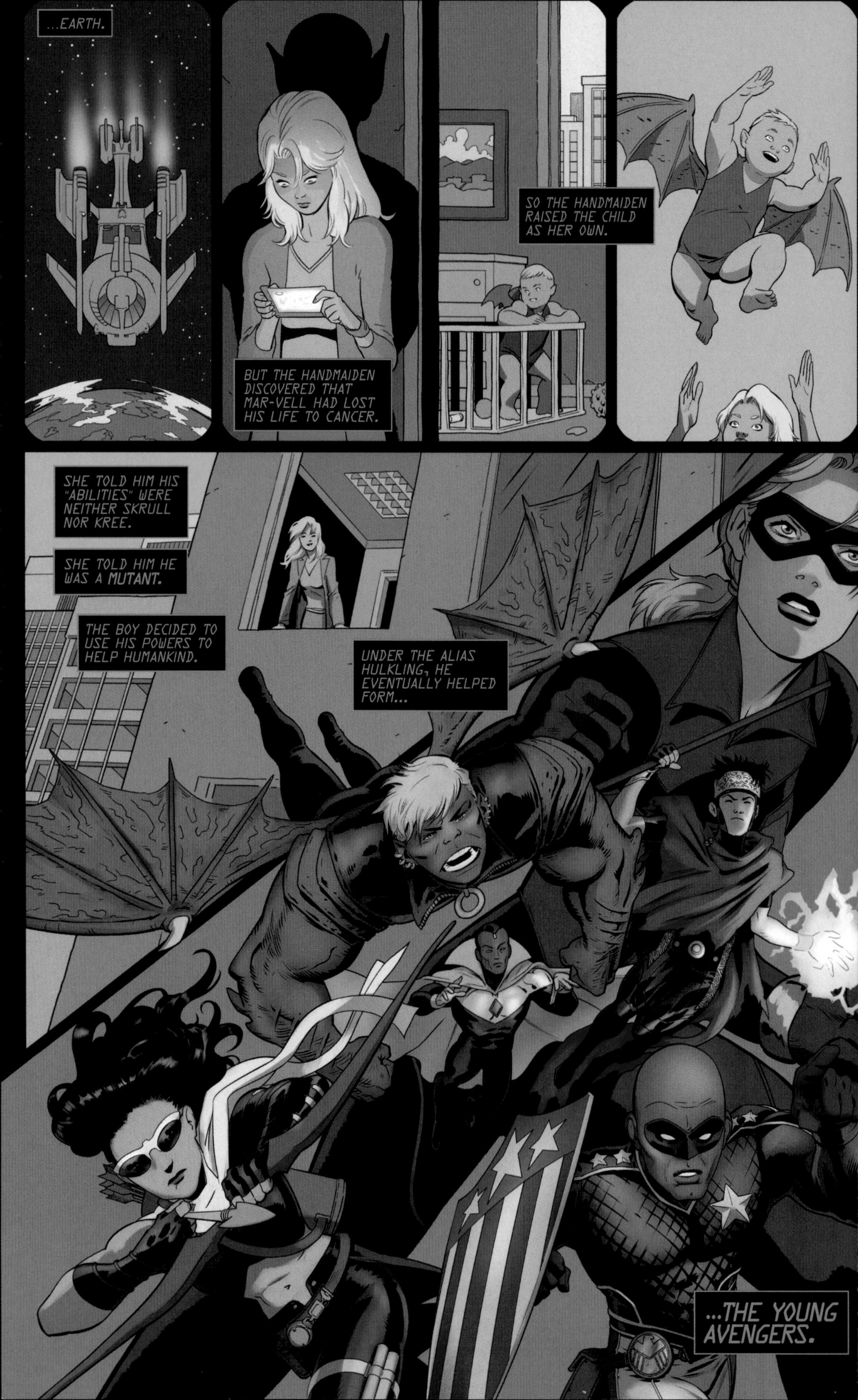
...EARTH.
BUT THE HANDMAIDEN DISCOVERED THAT MAR-VELL HAD LOST HIS LIFE TO CANCER.
SO THE HANDMAIDEN RAISED THE CHILD AS HER OWN.
SHE TOLD HIM HIS "ABILITIES" WERE NEITHER SKRULL NOR KREE.
SHE TOLD HIM HE WAS A MUTANT.
THE BOY DECIDED TO USE HIS POWERS TO HELP HUMANKIND.
UNDER THE ALIAS HULKLING, HE EVENTUALLY HELPED FORM...
...THE YOUNG AVENGERS.

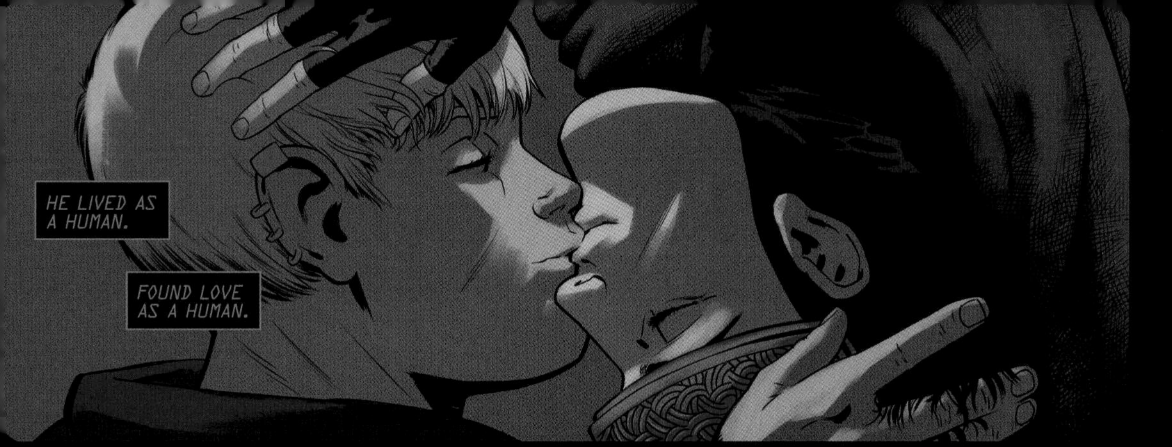
HE LIVED AS A HUMAN.
FOUND LOVE AS A HUMAN.

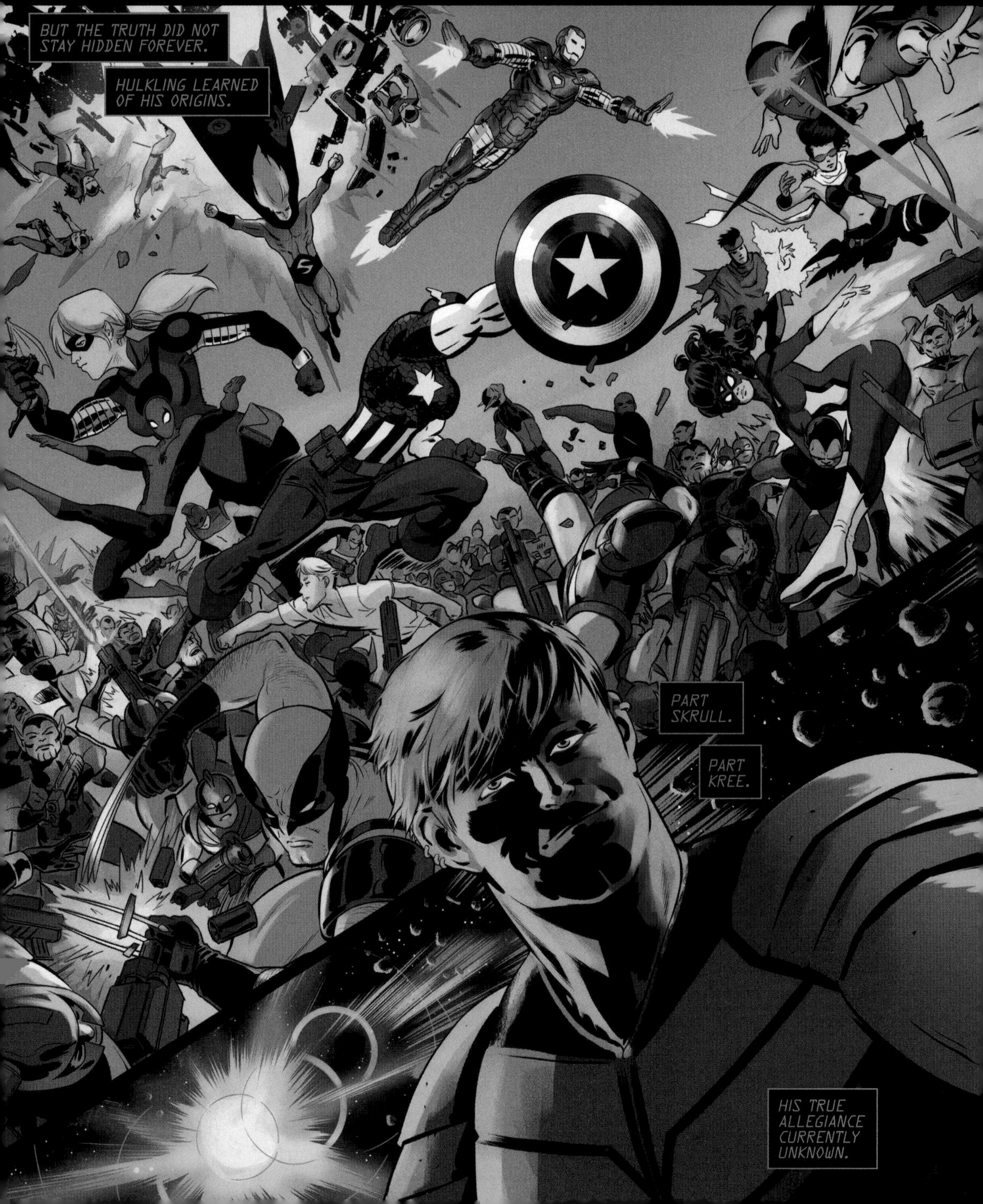
BUT THE TRUTH DID NOT STAY HIDDEN FOREVER.
HULKLING LEARNED OF HIS ORIGINS.
PART SKRULL.
PART KREE.
HIS TRUE ALLEGIANCE CURRENTLY UNKNOWN.

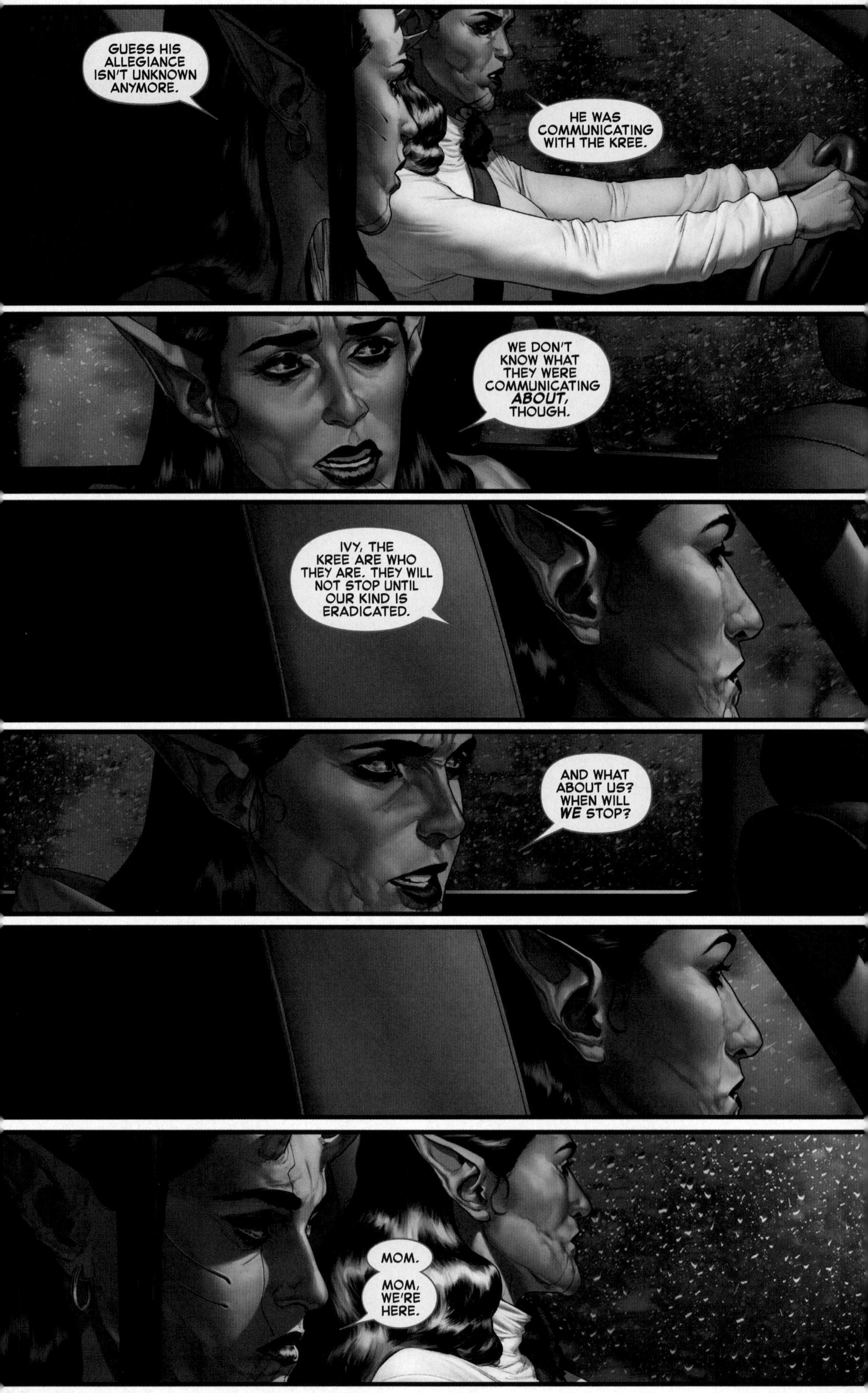
GUESS HIS ALLEGIANCE ISN'T UNKNOWN ANYMORE.
HE WAS COMMUNICATING WITH THE KREE.
WE DON'T KNOW WHAT THEY WERE COMMUNICATING *ABOUT,* THOUGH.
IVY, THE KREE ARE WHO THEY ARE. THEY WILL NOT STOP UNTIL OUR KIND IS ERADICATED.
AND WHAT ABOUT US? WHEN WILL *WE* STOP?
MOM.
MOM, WE'RE HERE.

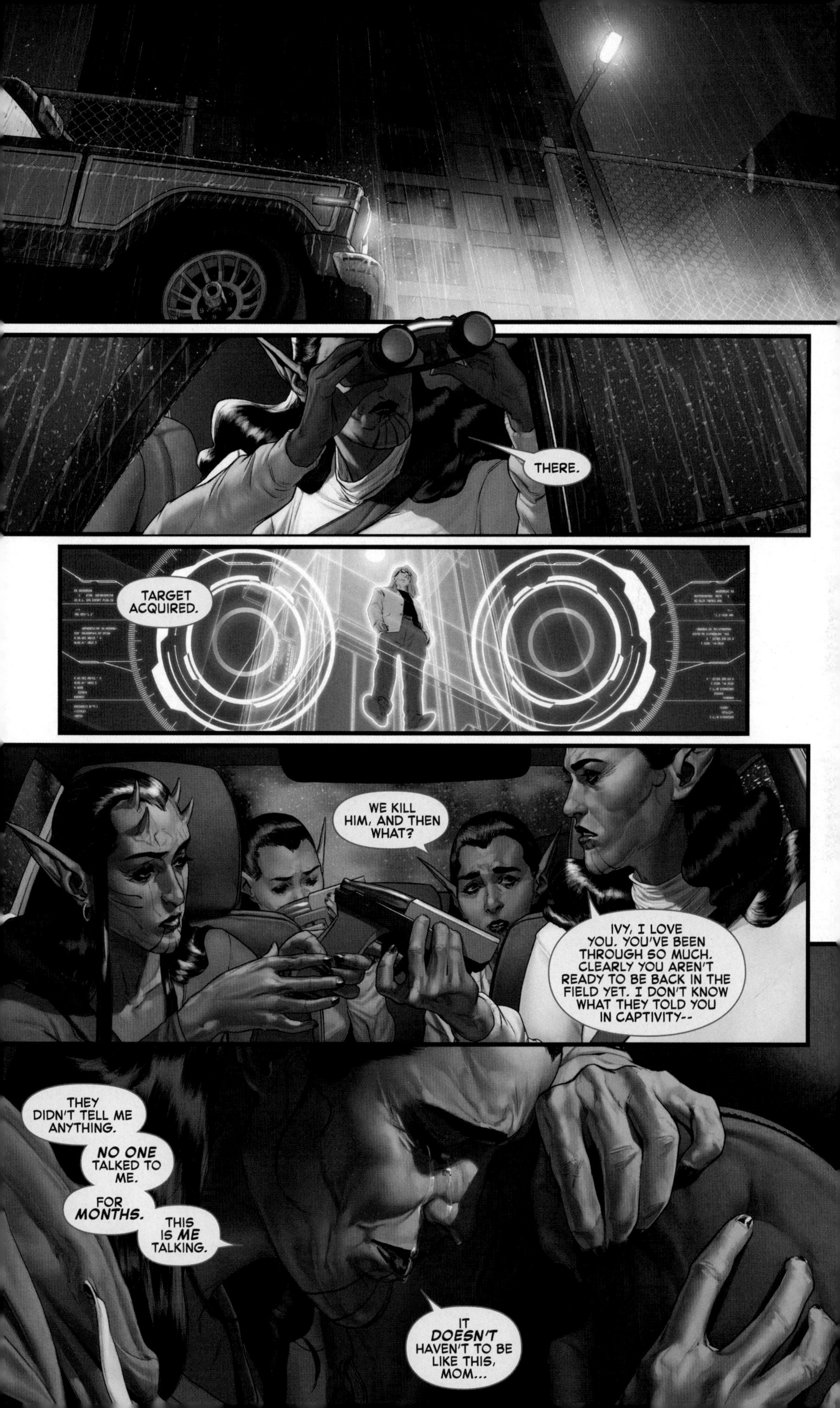
THERE.
TARGET ACQUIRED.
WE KILL HIM, AND THEN WHAT?
IVY, I LOVE YOU. YOU'VE BEEN THROUGH SO MUCH. CLEARLY YOU AREN'T READY TO BE BACK IN THE FIELD YET. I DON'T KNOW WHAT THEY TOLD YOU IN CAPTIVITY--
THEY DIDN'T TELL ME ANYTHING.
NO ONE TALKED TO ME.
FOR MONTHS.
THIS IS ME TALKING.
IT DOESN'T HAVEN'T TO BE LIKE THIS, MOM...

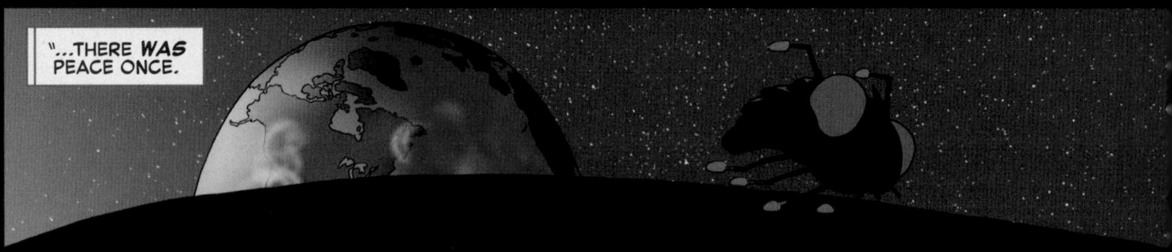
"...THERE *WAS* PEACE ONCE.

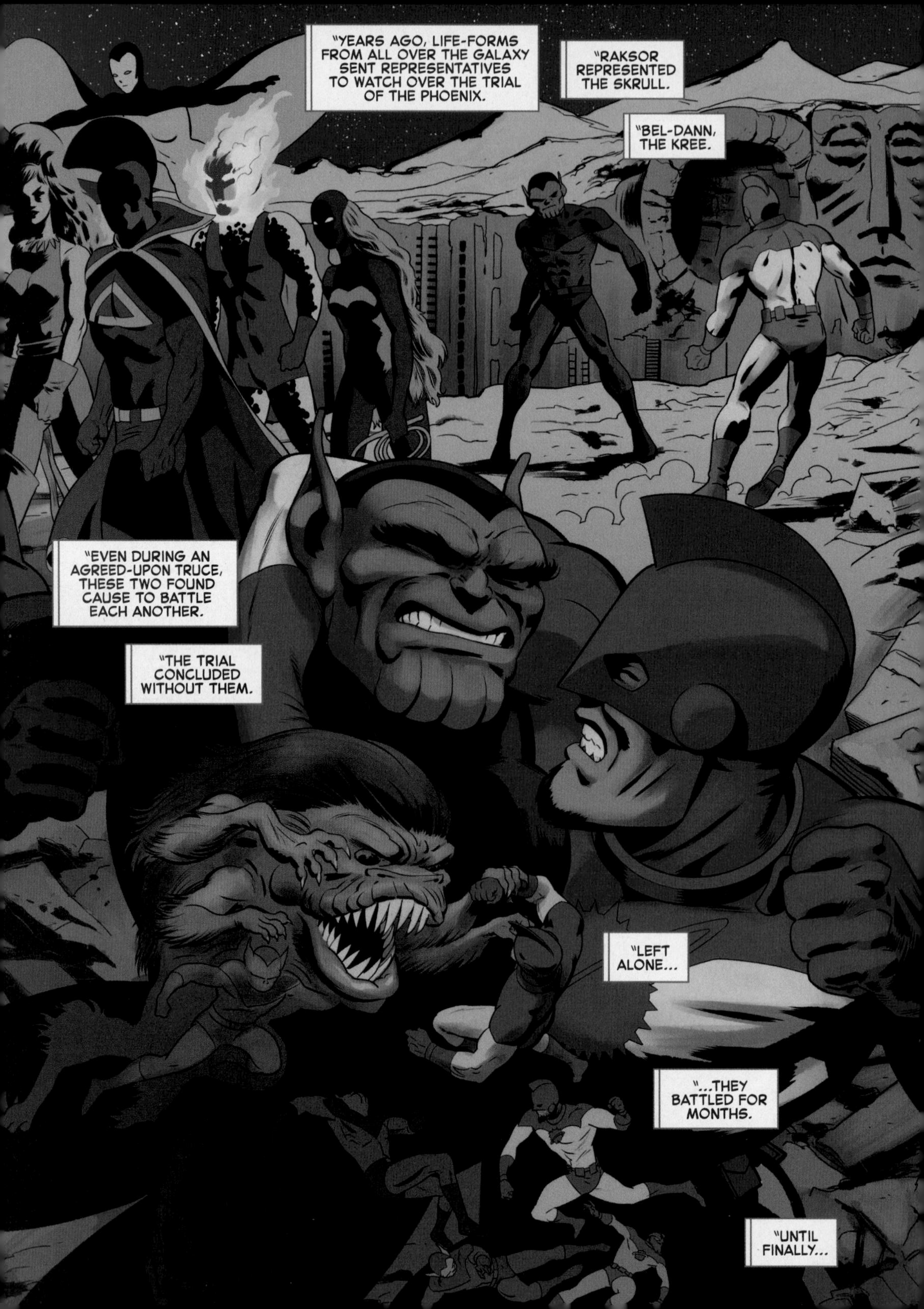
"YEARS AGO, LIFE-FORMS FROM ALL OVER THE GALAXY SENT REPRESENTATIVES TO WATCH OVER THE TRIAL OF THE PHOENIX.
"RAKSOR REPRESENTED THE SKRULL.
"BEL-DANN, THE KREE.
"EVEN DURING AN AGREED-UPON TRUCE, THESE TWO FOUND CAUSE TO BATTLE EACH ANOTHER.
"THE TRIAL CONCLUDED WITHOUT THEM.
"LEFT ALONE...
"...THEY BATTLED FOR MONTHS.
"UNTIL FINALLY...

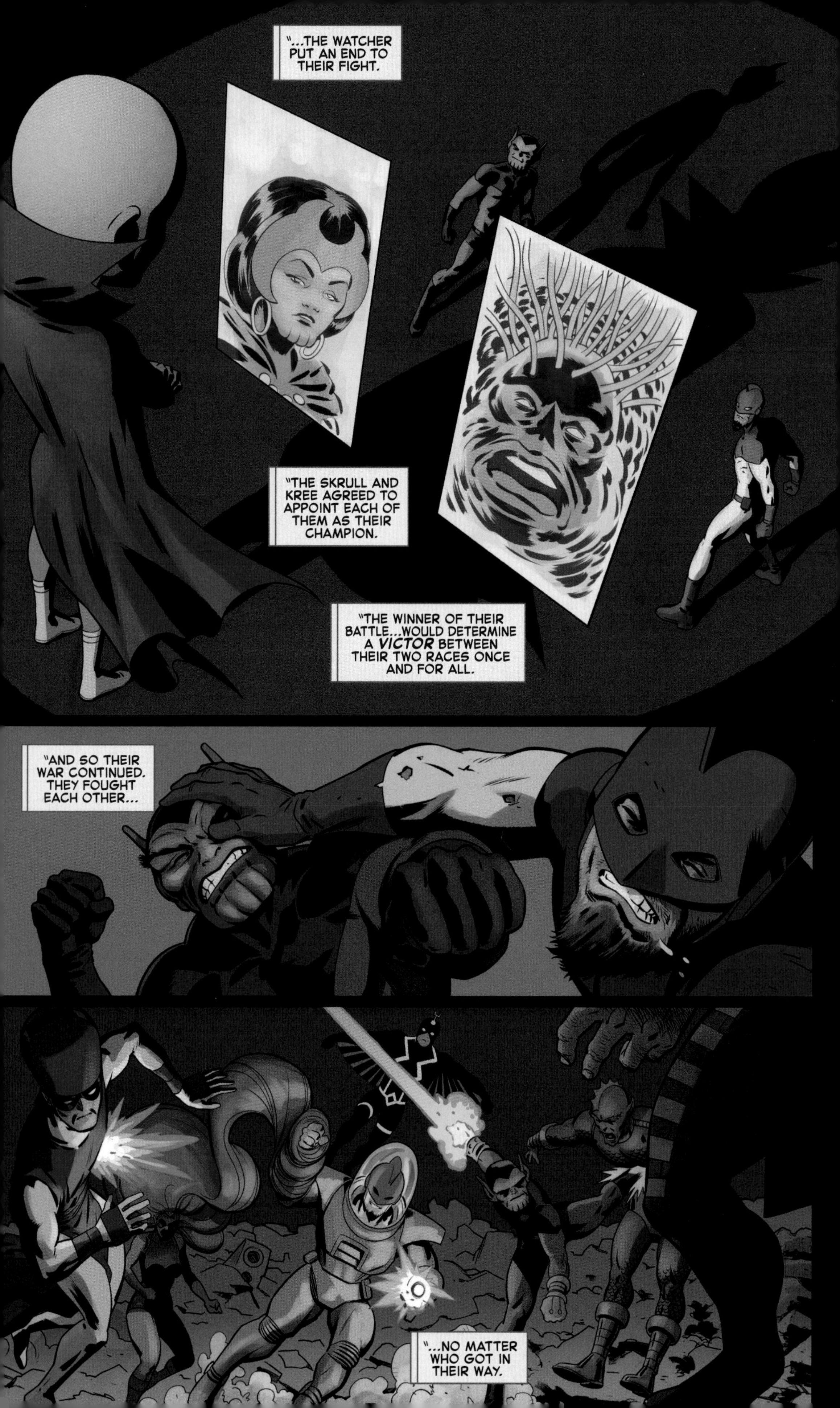
"...THE WATCHER PUT AN END TO THEIR FIGHT.
"THE SKRULL AND KREE AGREED TO APPOINT EACH OF THEM AS THEIR CHAMPION.
"THE WINNER OF THEIR BATTLE...WOULD DETERMINE A *VICTOR* BETWEEN THEIR TWO RACES ONCE AND FOR ALL.
"AND SO THEIR WAR CONTINUED. THEY FOUGHT EACH OTHER...
"...NO MATTER WHO GOT IN THEIR WAY.

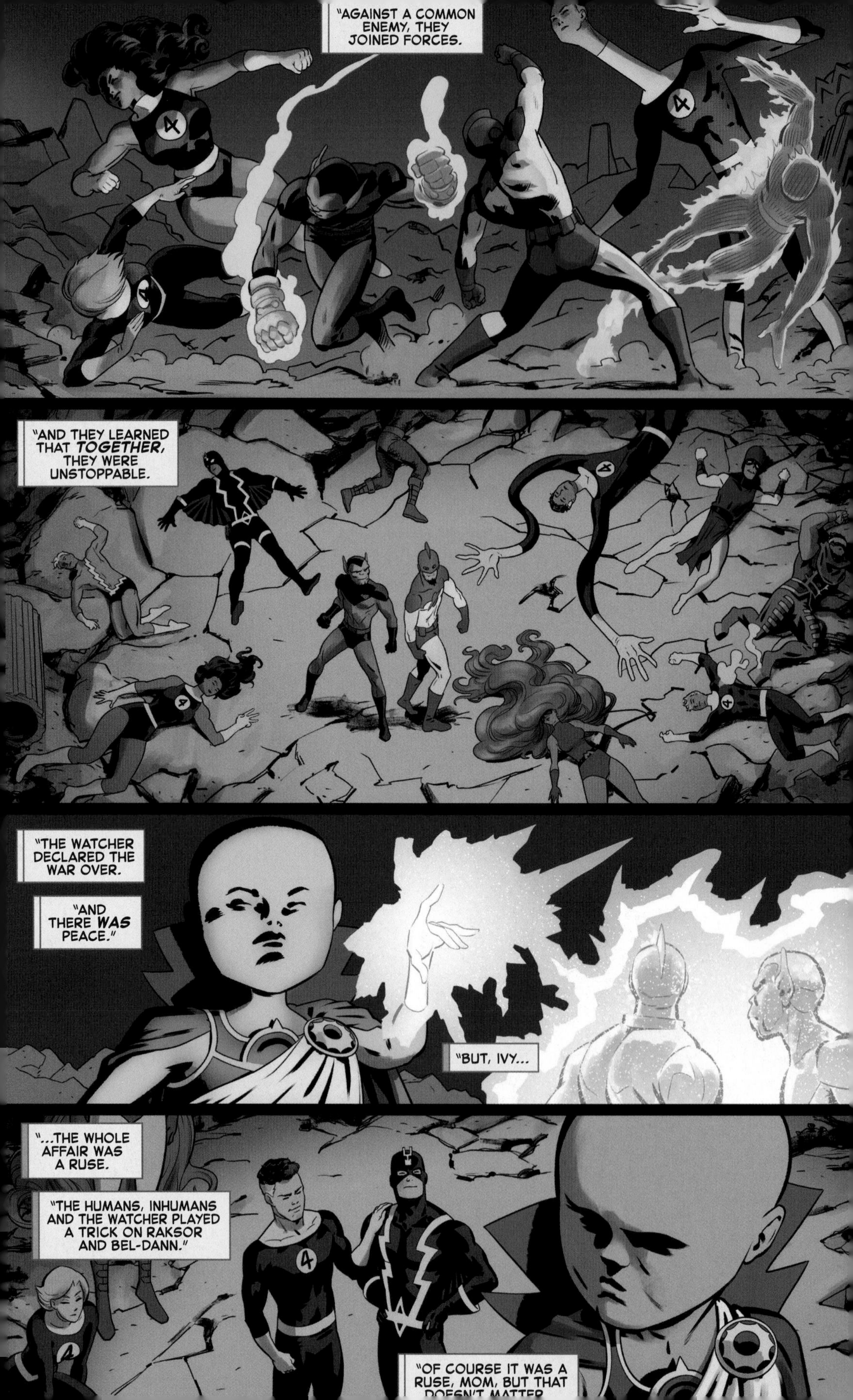
"AGAINST A COMMON ENEMY, THEY JOINED FORCES.
"AND THEY LEARNED THAT TOGETHER, THEY WERE UNSTOPPABLE.
"THE WATCHER DECLARED THE WAR OVER.
"AND THERE WAS PEACE."
"BUT, IVY...
"...THE WHOLE AFFAIR WAS A RUSE.
"THE HUMANS, INHUMANS AND THE WATCHER PLAYED A TRICK ON RAKSOR AND BEL-DANN."
"OF COURSE IT WAS A RUSE, MOM, BUT THAT

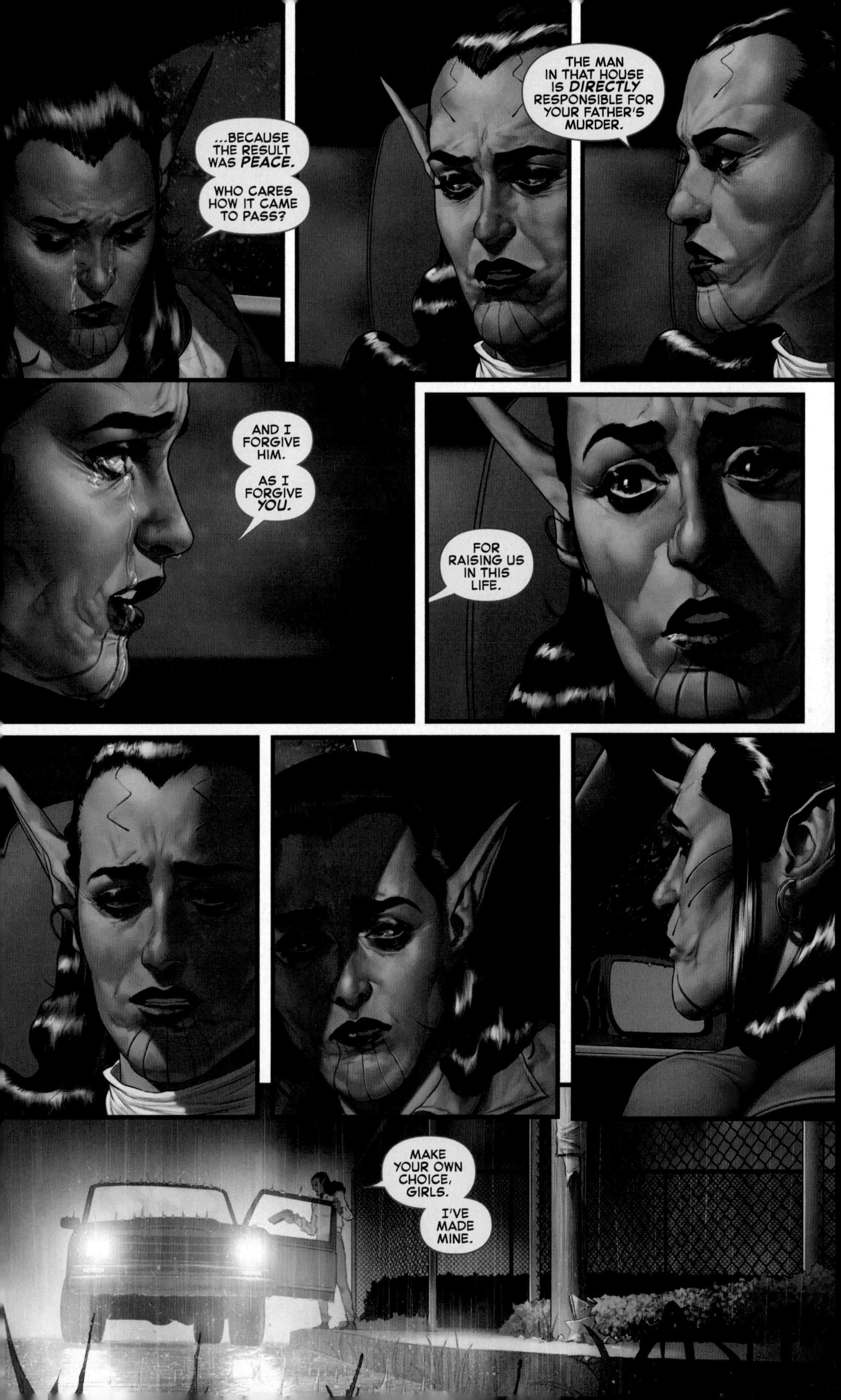
...BECAUSE THE RESULT WAS PEACE.
WHO CARES HOW IT CAME TO PASS?
THE MAN IN THAT HOUSE IS DIRECTLY RESPONSIBLE FOR YOUR FATHER'S MURDER.
AND I FORGIVE HIM.
AS I FORGIVE YOU.
FOR RAISING US IN THIS LIFE.
MAKE YOUR OWN CHOICE, GIRLS.
I'VE MADE MINE.

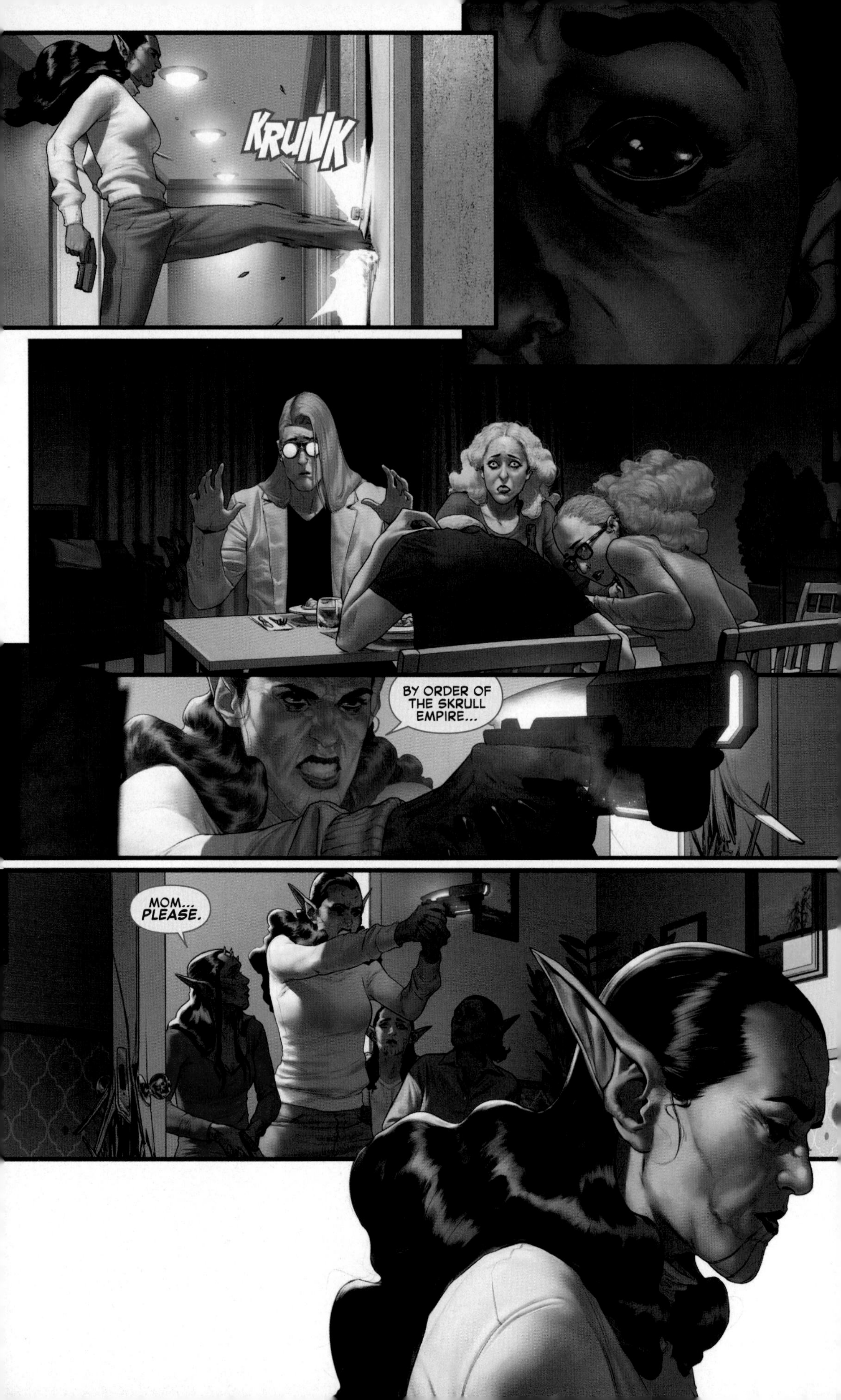
KRUNK
BY ORDER OF THE SKRULL EMPIRE...
MOM... PLEASE.

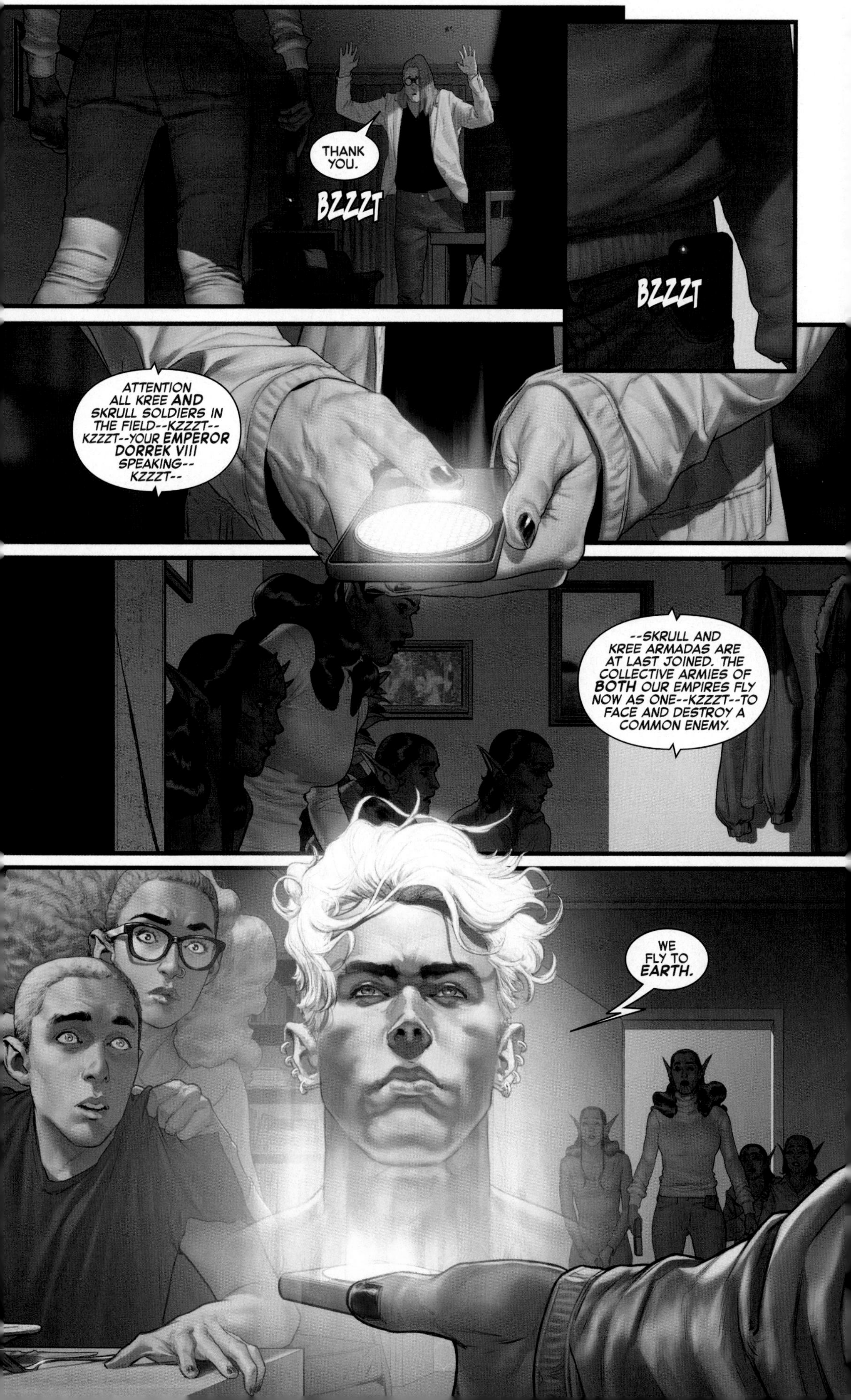
THANK YOU.
BZZZT
BZZZT
ATTENTION ALL KREE AND SKRULL SOLDIERS IN THE FIELD--KZZZT--KZZZT--YOUR EMPEROR DORREK VIII SPEAKING--KZZZT--
--SKRULL AND KREE ARMADAS ARE AT LAST JOINED. THE COLLECTIVE ARMIES OF BOTH OUR EMPIRES FLY NOW AS ONE--KZZZT--TO FACE AND DESTROY A COMMON ENEMY.
WE FLY TO EARTH.

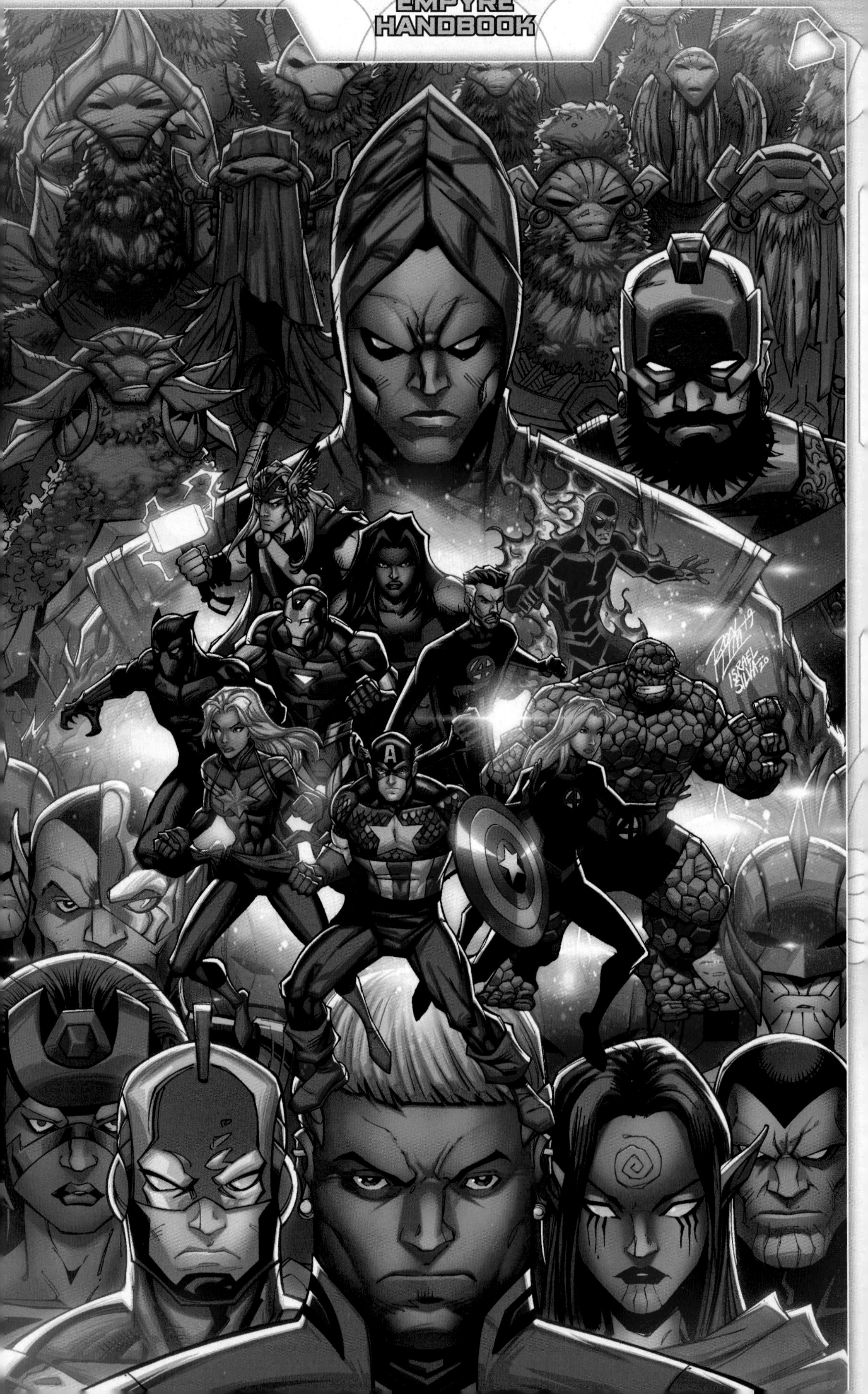

AVENGERS

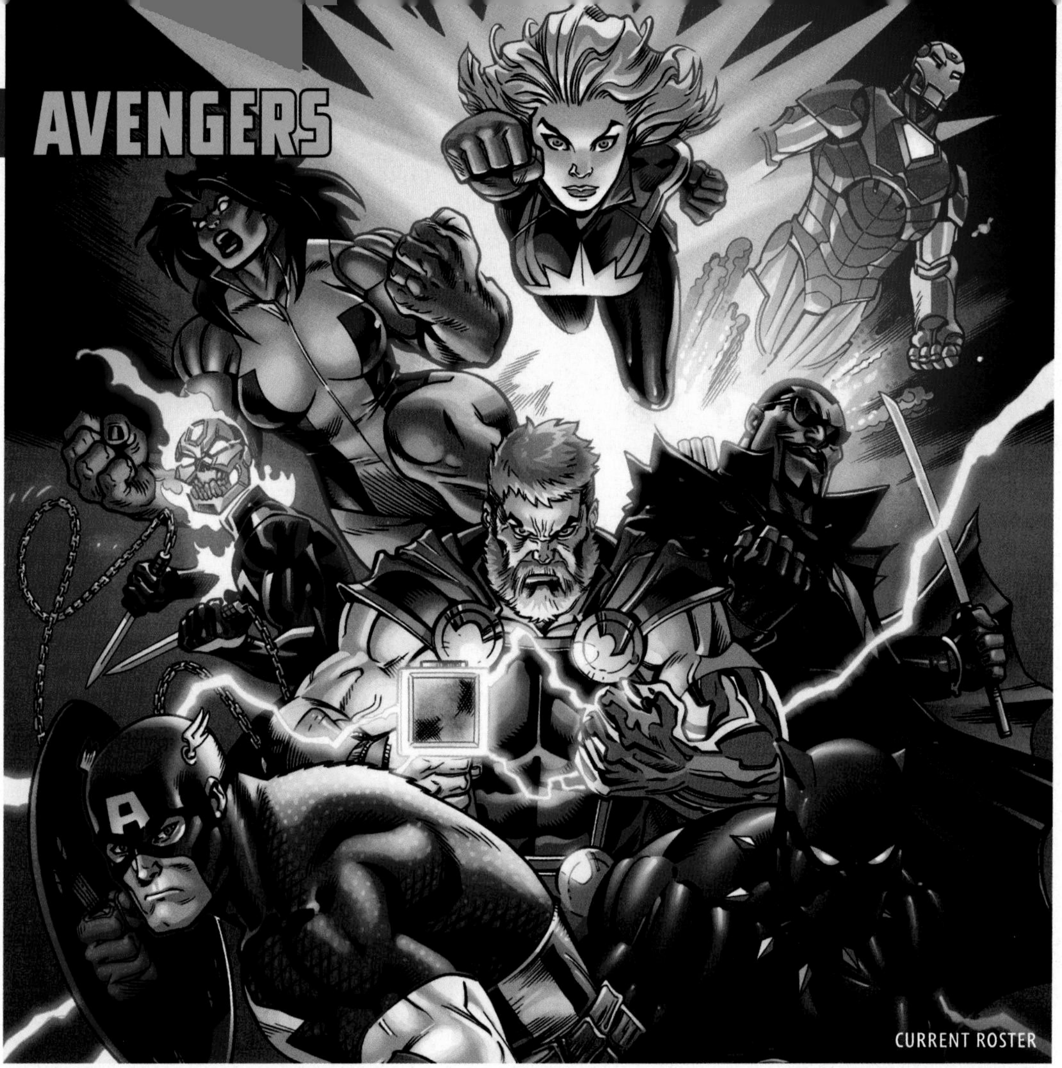

CURRENT ROSTER

HISTORY *UPDATE*: *Continued from the Avengers Update profile in the* Avengers Now! Handbook *(2014)*. In the Kooky Quartet era, the secretly corrupt, power-boosting Cressida helped the Avengers battle the enigmatic, cosmic Stranger. Unaware that she sapped bystanders' lives when using her powers, the Avengers made her a member, as Avenger X, but she soon turned on them, copying their powers and almost fatally draining them before being driven off. Avenger X subsequently encountered an angry Frightful Four, whom she previously manipulated against the Avengers. the Frightful Four vengefully entombed her alive.

More recently, after the Scarlet Witch (Wanda Maximoff) accidentally inverted heroes and villains, the inverted Avengers attacked the Mighty Avengers, halting only when they realized the public battle was harming their reputations. Meanwhile, the inverted Doctor Doom (Victor Von Doom) resurrected both Cassie Lang and Doctor Voodoo (Jericho Drumm). Hoping the inverted heroes could be restored, the still-elderly Steve Rogers' team of inverted villains recorded a video claiming responsibility for the heroes' misdeeds then stopped the inverted X-Men from detonating their human-killing DNA bomb. When the inverted Avengers joined the fray, Doctor Voodoo's ghostly brother, Daniel Drumm, possessed the Scarlet Witch, forcing her to assist Doctor Doom and the inverted Red Skull (Johann Shmidt) in restoring everyone, though Iron Man (Tony Stark) managed to shield himself and, accidentally, Havok (Alex Summers) and Sabretooth (Victor Creed). Sabretooth voluntarily placed himself in Avengers custody, Havok defected to Cyclops' militant X-Men, Doctor Voodoo joined the Avengers Unity Squad, and Steve Rogers gave Nova (Sam Alexander) provisional Avengers membership for helping during the crisis. Remaining inverted, Stark launched legal proceedings to block Luke Cage (born Carl Lucas) from using the Avengers name.

Seeking their true origins, the Scarlet Witch and Quicksilver (Pietro Maximoff) traveled to Counter-Earth, where the geneticist High Evolutionary (Herbert Wyndham) took credit for empowering them — not mutant genes — and revealed that Magneto (Max Eisenhardt) was not their father. Tracking the twins using Sabretooth, the Unity Squad followed, but the High Evolutionary's Master

STARK ENTERPRISES
AIRCRAFT HANGAR ROSTER

Scientist captured Rogue (Anna Marie) and suppressed the mind of Wonder Man (Simon Williams) within her. When the Unity Squad discovered the High Evolutionary was slaughtering millions of New Men he deemed obsolete, they helped his son, the Low Evolutionary, overthrow him. On Earth, the Mighty Avengers discovered Jason Quantrell's Cortex Incorporated was a front for the Beyond Corporation — malevolent entities from outside reality. To stop them, Blue Marvel (Adam Brashear) and his son Doctor Positron (Max Brashear) summoned Max's sibling, Kevin, whose travels outside the known Multiverse had changed him into a being more powerful than Quantrell.

Learning of Earth's imminent destruction due to an ongoing multiversal collapse caused by alternate-reality Earths colliding, and with Steve Rogers and the still-inverted Iron Man at odds, billionaire Sunspot (Roberto Da Costa) launched a hostile takeover of the scientific A.I.M. (Advanced Idea Mechanics). He drove out leaders Andrew Forson and Monica Rappaccini, and turned the terrorist group to researching the extradimensional threat. With other Avengers teams aiding S.H.I.E.L.D., Sunspot assembled his own unofficial Avengers, sending some — Hyperion (Marcus Milton), Thor Odinson, Starbrand (Kevin Connor), Nightmask (Adam Blackveil), Abyss (formerly of the Builders), and Ex Nihilo — across the Multiverse to seek a way to confront the threat.

Soon, former Avenger Namor (McKenzie) realized his error in allying with the brutal Cabal to stop the incursions, so he worked with the Avengers and the Illuminati brain trust to trap the Cabal on the already dead Earth-15340 then destroyed the planet.

In Reality-112006 Sunspot's multiversal team confronted the collapse's perceived cause, the vastly powerful Beyonders, but was slain, unaware that though the Beyonders sought the Multiverse's destruction as part of a grand experiment, the collapse had actually been triggered by Rabum Alal — secretly Earth-616's Doctor Doom — who sought to foil the Beyonders. The Multiverse's judge, the Living Tribunal, fell to the Beyonders before Doom, aided by Molecule Man (Owen Reece) and Doctor (Stephen) Strange, destroyed the Beyonders and stole their cosmic power. With the Multiverse's final collapse imminent, the Illuminati's Mister Fantastic (Reed Richards) and Black Panther (T'Challa) used the Living Tribunal's skin to construct a lifeboat to save some of humanity. An alliance of galactic empires, belatedly learning of the incursions, sought to destroy Earth to save the rest of Reality-616 but were destroyed by the Avengers, S.H.I.E.L.D., and Illuminati using a captured alien Builders' planet-killer, A.I.M.'s geothermal cannon, and Iron Man's Dyson sphere space station. Elsewhere, Stark's lawsuit against Cage concluded, forcing the Mighty Avengers to disband

officially mere minutes before the world ended. As the final incursion began between Earth-616 and Earth-1610, the heroes of each world battled futilely, and the Multiverse was destroyed.

Using his stolen power, Doom gathered beings from various realities and constructed a patchwork Battleworld from remnants of alternate Earths, ruling it as God-Emperor. Surviving aboard the life raft, Reed Richards eventually challenged Doom and usurped his godlike power. Richards then began rebuilding the Multiverse, assisted by his reality-warping mutant son, Franklin, and the Molecule Man. They were accompanied by Richards' wife, Invisible Woman (Susan Richards), their daughter, Valeria, and Richards' students, leaving Earth's population to believe them dead. Most within Earth-616, now dubbed the Prime Reality, did not recall their world ending or its subsequent resurrection. Only the Unity Squad remained active, now including Spider-Man (Peter Parker), Thor (Jane Foster), Giant-Man (Hank Pym), and Avengers prisoner Sabretooth. When the murderous robot Ultron returned, he took over the world with consciousness spores that transformed organic life into metallic beings he controlled and merged forms with his "father," Pym. Using his psychic powers, former Avenger Starfox (Eros) helped Pym regain control. Horrified by the merger, Pym fled into space.

Around this time, the Inhuman King Black Bolt (Blackagar Boltagon) blanketed Earth with the metamorphic Terrigen Mist, transforming those with Inhuman ancestry but poisoning mutantkind. To counter rising tensions between Inhumans and mutants, Steve Rogers decided to expand the Unity Squad by including Inhumans, ultimately consisting of himself, Deadpool (Wade Wilson), the Human Torch (Johnny Storm),

Doctor Voodoo, Rogue, Quicksilver, and newly empowered psychic Inhuman Synapse (Emily Guerrero), Rogers issued a new mission for the team: to retrieve the late Charles Xavier's mutant telepathic brain from the Red Skull. Meanwhile, Mr. Gryphon, a version of Kang the Conqueror (Nathaniel Richards) reached back in time from a few months in the future to covertly take over the Vision (Victor Shade).

Sunspot rebranded A.I.M. as Avengers Idea Mechanics, forming his own unsanctioned New Avengers team. Meanwhile, Iron Man returned after several months in space to find Stark Industries in dire financial straits and sold both Avengers Mansion and Avengers Tower, the former to become a themed hotel and the latter to Mr. Gryphon's Qeng Enterprises. Now funded by Deadpool, the Unity Squad relocated to a Manhattan speakeasy beneath the Schaefer Theater in Manhattan. Gryphon, his time travel limited, manipulated the alien Chitauri Warbringer into stealing an artifact to restore him, but Warbringer's rampage was stopped by Iron Man, the Vision, Nova, Captain America (Sam Wilson), Thor, Ms. Marvel (Kamala Khan), and Spider-Man (Miles Morales, formerly of Earth-1610). Stark convinced them to remain together as Avengers, insisting the other two teams were not strictly Avengers. Stark's Avengers headquartered out of a condemned Stark Industries aircraft hangar in New Jersey, with Edwin Jarvis resuming butler duties. The team's formation prompted Mr. Gryphon to reach back to before they had assembled and take over the Vision, an agent to destroy them from within, but Stark freed Vision, and Gryphon was driven off.

When the insane Inhuman Shredded Man attacked Boston, transforming the residents into plant creatures and seeking to create a dystopian future, the Unity Squad and time-traveler Cable (elder Nathan Summers)

confronted him. Discovering Shredded Man was Synapse's grandfather, Cable infected Synapse with the transformation plague, forcing Shredded Man to withdraw the contagion. Finding himself stranded in this era, Cable joined the Unity Squad to help capture the Red Skull. S.H.I.E.L.D. arrested former Avengers ally Rick Jones for leaking hacked documents regarding S.H.I.E.L.D.'s Pleasant Hill, a prison disguised as a town whose residents were actually super villains brainwashed by a sentient but naive Cosmic Cube, Kobik. While A.I.M.'s New Avengers broke Jones out, both the Unity Squad and Iron Man's Avengers investigated Pleasant Hill and were brainwashed into the populace. Rogue, trained by Xavier to resist mind control, broke free of Kobik's conditioning and released the others just as Baron (Helmut) Zemo similarly restored the villainous inhabitants. During the resultant battle, the penitent Kobik returned Steve Rogers to his prime but was duped by the Red Skull into also making Rogers a secret loyalist of the terrorist Hydra organization by rewriting

his history. Rogers subsequently resumed using the Captain America identity, sharing it with Wilson, and Pleasant Hill was shut down. Later, Ultron/Pym returned to Earth, claiming to now be ruled by Pym's mind, but the Unity Squad was dubious, and when Ultron's personality resurfaced, they trapped him aboard a ship sent flying into the sun. Trademark confusion temporarily resulted in the Great Lakes Avengers being given official Avengers status, but this was swiftly rescinded once the legalities were ironed out.

Learning of a precognitive new Inhuman, Ulysses Cain, Captain Marvel (Carol Danvers) favored acting on Cain's visions to prevent tragedy while Iron Man expressed concern over pre-emptively targeting people for crimes not yet committed. Vision, meanwhile, took proactive action against Kang, using the Fantastic Four's time machine to abduct the infant Kang and hide him in the pacifistic Priests of Pama's care. Working from Cain's predictions, Danvers led a mission against the mad Titan Thanos, during which

EXPANDED UNITY SQUAD

Avenger War Machine (James Rhodey), Danvers' lover and Stark's best friend, was killed. Grieving, Stark abducted Cain, determined to prove his visions unreliable. Tracking Stark, numerous Avengers and the superhuman Ultimates arrived just as Cain predicted the Hulk (Bruce Banner) would kill many of them. With Bruce Banner then depowered, Stark argued the heroes needed proof before condemning him. Confronting Banner, the heroes discovered he had been experimenting on himself. Believing a panicking Banner was about to transform, Hawkeye (Clint Barton) slew him, as Banner had asked him to, should he lose control. Stark blamed Danvers for precipitating this, splitting the hero community. Simultaneously, Cable and Deadpool, seeking a Terrigen poisoning cure, stole U.S. Army research. Secretly wanting to end their pursuit of the Red Skull, Rogers used this as a pretext to disband the Unity Squad, but the team decided to ignore his order. Backed by S.H.I.E.L.D., Captain Marvel began detaining people based purely on Cain's visions until Iron Man led his Avengers and other heroes to confront her, triggering a battle that ended when Cain shared a vision of Spider-Man (Morales) killing Captain America (Rogers). Though Rogers himself argued against punishing Morales for a crime not yet committed, Danvers and S.H.I.E.L.D.'s Maria Hill still unsuccessfully tried to apprehend the rebels. Haunted by the vision, Morales soon tried to surrender to Danvers, but Iron Man interceded. The ensuing battle left Stark comatose, but Morales escaped, rescued by Nova. Unhappy with the adult Avengers' actions during this "civil war," Morales, Nova, and Ms. Marvel quit and formed their own team, the Champions.

With Iron Man incapacitated, his Avengers relocated to the Fantastic Four's former headquarters, the Baxter Building, and accepted funding from the building's owner, Parker Industries. The Avengers

BAXTER BUILDING ROSTER

added returning members Spider-Man (Peter Parker) and Hercules (Heracles) and welcomed new member Wasp (Nadia Van Dyne, daughter of Hank Pym). Almost immediately, multiple iterations of Kang attacked, his now paradoxical existence dividing thanks to the Vision kidnapping Kang's infant self. After failing to extract the child's location from the Vision's mind, the Kangs traveled back in time to slay the Avengers as children. Only Hercules was spared, as the true details of his birth were lost to history, while a peaceful Kang iteration saved the others from oblivion by moving them to the timeless Limbo. Trying to return the infant to end the conflict, Wasp learned exposure to the child had given the Priests of Pama the power to devour time paradoxes, allowing them to restore the Avengers and destroy the pursuing Kangs. Wanting to end Kang's threat forever, the Avengers recruited Avengers from past eras and launched simultaneous surgical strikes to his strongholds across time before trapping multiple incarnations of the despot within a chronal absorption device. Freed by the conflict, Avenger X attacked

the Avengers but was defeated by Wasp, who was helped by a then heroic Victor Von Doom, together trapping Avenger X in the Microverse.

When the alien Leviathon Tide attacked Earth, the Avengers joined other heroes defending the planet until the monsters were repelled by the Inhuman Kid Kaiju. Meanwhile, having attained S.H.I.E.L.D. backing, A.I.M. launched their new U.S. Avengers, recognized by the government but not sanctioned by the Avengers proper. The Red Skull telepathically seized control of the Unity Squad, but Deadpool's insanity rendered him immune, allowing him to free Rogue. Capturing the Skull, Rogue had Beast (Hank McCoy) cut out the Skull's stolen telepathic brain center, which the Human Torch destroyed. Grateful for Deadpool's help, Rogue kissed him. Absorbing his regenerative powers had an unexpected side effect, expelling Wonder Man's ionic energy from her body and restoring him.

Before long, the Hydra-loyal Rogers sprung his trap, summoning the Avengers and many of America's

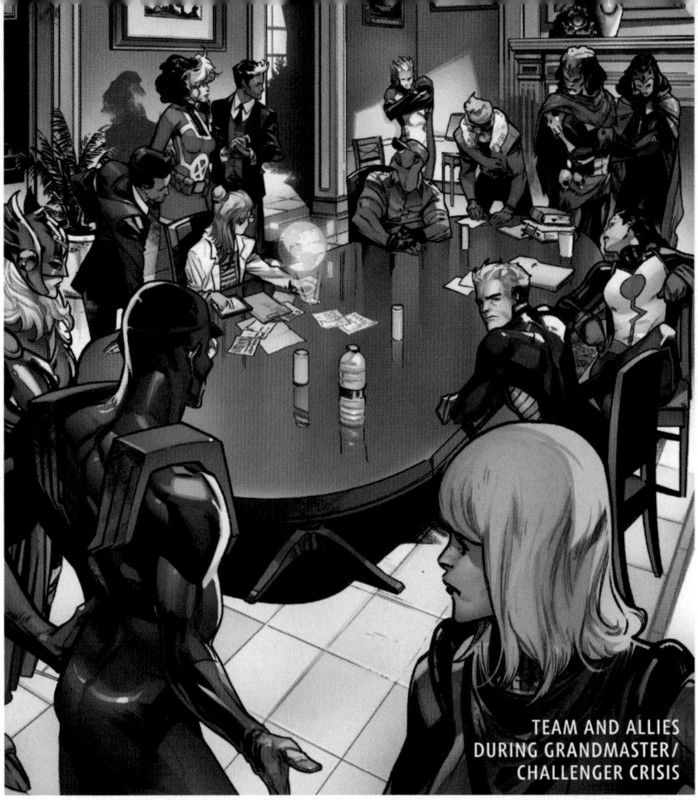

TEAM AND ALLIES DURING GRANDMASTER/ CHALLENGER CRISIS

other super heroes to New York, where an overwhelming Hydra force ambushed and defeated them. The Avengers went underground, joined forces with the Champions and other escaping heroes, and mounted a resistance while Hydra conquered the United States. Most of the Unity Squad remained in New York only for the entire city to be sealed in a Darkforce dome. For days, they dealt with panicking citizens, opportunistic super villains, and ravenous Darkforce creatures. Even though Hydra assembled their own team of Hydra-affiliated "Avengers," the heroic Avengers and their allies ultimately rallied to defeat Hydra's forces while Kobik restored the real Captain America. The true Captain America then defeated his fascist doppelganger.

Following this, the Avengers faced a crisis. To prevent Otto Octavius (formerly Doctor Octopus) from taking over his company's technology, Peter Parker destroyed the technology, bankrupting himself and leaving the Avengers without a financial backer or a headquarters. Sam Wilson relinquished the Captain America mantle back to the real Rogers and became the Falcon again. He also attempted to cede his position as Avengers leader to Thor, believing only his authority as Captain America kept the team together, but Jane convinced him to stay on. Soon, the team faced a crisis of Earth-shattering proportions when the High Evolutionary attempted to merge Counter-Earth with the Earth. With two worlds in the balance, the Avengers combined forces with the Champions again, mending some bridges with their former teammates in the process as they foiled the High Evolutionary's mad scheme. Meanwhile, the Unity Squad took possession of Avengers Mansion again, as its owners had abandoned it during the Hydra takeover, and attempted to solidify as a team. However, when Quicksilver's arrogance during a battle with Juggernaut (Cain Marko) led to Synapse's being critically injured, the team finally broke apart.

Seeking a game board for one of their games, two Elders of the Universe, Grandmaster (En Dwi Gast) and the Challenger, stole Earth, placed it into an extradimensional void, and pit the alien warriors of the Lethal Legion and Thanos' former minions the Black Order against each other. To ensure as little interference as possible, most of the Earth's superhumans were frozen in time by a hyper-fast, world-traversing beacon. Earth's civilizations were plunged into chaos. The few superhumans who remained — a ragtag assortment of Avengers from the Falcon's team, the Unity Division, and Sunspot's U.S. Avengers as well as ex-Avenger Lightning (Miguel Santos, formerly the Living Lightning) — were summoned to Avengers Mansion by Voyager (Valerie Vector). Voyager claimed to be a founding member of the Avengers who had been erased from history but had returned to rally them against their alien foes. However, she was actually Va Nee Gast, the Grandmaster's daughter, who had been sent by her father to manipulate the Avengers into winning the contest for him. As the leaders of the Avengers and their allies tried to come up with a strategy, the Black Order destroyed the mansion, forcing the Avengers to retreat to their long-vacant auxiliary/emergency headquarters somewhere outside New York City. Galvanized by the experience, the Avengers cohered into a single unit and divided their opponents' forces. Amid the chaos, Jarvis suffered a concussion, which, along with a quantum pathogen infection, put him into a coma. Wasp and the Beast (Hank McCoy) successfully revived him. Because the infection had blocked Voyager's memory implants, Jarvis recognized her as an imposter and revealed her deception to the team. The Challenger also resurrected the Hulk as one of his champions, forcing the Avengers to battle their former member. However, both the Hulk and Voyager soon turned against their masters. With his plans foiled, the Challenger launched a direct assault on Earth himself. To destroy the Elders' beacon and free Earth's other heroes, a recovered Synapse and the Scarlet Witch combined their powers to massively boost Quicksilver's speed, allowing him to catch and destroy it. Voyager then summoned

every nearby Avenger to do battle with the Challenger, who ultimately succumbed to their combined assault. Meanwhile, Lightning challenged the Grandmaster to a game of poker. Lightning outbluffed the Elder, forcing him to restore the Earth. In the wake of the battle's conclusion, the Avengers parted ways, disbanding again.

Sometime later, a revived Tony Stark met with Thor Odinson and Steve Rogers to talk about putting the Avengers back together. Their meeting coincided with longtime Avengers foe Loki (Laufeyson)

allying himself with the Final Host, a faction of evil and corrupted Celestials, to purge the Earth of humanity. As the Final Host rained chaos on Earth, the three heroes gathered an ad hoc collection of former Avengers, including the Black Panther, She-Hulk (Jennifer Walters), Captain Marvel, and Doctor Strange, and recruited Ghost Rider (Robbie Reyes) as a new member. Together, the eight heroes drove off the Final Host and saved the Celestial race from the corrupting Horde plague. The grateful Celestials raised a long-dead Celestial's corpse from the depths

of the Arctic Ocean to serve as the Avengers' high-tech headquarters in the North Pole, dubbed Avengers Mountain. The resulting team installed the Panther as chair and put the team under the purview of the Wakandan government. However, Doctor Strange chose to go to reserve status, leaving the eighth roster spot open for revolving members. With such a powerful Avengers team under the auspices of the Wakandan monarch, a super-team arms race erupted across the world. Russia assembled a new Winter Guard team to defend their sovereignty and exert their own influence worldwide while the United States government, represented by ex-S.H.I.E.L.D. agent Phil Coulson, backed the nationalistic Squadron Supreme of America, unaware that the demonic Mephisto was manipulating the team. Beneath the seas, Namor, asserting his dominance over the world's oceans, brought together his own aquatic super-squad, the Defenders of the Deep. The new Avengers team soon found themselves in conflict with

AVENGER X Active: *Avengers #2.1* (2017)	 **DOCTOR VOODOO** Active: *Axis: Avengers & X-Men #9* (2015)	 **NOVA** (SAM ALEXANDER) Active: *Nova #25* (2015)	 **MS. MARVEL** (KAMALA KHAN) Active: *Free Comic Book Day 2015 (All-New, All-Different Avengers) #1* (2015)	 **SPIDER-MAN** (MILES MORALES) Active: *Free Comic Book Day 2015 (All-New, All-Different Avengers) #1* (2015)	 **THOR** (JANE FOSTER) Active: *Free Comic Book Day 2015 (All-New, All-Different Avengers) #1* (2015)	 **DEADPOOL** Active: *Avengers #0* (2015)	 **HUMAN TORCH** (JOHNNY STORM) Active: *Uncanny Avengers #1* (2015)

CIVILIAN STAFF AND ASSOCIATES

SYNAPSE Active: *Uncanny Avengers #1* (2015)	 **CABLE** Active: *Uncanny Avengers #4* (2016)	 **WASP** (NADIA VAN DYNE) Active: *Avengers #1* (2017)	 **GHOST RIDER** Active: *Avengers #8* (2018)	**CONNIE FERRARI** Attorney Active: *Great Lakes Avengers #1* (2016)	**GORILLA-MAN** Active: *Avengers #12* (2019)	 **WASP** (JANET VAN DYNE) Active: *Avengers #12* (2019)	 **OKOYE** Active: *Avengers #12* (2019)

KA-ZAR Active: *Avengers #12* (2019)	 **BROO** Active: *Avengers #12* (2019)	 **AMERICAN EAGLE** Active: *Avengers #12* (2019)	 **DOCTOR NEMESIS** Active: *Avengers #12* (2019)	 **FAT COBRA** Active: *Avengers #12* (2019)	 **ROZ SOLOMON** Active: *Avengers #12* (2019)	 **BOY-THING** Companion to Blade Active: *Avengers #17* (2019)	 **MOCKINGBIRD** Active: *Black Panther and the Agents of Wakanda #4* (2020)

all three and in need of a dedicated staff to keep their operations running smoothly. Though Jarvis was now in semi-retirement, he helped T'Challa recruit a team of support staff and intelligence operatives, dubbed the Agents of Wakanda, to assist the Avengers whenever needed. This team came to include former Avengers such as the Wasp (Janet Van Dyne) and Mockingbird (Bobbi Morse).

The Avengers brought vampire-hunter Blade (Eric Brooks) back to fill their rotating eighth space when a civil war began brewing in the ranks of Earth's vampires — on one side, the traditional vampire leadership structure, as personified by venerable vampire lord Dracula, and on the other, the Legion of the Unliving, a vampiric strike force led by the Shadow General (Dracula's son Xarus). Unbeknownst to the Avengers, however, the entire war was a ruse, allowing Dracula to establish a new vampire nation in the radioactive wastelands of Chernobyl. Furthermore, Agent of Wakanda Gorilla-Man secretly cut a deal with Dracula, hoping to end his immortal life in exchange for serving as Dracula's mole inside the Avengers.

When the Dark Elf King Malekith conspired with rulers of seven of the Ten Realms to take possession of the seven continents of the Earth, the Avengers were pulled into one of the largest wars in history. Before long, Frost Giants were rampaging across North America, Fire Demons were burning cities in Asia, and the Dark Elves laid claim to Europe. While evacuating civilians poured into Avengers Mountain, the Avengers split up to traverse the realms, helping Thor Odinson and Jane Foster (who had relinquished her Thor identity) ultimately end Malekith's threat and repel the otherworldly invaders. With Earth safe once more, the Avengers faced a threat from within. Ghost Rider's supernatural Hell Charger car began acting suspiciously, so they called in Daimon Hellstrom (the Son of Satan) to exorcise it only for the spirit possessing it — an insane, cosmic-powered Ghost Rider (Frank Castle, the Punisher) from a far future — to possess Avengers Mountain. Meanwhile, Reyes was sucked into Hell and forced to race Hell's current ruler, another Ghost Rider (Johnny Blaze). Ultimately, Castle and the Avengers joined forces to aid Reyes' escape from Hell. Shortly afterward, the Starbrand, a planetary weapon formerly wielded by late Avenger Kevin Connor, re-emerged in the Ravenstarr prison galaxy. The Avengers, accompanied by the Black Widow (Natasha Romanoff), raced to find it before its immense power could be turned to evil.

NOTE: *The following groups, while either affiliated with the Avengers or even using the Avengers name, are not officially sanctioned Avengers franchises and their members do not hold Avengers membership: "A-Force," "Occupy Avengers," "Savage Avengers," Ultimates (Captain Marvel/Carol Danvers-led), West Coast Avengers (Hawkeye/Kate Bishop-led).*

IMPOSTERS

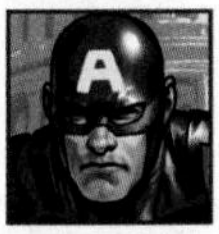

CAPTAIN AMERICA
(HYDRA STEVE ROGERS)
Active: *Captain America: Sam Wilson* #7 (2016)

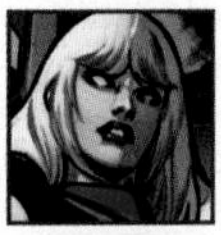

VOYAGER
Active: *Avengers* #675 (2017)

ACTIVE MEMBERS *UPDATE*:
Black Panther (T'Challa), Blade (Eric Brooks), Captain America (Steve Rogers), Captain Marvel (Carol Danvers), Ghost Rider (Robbie Reyes), Iron Man (Tony Stark), She-Hulk (Jennifer Walters), Thor Odinson

RESERVE MEMBERS *UPDATE*:
Doctor Strange (Stephen Strange)

INACTIVE MEMBERS *UPDATE*:
Black Widow (Natasha Romanoff), Blue Marvel (Adam Brashear), Luke Cage (born Carl Lucas), Cannonball (Sam Guthrie), Captain Universe (Tamara Devoux), Deadpool (Wade Wilson), Doctor Voodoo (Jericho Drumm), Falcon (Sam Wilson), Hawkeye (Clint Barton), Hercules (Heracles), Hulk (Bruce Banner), Human Torch (Johnny Storm), Hyperion (Marcus Milton), Jessica Jones (formerly Jewel), Kaluu, Manifold (Eden Fesi), Nightmask (Adam Blackveil), Power Man (Victor Alvarez), Quicksilver (Pietro Maximoff), Rogue (Anna Marie), Scarlet Witch (Wanda Maximoff), Shang-Chi, Smasher (Isabel Kane), Spectrum (Monica Rambeau), Spider-Man (Peter Parker), Spider-Woman (Jessica Drew), Sunspot (Roberto Da Costa), Synapse (Emily Guerrero), Thor (Jane Foster, now Valkyrie), Tigra (Greer Nelson), Vision (Victor Shade), Wasp (Janet Van Dyne), Wasp (Nadia Van Dyne), White Tiger (Ava Ayala), Wonder Man (Simon Williams)

FORMER MEMBERS *UPDATE*:
Abyss (formerly of the Builders, deceased), Avenger X (Cressida), Cable (elder Nathan Summers, apparently deceased), Ex Nihilo (deceased), Ms. Marvel (Kamala Khan), Nova (Sam Alexander), Hank Pym, Spider-Man (Miles Morales), Starbrand (Kevin Connor, deceased)

IMPOSTERS *UPDATE*:
Captain America (Hydra duplicate of Steve Rogers), Voyager (Va Nee Gast)

STAFF/ASSOCIATES *UPDATE*:
American Eagle (Jason Strongbow), Boy-Thing, Broo, Doctor Nemesis (James Bradley), Fat Cobra, Connie Ferrari, Gorilla-Man (Ken Hale), Ka-Zar (Kevin Plunder), Mockingbird (Bobbi Morse), Okoye, Roz Solomon, Wasp (Janet Van Dyne), numerous unidentified support staffers

BASES OF OPERATIONS *UPDATE*: Avengers Mountain, North Pole; formerly Avengers Auxiliary/Emergency Headquarters, somewhere outside New York City; Avengers Mansion, 890 Fifth Avenue, Manhattan, New York; Baxter Building, Manhattan, New York; Stark Industries airfield, New Jersey; Schaefer Theater, Manhattan, New York; Avengers Academy campus, 1800 Palos Verdes Drive, Palos Verdes, California; Lighthouse orbital space station; Gem Theatre, 42nd Street, Times Square, Manhattan, New York; Hank Pym's research laboratory, Crofton University, Washington, D.C.

ART BY MAHMUD ASRAR, SIMONE BIANCHI, OSCAR JIMENEZ, PEPE LARRAZ, DAVID MARQUEZ & ED MCGUINNESS

BEL-DANN

UNMASKED

HISTORY: Colonel Bel-Dann was born a pink-skinned Kree extraterrestrial. He and Raksor of the Skrull Empire were assigned to be interplanetary observers in the Shi'ar Empire's efforts to execute the destructive Phoenix entity. The pair monitored the trial by combat when Earth's X-Men fought against the Shi'ar Empire's Imperial Guard to save their teammate Phoenix in the habitable Blue Area of Earth's moon. However, the two observers' enmity toward each other, reflecting their empires' epoch-long war, resulted in fierce combat that continued for months in ancient underground Kree ruins. Both warriors remained oblivious to passing events, including the Inhuman city Attilan's relocation from Earth to the Blue Area. Meanwhile, the Kree and Skrull empires proved too evenly matched for any decisive victory, so both empires decreed the war's end would be decided by the outcome of the two soldiers' combat, with Uatu the Watcher, also based near the Blue Area, as a neutral arbiter. The warriors' combat intensified until it threatened peace in Attilan, so the Inhuman king, Black Bolt (Blackagar Boltagon), and Reed Richards of the Fantastic Four devised a plan to manipulate Bel-Dann and Raksor into allying against a feigned attack of the Inhumans and the Fantastic Four. Uatu judged the two victorious champions as joint winners and teleported them back to their respective empires, although hostilities between the empires eventually resumed. Later promoted to general, Bel-Dann survived the Nega-Bomb that decimated the Kree Empire, which was subsequently annexed by the Shi'ar Empire. Hoping to restore the conquered Kree's militaristic ways, Bel-Dann manipulated the adventurer Legacy (Genis-Vell, later Captain Marvel) into detonating a bomb on Shi'ar outpost Link 616 as part of fellow Kree Zey-Rogg's vengeful machinations. Eventually, Bel-Dann and Raksor reconciled and developed a close friendship, uniting in the secretive Kree/Skrull Alliance. Posing as humans, the two set up base on Earth in New York, using a hexadecimal code to communicate covertly. When Bel-Dann was mysteriously murdered, several of Earth's heroes recovered Bel-Dann's body and a cryptic message, one they learned advised him to "beware the trees."

REAL NAME: Bel-Dann

ALIASES: Unrevealed

IDENTITY: No dual identity

OCCUPATION:
Deep-cover operative; former soldier

CITIZENSHIP: Kree Empire

PLACE OF BIRTH: Unrevealed location in the Kree Empire

KNOWN RELATIVES: None

GROUP AFFILIATION:
The Kree/Skrull Alliance; formerly Kree Consolidated Peace Battalion, Kree military

EDUCATION: Kree military training

HEIGHT: 6'

WEIGHT: 220 lbs.

EYES: Black   **HAIR:** Black

ABILITIES/ACCESSORIES:
Bel-Dann had Kree superhuman durability and twice the strength of a comparably built human. Kree military training made him an accomplished leader also skilled in subterfuge, and intensive experience advanced his combat abilities and familiarity with Kree weapons, including an armored suit of unrevealed specifications. While in the Kree military, Bel-Dann carried a standard issue Uni-Blaster.

| ① | ② | ③ | ④ | ⑤ | ⑥ | ⑦ |

INTELLIGENCE
STRENGTH
SPEED
DURABILITY
ENERGY PROJECTION
FIGHTING SKILLS

FIRST APPEARANCE:
X-Men #137 (1980)

ART BY ED BENES, MARK BRIGHT, & HUMBERTO RAMOS

ARMORED

BLUE AREA OF THE MOON

KREE CITY RUINS IN MODERN TIMES

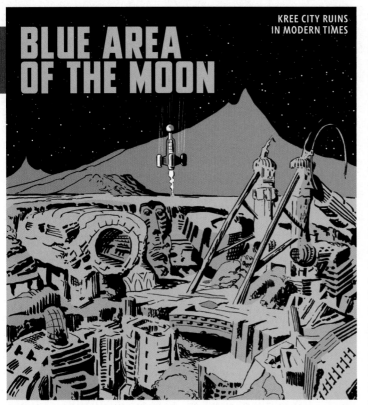

HISTORY: Billions of years ago, Uatu, a member of a cosmically powered race of observers called the Watchers, chose Earth's solar system as the place to mentally record what he saw and transfer it to the collective knowledge of the universe: *The Cyclopedia Universum*. He built his citadel on the moon and began his observation of Earth. Between one and ten million years ago, the technologically advanced Skrull race visited planet Hala, where the barbaric Kree cohabitated with the Cotati, a humanoid plant race. The Skrulls announced a contest to see who could make the most impressive creation in a year's time, offering to provide knowledge and technology to the winning race. Presumably unaware the Watcher lived there — likely due to the Watcher cosmically hiding his presence — the Skrulls took seventeen Kree to the dark side of Earth's moon, where technology was used to create a breathable atmosphere in a 200-mile-wide area filled with craters and gravity one-sixth that of Earth's. By year's end, the Kree had built a blue city of unimaginable size while the Cotati had raised an ornate garden on a distant barren planet. Upon returning to Hala, the Kree were enraged to learn they had lost the contest and slew the Skrulls and Cotati, beginning the Kree/Skrull War that continued to the present time. Over the subsequent centuries, though largely hidden from Earth's view by lunar dust, the city fell into disrepair, and the area was eventually named the Blue Area due to the bluish hue the city's remains created.

In 1949, Namor McKenzie (the Sub-Mariner) was inadvertently taken to the Blue Area when a portion of the Pacific Ocean was seized by moon-based robots who were collecting water for their system's operations. The robots claimed they had been created ages prior by the late, "original Moon-Men." To avoid humanity's hostility and possibly being charged for the water, the robots erased Namor's memories of them before returning him to Earth. In the 1950s, publisher Whitney Hammond assigned Venus, actually the Olympian goddess of love and beauty, to accompany Randall "Randy" Dover to the moon in his self-designed rocket ship so she could document the trip. While in the Blue Area, Luna-Thing creatures and a volcano eruption threatened them, but Venus saved Dover before they returned to Earth. What became of the robots, their system, the Luna-Things, and the volcano is all unrevealed. In 1962, the Blue Marvel (Adam Brashear) visited the Blue Area and encountered the Watcher, shortly before destroying an alien invasion fleet heading towards Earth. Later, both the time-traveling Cassandra Locke and Earth's Sorcerer Supreme Doctor Stephen Strange joined the Watcher in witnessing Earth's defenders obliterate a Skrull Armada over the Blue Area, however, the victory came at the cost of almost an entire generation of costumed heroes.

In recent years, Mister Fantastic (Reed Richards) sought to explore the Blue Area and brought his super-powered Fantastic Four (F4) family with him. There, the team met the Watcher and was attacked by the space-pioneering, cosmic-ray-empowered Red Ghost (Ivan Kragoff), who wanted to claim the moon for the Communist empire. During the battle, both the Red Ghost and Mister Fantastic found that technology in the dead city still worked and utilized it. Sometime after the Red Ghost's defeat, the Gardener, a member of the age-old Elders of the Universe, grew a garden in the Blue Area using the Time Gem, one of the immensely powerful Infinity Gems. However, when a battle between Spider-Man (Peter Parker), Adam Warlock, and the enigmatic Stranger erupted there, the Gardener was forced to use the Time Gem against the Stranger, which caused the garden to wither and die.

WATCHER'S CITADEL

THE WATCHER

When the cosmic force of rebirth and destruction, the Phoenix Force, impersonated the mutant X-Man Jean Grey as the Phoenix, it was overwhelmed by primal urges and consumed the star D'bari, killing five billion beings in its system. When the Shi'ar Empire sought to impose capital punishment upon "Jean Grey," the X-Men demanded a trial by combat, which subsequently took place in the Blue Area with representatives of the long-warring Skrull and Kree empires (Raksor and Bel-Dann, respectively) as observers. Ultimately, fearing it would destroy again, the Phoenix triggered a long-buried Kree weapon in the city's ruins, destroying its mortal shell. Unaware that the trial had ended because a fight had erupted between them, Raksor and Bel-Dann continued fighting in the Blue Area for months. The two utilized machinery found in the ruins and littered the vast underground cavern system with booby traps and escape hatches.

Seeking to end the age-long war, rulers of both empires decreed the war's end would be decided by the victor of the Raksor/Bel-Dann rivalry. Uatu agreed to arbitrate. The two warriors were so consumed by their months-long duel, they remained oblivious that the city of Attilan, home to a genetic offshoot of humanity called the Inhumans, had been relocated to the Blue Area by Mister Fantastic in order to save the Inhumans from Earth's pollution and potential hostility. When the duo's battle unintentionally threatened the Inhumans, the visiting F4 and the Inhumans' royal family tricked Raksor and Bel-Dann into working together to battle them. Consequently, Uatu ruled the two combatants to be co-champions and decreed that the end of the Kree/Skrull War should come about through cooperation between the two empires; Bel-Dann and Raksor were then returned to their empires. Around this time, the Inhumans discovered a vast system

of sublunar channels filled with water as well as a small crystal sculpture of unrevealed origin that created mass hallucinations for the Inhumans before it was destroyed.

Over subsequent years, the Blue Area was the site of numerous events involving Earth's superhuman population. Age-old mutant Apocalypse (En Sabah Nur) took over Attilan until he was beaten back by the Inhumans and mutant X-Factor led by Cyclops (Scott Summers). The Elder of the Universe named the Collector (Taneleer Tivan) staged a failed attempt to destroy Earth's population from the Blue Area. The X-Men returned to fight Stryfe, a clone of the fully grown, time-traveling son of Cyclops, Cable (elder Nathan Summers). The F4 and Inhumans battled Doctor Doom (Victor Von Doom) after he stole the power of Uatu's fellow Watcher, Aron the Rogue, then later the F4 battled Aron the Rogue himself. When the lives of the Inhumans were threatened

KREE CITY

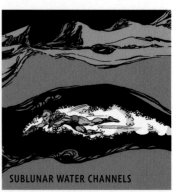

SUBLUNAR WATER CHANNELS

by the temporary dissipation of the Blue Area's atmosphere, the F4 used Doctor Doom's shrink-ray technology to miniaturize Attilan and transport it to Earth. The heroic Avengers battled Kree guerrillas who apparently restored the atmosphere-generating machinery, built a base below the Blue Area, relocated their Supreme Intelligence (SI) ruler there, and planned to transform humanity to Kree. Following the battle, the security agency S.H.I.E.L.D. (Strategic Hazard Intervention Espionage Logistics Directorate) and the scientific Starcore agency established a research laboratory where they could study the captured SI while it was in their custody. The F4 also prevented the Kree Ronan the Accuser from stealing weaponry from the Watcher's citadel.

Sometime after this, unwelcome in any nation due to humanity's mistrust of them, the Inhumans were forced by the United Nations to relocate Attilan back to the Blue Area. Despite this, the F4 maintained close ties with the Inhumans, often leaving the children of Reed and Susan Richards (Invisible Woman) with them for babysitting when the F4 were away. Repeated negative interactions with humanity resulted in the Inhumans declaring war on the United States when the sacred transformative Terrigen crystals in their possession

were not returned. A group of Terrigen-mutated U.S. Marines invaded Attilan and, in the process, one Marine exploded, destroying Attilan. Sometime after rebuilding, the Inhumans converted Attilan to a spacecraft and departed the Blue Area to pursue war against the Skrull Empire. However, they left behind a large warehouse of weaponry called the Storehouse for future use. The Blue Area later became a battleground between the Avengers and X-Men when they went to war over how to handle the impending return of the Phoenix Force.

When the F4's Special Class of students temporarily stayed at the Watcher's citadel, two aquatic members of the class (Wu & Vil) learned they could breathe the Blue Area's atmosphere, surmising it was because it was non-homogenous and tailored to individual respiratory requirements — this supposition remains unverified. Not long after this, when World War II era super-spy Nick Fury learned powerful weapons had been pilfered from the Watcher's citadel, the Watcher refused to break his oath of non-interference to reveal the suspect so Fury

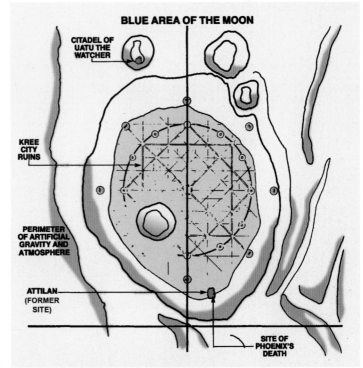

BLUE AREA OF THE MOON

CITADEL OF UATU THE WATCHER

KREE CITY RUINS

PERIMETER OF ARTIFICIAL GRAVITY AND ATMOSPHERE

ATTILAN (FORMER SITE)

SITE OF PHOENIX'S DEATH

could track down the weapons. During a subsequent argument, the Watcher appeared ready to attack Fury, who then killed the Watcher and took his eye to gain the knowledge the Watcher possessed. After stopping the orchestrator of the thefts — the power-hungry Doctor Midas — Fury was chained to the Blue Area by Uatu's fellow Watchers and forced to take up Uatu's role of cosmic observer as the Unseen. When Thor Odinson came to believe that gods were not worthy of worship, he became unworthy of wielding his hammer, Mjolnir. The hammer remained in the Blue Area until Thor's human ally Jane Foster proved worthy of Mjolnir and took it up for a time as a replacement Thor. After learning of the Watcher's murder, his friend Nova (Sam Alexander) carved a bust of the Watcher on a moon rock to pay tribute to his lost confidant. Later, Spider-Woman (Jessica Drew) was sent by Captain Marvel (Carol Danvers) to confront a semi-sentient fungus creature living in the Blue Area. It is unclear if the fungus still survives after Spider-Woman reduced it to liquid by punching it, or if there are others

like it. When a being called the Time Eater began consuming timelines, the Unseen worked with a new iteration of the inter-reality Exiles to stop it. This group then battled a group of rogue Watchers in the Blue Area until the zealot Watchers were taken away by their brethren for violating their race's sacred laws. Later, using a sapling taken from the sentient island Krakoa, the X-Men created an outpost one lunar mile from the Blue Area — named the Summer House, a number of X-Men (including Cyclops) took up residence there, accessing the facility through teleportation.

NOTE: *Other recorded events on the moon prior to* Fantastic Four #13 *(1963) depict beings requiring space suits or oxygen during their visits. Since these items were necessary for survival, it is unlikely the events took place in the Blue Area's atmosphere. "Moon-Men" claiming to be from floating cities on the moon visited Earth in* Strange Tales #42 *(1956), but these claims (and their location on the moon) remain unverified.*

THE UNSEEN

MEMORIAL FOR THE WATCHER

OFFICIAL NAME: Blue Area
POPULATION:
1 (possibly more)
CAPITAL CITY: None
PLACES OF INTEREST:
Inhumans' Storehouse, dormant volcano, long-dead Kree city, former citadel of and memorial for Uatu the Watcher, sublunar water channel system; formerly Attilan, S.H.I.E.L.D. research center, settlement maintained by robots

GOVERNMENT: None

MAJOR LANGUAGES: None

MONETARY UNIT: None

MAJOR RESOURCES: None

NATIONAL DEFENSE: None

INTERNATIONAL RELATIONS: None

NONHUMAN POPULATION:
Semi-sentient fungus creature (possibly deceased), Luna-Things (unconfirmed), the Robots (unconfirmed); formerly Uatu the Watcher

DOMESTIC SUPERHUMANS: None

PROMINENT CITIZENS:
The Unseen, Formerly Uatu the Watcher, the Inhumans, the "original Moon-Men" (allegedly), possibly others

SUPERHUMAN RESIDENTS:
The Unseen; formerly Uatu the Watcher, the Inhumans

DOMESTIC CRIME: None

INTERNATIONAL CRIME:
The murder of the Watcher by Nick Fury

FIRST APPEARANCE:
Blonde Phantom Comics #21 (1949); (identified) *Fantastic Four* #13 (1963)

ART BY ELIOT R. BROWN, SAL BUSCEMA, JOHN BYRNE, MIKE DEODATO JR., ANDREA DI VITO, JACK KIRBY, PAUL PELLETIER & FEDERICO SANTAGATI

CAPTAIN GLORY

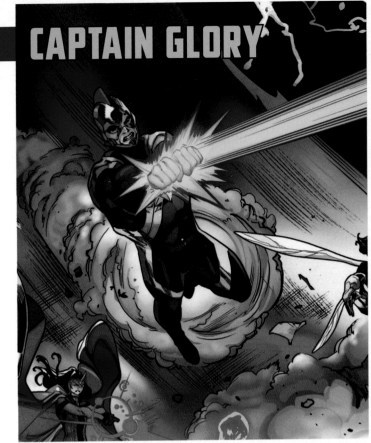

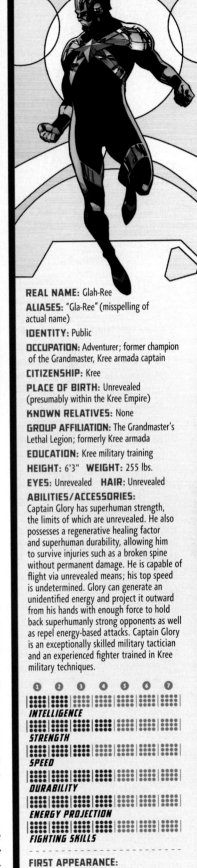

HISTORY: A proud captain in the alien Kree armada, Glah-Ree (codenamed Captain Glory) and his squadron were sent up against the brutal alien Takolians, who slaughtered most of Glah-Ree's squadron during the confrontation. The last survivor, Glory prepared for a final stand against the Takolians but was taken from the battlefield by Elder of the Universe Grandmaster (En Dwi Gast). The Grandmaster had chosen Glory and other extraterrestrials for the Lethal Legion, a team of mortal representatives he would use in his gaming contests. Told he would be returned to face certain death if he refused to act as the Grandmaster's champion in a game against the Grandmaster's fellow Elder the Challenger, Glory agreed to lead the Lethal Legion against the Challenger's champions, the Black Order (former servants of the mad Titan Thanos). The teams competed to find Pyramoids, powerful elemental objects hidden in various places on Earth. When the Pyramoids began disrupting global weather patterns, Earth's Avengers intervened in the Elders' game, clashing with both sides. During a subsequent battle with the Avengers, Glory overwhelmed the telepathic Synapse (Emily Guerrero) by allowing her full access to his harsh, tactical mind. Captain Glory continued to lead the Lethal Legion until the Challenger unleashed his mentally coerced secret champion, the Hulk (Bruce Banner), who sidelined Glory with a broken spine. Following his recovery after the game's end, Glory reunited with the Lethal Legion and decided to remain with the group rather than return to the Kree armada and face execution for desertion — the team apparently freed from the Grandmaster's service.

NOTE: *Captain Glory (Glah-Ree), of the Prime Reality, is not to be confused with Captain Glory (Earth-200080), father of that reality's Marvel Boy (Noh-Varr).*

REAL NAME: Glah-Ree
ALIASES: "Gla-Ree" (misspelling of actual name)
IDENTITY: Public
OCCUPATION: Adventurer; former champion of the Grandmaster, Kree armada captain
CITIZENSHIP: Kree
PLACE OF BIRTH: Unrevealed (presumably within the Kree Empire)
KNOWN RELATIVES: None
GROUP AFFILIATION: The Grandmaster's Lethal Legion; formerly Kree armada
EDUCATION: Kree military training
HEIGHT: 6'3" **WEIGHT:** 255 lbs.
EYES: Unrevealed **HAIR:** Unrevealed
ABILITIES/ACCESSORIES:
Captain Glory has superhuman strength, the limits of which are unrevealed. He also possesses a regenerative healing factor and superhuman durability, allowing him to survive injuries such as a broken spine without permanent damage. He is capable of flight via unrevealed means; his top speed is undetermined. Glory can generate an unidentified energy and project it outward from his hands with enough force to hold back superhumanly strong opponents as well as repel energy-based attacks. Captain Glory is an exceptionally skilled military tactician and an experienced fighter trained in Kree military techniques.

INTELLIGENCE
STRENGTH
SPEED
DURABILITY
ENERGY PROJECTION
FIGHTING SKILLS

FIRST APPEARANCE:
Avengers #676 (2018)

ART BY SEAN IZAAKSE & PEPE LARRAZ

CAPTAIN MARVEL

HISTORY *UPDATE :* *Continued from the Captain Marvel profile in the* Captain Marvel: In Pursuit of Flight *trade paperback (2013).* Shortly after taking the name Captain Marvel and rejoining the Avengers, Carol Danvers battled Magnitron (Yon-Rogg), who created a flight-limiting brain lesion in Danvers. Captain Marvel used a flying cycle provided by Captain America (Steve Rogers) to avoid flying. Though she defeated Magnitron, the lesion ruptured during the battle, robbing Danvers of many memories. Later, Danvers and the Avengers battled the Builders race in deep space, stopping their invasions of various interstellar powers. During the ordeal, Danvers briefly re-accessed her cosmic-level Binary powers. Finding a camaraderie with fellow armed services veteran and Avenger Iron Patriot (James Rhodes, formerly War Machine), Danvers began a romance with him shortly before she was assigned to space by the Avengers. They continued their relationship long-distance. During her time in space, Danvers learned her cat, Chewie, was a Reality-58163 native known as a Flerkin, a carnivorous alien creature with extendable internal tentacles from within her mouth, and also joined Star-Lord's the Guardians of the Galaxy led by Star-Lord (Peter Quill), helping them keep the Black Vortex — an object that unleashes cosmic potential in those who use it — out of the hands of those who would abuse it. However, the Kree homeworld, Hala, was destroyed by J'son, king of the Spartax Empire, who sought the Vortex for himself.

Later, the Multiverse faced destruction when the nigh-omnipotent Beyonders engineered the Incursions, cataclysmic events where alternate Earths smashed together, destroying their realities. Returning to Earth, Danvers joined S.H.I.E.L.D. to help efforts to prevent Earth's destruction. During this time, Danvers, wanting to meet the successor to her first costumed identity, introduced herself to Ms. Marvel (Kamala Khan), a teenage Inhuman who idolized Captain Marvel and underwent Terrigenesis following exposure to the Inhumans' Terrigen Mist, which was now loose in Earth's atmosphere. Impressed with Ms. Marvel's handling of riots in Jersey City, Danvers gave her a medallion with both their insignias on it as a show of hope for the future. Following the final Incursion between the last two remaining Earths, Earth-616 (Danvers' own) and Earth-1610, Danvers and a handful of other heroes survived thanks to a life raft created by the Fantastic Four's Mister Fantastic (Reed Richards). Eight years later, Earth-616's survivors were awakened by Doctor Stephen Strange on Battleworld, a planet created by the now near-omnipotent Doctor Victor Von Doom from remnants of destroyed realities. Doom ruled Battleworld as god emperor with Strange as his sheriff and Molecule Man (Owen Reece) as the power source. When discovered, Strange scattered the survivors across Battleworld before Doom murdered him for the betrayal. Danvers and the survivors inspired Battleworld's residents to rebel against Doom.

FLYING CYCLE

Mister Fantastic eventually defeated Doom with Molecule Man's help, then re-created Reality-616 and set out to restore the Multiverse.

Back on Earth, Danvers was recruited by the Alpha Flight Space Program to be the commander of the Alpha Flight Low-Orbit Space Station, Earth's first line of defense against extraterrestrial threats. Under Danvers' direct supervision were Abigail Brand as her lieutenant commander and Alpha Flight team members Aurora (Jean-Marie Beaubier), Puck (Eugene Judd), and Sasquatch (WalterLangkowski). Danvers and Rhodes (once again War Machine) resumed their romance. Danvers proposed the Ultimates, a proactive task force dedicated to uncovering potential threats and resolving them with nonviolent solutions. Black Panther (T'Challa) agreed to join, as well as Blue Marvel (Adam Brashear), Spectrum (Monica Rambeau), and Ms. America (America Chavez). An early Ultimates mission was to solve the hunger of the planet-devouring Galactus (Galan). They forced an evolution that transformed him into the Lifebringer, seeder of worlds. Around this time, Danvers also joined She-Hulk (Jennifer Walters), Medusa (Medusalith Boltagon), and a number of other women in an informal female hero group. When Danvers' best friend Spider-Woman (Jessica Drew) gave birth to her son, Gerry Drew, Danvers was elated to become "Auntie Carol" and babysat from time to time.

Learning of Ulysses Cain, an Inhuman with precognition abilities, Danvers wanted to use his power to proactively deal with threats before they could develop. Danvers' fellow Avenger Iron Man (Tony Stark) opposed the idea, arguing the morality of punishing someone for something they hadn't done, and if Cain's visions could be averted, Stark doubted their accuracy. Danvers was buoyed by Rhodes' admittance that he trusted her instincts. Soon after, Danvers learned the Kree scientist Doctor Minerva had constructed a

biological weapon on Earth. Unable to stop Minerva and furious about the deaths resulting from Minerva's weapon, Danvers cemented her decision to use Cain's power to profile the future. Unfortunately, while acting on a vision to ambush the mad Titan Thanos, Danvers' friend She-Hulk was beaten into a coma and Rhodes was killed, devastating Danvers. Soon after, another vision foretold Bruce Banner losing control of his superstrong Hulk persona, resulting in Hawkeye (Clint Barton) killing him at the request of Banner with a special arrow constructed by Banner. Angry over the Hulk's death and Hawkeye's arrest, Spider-Woman ended her friendship with Danvers.

Cain then had a premonition of finance banker Alison Green being a Hydra agent, but after Danvers arrested Green, the premonition was proven wrong. Iron Man and other super heroes who opposed Danvers' use of Cain attacked S.H.I.E.L.D.'s Triskelion facility and rescued Green, resulting in a massive battle between those who

supported Iron Man and Danvers. During the melee, a new vision was suddenly broadcast, one of Spider-Man (Miles Morales of Earth-1610, now living on Earth-616) holding the corpse of Captain America. When Danvers tried to detain Spider-Man, several of her compatriots decided they could no longer support her course of action and defected, including Black Panther, Medusa, and Ms. Marvel. Feeling abandoned and reflecting on all she had lost, including friendships and Rhodes, Danvers convinced herself that all she'd accomplished using Cain's power was worth her losses.

When Captain America and Spider-Man met to disprove the vision, Danvers joined them to keep Spider-Man safe. Before Spider-Man could answer Danvers' request he work with her, Iron Man attacked. Danvers defeated him, but Stark was left in a coma at the battle's end. Meanwhile, Cain's powers evolved, and he left Earth to ascend to a higher plane of existence, ending Danvers'

WITH ALPHA FLIGHT

MAINE HEADQUARTERS

CAPTAIN MARVEL

CHEWIE

BATTLING POSSESSED CHEWIE

future profiling. Despite this, the president of the United States was impressed with Danvers' results and asked if she had any other plans to protect the Earth. She proposed a planetary defense shield that was quickly approved.

Now hating super heroes and wanting revenge on Danvers for arresting her, Alison Green abducted Danvers' friend Jessica Jones in a plot to lure Danvers to her. Green revealed her plan to stage a catastrophe that would be blamed on superhumans, but Jones secretly recorded Green's monologue, which led to her arrest. Danvers began repairing her friendships, beginning with Spider-Woman. Despite now being considered the world's most popular super hero, one even immortalized by a television show dramatizing her exploits, Danvers began seeing a psychiatrist to deal with her recent losses. Meanwhile, Doctor Eve, a Kree scientist, arranged for the abduction of a dozen Kree children — one of whom Danvers named "Bean" — from an Alpha Flight Displaced Alien Refugee Camp so she could obtain their unique genetic human leukocyte antigen (HLA) markers for her efforts to return the Kree Empire to glory. Eve distilled the twelve HLA markers into a single composite, HLA-12, which she used against Danvers. The composite affected Danvers' hybrid physiology and drove her into a mindless rage. Satisfied with the result, Eve planned to

use the HLA-12 to make herself the most powerful person in the universe and escaped. As a result of the experiments, Bean was transformed into an energy being and left to explore space.

When the extraterrestrial Chitauri attacked Earth, Danvers led her allies to battle them in space. Captain America — transformed by Kobik, a sentient reality-altering Cosmic Cube to have been loyal to the terroristic Hydra his entire life — used Danvers' planetary defense shield to lock Danvers and her allies outside Earth's atmosphere. Meanwhile, he staged a fascist takeover of the United States. Stranded in space with the Chitauri hordes still attacking, Danvers led Earth's defense, but attrition took its toll. The Guardians of the Galaxy helped with supply runs for the Alpha Flight Low-Orbit Space Station, but no other alien race was willing to assist Earth. Eventually breaching the shield by sacrificing the space station, Danvers joined the rest of Earth's heroes in defeating Captain America, now the Hydra Supreme, and witnessed Kobik's restoration of the true Captain America. Afterward, Danvers was at a loss. Her space station was destroyed and, Alpha Flight was placed on indefinite paid leave. Spider-Woman allowed Danvers to stay in her baby's room until she could find new living arrangements. Later, Danvers was contacted by Bean, who warned her that she was in danger. Danvers prepared to investigate but was attacked by

Doctor Eve, who lured Danvers into an alternate reality. There, Eve acquired the reality-altering Reality Stone, one of the immensely powerful Infinity Stones. Meanwhile, Danvers encountered Zeta Flight, this reality's mercenary version of Alpha Flight, and Lord Starkill (Peter Quill). Eve attempted to merge Bean with Danvers to enable her to use the Reality Stone to move this reality's Hala to Eve's native reality. The pair broke free of Eve's control and instead restored the Alpha Flight Low-Orbit Space Station in their native universe. Captain Marvel kept the Reality Stone safe until it was taken by Guardian of the Galaxy Gamora in her quest to reunite all six Infinity Stones.

When her brother Joe was left comatose following a drunk-driving accident, Danvers retired from the Avengers and Alpha Flight for months while she and her mother took care of him. While there, Danvers and Tony Stark built a high-tech underwater headquarters for her Captain Marvel endeavors, and she unintentionally activated a homing beacon among her parents' belongings that summoned a Kree Kleaner. Sometime after Joe regained consciousness, the Kleaner arrived. While preparing to battle the Kleaner, Danvers learned her mother, Marie, was actually Mari-Ell, a Kree soldier, making Danvers a human-Kree hybrid whose true name was Car-Ell. The two Danvers women battled the Kleaner together, but Mari-Ell was killed. Once Joe was able to function on his own again, Danvers returned to adventuring while a revived Tony Stark helped Danvers improve Captain Marvel's public image. Around this time, Danvers began mentoring Avenger Third Grade Hazmat (Jennifer Takeda) and was reunited with Rhodes, who was saved from death by Tony Stark when he used untested technology and undocumented science to "reboot" Rhodes' biological systems. Danvers fought to protect Earth when it became embroiled in the Asgardian War of the Realms.

Following the war, Danvers spent some rare downtime with the Avengers, specifically connecting with new recruit Ghost Rider (Robbie Reyes) by helping him address his fear over being an Avenger by revealing that fear is something she grapples with as well. Danvers later joined a number of prominent female crimefighters as guest speakers at Camp Gloriana Leadership Camp for Young Girls, then learned that Walter Lawson, the man Mar-Vell based his secret identity upon when he arrived on Earth, was alive and had been gathering Kree tech for years, hoping to take revenge on the Kree for ruining his life. With the help of Ms. Marvel and the Kree Starforce Blue criminal justice enforcement group, Danvers defeated Lawson's plans and allowed Starforce Blue to remove him from Earth to serve ten years of community service on Kree. Danvers' public image took a serious hit as the public learned of her Kree heritage, causing some to consider her a threat or an alien spy. Unknowingly, Danvers' longtime foe Doctor Minerva, trying to drive Danvers to Kree loyalty, was responsible for leaking the information to the press. Minerva also empowered reporter Ripley Ryan. Ryan had interacted with Captain Marvel and become bitter after being trapped in a reality warp

VOX SUIT

by a super villain for an extended time. Ryan used nanotechnology to sap Danvers' powers so Ryan could be the super hero Star. Eventually, Danvers learned of Minerva's actions, and she challenged Star to a public battle where Danvers tore the power-transferring device from both their chests before Star could use it to drain energy from countless New Yorkers. Danvers' triumph over Star restored Danvers' reputation in the public eye, which returned her to one of Earth's premier heroes, but the revelation she was half-Kree resulted in Danvers' formal dismissal from the U.S. Air Force; Danvers also resigned from Alpha Flight to preserve its government funding.

With the Avengers, Danvers traveled to Hell to rescue Robbie Reyes from a previous Ghost Rider, Johnny Blaze, who now ruled Hell, then also went to outer space to locate the previously missing Starbrand power. Danvers returned to Earth to learn Chewie had been possessed by a portion of an alien symbiote as part of an attempt by the murderous Carnage (Cletus Kasady) to awaken the god of Symbiotes, Knull, and bring him to Earth. After being swallowed by "Carnage-Chewie," Danvers battled the symbiote in the pocket dimension, ultimately causing Chewie to vomit Danvers and the symbiote out for Danvers to apparently destroy. After these events, Chewie returned to normal life as Danvers' beloved companion. Later, when the Kree Vox Supreme — a member of the powerful beings who apparently killed the Inhumans, now merged with part of the Kree Supreme Intelligence — sought to kill the Avengers and use their genetics to create a Kree master race, he planted bombs in Kree refugee camps around Earth and forced Captain Marvel to attack her teammates in a dramatic red-and-black outfit. However, using deceased clones of the Avengers she procured from an abandoned S.H.I.E.L.D. project, Danvers tricked Vox Supreme into believing she killed her teammates, whom, in actuality, she secreted away inside

the stellar body of Danvers' friend Singularity. During the inevitable battle between Vox Supreme and Danvers, the Avengers disarmed the bombs, upending Vox Supreme's plans. Later still, a Kree symbol found at the murder of Kree member Bel-Dann pulled Danvers into an investigation that ultimately led to confronting the Skrull Raksor, whom Danvers and other heroes believed responsible for the murder. However, after they learned Raksor and Bel-Dann were actually partners in trying to unite the long-warring Skrull and Kree empires, Raksor was killed by a rapidly emerging tree bursting from his body. Raksor's final words to the heroes were "empires will fall."

REAL NAME *UPDATE*: Car-Ell

OCCUPATION *UPDATE*:
Formerly Alpha Flight Commander

KNOWN RELATIVES *UPDATE*:
Steven J. Danvers (half brother, deceased), Joseph "Joe" Danvers, Jr. (half brother)

GROUP AFFILIATION *UPDATE*:
Formerly Alpha Flight, Ultimates, informal female hero group, S.H.I.E.L.D., Guardians of the Galaxy

ABILITIES / ACCESSORIES *UPDATE*:
Captain Marvel constantly emits electromagnetic radiation, limiting the effectiveness of X-rays, MRIs, and CT scans. She claims to have a Kree metabolism, which is faster than a human's. While her flight power was limited, Captain Marvel utilized Captain America's custom-designed flying cycle that came equipped with a bolo/net weapon and could cast a smokescreen.

ART BY FILIPE ANDRADE, KRIS ANKA, ANDREA BROCCARDO, SIMONE BUONFANTINO, CARMEN CARNERO, LEE GARBETT & DIEGO OLORTEGUI

CHIMERA

IN ATTACK FORM

HISTORY: Skrull 21st Observation Corps Commander Zuhn accompanied Lieutenant Velmax on a 1947 mission to Earth. Spotted, Velmax engaged a U.S. Air Force jet over the American Southwest; ultimately, both ships crashed, and the jet's human pilot barely survived. With their ship's major systems down, Zuhn roused the stunned Velmax to assess damages. Upon exiting, Zuhn was shot in the chest by drunken U.S. Army veteran Jacob Scott. Instructed to follow Priority Seven (disposing of witnesses), Velmax pursued Scott, who fled in his truck but fatally crashed. Velmax placed the dying Zuhn in a med-pod, but before he could get undercover, U.S. soldiers arrived. Adopting Scott's form, Velmax convinced authorities he had shot aliens that dissolved; he subsequently used Scott's identity to become a federal agent. Reviving and setting the med-pod afire, Zuhn escaped but was believed dead by Velmax when he gained clearance to investigate. Their ship was brought to Long Island, New York, and in 1958, Zuhn (in human form) attempted to reclaim it. When "Scott" (Velmax) led a group of costumed heroes to investigate the facility, the ship's bio-moleculizer mutated investigator Earl Schreiber into a rampaging monster. As the heroes arrived, Zuhn fled into the ship, and Velmax pursued (with neither Skrull recognizing the other). Attempting to create another monstrous diversion, Zuhn used the bio-moleculizer on Velmax then escaped in a new human form. The weapon's effects allowed Scott to feign mutation into a metamorph; he became the heroic Effigy, ultimately becoming leader of the First Line super-team. At some point, Zuhn, as human Roger Winget, established Winget Co. in Dallas, Texas, to develop electronic aerospace components while using the metamorphic Chimera identity against competitors when more scrupulous tactics failed. In November 1963, Winget enlisted the lycanthropic Howler (Luke Garrow) to loot a Stark Industries facility for a new guidance system. Alerted by teammate Nightingale's prophecy of tragedy in Dallas, where U.S. President John F. Kennedy was to speak, Effigy led the First Line to investigate and confronted Chimera, who slew member Liberty Girl. Effigy engaged and fatally wounded Chimera just as they recognized each other. Dying, Zuhn condemned Velmax as a traitor. 🜨

REAL NAME: Zuhn
ALIASES: Roger Winget; others unrevealed
IDENTITY: Secret
OCCUPATION: Founder and presumably C.E.O. of Winget Co.; former commander in 21st Observation Corps
CITIZENSHIP: Skrull Empire; possibly falsified U.S. citizen under Winget or other identity
PLACE OF BIRTH: Presumably the Skrull Empire within the Andromeda Galaxy
KNOWN RELATIVES: None
GROUP AFFILIATION: Formerly Skrull 21st Observation Corps
EDUCATION: Skrull military training
HEIGHT: 5' 1" (variable)
WEIGHT: 180 lbs. (possibly variable)
EYES: Pink (apparently each with paired, concentric irises; variable)
HAIR: Unrevealed (likely none; variable)
ABILITIES/ACCESSORIES: Like most Skrulls, Zuhn could take the appearance of other beings or objects up to at least thrice his volume; he could create functioning wings, sharp claws, etc. Zuhn also used a Skrull bio-moleculizer, transforming humans into rampaging monsters and temporarily destabilizing metamorphs, and a moonlight-simulating device to improve lunar-powered creatures' conscious control.

1	2	3	4	5	6	7
INTELLIGENCE
STRENGTH
SPEED
DURABILITY
ENERGY PROJECTION
FIGHTING SKILLS

FIRST APPEARANCE:
Marvel: The Lost Generation #4 (2000)

TRUE FORM

AS WINGET

ART BY JOHN BYRNE

COTATI

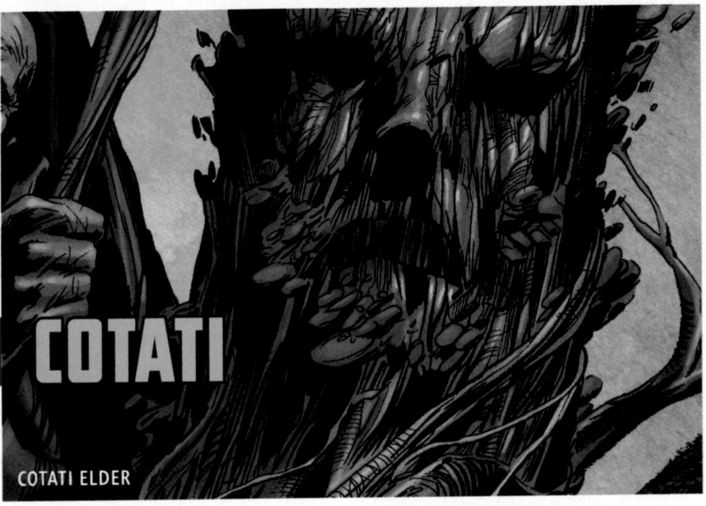

COTATI ELDER

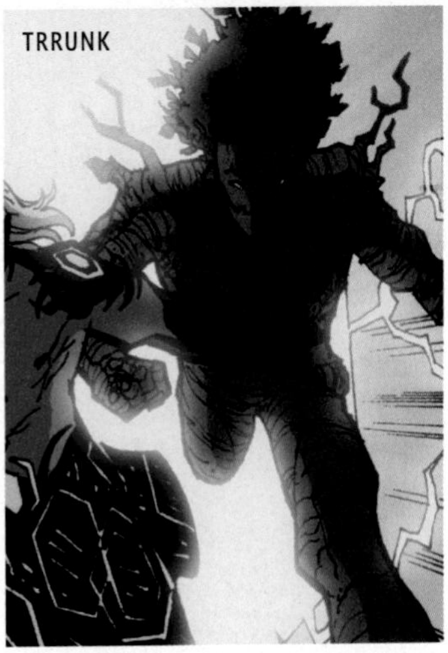

TRRUNK

HISTORY *UPDATE*: *Continued from the Cotati profile in the* Official Handbook of the Marvel Universe A-Z Vol. 2 *trade paperback (2011).* When the insidious techno-organic Phalanx race attacked the Kree Empire in their quest for domination, hybrid Kree hero Quasar (Phyla-Vell) was forced to flee to a Kree fringe world. There she found the pacifist Priests of Pama tending to a plantlike Cotati elder whose entire body formed a peaceful sanctuary and whose exposed roots and trunks provided accommodation and limited walled defenses for the priests and their guests. Even after reuniting with her lover, Moondragon (Heather Douglas), Quasar was troubled by recent conflicts. When the Cotati elder telepathically linked with Quasar, Moondragon, and a Pama Priest to help ease Quasar's negative emotions, they discovered the extent of the Phalanx threat as well as the opportunity to counter it through the reborn, genetically engineered Adam Warlock. However, within hours, the Phalanx, aided by the android Super-Adaptoid, who had been infected with a techno-organic virus, burned the Cotati elder, fatally wounding it and killing the priests. The information gained through the Cotati's telepathy eventually helped defeat the Phalanx. Sometime after the war, an individual Cotati named Trrunk (who was apparently separated from the usually pacifist Cotati collective) on the planet Kree-Pama was cosmically chosen as one of the four Kree Heralds for the planet's impending White Event. The event would replace Earth with Kree-Pama as the heart of Eternity (the cosmic embodiment of reality) and empower the Kree Va-Sohn with the Starbrand (Kree-Pama's planetary defense system). This replacement would restore cosmic balance but also destroy Earth. Trrunk's role was that of Justice, acting as the Starbrand's conscience. Together with two other Heralds, the Nightmask (Mar-Sohn, Va-Sohn's brother) and Cipher (Joras-Kyl), Trrunk searched for Va-Sohn. Va-Sohn sought to protect only Kree at all costs, and she destroyed Trrunk and Mar-Sohn, as she did not want any interference with her extremist and lethal work making the Kree Empire reign supreme. Her efforts to destroy Earth were ultimately foiled by Earth's Starbrand (Kevin Connor) and Nightmask (Adam Blackveil). Later, the Kree Bel-Dann and the Skrull Raksor, agents of the Kree/Skrull Alliance living on Earth, had uncovered an apparent Cotati presence on Earth but were murdered before being able to act on their findings, leaving behind a cryptic message: "Beware the trees."

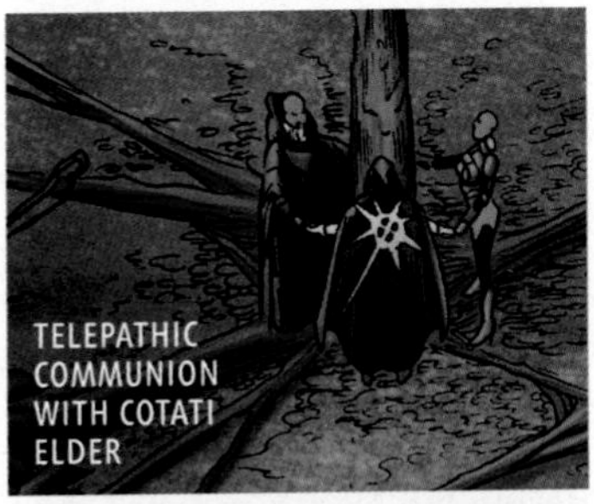

TELEPATHIC COMMUNION WITH COTATI ELDER

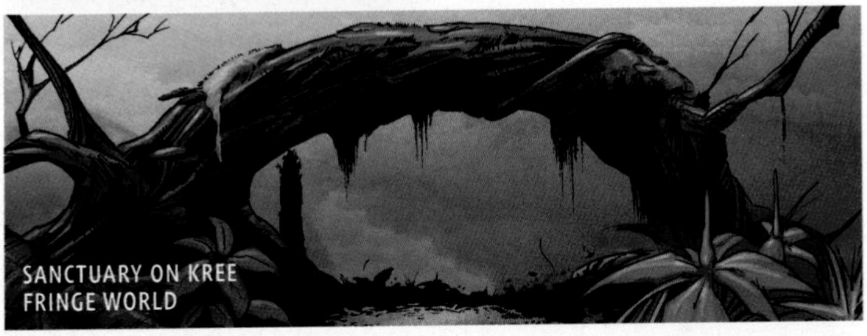

SANCTUARY ON KREE FRINGE WORLD

KNOWN MEMBERS *UPDATE*:
Trrunk

BASE OF OPERATIONS *UPDATE*:
Possibly Earth, an unidentified Kree fringe world

TRAITS *UPDATE*:
The Cotati elder on the Kree fringe world had mutated its form to become a series of incredibly large, twisted, interconnected, and hollow trees, which supported accommodation. Trrunk, another Cotati that had cosmically separated from the collective, appeared to gain independent thought and identity (including a name).

FIRST APPEARANCE *UPDATE*:
(Cotati elder): *Annihilation: Conquest—Quasar #1* (2007); (Trrunk): *Starbrand & Nightmask #4* (2016)

ART BY MIKE LILLY, VALERIO SCHITI, & DOMO STANTON

FANTASTIC FOUR

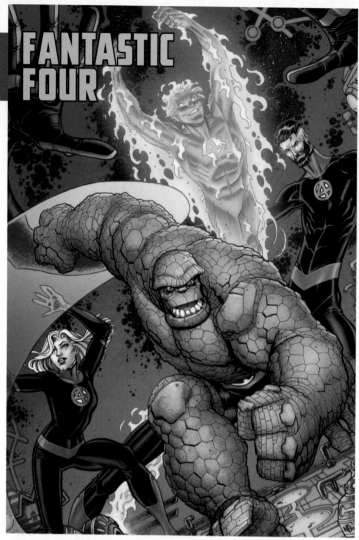

HISTORY *UPDATE*: *Continued from the Future Foundation profile in FF: 50 Fantastic Years (2011).* Throughout their conflict with the Interdimensional Council of Reeds, the Future Foundation (FF) became embroiled in a number of unrelated threats. There was an invasion of Earth by the fear-mongering Asgardian Cul the Serpent, whose minion Angrir, Breaker of Souls, briefly took possession of the Thing (Ben Grimm). The team also helped against a pandemic engineered by the Queen (Ana Soria) and aided the mutant X-Men in responding to an interdimensional distress call received by James Scully (Skull the Slayer). During this time, the FF remained unaware Annihilus had resurrected the Human Torch (Johnny Storm) as a gladiator for sport in the Negative Zone.

Alongside other gladiators, the Torch fostered a rebellion that succeeded when the Torch seized the Cosmic Control Rod away from Annihilus.

Shortly after, the council's machinations caused the War of Four Cities to erupt between the Lost City of the High Evolutionary (Herbert Wyndham), the Old Kingdom of Atlantis, the Inhumans' Universal City, and a city created out of the Negative Zone's former Prison 42. This war was inflamed when the Inhumans from Earth and four other extraterrestrial races (the Universal Inhumans) joined the fray. Though the FF's Mister Fantastic (Reed Richards) finally enlisted the aid of New York's heroes against the Council, a Kree armada, on the order of a reborn Supreme Intelligence, attacked New

York City in rebellion against the Inhumans' rule of the Kree Empire. As the gathered heroes resisted the invasion, Valeria, the super-genius daughter of the FF's Reed and Invisible Woman (Susan Richards), was directed by her time-traveling grandfather Nathaniel Richards to lead the FF's Special Class students to teleport themselves and the Baxter Building's top three floors to safety in Latveria. In New York, the Human Torch emerged from the FF's Negative Zone portal, now in command of Annihilus' armies. Elsewhere while protecting the FF students from Mad Celestials of Reality-10235 who wanted to destroy every Reed Richards in the Multiverse, Doctor Doom (Victor Von Doom) was believed killed, though Valeria knew he still lived but did not reveal this to anyone. Despite aid from the Torch's forces, the Inhumans, and the world-consuming Galactus (Galan), whom the FF's Reed summoned, the Kree only withdrew when the Mad Celestials arrived in Earth's atmosphere, intent on killing Reed. Both Galactus and the use of the council's Sol's Anvil weapon proved futile against the Mad Celestials, but the arrival of an adult Franklin Richards (the son of Reality-10235's Reed and Susan) turned the tide when he bolstered his own powers with energies from his younger Reality-616 counterpart and destroyed the Mad Celestials. The Torch rejoined the team—which re-assumed the Fantastic Four (F4) name and iconography, granting numbered uniforms to the Special Class as well (who continued using the Future Foundation name)—while Spider-Man (Peter Parker) resigned his full-time involvement. Hoping to establish democracy, the Torch allowed free elections to decide the Negative Zone's next ruler; Annihilus won by a landslide write-in vote.

During a time-travel excursion to prehistoric Earth, the F4 were exposed to a flare sent through space and time by an alternate F4 of a so-called "Doomed Universe." This

F4 sent the essence of their powers into the Multiverse to prevent them from being misused by their Earth's rulers: Doctor Doom, Annihilus and Kang. Exposure to this F4's powers caused the powers of Reality-616's F4 to "overload." Detecting the overload as a degradation of his cellular structure and rightly fearful that his teammates were similarly affected, Reed proposed an educational vacation through space and time for the F4 and his children using the Torch's Negative Zone flagship, *Pestilence*, that would allow Reed to secretly research a cure. Assembling a replacement F4 composed of Ant-Man (Scott Lang), the Inhuman Medusa, She-Hulk (Jen Walters), and the Torch's girlfriend, Darla Deering—who utilized a Thing exoskeleton as Miss Thing—to safeguard the FF Special Class, the Richards family departed, visiting multiple worlds and periods in Earth's history while Reed attempted to develop a cure for the ailment. His teammates

and children eventually learned of the trip's true purpose, earning their justifiable irritation, but they eventually set aside their hurt feelings to mutually search for a cure. The Human Torch of the Doomed Universe's future brought the F4 to his past, where his teammates restored the abilities of both teams and defeated the alternate Doom, who had absorbed the abilities of Kang and Annihilus. Upon their return home, Valeria, still angry with Reed, left home to live with Doctor Doom, her godfather, in Latveria. After Ant-Man's team disbanded, Richards' team changed their uniform design to a red-and-black motif.

The Quiet Man, a scientist harboring a years-long grudge against Reed for robbing him of his opportunity to pursue a relationship with Susan, enacted a scheme to ruin the F4's public image. Aided by his vast financial and political networks and through

alliances with the evil genius Wizard (Bentley Wittman) and the emotion-manipulating Psycho-Man, the Quiet Man corrupted the pocket universe created by Franklin Richards during the Onslaught crisis, enslaved that universe's heroic Avengers, and turned the reality's populace into a winged insectoid army. By triggering a failure of one of Reed Richards' interdimensional portals, the Quiet Man unleashed his insectoids on New York and then set forth a chain of events that robbed the Torch of his powers and saw the team convicted of reckless endangerment—leading to the seizure of the team's assets and the relocation of Franklin, Valeria, and the FF Special Class into S.H.I.E.L.D. custody. He also framed the Thing for the murder of the Puppet Master (Phillip Masters) by luring him into a room with the pocket universe's Puppet Master's corpse, while the Psycho-Man also awakened Susan's repressed Malice persona at inopportune

SPACE-TIME VOYAGE UNIFORMS

REPLACEMENT TEAM (RED AND BLUE UNIFORMS, FROM LEFT): MEDUSA, ANT-MAN, SHE-HULK, MISS THING

occasions, making Valeria fearful of her. The team and their allies, including Ant-Man's substitute F4, Spider-Man, and Wyatt Wingfoot, noticed a design behind the team's troubles when Reed and the Special Class were taken prisoner by the Quiet Man and his Avengers and the Wizard used Franklin's powers to expand the pocket universe to start a global invasion. The team — donning new blue uniforms from Susan — and their allies, now including the Special Class' S.H.I.E.L.D. guardian Jim Hammond (the android Human Torch) and dream guardian Sleepwalker, divided their resources between combatting the insectoids and entering the pocket universe, where Franklin was able to destroy the universe from within. The energies released from its destruction restored the Torch's powers. The F4 was exonerated from all wrongdoings, though the Quiet Man escaped.

In preparation for an imminent incursion with Reality-1610 that would annihilate both universes, Reed constructed interdimensional "life rafts" to carry survivors into what thereafter remained of reality. On the day of the final incursion, only two life rafts survived the cataclysm: Reed's, which carried the rest of the F4, his children, Spider-Man, Thor (Jane Foster), Captain Marvel (Carol Danvers), Star-Lord (Peter Quill), Cyclops (Scott Summers), and the FF Special Class. Another raft commandeered by Namor the Sub-Mariner held his Cabal (including the mad Titan Thanos and Reality-1610's evil counterpart to Reed Richards, the Maker), who had stopped multiple incursions by pre-emptively destroying universes. As the ships launched, however, the section of the life raft carrying Reed's teammates, family, and the FF broke off when struck by lightning, and all aboard were incinerated. As Reed and his passengers lay in stasis for the next eight years, Doctor Doom used the powers of the extraterrestrial Beyonders and the matter-shaping Molecule Man (Owen Reece) to craft Battleworld, a patchwork planet comprising fragments of destroyed realities, with himself installed as its emperor and deity. He created versions of Susan, Franklin and Valeria Richards who considered him their family patriarch. He resurrected the Torch as the planet's living sun and the Thing as the Shield, an immobile living wall separating Battleworld's more volatile regions from those more civilized. Unbeknownst to Doom, Doctor Stephen Strange, whom Doom appointed his sheriff, had kept Reed's life raft secreted in his home, while the Cabal's life raft was discovered by the Future Foundation, a science ministry led by Doom's replica of Valeria. After the occupants of the life raft hidden by Strange were freed and Doom discovered his treachery, Doom killed Strange but blamed the Reality-616 survivors. However, Valeria doubted Doom's version of events. Reed's fellow survivors and the Cabal allied to destabilize Battleworld and learn its origins, leading to a confrontation between Doom and Reed, wherein Reed succeeded in getting Doom to admit Reed could have crafted a better world. With Doom's power subsequently taken from him by the Molecule Man and given to Reed, Battleworld exploded, but Reed survived and resurrected his wife, children, and the FF Special Class. Reunited with his loved ones, Reed employed the Molecule Man's and Franklin's abilities to rebuild the Multiverse, beginning with the Prime Universe, a re-creation of Reality-616 with elements introduced from other realities. As a parting gift to Doom, Reed restored Doom's facial features and urged him to find a new purpose.

Earth's population, including the Thing, believed the Richards family and FF Special Class to be dead. Grimm joined the Guardians of the Galaxy and later S.H.I.E.L.D. The Torch, refusing to believe the Richards family dead, also found new heroic alliances with the Avengers Unity Squad and the Inhumans. Doom began a new life as a semi-benevolent sorcerer and even became a substitute Iron Man following Tony Stark's descent into a comatose state, but

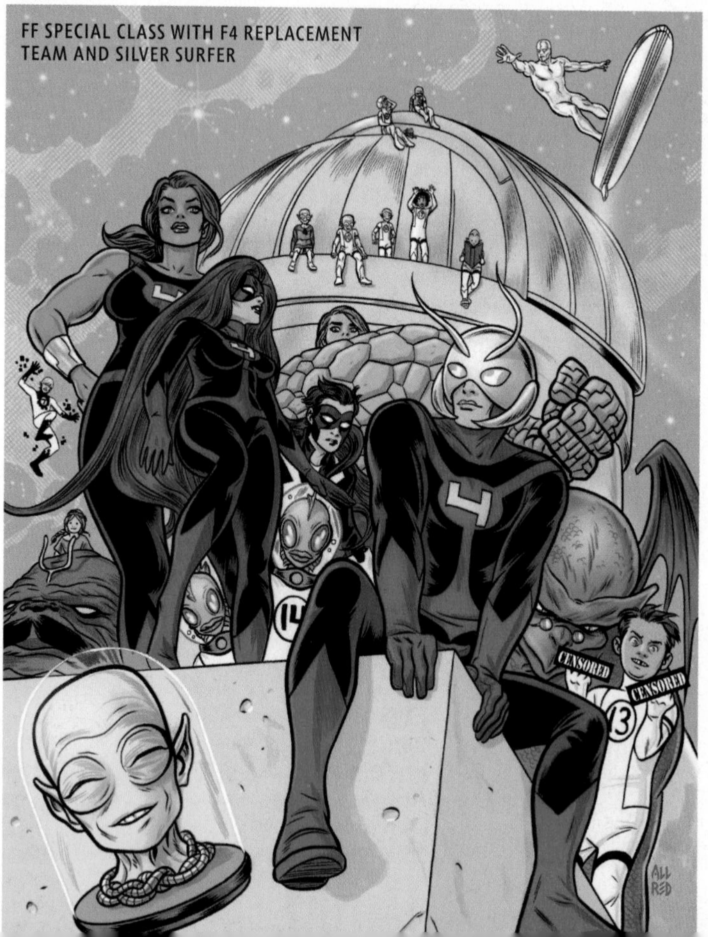
CENSORED
CENSORED
FF SPECIAL CLASS WITH F4 REPLACEMENT TEAM AND SILVER SURFER

he ultimately returned to villainous form. During a later sojourn of multiple alternate realities using Reed's Multisect device, the Thing hoped the Torch would shake his belief that the Richards family still lived, but the Torch remained steadfast. During this time, the team's powers proved unstable due to their extended separation. Peter Parker, then Parker Industries (PI) C.E.O., purchased the Baxter Building, both to use as PI's New York headquarters and to hold on to the building for the Richards family, should they return, but PI's collapse resulted in the building's purchase by another super-team, the Fantastix.

Time passed more quickly for the Richards family and the FF Special Class during their re-creation of the Multiverse, with Franklin and Valeria growing into adolescence and assuming the respective codenames of Powerhouse and Brainstorm over the five years of their travels. Powerhouse and the Molecule Man created hundreds of new universes, earning the enmity of the Griever, a self-described embodiment of entropy infuriated by their reconstruction efforts. When Powerhouse became unable to create new realities, the Griever discorporated the Molecule Man and pursued the Richards family and their students throughout the Multiverse, destroying each new universe through which they passed. When Reed taunted the Griever with the notion that she couldn't defeat the F4's full roster, she arrogantly gave him a device to allow him to gather them, unprepared for Reed's summoning of not only the Human Torch and the Thing but also all of the team's former members. After driving off the Griever and learning of the Thing's engagement to Alicia Masters, the team returned their comrades to Earth, leaving Alex Power in charge of the Future Foundation, who chose to search for any remaining molecule of the Molecule Man instead of returning to Earth.

Once on Earth, the reunited F4 assented to the Fantastix's ownership of the Baxter Building and moved into the Thing's brownstone at 4 Yancy Street, which Reed and Valeria modified through dimensional engineering to house a massive base of operations that maintained the brownstone's smaller exterior size. The family then traveled to Benson, Arizona, home of the Thing's Uncle Jake and Aunt Petunia, for the Thing and Masters' wedding. Though a broadcast by Doctor Doom announcing that Galactus had arrived in Latveria disrupted the ceremony, Reed activated a device that froze time outside the altar for four minutes, allowing the wedding to commence unabated. The F4 then traveled to Latveria to face not only Doom and Galactus but Doom's new disciple, Victorious. Doom empowered himself and Latveria with Galactus' energies, captured the F4, and ordered their execution for violating Latverian sovereignty,

but the team escaped with the use of a teleportation device Valeria built out of Jake's truck. Despite their appreciation for Valeria's aid, the F4 were displeased to learn that she and Franklin took apart Jake's truck without permission and that Franklin, suffering from depression and nightmares over the universes the Griever destroyed, had disobeyed and disrespected Alicia while in her care. The two were consigned to volunteer at a nearby community center, where the Thing noticed Franklin and Valeria's unease since returning from Multiversal space. The Thing decided to organize a block party to let the two get acquainted with their new neighborhood, but the party was disrupted by an invasion of trolls attacking New York as part of the global invasion of Earth led by the Dark Elf Malekith. Recognizing that the trolls were drawn to an enhanced communications antennae created by Valeria, Franklin destroyed it, driving the creatures off.

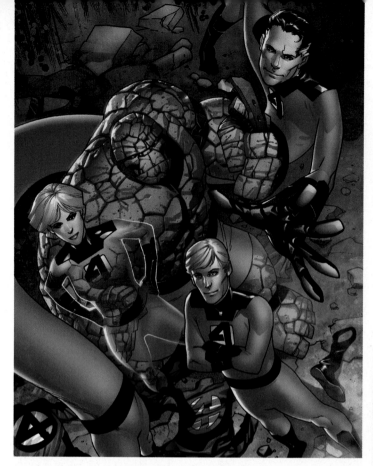

Spyrean hero Sky (Kaila), who, after being identified by Spyrean technology as the Human Torch's soul mate, relocated to Earth so they could be together. Soon after, Mister Fantastic was asked to assist in a mysterious murder investigation with the only clue a hexadecimal code. After recognizing the corpse as the Kree warrior Bel-Dann, Mister Fantastic realized the code was a cypher that translated into "beware the trees." Wrongly assuming Bel-Dann's former adversary Raksor to be the murderer, Mister Fantastic and other heroes confronted him only to witness his death as a rapidly expanding tree ripped Raksor apart from within; his dying words were "empires will fall." ✎

After the Grimms returned from their honeymoon, which was disrupted by a Puppet Master-controlled Hulk (Bruce Banner), the team dealt with the Urchin, an infectious fungi native to the extradimensional K'un-Lun realm that enveloped the majority of New York's inhabitants, including Reed, Susan, and the Torch. Allying with New York's remaining uninfected heroes, Grimm helped free the populace from the Urchin, which Reed contained within a Vibranium-reinforced terrarium. The team then fought off an invasion of the Negative Zone by the forces of the Cancerverse, including their own Cancerverse counterparts, who destroyed themselves when they viewed the Torch's memories of their happier lives.

Later, the team attended the installation of the *Marvel-1*, the spacecraft that carried them on the flight that empowered them, as an exhibit at the Air and Space Museum. Inspired by the exhibit, Reed and the Torch constructed

the *Marvel-2*, an improvement on the original design. On its maiden flight, the team traveled to the *Marvel-1*'s intended destination, an Earthlike planet called Spyre, for whose populace the F4 were a fabled band of alien invaders dubbed "the Four-Told." The team learned that planetary leader, Revos the Overseer, had not only been experimenting with cosmic radiation on his own people — resulting in the creation of super-beings and monstrous mutates, the latter consigned to life underground — but that Revos had intensified the cosmic ray storm through which the *Marvel-1* had flown in an attempt to destroy the ship, only to bestow the F4 with their powers. Initially angered by Revos' actions, Reed made peace with him and agreed to help him better master cosmic radiation. Reed also provided Spyre's people the formula that allowed the Thing to annually regain human form so Spyre could repair its society. The F4 thereafter returned to Earth, accompanied by the winged

MEMBERS *UPDATE*:

MISS THING (DARLA DEERING)
Active: *Fantastic Four #2* (2013)
ICEMAN (BOBBY DRAKE)
Active: Unchronicled, mentioned as formerly active in *Fantastic Four #3* (2019)

- -

ACTIVE MEMBERS *UPDATE*: Human Torch (Johnny Storm), Invisible Woman (Sue Richards), Mister Fantastic (Reed Richards), Thing (Ben Grimm)
FORMER MEMBERS *UPDATE*:
(F4) Iceman (Bobby Drake), Miss Thing (Darla Deering); (FF) Human Torch (Johnny Storm), Invisible Woman (Susan Richards), Mister Fantastic (Reed Richards), Doctor Doom (Victor Von Doom), Franklin Richards, Valeria Richards, Spider-Man (Spider-Man), Thing (Ben Grimm)
BASE OF OPERATIONS *UPDATE*:
Grimm residence, 4 Yancy Street, Lower East Side, Manhattan; formerly the Baxter Building
NOTE: When Reed transported all past F4 members to help battle the Griever, the assemblage included the X-Man Iceman (Bobby Drake), who claimed the team granted him membership during an as-yet-undocumented adventure involving Namor. As revealed in *Avengers #10* (2019), the Wolverine who assisted the F4's battle against the Griever was in actuality a Wolverine from the future of Reality-14412 who was empowered by the Phoenix Force.

_____

ART BY ARTHUR ADAMS, MICHAEL ALLRED, MARK BAGLEY, NICK BRADSHAW, & LEONARD KIRK

HULKLING

HISTORY *UPDATE*: *Continued from the Hulkling profile in the* Official Handbook of the Marvel Universe A-Z Vol. 5 *trade paperback (2012).* During the Skrulls' secret invasion of Earth, the hybrid Hulkling was marked for death by fanatical Skrull invaders but escaped with the aid of the Young Avengers' occasional allies, the teenage Runaways and their Skrull member, Xavin. Together with his teammates, Hulkling joined dozens of Earth's heroes and villains in a Central Park battle with the Skrull invasion force, eventually defeating them. After criminal mastermind Norman Osborn killed the Skrull Queen Veranke, the public lionized him. He was given the reins of America's super-human infrastructure, replacing the disgraced S.H.I.E.L.D. organization with H.A.M.M.E.R. and forcing Hulkling and his teammates even further underground. As Osborn's dark reign began, Hulkling and his teammates encountered a new team of young vigilantes that had also claimed the title of Young Avengers. Though Hulkling and Wiccan befriended one member of the team, Enchantress (Sylvie Lushton), all of the team was deemed dangerously unstable. Eventually, the other team betrayed the original Young Avengers to Osborn and his secretly evil Avengers team. Chaos ensued, with the new Young Avengers dubbing themselves the Young Masters and escaping while Hulkling and the original Young Avengers reached a stalemate with Osborn's team.

Hulkling and his teammates later joined a massive gathering of the true Avengers in opposing the Unspoken, a deposed Inhuman monarch who wished to enslave all of humanity, and helped their friend Nomad (Rikki Barnes) quell a riot induced by the subversive Secret Empire. When Osborn besieged Asgard, then located outside of Broxton, Oklahoma, Hulkling and his teammates aided the Avengers to publicly defeat and expose Osborn, who was then deposed. When unrest over his missing mother, the Scarlet Witch (Wanda Maximoff), led Wiccan to travel to Latveria, Hulkling and his teammates followed and found themselves embroiled in a plan enacted by Doctor Doom (Victor Von Doom) to usurp the Witch's power and attain godhood. The Scarlet Witch was ultimately liberated, but Doom's wrath resulted in the apparent death of Hulkling's teammate Stature (Cassie Lang) and the destruction of Vision (Jonas). Traumatized and saddened by the experience, Hulkling and Wiccan quit super-heroics, choosing to focus on their personal lives and their relationship. A guilt-ridden Wiccan isolated himself for months until Hulkling proposed marriage. Soon afterward, the Young Avengers were all named honorary Avengers.

AVENGERS IDEA MECHANICS
OUTFIT (WITH WICCAN)

(David Alleyne). When they accidentally ended up in Mother's void-like home dimension, Hulkling and Prodigy became trapped and shared a kiss while separated from the team. When their teammates rescued them, Hulkling told Wiccan that he needed to take a break from their relationship and left the team. Eschewing heroics, Hulkling began seeing a therapist, unaware she was a projection of Loki's subconscious. Eventually, Hulkling was captured by Mother and returned to her home dimension, where she agonizingly reshaped him into a living throne for herself. The Young Avengers mounted a rescue of Hulkling, who realized the love he felt for Wiccan was true, no matter the origin. Hulkling happily resumed his relationship with Wiccan. Buoyed by Hulkling's love, Wiccan marshaled the magical strength to defeat Mother at last.

Later, when an attempted heist of the eyes of the deceased all-seeing Uatu the Watcher resulted in the citizens of Manhattan being buffeted by Uatu's knowledge, Hulkling and his Young Avengers teammates Marvel Boy and Prodigy leaped into the fray to help stem the chaos. They found a tenement building occupied by drug addicts, whose already addled minds allowed them to absorb vast amounts of knowledge, causing the addicts extreme distress. However, deposed crime lord the Hood (Parker Robbins) had also found the addicts. Claiming to be looking for a cure for his ailing mother, he enlisted the trio to help him build a device to extract the knowledge from the addicts; however, the Hood also wanted to build a blackmail file to assist his criminal endeavors. When the Hood betrayed the heroes, Prodigy encrypted the data before the Hood could use it; the Hood subsequently escaped.

The urge to do good nagged at the kindhearted Hulkling, however, and he began sneaking out at night to fight crime, impersonating other heroes with his shape-shifting abilities to avoid detection. When Wiccan eventually discovered Hulkling's activities, a rift formed between the two. In an attempt to reconcile (and unaware he was being manipulated by a young incarnation of the Asgardian God of Mischief Loki Laufeyson, who wanted to control someone destined to have great influence over magic), Wiccan tried to summon Hulkling's foster mother moments before her death. Instead, he accidentally summoned the extradimensional shape-shifting parasite Mother, who infested parents and bent them to her will. Fleeing Mother and her minions, Hulkling and Wiccan acquired allies to form a new Young Avengers team, including Hawkeye (Kate Bishop), her extraterrestrial Kree boyfriend, Marvel Boy (Noh-Varr), Loki and the dimension-hopping America Chavez. During their battle with Mother, Loki noted Hulkling was almost too perfect a boyfriend for Wiccan and suggested Wiccan's powers may have created Hulkling or influenced his feelings, sending Wiccan into an existential crisis. Hulkling and his teammates soon fled New York to protect their loved ones from Mother, spending several months adventuring through space and around the globe, also gaining a new member with Prodigy

DRAWING THE STAR-SWORD

held them off, giving Wiccan the chance to summon the willpower to expel Moridun.

When longtime Avengers ally Rick Jones was arrested by S.H.I.E.L.D. for leaking information about their unethical Cosmic Cube experiments, Sunspot put Hulkling and the team to a vote on whether to liberate Jones from custody. When Hulkling, Wiccan, and teammate Squirrel Girl (Doreen Green) voted against direct action, they were immediately dismissed from the team and teleported away. As they attempted to assess their situation, they were joined by Hawkeye (Clint Barton), who left the team shortly after they did. Deciding to live up to the Avengers name, the foursome began crimefighting in New York, clashing with the felonious Plunderer (Parnival Plunder) and, alongside other heroes, battling a massive Celestial Destructor. Soon afterward, Sunspot called them back to repel an attack by the Maker (Reality-1610's corrupt counterpart to Reed Richards/Mister Fantastic) and his New

After billionaire super hero Sunspot (Roberto Da Costa) bought the subversive scientific organization A.I.M. (Advanced Idea Mechanics) and transformed it into the benevolent Avengers Idea Mechanics, he recruited Wiccan, Hulkling and several other heroes into their super-heroic division. Operating out of A.I.M's own island, Hulkling and Wiccan were soon abducted by the Knights of the Infinite, a society of fellow Kree-Skrull hybrids who believed Hulkling to be the reincarnation of their founder, Dorrek Supreme. Humoring them, Hulkling cooperated but was surprised when he withdrew the Star-Sword from the Light of Truth, fulfilling their prophecy. Unknown to all, the knights' leader, M'ryn the Magus, had been secretly possessed by the horrific alien wizard Moridun, who had orchestrated Hulkling's abduction as a way to bring Wiccan into his presence; Moridun successfully possessed Wiccan. After Hulkling and Wiccan returned to Earth, Moridun remained undetected

within Wiccan until King Hulk (a counterpart of Hulkling) and the future Avengers of Reality-15061 (where Moridun had fully seized control of Wiccan) came to kill Wiccan before he could become the horrific Demiurge. Unwilling to let Wiccan die, Hulkling and his A.I.M. division teammates

WITH WICCAN

AS EMPEROR

Revengers. Hulkling defeated the Revenger Paibok the Power Skrull then took Sunspot's form to foil a S.H.I.E.L.D. assassination attempt. To repay Hulkling and Wiccan for their troubles in his service, Sunspot bought them an apartment in New York City.

The duo largely steered clear of super-heroics for a time, although they helped combat the Frost Giant invasion of New York and mooted a Young Avengers reunion while catching up with their old teammates. Wiccan, longing for a return to the excitement of the Avengers, viewed a number of possible futures where the Young Avengers allied with an advanced robotic Death's Head prototype dubbed "Vee." When Wiccan stole Vee from his creator, obsessive roboticist Dr. Evelyn Necker, Hulkling became frustrated that he was once again drawn into a dangerous situation. Hulkling nevertheless joined Wiccan and Kate Bishop

to deal with Vee's progenitor, the freelance peacekeeping agent Death's Head and Necker herself. Ultimately, Necker and Death's Head embarked on a partnership of their own while Vee became Billy and Hulkling's new roommate.

Later, apparently having accepted his perceived destiny, Hulkling united the warring Kree and Skrull empires, serving as their new emperor and taking on his birth name, Dorrek VIII. Putting aside his distaste for a number of his new allies, including the Super-Skrull (Kl'rt), who had killed his foster mother, Hulkling led the combined races on a mission to Earth to face a menace that apparently threatened Kree and Skrull alike. 🪐

OCCUPATION *UPDATE*: Emperor
KNOWN RELATIVES *UPDATE*:
Billy Kaplan (Wiccan, fiancé), Minister Marvel (cousin, deceased), Marvel Mind (first cousin once removed, deceased); numerous ancestors through the Dorrek line, including Dorrek I, Soh-Larr, and Ryga'a (distant relatives, all deceased)
GROUP AFFILIATION *UPDATE*:
The Kree/Skrull Alliance, Avengers (honorary); formerly Avengers Idea Mechanics, Young Avengers
ABILITIES/ACCESSORIES *UPDATE*:
Hulkling is apparently immune to pheromones. He wields the Star-Sword, a magical sword capable of firing cosmic energy blasts and absorbing and dispelling magical energy — Hulkling can summon it at will.

① ② ③ ④ ⑤ ⑥ ⑦

INTELLIGENCE

STRENGTH

SPEED

DURABILITY

**ENERGY PROJECTION
[WITH THE STAR-SWORD]**

FIGHTING SKILLS

ART BY JIM CHEUNG, JAMIE McKELVIE, PACO MEDINA, HUMBERTO RAMOS, VALERIO SCHITI, DECLAN SHALVEY

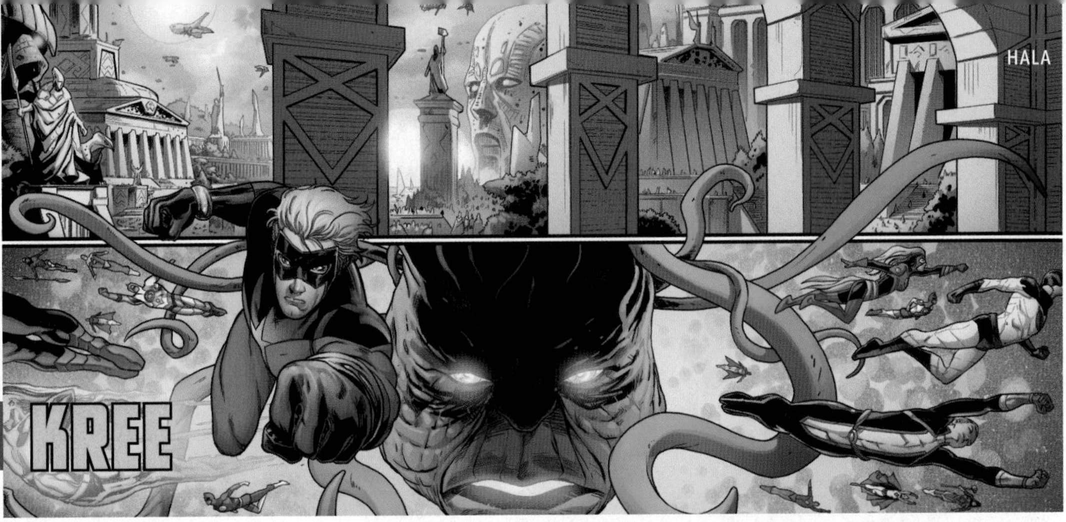
HALA

KREE

HISTORY *UPDATE*: *Continued from the Kree profile in the* Official Handbook of the Marvel Universe A-Z Vol. 6 *hardcover (2009).* 66 million years ago, a Kree Accuser and troops fought a Starbrand-empowered Tyrannosaurus rex on Earth, presumably via time travel. Millennia ago, the Kree Supreme Intelligence (SI) abruptly halted the Kree Empire's program to create a race of subservient super-beings through experimentation on other species across the universe when he learned from a religious leader within his hive mind of a prophecy that one such super-being would eventually revolt and destroy the SI. In his haste to execute the scientists involved and exterminate the test-bed species, the SI unwittingly spared five of the subject species, each of which would spawn a race of Inhumans—the Badoon, the Centaurians, the Dire Wraiths, the Kymellians and the humans of Earth. The SI also created and entrusted to its head Accuser a Supremor Seed, which, when bonded with living minds, would re-create the SI in the event of its destruction. The Kree later created the God's Whisper, a device that could psionically enthrall beings of cosmic power, but their test subject, the Asgardian Balder the Brave, freed himself and hid the Whisper on Earth.

At some point during the Kree/Skrull War, Kree ultra-warrior Soh-Larr and Skrull war-queen Ryga'a fell in love and vanished. The pair's rumored offspring, Dorrek Supreme, later founded the Knights of the Infinite, a heroic order of Kree-Skrull hybrids dedicated to uniting the two races. Later, in Earth's 20th century, Kree captain Mari-Ell crashed on Earth during a survey mission and fell in love with her rescuer, widower Joseph Danvers. Renaming herself Marie, Mari-Ell renounced the Kree and married Danvers, with whom she later bore a daughter. Marie named the child both Car-Ell ("champion" in Kree) and the human name Carol Susan Jane Danvers.

In recent years, Earth's Inhumans relocated their city-ship of Attilan to Hala and declared their monarch, Black Bolt (Blackagar Boltagon), ruler of the Kree Empire. Then-leader Ronan peacefully ceded his office, out of both weariness of politics and love for Black Bolt's sister-in-law Crystal (Crystalia Amaquelin), whose hand in marriage Ronan took as part of the Kree-Inhuman alliance against the Skrulls. Despite the Inhumans' promises to accelerate Kree evolution through Terrigenesis, the Kree proved immune to the Terrigen Mist's mutative effects. The Inhuman monarchy became divisive for the Kree, with some resorting to acts of terrorism in protest. The Shi'ar Empire and its power-mad Earth mutant ruler Vulcan (Gabriel Summers), angered that the Inhumans granted political asylum to the deposed Shi'ar empress Lilandra Neramani, attacked Hala during Ronan and Crystal's wedding. In response, the Inhumans declared war on the Shi'ar, causing anti-Inhuman sentiment among the Kree to grow into open revolt, but the genuine concern and care Crystal displayed for those wounded in the attack, including Ronan, warmed the Kree to the Inhumans. Bolstered by Inhuman technology and labor, the Kree and Inhumans achieved a pyrrhic victory — the use of an Inhuman-made Terrigen Bomb decimated much of the Shi'ar armada but also created the Fault, a growing tear in the fabric of space-time light-years in size. The Kree later allied with other star-faring armadas to battle the Many-Angled Ones, a Reality-10011 race of celestial demons using the Fault as a gateway. Though the Fault was eventually sealed, the Kree lost nearly half their fleet in the effort.

The Inhumans again angered the Kree when Black Bolt, spurred by a genetic compulsion to unite the Inhumans of other species in the universe, ordered Attilan to return to Earth, leaving Ronan as regent. Urged by his people and supported by Crystal, Ronan used the Supremor Seed and a pair of alternate-universe versions of Earth scientist Mister Fantastic (Reed Richards) to spawn a new SI, who immediately ordered a genocidal attack on Earth in retaliation against the Inhumans, an action only halted by the sudden arrival of the Reality-4280 Mad Celestials. On the suggestion of an adult

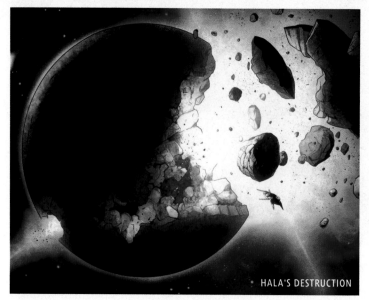
HALA'S DESTRUCTION

teammates by stealing a Phoenix Force energy fragment, thinking the SI could formulate a way to help Earth. He then earned the Kree's enmity when he fled with the fragment after learning the SI was not intending to assist Earth. The fragment was ultimately reclaimed by the angered Avengers.

Later, the Kree allied with a coalition of star-faring races, which included the Avengers, to combat the Builders, a race bent on controlling the evolution of all life. Hala and other worlds fell under Builder rule, but a revolt sparked by Asgardian Avenger Thor Odinson inspired the Kree and other subjugated cultures to fight back and eventually rout the Builders. Following the coalition's victory, the SI dispatched the Accuser Tanalth to locate the God's Whisper by probing the memories of a trio of Earth heroes—Namor the Sub-Mariner, the Human Torch (Jim Hammond) and the Winter Soldier (Bucky Barnes)—who, during World War II, wrested the device from Nazi scientist Baron Wolfgang Von Strucker and hid the three pieces of it around Earth. Despite

version of Richards' son Franklin from Reality-10235, Black Bolt and the SI mutually agreed to end their feud, with the proviso that Ronan return to Hala, effectively ending his marriage to Crystal.

Upon the re-emergence of the Phoenix Force, the feared embodiment of death and rebirth, the Kree used a fragment of the reality-shaping M'Kraan Crystal to procure a sample of the Force's energies, lure the Force to Hala and

resurrect the long-dead defector Mar-Vell as part of the SI's plan to use the Force to accelerate Kree evolution. SI used Mar-Vell's presence and the psionic abilities of his grandnephew Marvel Mind to calm the populace into accepting the Force's arrival. A team of Earth's heroic Avengers that was sent to redirect the Force away from Earth halted the SI's scheme, but one of the team's members, Protector (Noh-Varr of Reality-200080's Kree race), betrayed his

---

AL-VOKK
Politician
FF #6 (2011)

BAR-KONN
Captain, Kree Military;
Alpha Flight
Board of Governors
Captain Marvel #6 (2016)

CADMI-M
Pursuer, Starforce Blue
Marvel Team-Up #5 (2019); (identified) *Marvel Team-Up #6* (2019)

DEA-SEA
Captain, Kree Military
Infinity Countdown: Darkhawk #3 (2018)

DOCTOR EVE
Renegade scientist
Mighty Captain Marvel #4 (2017)

FENN-RA
Reformed anti-Inhuman terrorist
War of Kings: Warriors #2 (2009)

GLAH-REE
(CAPTAIN GLORY)
Ex-captain, Kree Military;
Lethal Legion member
Avengers #676 (2018)

HALA
Accuser
Guardians of the Galaxy #1 (2016)

KAH-REHZ
Mar-Sohn's betrothed
Starbrand and Nightmask #2 (2016)

KAR-VOKK
Lieutenant, Kree Military
Moon Girl and Devil Dinosaur #10 (2016)

LIEV-RA
Fenn-Ra's daughter
War of Kings: Warriors #2 (2009)

MAJOR-L THE ULTIMUS
Judge, Starforce Blue
Marvel Team-Up #5 (2019); (identified) *Marvel Team-Up #6* (2019)

MAR-KOLL
(CAPTAIN MIRACLE)
Salesman
Ms. Marvel Annual #1 (2019)

MAR-SOHN
(NIGHTMASK)
Empowered by Kree-Pama White Event
Starbrand and Nightmask #2 (2016)

MARI-ELL
(MARIE DANVERS)
Former Captain, Kree Intelligence Elite Guard; Carol Danvers' mother
Ms. Marvel #13 (1978)

PRAMA
Captain, Kree Colonial Vanguard
Chaos War: Dead Avengers #2 (2010)

RY-NOOR
Weaponized biologist
FF #6 (2011)

SERULY-N THE SHATTERAX
Detainer, Starforce Blue
Marvel Team-Up #5 (2019); (identified) *Marvel Team-Up #6* (2019)

SINTA
Accuser
Avengers #27 (2012)

SOH-LARR
Ultra-warrior, rumored father of Dorrek Supreme
New Avengers #4 (2016)

STELLA NEGA
Leader of Guardians of the Galaxy of 1016 A.D.
Guardians of Infinity #1 (2016); (identified) *Guardians of Infinity #2* (2016)

STORMRANGER ZO-14
Kree Military
Magnificent Ms. Marvel #5 (2019)

TANALTH
Chief-High Pursuer
All-New Marvel Now! Point One #1 (2014)

the Kree having the Earth Eternal Ikaris under the Whisper's control, the three heroes and their allies—the Vision (Aarkus) and Captain America (Steve Rogers)—halted the SI's plan of using the Whisper to aid the Empire's expansion.

The Kree became embroiled in the search for the Black Vortex, an ancient artifact capable of bestowing immense cosmic power to someone at the price of corrupting their better nature. As the various parties on Hala battled to attain possession of the Vortex, J'son, king of the Spartax Empire, unleashed a strike against Hala that destroyed the planet in his own bid for the Vortex—the SI apparently died in the assault. Though the attack did not cause the Kree's extinction, the Kree Empire fragmented into numerous factions without a central government. Ronan, empowered by the Black Vortex, survived the planet's fall and roamed its surface recording the names of the dead. Several Kree saw fit to visit vengeance on those they considered at fault for Hala's destruction. The Accuser Hala launched an assault on Spartax's current king, J'son's son and former Guardian of the Galaxy Peter Quill (Star-Lord). Va-Sohn, a Kree warrior empowered during a "White Event" to be a cosmically powered Starbrand, sought to destroy Earth as a potential threat to the Kree Empire but was driven off by the human Starbrand Kevin Conner. Another Kree faction exterminated tens of thousands of Inhumans using the Vox, a race of living and dead Inhumans engineered into lethal assassins.

After Earth's Terrigen supply was destroyed, Noh-Varr helped a crew of Inhumans travel to Hala's remains to seek a way to restart the propagation of the Inhuman race. There, Noh-Varr combined the SI's remains with the Plex Seed (what remained of his universe's SI) to create the Plex Intelligence, who began restoring the planet, a sure but slow process estimated to take years. Ronan took little solace in the gesture and was later deemed unfit as one of the "old Kree" by the Kree soldiers who were utilizing the Vox against the Inhumans. They abducted Ronan and began transforming him into a Vox. When Black Bolt encountered Ronan, he honored the Accuser's request to euthanize him. Some time after this, the Plex Intelligence — now called the Extreme Intelligence — dispersed Kree forces across the universe to search for the all-powerful Infinity Stones, hoping to use them to restore the Kree Empire.

Later, upon learning of the Earth-based Kree-Skrull hybrid hero Hulkling (Teddy Altman/Dorrek VIII), the Knights of the Infinite escorted him and his fiancé Wiccan (Billy Kaplan) to their stronghold, Castle Tarnala, in the Andromeda galaxy. There, Hulkling fulfilled their prophecy by retrieving the Star-Sword from its protective energy field, the Light of Truth, establishing him as the future king of the Kree and Skrull Empires. Hulkling later answered a summons by the Kree/Skrull Alliance and assumed its throne, vowing to destroy the Alliance's enemies.

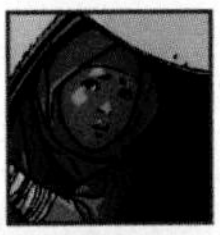

HALA CHILD NINE
("BEAN")
Refugee
Mighty Captain Marvel #1 (2017)

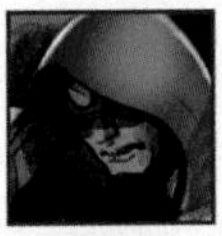

HURAN
Accuser
FF #6 (2011)

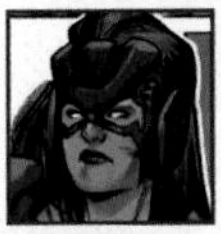

INNDIG-O
Accuser, Starforce Blue
Marvel Team-Up #5 (2019); (identified) *Marvel Team-Up* #6 (2019)

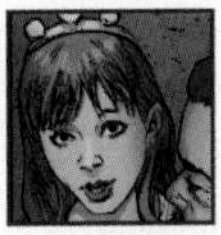

JAL-HA
Witness of the Phoenix's approach to Hala
Secret Avengers #27 (2012)

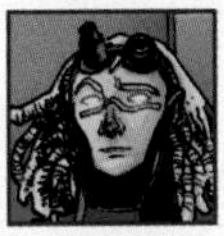

JORAS-KYL
(CIPHER)
Empowered by Kree-Pama White Event
Starbrand and Nightmask #3 (2016)

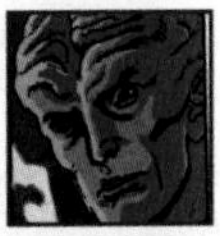

MARVEL MIND
Psionic, Minister Marvel's son
Secret Avengers #26 (2012)

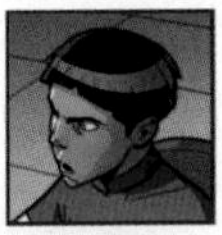

MEL-VARR
(KID KREE)
Would-be super hero
Moon Girl and Devil Dinosaur #7 (2016)

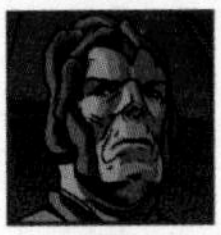

PHIL
Cameraman
Skrull Kill Krew #4 (2009)

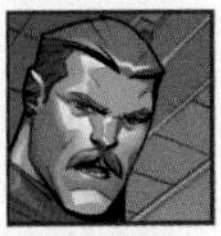

PAD-VARR
General, Kree military; Mel-Varr's father *Moon Girl and Devil Dinosaur* #7 (2016); (identified) *Moon Girl and Devil Dinosaur* #10 (2016)

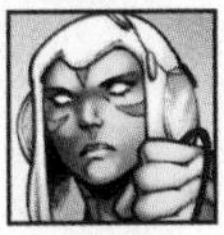

PAM'A
Intelligence Empress
Life of Captain Marvel #3 (2018)

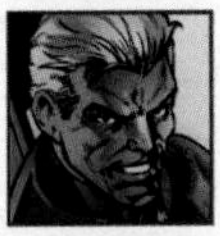

TEL-KAR
Covert operative, prior host of Venom symbiote
Venom: First Host #1 (2018)

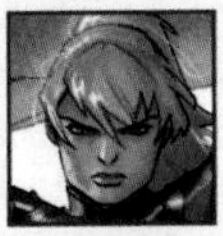

VA-SOHN
(STARBRAND)
Empowered by Kree-Pama White Event
Starbrand and Nightmask #5 (2016)

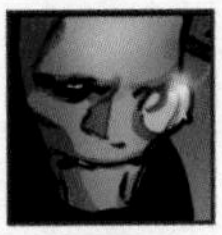

VON-WARR
Science officer
FF #6 (2011)

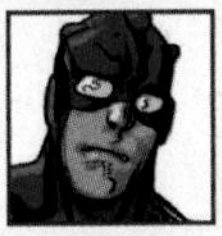

YOND-R
Protector, Starforce Blue
Marvel Team-Up #5 (2019); (named) *Marvel Team-Up* #6 (2019)

KNOWN MEMBERS *UPDATE*: Al-Vokk, Ar-Dann, Bar-Konn, Cadmi-M, Dea-Sea, Doctor Eve, Ell-Vokk, Fenn-Ra, Gar-Nonn, Glah-Ree (Captain Glory), Hala, Hala Child Nine ("Bean"), Huran, Inndig-O, Jal-Ha, Jan-Takk, Joras-Kyl (Cipher), Kah-Rehz, Kar-Vokk, Liev-Ra, Major-L, Mar-Koll (Captain Miracle), Mar-Sohn (Nightmask), Mari-Ell (Marie Danvers), Marvel Mind, Mel-Varr (Kid Kree), Minister Marvel, Pad-Varr, Pam'a, Prama, Ry-Noor, Seruly-N, Sinta, Stella Nega, Stormranger 20-14, Tanalth, Va-Sohn (Starbrand), Vay-Larr, Vok-Larr, Von-Warr, Yond-R, Yva-Larr

KNOWN HYBRIDS *UPDATE*: Car-Ell (Carol Danvers, Captain Marvel), K'kyy, Lan-Zarr, M'ryn the Magus, Mur-G'nn

BASE OF OPERATIONS *UPDATE*: Various colony worlds; formerly Hala, Pama System, Great Magellanic Cloud Galaxy

TRAITS *UPDATE*: Kree are immune to the mutative effects of Terrigen crystals.

ART BY VALERIO SCHITI

MANTIS

MANTIS' SHIP

HISTORY *UPDATE* **:** *Continued from the Mantis profile in the* Annihilation Conquest Omnibus *hardcover (2015).* Leaving her civilian life on Rigel-7, Mantis joined the Knowhere Corps, a peacekeeping force on the space station Knowhere. The severed head of a Celestial serves as a port of call from the edge of the known universe to realms beyond. Alongside her teammates Bug, Cosmo, Moondragon (Heather Douglas), and the Majesdanian Prism, Mantis intervened in a battle on Knowhere between the Guardians of the Galaxy and the criminal Yotat, whom the Knowhere Corps quickly defeated and imprisoned. Later, Mantis responded to a distress call from the Guardians of the Galaxy and picked them up in her ship after they escaped imprisonment by the Collector (Taneleer Tivan).

During the fascist Hydra's takeover of the USA, an energy shield around Earth kept the Guardians of the Galaxy off the planet. Unwilling to help personally or involve the Knowhere Corps, Mantis instead told the Guardians of the Galaxy of a repository of weapons built by various alien species to battle the planet-consuming Galactus (Galan). She suggested one of the weapons, the Transluminal Tuning Fork, could be used to disrupt the shield around Earth. Unfortunately, the weapons were located in the Jojola Nebula, a sector of space notorious for travelers becoming

lost and rarely returning from the area. Luckily, Mantis knew of someone who had returned from the Jojola Nebula: Yondu Udonta, the estranged mentor of Star-Lord (Peter Quill). Mantis arranged for Yondu's release from Knowhere's detention complex on the condition that Yondu guide the Guardians of the Galaxy's journey.

When the Universal Church of Truth, led by Patriarch—a future version of Star-Lord's father, J'Son of Spartax—returned on a quest to destroy Death, Mantis, the Knowhere Corps, and others fell under the Church's mind control. Mantis initially assisted the church on its mission to power its flagship's engines with the life energy of Earth's population, but when Rocket Raccoon freed those enthralled by the church, Mantis joined the Guardians of the Galaxy and others to defeat the Universal Church of Truth by sending it back to its original timeline. 🚀

WITH KNOWHERE CORPS

OCCUPATION: Peacekeeper
GROUP AFFILIATION *UPDATE***:** Knowhere Corps; formerly Guardians of the Galaxy, Star-Lord (Peter Quill)'s unnamed squad

ART BY DANILO S. BEYRUTH, EDGAR SALAZAR & VALERIO SCHITI

ALICIA (MASTERS) GRIMM

HISTORY *UPDATE:* *Continued from the Alicia Masters profile in the* Women of Marvel: Celebrating Seven Decades Handbook *trade paperback (2010).* Motivated by a visit from the Thing (Ben Grimm) after he attained the ability to regain human form for 24 hours every year, Alicia Masters began to interact with him again. The renewal of their friendship suffered an early setback when the Thing, possessed by the destructive Asgardian Angrir, Breaker of Souls, viciously struck her when she tried to appeal to his better nature. Revived from unconsciousness by the Thing's teammate the Invisible Woman (Susan Richards), Alicia was assured by the fear she heard in the Thing's voice that his true nature still survived within him. Soon afterward, Franklin Richards psychically purged the Thing of Angrir's influence. During an epidemic engineered by the Queen (Ana Soria) and the Jackal (Miles Warren), which transformed Manhattan's population into feral spider-creatures, Alicia was immune due to a previous transformation into a spider-creature by the terror organization Hydra. This was noted by the leader of the Fantastic Four (F4), Mister Fantastic (Reed Richards), in his research for a cure and by the Queen herself, who sought to

keep Alicia out of Richards' hands. Despite the efforts of the Queen's agent Gypsy Moth (presumably Sybil Dvorak), Alicia was rescued and brought to Richards by the Thing and Spider-Woman (Jessica Drew), whose blood had been used to mutate Alicia years earlier.

After the Queen's defeat, the Thing and Alicia eventually decided to pursue their romance once again, but the Quiet Man, a scientist bent on ruining the public image of the F4, arranged for Alicia's abduction by a pocket-universe counterpart of her stepfather, the Puppet Master (Phillip Masters). The Quiet Man then killed the alternate Puppet Master and arranged for Richards to find the Thing standing over the corpse, framing him for the murder. To Alicia's relief, the F4 exposed the Quiet Man's plans, and the Thing was exonerated.

Following the destruction and restoration of the Multiverse and the presumed death of the Richards family, Parker Industries CEO Peter Parker, A.K.A. longtime F4 ally Spider-Man, bought the F4's Baxter Building residence. He commissioned Alicia to sculpt a life-size replica of the F4 and the Richards children, which he installed in the lobby to signify that the building would be waiting for the F4 if they returned. During a Zenn-Lavian assimilation of Earth, the Silver Surfer (Norrin Radd) and his human companion, Dawn Greenwood, sought Alicia's aid in amassing Earth's heroes to the planet's defense. When the Surfer was rendered unconscious after expending his Power Cosmic to repel the invaders and their leader, his former betrothed, Shalla Bal, Alicia, and Greenwood defended the Surfer, but to their

FIGHTING BATONS

relief, Bal simply declared the Surfer exiled from his people, and she departed.

Emboldened by his memories of the Richards family, the Thing proposed marriage to Alicia, who quickly accepted. As the pair approached F4 member and longtime friend the Human Torch (Johnny Storm) about acting as the Thing's best man, the Richards family signaled Earth from multiversal space, through which they had traveled for subjective years rebuilding the Multiverse. They teleported the Torch, the Thing, and the other former F4 members to their location to battle the Griever, an extradimensional entity who destroyed many of the new universes they had created. Upon their return, Alicia, inspired by the Thing's sudden departure, suggested that they get married the following weekend and not wait for a future date that might not come. The wedding was held in Benson, Arizona, home of the Thing's uncle Jake and aunt Petunia, but a worldwide broadcast from Dr. Doom (Victor Von Doom) warning of the arrival of the planet-devouring Galactus (Galan) was received before the couple could exchange their vows. Reed activated a device that froze time outside the altar for four minutes, allowing the ceremony to proceed. The F4 left Alicia (now Alicia Grimm, though she continued using her Masters surname in her professional life), F4 ally Wyatt Wingfoot, Jake, and Petunia to care for the Richards' children, Franklin and Valeria, while the F4 traveled to Latveria. Alicia had difficulty doing so as Valeria, in her desire to help her parents, was willful toward Alicia and Franklin was surly from secretly suffering from depression and nightmares after the Griever's destruction of the universes he created.

After preventing the threats posed by Doom and Galactus, the Grimms scheduled their honeymoon to coincide with one of the Thing's annual transformations and spent it at the tropical resort of Koma Koi, an occasion Alicia further commemorated by giving the Thing a human-sized wedding band. Their honeymoon was disrupted when the Hulk (Bruce Banner), under the Puppet Master's control, attacked the Thing. A landslide caused by their ensuing brawl trapped Alicia and the resort's other guests, but Alicia guided them to safety and encouraged her badly beaten husband to fight on. Though the Thing defeated the Hulk, his injuries left him unconscious for a week, robbing the pair of the opportunity to consummate their marriage, but Alicia assured the Thing that they had a lifetime of future opportunities.

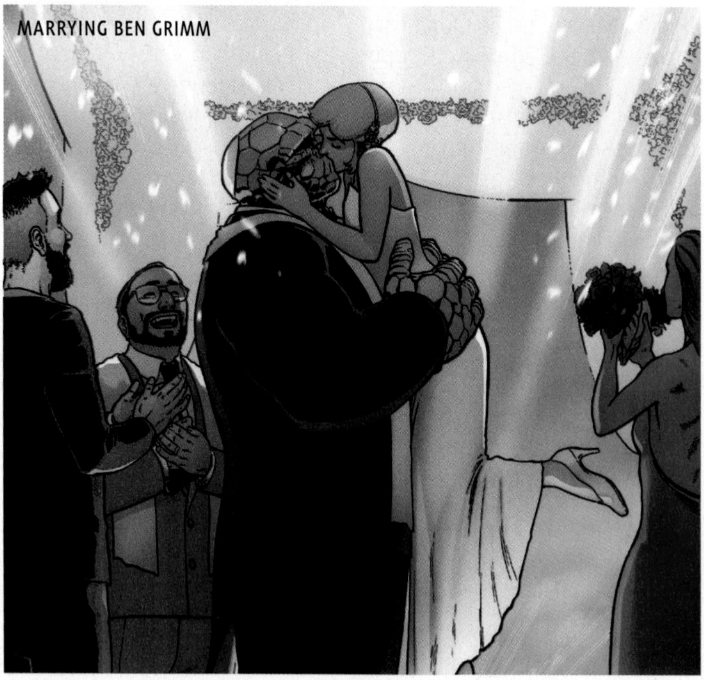
MARRYING BEN GRIMM

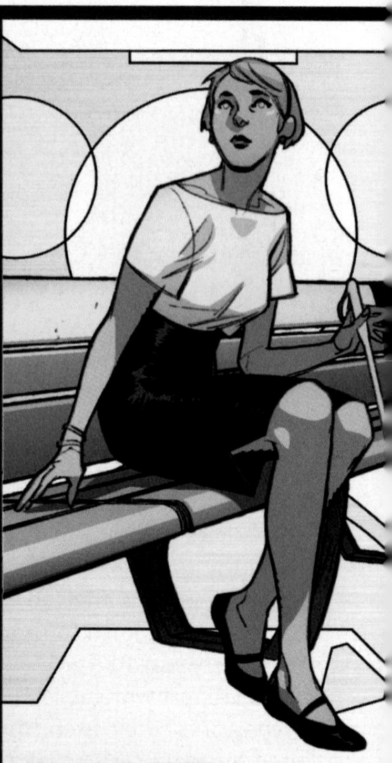

REAL NAME *UPDATE*:
Alicia Reiss Grimm (*née* Masters)

OCCUPATION *UPDATE*:
Art teacher

KNOWN RELATIVES *UPDATE*:
Benjamin Jacob Grimm (Thing, husband), Jacob Grimm (uncle-in-law), Petunia Grimm (aunt-in-law)

ABILITIES/ACCESSORIES *UPDATE*:
In addition to her standard identification cane, Alicia sometimes carries a customized cane she received as a birthday gift from the secretly blind Daredevil (Matt Murdock). Much like the billy club Daredevil wields, Alicia's customized cane can separate into a pair of fighting batons, with which Alicia has attained a modest degree of expertise.

	Rating (1–7)
INTELLIGENCE	3
STRENGTH	2
SPEED	2
DURABILITY	2
ENERGY PROJECTION	1
FIGHTING SKILLS	3

ART BY MICHAEL ALLRED, JIM CHEUNG, AARON KUDER, & SARA PICHELLI

QUOI

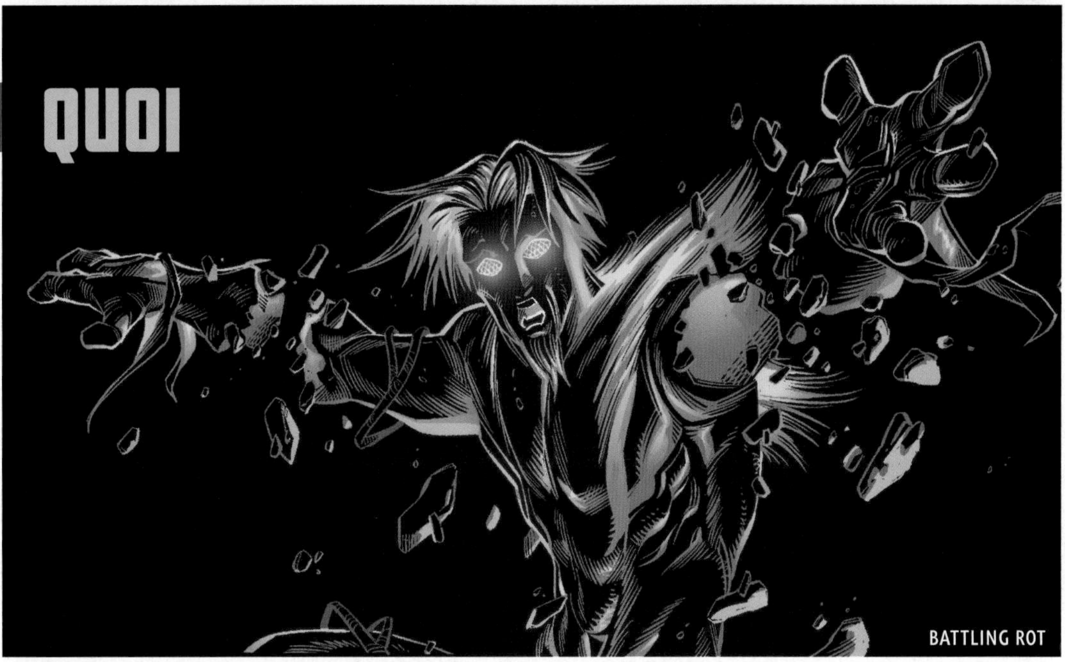
BATTLING ROT

HISTORY: A prophecy of unrevealed origin foretold that a perfect human would come to be known as the Celestial Madonna and give birth to the perfect child, a Celestial Messiah who was destined to change the universe. In recent years, the Celestial Madonna was revealed as the human female Mantis, a member of Earth's superhuman Avengers. She married the Supreme Exemplar, a perfect plant of the alien Cotati race, who re-animated the body of Mantis' dead lover, the Avenger Swordsman (Jacques Duquesne). In energy form, the couple conceived a child, then Mantis created a plant simulacrum with a womb perfectly suited to carry a hybrid child to house her own spirit. In this form, Mantis eventually gave birth to a boy, whom she named Sequoia ("Quoi" for short) after the noblest of Earth trees. She then secretly raised Sequoia for one year in Willimantic, Connecticut, keeping his existence hidden from the world. Sometime later, the Supreme Exemplar took the rapidly aging boy to the planet Tamal (as the couple had agreed would happen) so Sequoia could explore his plant nature. Sometime after this, Quoi, now housed in a pod that was presumably part of his plant nature, accompanied the Cotati High Council to Earth to convince a then amnesiac Mantis — who wrongly believed Quoi had been stolen from her — that he needed to remain with the Cotati. The meeting ended with an enraged Mantis driving the Cotati away with her mental powers; Sequoia accompanied them.

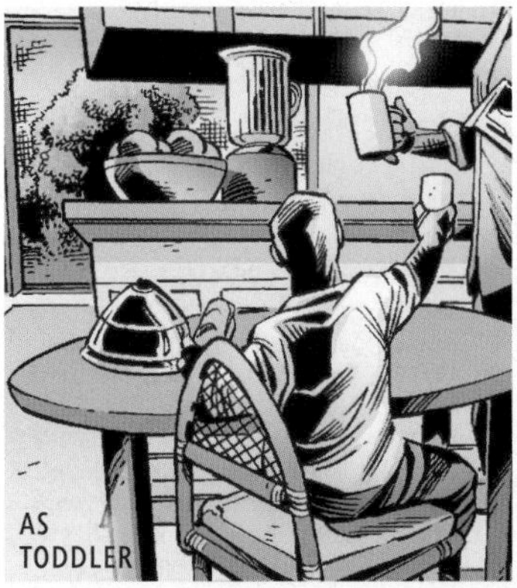
AS TODDLER

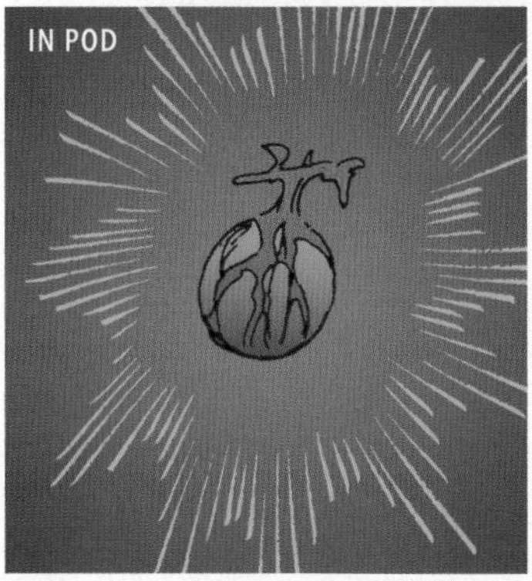
IN POD

A few years after visiting Earth, Sequoia attracted the attention of a Thanosi (one of the androids/clones/mystical doppelgängers of the mad Titan Thanos, who apparently believed it was the true Thanos.) Wanting to show his power over life and death, the Thanosi sought to kill the Celestial Messiah. When Mantis (now apparently back in her true body and her memories restored)

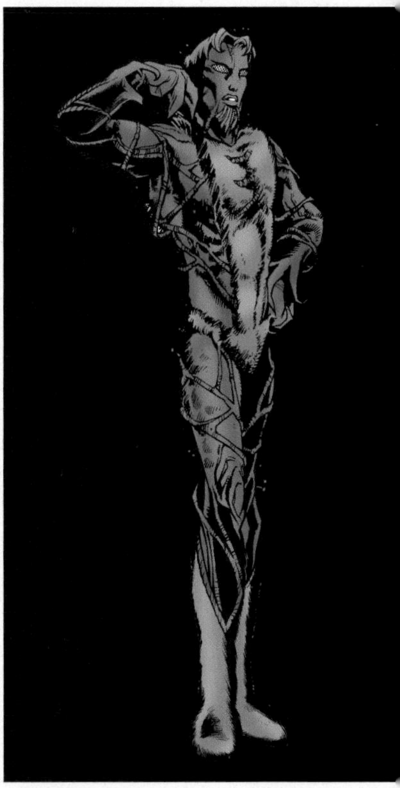

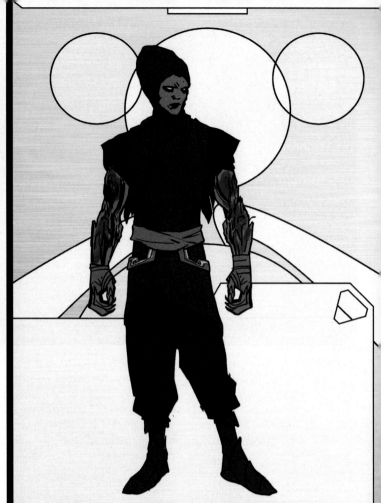

learned of this, she journeyed to Tamal with a group of Avengers to protect Quoi from the Thanosi. There, they discovered that Quoi, now an angst-ridden teen calling himself Q — the "weirdest of the Earth letters" — rejected Mantis, wrongly accusing her of abandoning him. The Thanosi sent several servants to bring him the Celestial Messiah. One, the reptilian pirate Raptra, succeeded in capturing Quoi. However, when the Thanosi refused to negotiate with Raptra the pirate and Quoi entered an uneasy alliance. The two hid from the Thanosi near a region of space known as the Rot, the apparent all-consuming, growing spawn of the personification of Death and the true Thanos. When found by both the Avengers and the Thanosi, Quoi battled the Thanosi on the astral plane, then also finally made peace with Mantis. After Quoi failed in his attempt to drive back the Rot, the Thanosi and Death realized the Rot would also end death itself, so they destroyed it with their vast power. Afterward, Quoi began his work as the Celestial Messiah in trying to bring new life to the region of space that was decimated by the Rot. He was accompanied in this work by Raptra, whom Quoi now loved.

REAL NAME: Sequoia
ALIASES: Q, One Who Would Change the Universe, Celestial Messiah
IDENTITY: No dual identity
OCCUPATION: Messiah
CITIZENSHIP: Tamal, possibly dual citizenship on Earth
PLACE OF BIRTH: Unrevealed location on Earth
KNOWN RELATIVES: Mantis (surname presumably Brandt, mother), Supreme Exemplar of the Cotati (father), Gustav Brandt (A.K.A. Lloyd Willoughby, Libra, maternal grandfather), Lua Nguyen Brandt (maternal grandmother, deceased), Khruul (maternal great-uncle, deceased), numerous Cotati relatives on paternal side
GROUP AFFILIATION: None
EDUCATION: Unrevealed
HEIGHT: 5'8"
WEIGHT: 190 lbs.
EYES: Yellow (compound)
HAIR: Green

ABILITIES/ACCESSORIES: A hybrid plant-human, Quoi can breathe oxygen for respiration or carbon dioxide for photosynthesis, does not require food, and can survive in a vacuum. Quoi shares an empathic bond with his mother and has tremendous mental strength, enough to battle a Thanosi to a standstill on the astral plane. He has powers over the basic forces of life itself, allowing him to absorb universal energy (including from other beings) and channel it into energy blasts or heal his surroundings. Presumably, as he grows, more abilities will be revealed.

①	②	③	④	⑤	⑥	⑦

INTELLIGENCE

STRENGTH

SPEED

DURABILITY

ENERGY PROJECTION

FIGHTING SKILLS

FIRST APPEARANCE: (Partial) *Silver Surfer* #4 (1987); (in pod) *Fantastic Four* #325 (1989); (as Quoi) *Avengers: Celestial Quest* #3 (2001)

ART BY RICH BUCKLER, JORGE SANTAMARIA, VALERIO SCHITI

RAKSOR

HISTORY: Not content to be Empress R'Klll's observer at the Shi'ar Empire's trial of the Phoenix Force (then posing as the X-Man Jean Grey) on Earth's moon, distinguished Skrull warrior Raksor entered the battlefield and attacked Phoenix's teammate Wolverine (Logan/James Howlett). However, when Raksor's hated Kree counterpart Bel-Dann interrupted, stunning Wolverine, an enraged Raksor attacked Bel-Dann, beginning a months-long conflict in the region's catacombs. Consumed by their conflict, the pair remained oblivious to the arrival of the Inhuman city Attilan when it was relocated from Earth. Intrigued by Bel-Dann and Raksor's duel and seeking to end the costly millennia-long Kree/Skrull War, the empires' respective rulers, the Supreme Intelligence and R'Klll agreed to let single combat decide the war's disposition, with the moon's resident Watcher, Uatu, arbitrating. When the battle drew the attention of the Inhumans and visiting Fantastic Four, they were informed by Uatu of the duel's significance, so they harried the alien warriors then feigned defeat when the duo united against them. Before the feud could resume, Uatu pronounced them joint winners, declaring the solution to the Kree/Skrull war lay in cooperation. Reluctantly accepting this, the pair were returned to their respective galaxies. Finding the Skrull Empire in chaos following the destruction of their throneworld by the world-eating Galactus (Galan), Raksor freed Prince Dezan (imprisoned for pacifism), who assisted the Avengers in a failed effort to halt Dezan's revolutionary former ally Zabyk from detonating a Skrull metamorphosis-neutralizing bomb. During this time, as a member of the Slaughter Squad employed by Mister Knife (Star-Lord's father, J'son of Spartax) Raksor briefly participated in a conflict against the Guardians of the Galaxy led by Star-Lord (Peter Quill) and members of the X-Men. At some point, while various coups and interstellar wars disrupted their empires, Raksor and Bel-Dann hid on Earth, seeking a way to unite both races. Later, with their empires now led by rulers receptive to unification, Bel-Dann and Raksor helped convince royal Kree-Skrull hybrid Hulkling (Teddy Altman/Dorrek VIII) into ascending the throne. When Bel-Dann was found mysteriously murdered, investigating Earth heroes assumed Raksor was the guilty party, but he was torn apart when a rapidly growing tree burst from within him; as he was dying, Raksor warned the heroes that "empires will fall."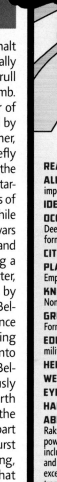

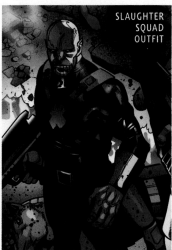

SLAUGHTER
SQUAD
OUTFIT

REAL NAME: Raksor
ALIASES: Lucien; impersonated many others
IDENTITY: No dual identity
OCCUPATION: Deep cover operative; former warlord, soldier
CITIZENSHIP: Skrull Empire
PLACE OF BIRTH: Presumably the Skrull Empire, Andromeda Galaxy
KNOWN RELATIVES: None
GROUP AFFILIATION: Formerly Slaughter Squad, Skrull military
EDUCATION: Presumably the Skrullian military academy
HEIGHT: 6'; variable
WEIGHT: 180 lbs. (possibly variable)
EYES: Green; variable
HAIR: None; variable
ABILITIES/ACCESSORIES: Raksor's highly developed metamorphic powers allowed him to exact impersonations, including physically powerful alien species, and to shape his limbs into weapons. An exceptional combatant, Raksor could rapidly transform to exploit different creatures' abilities in unarmed combat. He was also an expert with Skrullian armaments, including power gauntlets.

❶	**❷**	**❸**	**❹**	**❺**	**❻**	**❼**

INTELLIGENCE

STRENGTH

SPEED

DURABILITY

ENERGY PROJECTION

FIGHTING SKILLS

FIRST APPEARANCE:
X-Men #137 (1980)

ART BY JOHN BYRNE, PACO MEDINA & CARLOS PACHECO

SKRULLS

HISTORY *UPDATE* **:** *Continued from the Skrulls profile in the* Official Handbook of the Marvel Universe A-Z Vol. 10 *hardcover (2009).* Early in their history, the Skrulls and the heavily plumed Shi'ar fought in the Darkforce Dimension's Null Space region over the Elder of the Universe Gardener's Tree of Shadows until its seeds transformed a Shi'ar into the first of the vastly powerful Fraternity of Raptors. Instinctively copying the Skrulls' shape-shifting ability, the Raptor Prime then slaughtered them. Subsequent Raptors served to advance the Shi'ar Empire through history.

Sometime early during the Glorious War (A.K.A. the Kree/Skrull War), Skrull war queen Ryga'a and "ultimate" Kree warrior Soh-Larr fell in love while battling on the planet Xaccus. The resultant child, allegedly the first Kree-Skrull hybrid, was named Dorrek Supreme, after the two empires' respective rulers, and inherited his parents' ancestral swords, merging them to form the Star-Sword. He gathered other hybrids, the Knights of the Infinite, who dedicated themselves to uniting the two warring dominions. Hunted by both empires, the Knights hid in Castle Tarnala amid the Forbidden Asteroids on Andromeda Galaxy's edge.

When a Skrull Dark Throne military installation hidden in the D'karr Nebula developed an incurable plague programmable to target specific species, the Skrulls balked at unleashing such an apocalyptic weapon and mothballed it. However, the Kree Tel-Kar, using a Klyntar symbiote's shape-shifting abilities to infiltrate the Skrulls, learned of the plague. Forced to break cover to save Kree refugees before he could report back to his superiors, Tel-Kar hid the base's location within the Klyntar's subconscious and entrusted the symbiote to the refugees while he covered their escape. Tel-Kar was captured by Skrull War Sisters, led by M'lanz, while the

refugees lost the symbiote, which eventually made its way to Earth and became Venom.

Though the Skrull Empire had renounced magic following the divergence of the malignant, sorcerous Dire Wraith subspecies, a few practitioners remained, including the magus Mt'nox and Klobok, a scholar sent to a penal colony for researching forbidden arcane arts. The Knights of the Infinite's own sorcerer, M'ryn the Magus, prophesied both Kree and Skrull Empires collapsing, with their survival dependent on the Knights and a "once and future king."

Over the years, Earth gradually accumulated a Skrull population. Some were deserters, integrating peacefully with the human populace of remote towns such as

MT'NOX
Sorcerer
*DOCTOR STRANGE
#3 (2018)*

Dungston, Iowa, and others were descended from the spies captured by the Fantastic Four (F4) during that team's first encounter with Skrulls. After they were hypnotized into becoming cows, the F4's prisoners interbred with Earth cattle, producing hybrid offspring born as cows but with dominant Skrull DNA — while some never developed sapience, others took on human form and hid among humanity, often peacefully but sometimes preying on humans for food and entertainment. Another Skrull, hypnotized into duck form, was eaten by young Tara Tam. Developing shape-shifting powers, Tam believed herself a mutant until the Skrull Kill Krew disabused her.

In recent times, several Skrulls defected during Veranke's "Secret Invasion" — including the mutant G'illian Blax'zthor, around half a dozen soldiers who fled to the remote Bide-A-Wee RV camp, and an unidentified Skrull who later joined the Chinese government's Ascendants team as the armored Devastator. Learning of the Skrull-cow hybrids, the Thunderbolts' corrupt leader, Norman Osborn, cut a deal with these Skrull-Americans, his "Native Protocol," granting protection in return for spying on the invaders and helping paint Osborn as a hero of the conflict. Meanwhile, the mutant Skrulls group Cadre K learned of the non-sapient Skrull-cow hybrids and gathered them at the Sagittarian Farms in South Dakota, for protection. Also hiding on Earth were the Skrull Raksor and his Kree counterpart, Bel-Dann, working to unite their races after Uatu the Watcher had convinced them their species' survival depended on it.

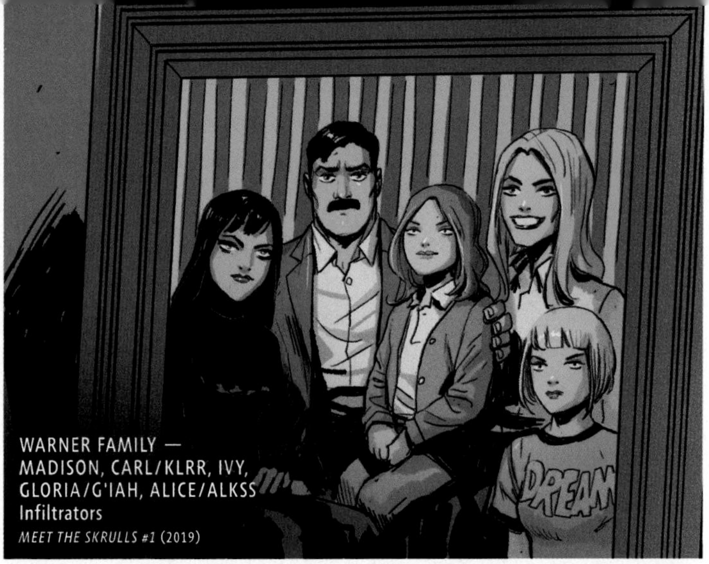
DREAM
WARNER FAMILY — MADISON, CARL/KLRR, IVY, GLORIA/G'IAH, ALICE/ALKSS
Infiltrators
MEET THE SKRULLS #1 (2019)

Veranke's demise left the Skrull Empire in further disarray, with rival warlords — including Gy'pl, My'rl, Dm'yr, and the Super-Skrull (Kl'rt) — seizing control over the fractured remnants. On Earth, fugitive Skrulls were hunted by Norman Osborn's newly formed H.A.M.M.E.R. and Abigail Brand's S.W.O.R.D. Deeming the Skrull-Americans' usefulness ended, Osborn had H.A.M.M.E.R. agent Viola Reichardt direct the resurrected Skrull Kill Krew to eliminate them. However, the Krew re-evaluated their anti-Skrull hatred. Realizing many of Osborn's targets were peaceful, the Krew declared the Skrull-Americans were under their protection.

One Skrull faction planted new sleeper cells on Earth, including the Warners of Stamford, Connecticut, and their handler, Moloth, preparing for Earth's subjugation and disrupting humanity's anti-Skrull research, such as Project Blossom. Having escaped penal servitude during the galaxies-destroying Annihilation Wave, Klobok summoned the slain Dire Wraith mage Doctor Dredd's spirit to teach him Wraith sorcery, then posed as Dredd to free the Wraiths from Limbo, intending to magically transform them into Skrulls, the foundation of a new empire, but an alliance of cosmic heroes, the Annihilators, thwarted his plans.

Long viewed by the Skrull Empire as a cultural laboratory, the Kral system experimented with ideas disallowed elsewhere, such as mimicking 1930s Earth gangster movies. While trying to pick up new broadcasts from Earth, the elder son of Kral X's Don Scarpone discovered transmissions of *The Ritchie Redwood Show* sitcom, set in the wholesome 1950s town of Glendale. Becoming obsessed, the son adopted the title character's persona and spread Redwoodism through the colony, forced his father into exile, and rebuilt Kral X into a Glendale replica.

Universe-wide attacks by the world-destroying Builders' armies forced the Skrull warlords to set aside their differences and ally with other interstellar powers against the common foe. Though others with claims to the imperial throne

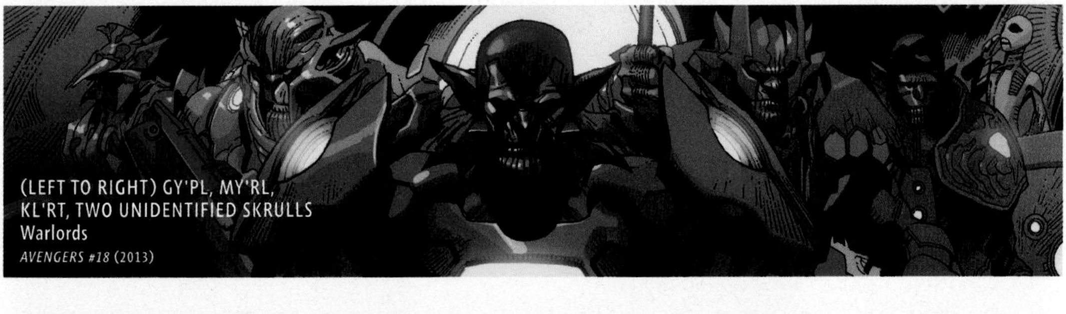
(LEFT TO RIGHT) GY'PL, MY'RL, KL'RT, TWO UNIDENTIFIED SKRULLS
Warlords
AVENGERS #18 (2013)

mutant X-Men and the heroic Avengers. While tracking down Cadre K, the heroes discovered the maniacal Doctor Doom (Victor Von Doom) was experimenting with captive Skrulls, hoping to create shape-shifting Doombots. Finding Cadre K peaceable, the heroes worked with them to free the Skrull-like prototype Doombot "from Beyond" and destroyed Doom's research. Cadre K returned to their ranch, with Captain America (Steve Rogers) promising to help them obtain U.S. citizenship.

Later, the Kree Empire suddenly collapsed when its homeworld, Hala, was destroyed by J'son, king of the Spartax Empire. Believing M'ryn's prophecy underway, the Knights of the Infinite declared Hulkling the re-incarnation of Dorrek Supreme, giving him the Star-Sword and promising to fight by his side when the time came to unite the empires. Meanwhile,

MR. WASPWIND,
RITCHIE REDWOOD, BIFF BISON
Glenbrook tyrant and enforcers
(BIFF, RITCHIE) U.S. AVENGERS #11 (2017);
(WASPWIND) U.S. AVENGERS #12 (2017)

BIFF

remained — including Dezan, thirteen-year-old Klundirk, and the Kree-Skrull hybrid Hulkling (Teddy Altman/Dorrek VIII) — Kl'rt's leadership during the crisis

prompted his coronation, reunifying the Skrull Empire. Mistakenly believing Cadre K was about to disrupt the fragile peace with Earth, the Skrull K'thron alerted Earth's

ALKSS (ELDER)
Warrior
Meet the Skrulls #2 (2019)

G'ILLIAN BLAX'ZTHOR
Skrull mutant
Unbeatable Squirrel Girl #37 (2018)

BECKY
Glenwood resident
U.S. Avengers #11 (2017)

BUGFACE BROWN
Glenwood resident
U.S. Avengers #11 (2017)

DEVASTATOR
Chinese state hero
Avengers World #7 (2014)

DEVASTATOR... D'LUTZ
Soldier
Venom: First Host #1 (2018)

GENERAL OM'YR
Warlord
Avengers #18 (2013)

DOOMBOT "FROM BEYOND"
Skrull/Doombot amalgam
A+X #17 (2013)

HURK
Warrior
Infinity Against the Tide Infinite Comic #1 (2013)

IRIS
Dungston waitress
Occupy Avengers #5 (2016)

JERRY McGILL
Rodeo rider
Skrull Kill Krew #2 (2009)

KORU KAVITI
Soldier
Spider-Woman #7 (2010)

K'KYY
Paladin of the Infinite
New Avengers #3 (2016)

KLOBOK (DR. DREDD)
Sorcerer
Annihilators #1 (2011)

PRINCE KLUNDIRK
Prince
Spider-Woman #3 (2016)

K'TAN
Experimental subject
A+X #14 (2014)

HOWARD MASON
Glenwood resident
U.S. Avengers #8 (2017)

VANESSA MASON
Glenwood resident
U.S. Avengers #11 (2017)

MAXOR
Deep-cover operative
Guardians of Infinity #5 (2016)

GERRY MAYS
Glenwood resident
U.S. Avengers #11 (2017)

M'LANZ
Warrior
Venom: First Host #2 (2018)

MOLOTH
Infiltrator
Meet the Skrulls #1 (2019)

M'RYN
Magus of the Infinite
New Avengers #3 (2016)

MUR-G'NN
Magic-user of the Infinite
New Avengers #3 (2016)

RHENA
Royal Science Officer
Infinity Against the Tide Infinite Comic #1 (2013)

RYGA'A
Skrull war-queen
New Avengers #4 (2016)

SABINE THE SORCERESS
Glenwood resident
U.S. Avengers #11 (2017)

SAV'RKK
Mercenary
Yondu #1 (2020)

DON SCARPONE
Kral X deposed ruler
U.S. Avengers #11 (2017)

SKRULL COW
Grazer, Evolutionary Trailblazer
A + X #16 (2014)

SKRULLTASTIC ONE
Super-Skrull
Fantastic Four Negative Zone #1 (2019)

SOFT TEETH
Smuggler
Rocket Raccoon #1 (2017)

Skrull rebels attempted to kidnap Prince Klundirk to make him a puppet-king in opposition to Kl'rt's rule but were stopped by Spider-Woman (Jessica Drew). Super-Skrulls dispatched to Earth to eliminate deserters hiding there wiped out hidden communities across the United States before finally being stopped in Dungston, Iowa, by Hawkeye (Clint Barton) and his allies.

On Kral X, Ritchie Redwood had imprisoned several Glendale residents, including his brother, Bugface Brown, for seeking to update their community in line with episodes from a 21st century *Ritchie Redwood Show* revival. Intent on maintaining Glendale's authenticity, he procured the mutant Cannonball (Sam Guthrie) from an alien slave auction to be the town's geography teacher. Cannonball broke out Bugface's dissidents just as his Avengers teammates arrived looking for him, and together, they deposed Ritchie.

Hoping one of the immensely powerful Infinity Stones could restore his empire, Kl'rt tracked down the Time Gem and entrusted it to Mt'nox, only for Earth's Sorcerer Supreme, Doctor Strange (Stephen Strange), to steal it for safekeeping. Elsewhere, having escaped Skrull custody, Tel-Kar forcibly retrieved the Venom symbiote from its human host, Eddie Brock, then breached the D'karr Nebula research base, intent on unleashing the Skrulls' plague against its creators, but was stopped by a pursuing Brock and M'lanz. Meanwhile, on Earth, G'illian Blax'zthor had adopted the human identity Gillian Blythe but learned she was being hunted as a deserter. She faked her death with help from Earth heroes Squirrel Girl (Doreen Green) and Iron Man (Tony Stark).

When Moloth sold out his operatives to Project Blossom, the result was the deaths of several undercover Skrull family spy cells. After he slew Carl Warner, the remaining Warners killed him in turn and went on the run. In space, deciding the Kral system was weakening the empire, Skrull High Command caused its sun to go supernova. Forewarned, a few residents escaped, including Bugface Brown, Prince Dezan, and Boss Barker. Soon afterward, the work of Raksor, Bel-Dann, and the Knights of the Infinite came to fruition: Kl'rt and his Kree counterpart, Tanalth the Pursuer, willingly stepped aside so that Hulkling could be crowned Emperor Dorrek VIII. Declaring his two peoples no longer Kree or Skrulls but the Kree/Skrull Alliance, he launched their fleet toward Earth for what he ominously declared "the Final War."

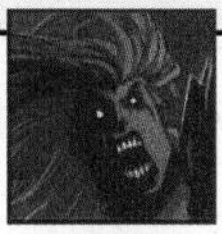

DORREK SUPREME
Skrull-Kree hybrid
New Avengers #3 (2016)

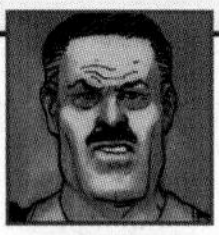

DUNGSTON SHERIFF
Dungston resident
Occupy Avengers #5 (2016)

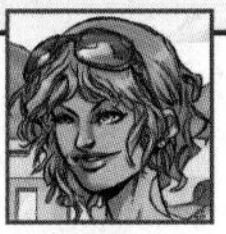

EVA
Infiltrator
Skrull Kill Krew #3 (2009)

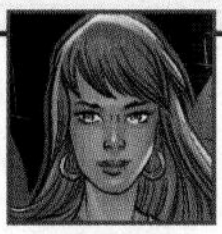

APRIL FLOWERS
Glenwood resident
U.S. Avengers #11 (2017)

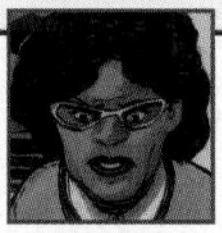

GERTIE
Dungston motel owner
Occupy Avengers #5 (2016)

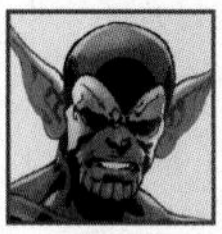

K'THRON
Hunter
A+X #13 (2013)

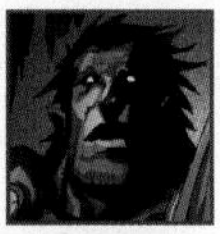

LAN-ZARR
Knight of the Infinite
New Avengers #3 (2016)

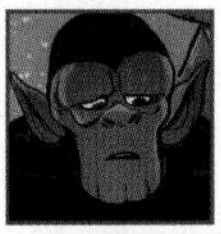

LAZ
Inept invader
Groot #1 (2015)

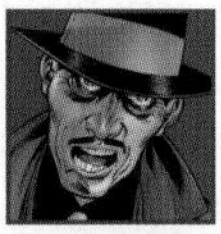

LITTLE RICO
Kral X gangster
U.S. Avengers #11 (2017)

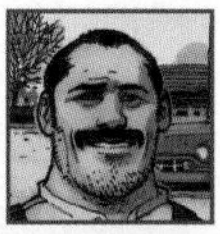

LOWELL LOVETT
Dungston mechanic
Occupy Avengers #5 (2016)

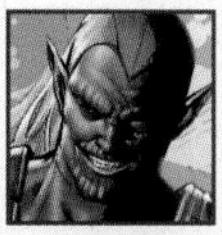

NAZUM
Soldier
X-Men #28 (2009)

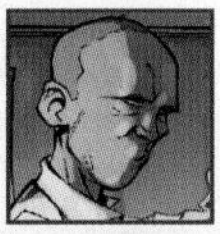

PHIL
Cameraman
Skrull Kill Krew #4 (2009)

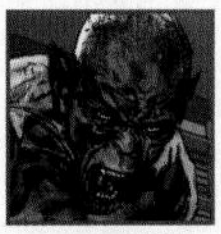

PILLI
Soldier
Spider-Woman #4 (2010)

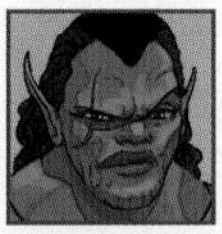

RAAVA
Warrior
Black Bolt #2 (2017)

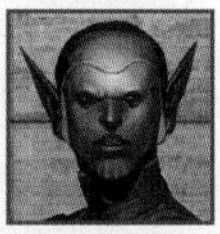

K'EEL R'KT
Royal Science Officer
Infinity Against the Tide Infinite Comic #1 (2013)

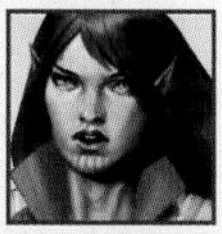

TARNA
Agent of the Cosmos
Venom: Space Knight #2 (2016)

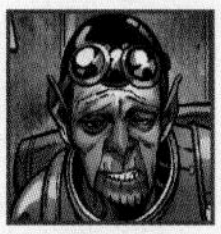

TINKERER
Spaceship mechanic
Nova #12 (2014)

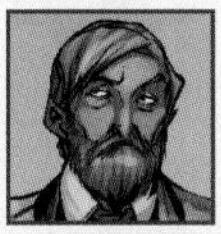

BILL TOMLINSON
Media mogul
Skrull Kill Krew #5 (2009)

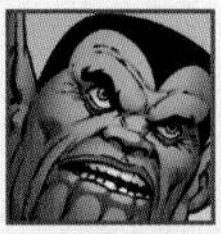

XELOR
Fight promoter
Thanos: Infinity Relativity #1 (2015)

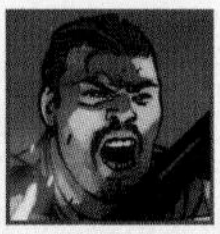

ZANDER
Dungston deputy
Occupy Avengers #6 (2016)

KNOWN MEMBERS *UPDATE*:
Alkss, Alkss (Alice Warner), Barry, Becky, Biff Bison, G'illian Blax'zthor (Gillian Blythe), Bl'rt, Bugface Brown, Bryson, Bt'nx, Clay, Rox'anne D, Devastator, D'lutz, Dm'yr, Doombot "from Beyond," Dorrek Supreme, Dr'zzt, Adam Felber, Flo, April Flowers, Gertie, G'iah (Gloria Warner), Pappy Guggenheim, Gy'pl, Hector, Horff, Iris, Beth Johnson, Koru Kaviti, Brandon Kay (Spider-Man), Keith, K'kyy, Klobok (Doctor Dredd), Klrr (Carl Warner), Klundirk, K'tan, K'thron, Lan-Zarr, Laz, Lowell Lovett, Mark, Marie, Howard Mason, Vanessa Mason, Gerry Mays, Jerry McGill, Eva Mendes, M'lanz, Moloth, M'ryn, Mt'nox, Mur-G'nn, My'rl, Nazum, Phil, Pilli Natu, Nina, J'olene R, Raava, Raavaka, Ratzo, Ritchie Redwood, Rhena, Little Rico, K'eel R'kt, Ryga'a, Sabine the Teen Sorceress, Sav'rkk, Don Scarpone, Skragg, Skrak, Skrulltastic One, Soft Teeth, Sol, Star-Kat Squadron, Tarna, Tinkerer, Bill Tomlinson, Varra, Ivy Warner, Madison Warner, Mister Waspwind, Y'olan'da X., D'rango Y., Pe'te'r Z, Zander; impersonators of Ben Franklin, Hawkeye (Clint Barton), Thor Odinson, and another Wolverine (Logan/James Howlett)

BASE OF OPERATIONS *UPDATE*:
Castle Tarnala, Tarnax II; formerly D'karr Nebula, Hy'lt Minor, Kly'tresz

ART BY DANIEL ACUÑA, TOM GRUMMETT, NIKO HENRICHON, PACO MEDINA & JESUS SAIZ

SUPER-SKRULL

WITH TIME STONE

HISTORY *UPDATE*: *Continued from the Super-Skrull profile in the* Official Handbook of the Marvel Universe A-Z Vol. 11 hardcover (2009). At some point, Kl'rt was apparently incarcerated and considered for Luke Cage's Thunderbolts Beta Squad but likely escaped during a jailbreak at Ryker's "Power House" wing, orchestrated by the wrongly imprisoned Thing (Ben Grimm). After this, Kl'rt became a Skrull warlord, reuniting much of the fractured Skrull Empire. Kl'rt united his fellow warlords when the planet-destroying Builders killed billions on several Skrull worlds. When he sought to join the Galactic Council, J'Son of Spartax vouched for Kl'rt, guaranteeing him a seat. Kl'rt provided the council with footage obtained from Warlord Dm'yr's successful battle against the Builders' advance fleet, proving the Builders weren't invincible. Though some of his allies believed a warrior's death against such formidable adversaries was noble, Kl'rt wanted to live, after having sacrificed so much to reunite his people. After the Builders' defeat, Kl'rt deployed his fleet to defend Earth against the mad Titan Thanos and fought alongside other council members to defeat Thanos' general, Black Dwarf, while the Avengers defeated Thanos. Kl'rt was subsequently crowned Emperor on Tarnax II. Later, angry with the universe's heroes for not preventing the destruction of the Skrull Empire, Kl'rt summoned the universe-devouring Omnipotentis on Earth, intending to destroy all planets in the universe. Child super-genius Moon Girl (Lunella Lafayette) worked with the Thing and the Human Torch (Johnny Storm) to stop him. Kl'rt then obtained the infinitely powerful Time Stone from deep beneath the planet Sakaar's crust and employed Skrull sorcerer Mt'nox to amplify the stone's power to restore the Skrull Empire. Sorcerer Supreme Doctor Stephen Strange challenged him for the stone, and succeeded by using the stone to strike Kl'rt with a dozen spells simultaneously. When the planet-devouring Galactus (Galan) threatened universal destruction by consuming all magic, Kl'rt joined the fight against him. Eventually, the Kree Mar-Koll enticed Kl'rt to restore the destroyed Skrull throneworld, Tarnax IV, by using a shape-shifter's amplified metamorphic energy to remake Earth with the Extractor device; but rather than sacrifice a Skrull, Mar-Koll targeted the metamorphic Inhuman Ms. Marvel (Kamala Khan). Kl'rt reassumed the Captain Hero identity to lure her into a trap, but his brutality ultimately exposed him. The Extractor was destroyed before Kl'rt's plan was realized, and Ms. Marvel convinced Kl'rt to abandon vengeance and move toward a brighter future. Kl'rt soon pledged himself to the prophesied Kree/Skrull hybrid Hulkling (Teddy Altman/Dorrek VIII), who merged the warring Skrull and Kree races into an alliance against their mutual enemies. 🜨

AS EMPEROR

AS CAPTAIN HERO

ARMORED

OCCUPATION *UPDATE*: Warrior; former emperor, warlord
GROUP AFFILIATION *UPDATE*: The Kree/Skrull Alliance, the Galactic Council (continued membership is presumptive); formerly the United Front

ART BY JIM CHEUNG, JON LAM, GREG LAND, HUMBERTO RAMOS & LEINIL FRANCIS YU

SWORDSMAN
(SUPREME EXEMPLAR)

HISTORY: Millennia ago, extraterrestrial Kree pacifists, the Priests of Pama, transported members of the Cotati, a telepathic plant race they revered, to hundreds of planets, including Earth, where the priests planted several Cotati in the land that would become Vietnam. In recent years, the Avenger Mantis, a disciple of the priests, buried her lover and teammate, Swordsman (Jacques Duquesne), near a tree in the priests' temple, unaware it was the eldest Cotati, the Supreme Exemplar, a perfect tree. The Exemplar inhabited Swordsman's corpse so it could mate with the Celestial Madonna, the human destined to produce the Celestial Messiah, who would bring enlightenment to the universe. After the Exemplar revealed to Mantis that she was the Madonna, the couple married, converted their consciousnesses into psionic energy, and left Earth. After conceiving a child, the two spirits returned. The Exemplar reclaimed its tree form, and Mantis created a plant simulacrum to give birth to Sequoia (Quoi) while her body lay in Swordsman's grave. Later, after Quoi had been sent to the planet Tamal to continue to be raised by the Cotati, Mantis' soul was fragmented in conflict against the age-old Elders of the Universe. When Mantis' simulacrum sought answers in Vietnam, the Exemplar used Swordsman's corpse to slay the simulacrum so its soul fragment could revive Mantis' original body. Swordsman's body crumbled when the Exemplar transferred his consciousness to a simulacrum on Tamal. Years later, a Thanosi doppelgänger of the death-obsessed Thanos sought to kill the teenage Sequoia, believing him a threat to fatality. A fully restored Mantis and the Avengers traveled to Tamal to protect Sequoia. The Cotati blamed the Avengers for the threat to the Messiah, so they seized control of the Exemplar's Swordsman simulacrum and attacked them, but they defeated him. Following the Thanosi's defeat, Sequoia began his universal mission of promoting life, apparently leaving the Exemplar on Tamal.

NOTE: *The Supreme Exemplar active during "The Crossing" conspiracy was later revealed as a shape-changing Space Phantom from Limbo.*

TRUE FORM

REAL NAME: None
(Cotati traditionally have no individual names.)
ALIASES: Supreme Exemplar, Prime One, Eldest Cotati on Earth, Prime Cotati, Most Perfect Cotati, Verdant One
IDENTITY: No dual identity
OCCUPATION: Supreme Exemplar of the Cotati, guardian of the Celestial Messiah
CITIZENSHIP: Planet Tamal
PLACE OF BIRTH: The planet Hala in the Pama Star System (presumably)
KNOWN RELATIVES:
Sequoia (Quoi, son), Mantis (surname presumably Brandt, wife, separated)
GROUP AFFILIATION:
High Council of the Cotati
EDUCATION: Unrevealed, presumably well educated through millennia of telepathic contact with others
HEIGHT: (Swordsman) 6'4"; (true form) 20'
WEIGHT: (Swordsman) 250 lbs.; (true form) 3,702 lbs.
EYES: (Swordsman) Green; (true form) none (presumably)
HAIR: (Swordsman) Green; (true form) none
ABILITIES/ACCESSORIES:
A Cotati, the Supreme Exemplar is telepathic, has a mental connection to all Cotati, and can project his consciousness across interstellar distances. He can create plant simulacra of other beings and animate them with his spirit. By inhabiting Swordsman's body, he became an acrobat, a strategist, a master of bladed weapons, and an exceptional combatant with fast reflexes. He carries an apparent simulacrum of a sword he previously wielded that projected concussive force, disintegrating rays, flames, electrical/sonic shock, and nerve gas; whether the simulacrum has the same abilities is unrevealed.

1	2	3	4	5	6	7
INTELLIGENCE
STRENGTH
SPEED
DURABILITY
ENERGY PROJECTION
FIGHTING SKILLS

FIRST APPEARANCE: (True form) *Avengers* #130 (1974); (Swordsman form) *Avengers* #131 (1974); (identity revealed) *Giant-Size Avengers* #4 (1975)

TALOS

WITH ABUNDANT GLOVE

HISTORY *UPDATE*: *Continued from the Talos profile in the* Official Handbook of the Marvel Universe A-Z Vol. 11 *hardcover (2009)*. Craving acceptance due to the genetic anomaly that left him unable to shape-shift like most alien Skrulls, Talos became determined to prove his worth to the Skrull Empire. Deciding to enslave Earth to garner attention, Talos set about acquiring the marginally powerful Abundant Gems. Among them were the gems of compassion, laughter, respect, and two of dance. After finding three gems, Talos learned that the Respect Gem was in a necklace on Earth in the possession of the thief Black Cat (Felicia Hardy). Talos disguised himself as a human named Jonathan Richards to hire private investigator Howard the Duck to retrieve the necklace, claiming it was a family heirloom stolen by Black Cat. Soon growing impatient at the hapless Howard's failure to obtain the necklace, Talos followed Howard. He tracked the necklace to the hideout of criminal hypnotist Ringmaster (Maynard Tiboldt), where

Talos revealed his identity and absconded with the gem. Talos then located the Laughter Gem at the former site of the Fantastic Four's Pier Four headquarters, where he found Howard, his shape-shifting ally Tara Tam, Sorcerer Supreme Doctor Stephen Strange, and the Fantastic Four's Human Torch (Johnny Storm) also investigating the site. Talos attacked the foursome and took the gem, completing the Abundant Glove, which he used to summon the Abundant Warriors, manifestations of the gems' powers. Talos' assaults drew the attention of New York's super hero community. After Talos defeated Mister Fantastic (Reed Richards), Tara Tam posed as Skrull Emperor Kl'rt (the Super-Skrull) to distract Talos with commendations on his perceived victory. But Talos overcame his need for acceptance and nearly killed Tara, believing she was Kl'rt, before Howard stole the Abundant Glove from Talos and used it to banish the Abundant Warriors as the assembled heroes apprehended Talos.

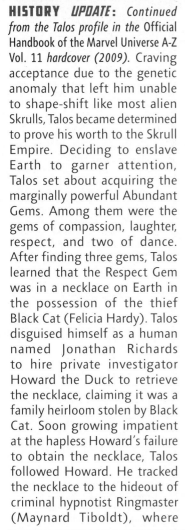

ALIASES *UPDATE*: Talos the Tamer, Jonathan Richards

ABILITIES/ACCESSORIES *UPDATE*: Talos is a capable disguise artist, using makeup, clothing, and other items to conceal his extraterrestrial appearance and pass as a human. Talos is able to resist hypnotic commands, but whether this is innate or is through technology is unrevealed. The Abundant Glove allowed Talos to levitate and to summon superhumanly strong and durable manifestations of the Abundant Gems' powers called the Abundant Warriors. Using the Respect Gem, Talos could project energy knives, powerful energy blasts, and force-fields capable of holding back multiple superhumans at once. He could also project unidentified energy using the Laughter Gem.

ART BY JOE QUINONES

TANALTH THE PURSUER

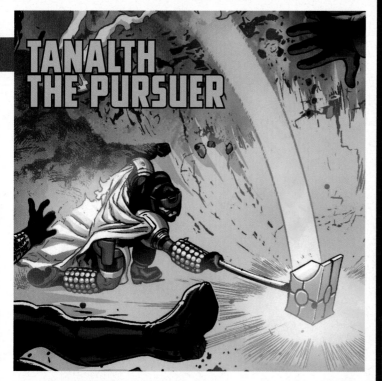

HISTORY: After the Kree warrior Korath the Pursuer was killed by Ultron during the war against the techno-organic Phalanx, the merciless and ambitious Tanalth succeeded him as leader of the Pursuers Elite Corps. With the galaxy in political turmoil due to maneuvering by the Shi'ar and Skrull empires and Earth's Inhumans, the Kree Supreme Intelligence directed Tanalth to Earth to recover the Gods' Whisper, a god-controlling Kree weapon lost on Earth millennia ago. The weapon had briefly resurfaced during the 1940s and three members of the heroic Invaders team split it into three pieces. Despite misgivings about the mission, which she suspected would ultimately harm the empire, Tanalth dutifully pursued it, seeking the three former Invaders: the android Human Torch (Jim Hammond), the Atlantean Namor, and cyborg secret agent Winter Soldier (James Barnes). Extracting memories from all three, she located the device then captured Namor for further interrogation on Hala. Hammond, Barnes, and another former Invader, Captain America (Steve Rogers), pursued Tanalth

to Hala, but she used the Gods' Whisper to enslave the Eternal Ikaris, whom she had brought to Hala, and set him against the heroes. Captain America infected the Supreme Intelligence with a computer virus, forcing Tanalth to surrender the Gods' Whisper to him to save the Intelligence. In the mission's aftermath, Tanalth investigated the Supreme Intelligence's inner circle, whom she did not trust. When she looked into one of them, Yan-Drall, she was nearly assassinated by aliens impersonating her own men. She privately met with another Eternal, Makkari, who suspected similar treachery among his people. When they survived a joint assassination attempt by the aliens, they agreed to collaborate on an investigation. The reasons behind these assassinations remain unrevealed. Later, Tanalth and several Kree soldiers joined forces with human super villain Moonstone (Karla Sofen) on Earth to battle the Avengers for unrevealed reasons. She subsequently aligned herself with the united Kree and Skrull empires, under the new emperor, Kree-Skrull hybrid Hulkling (Teddy Altman/Dorrek VIII).

REAL NAME: Tanalth
ALIASES: None
IDENTITY: No dual identity
OCCUPATION: Chief-High Pursuer
CITIZENSHIP: Kree Empire
PLACE OF BIRTH: Unrevealed location in Kree Empire
KNOWN RELATIVES: None
GROUP AFFILIATION: Pursuers Elite Corps
EDUCATION: Unrevealed
HEIGHT: 7'1"
WEIGHT: 400 lbs.
EYES: Green
HAIR: Auburn
ABILITIES/ACCESSORIES:
Tanalth can lift 60 tons, is superhumanly durable, can survive in outer space, and can fly in both an atmosphere and through space. She is a skilled and brutal combatant, and she wields a war hammer that fires powerful energy blasts. She also uses a desiccating rifle and a memory-extraction device.

| ❶ | ❷ | ❸ | ❹ | ❺ | ❻ | ❼ |

INTELLIGENCE
STRENGTH
SPEED
DURABILITY
ENERGY PROJECTION
FIGHTING SKILLS

FIRST APPEARANCE: *All-New Marvel Now! Point One #1* (2014)

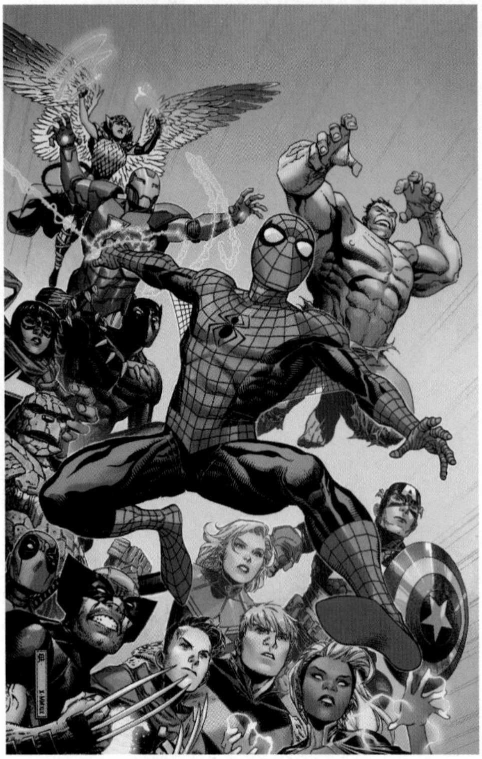

INCOMING! VARIANT BY
Jim Cheung & **Romulo Fajardo Jr.**

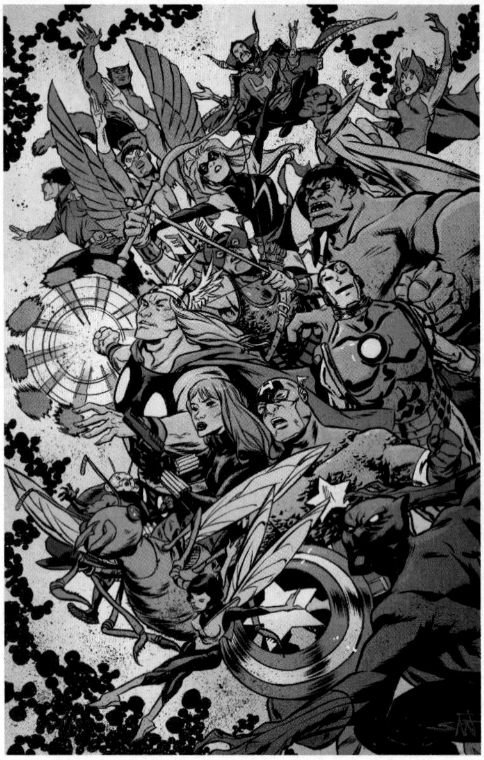

INCOMING! VARIANT BY
Sanford Greene

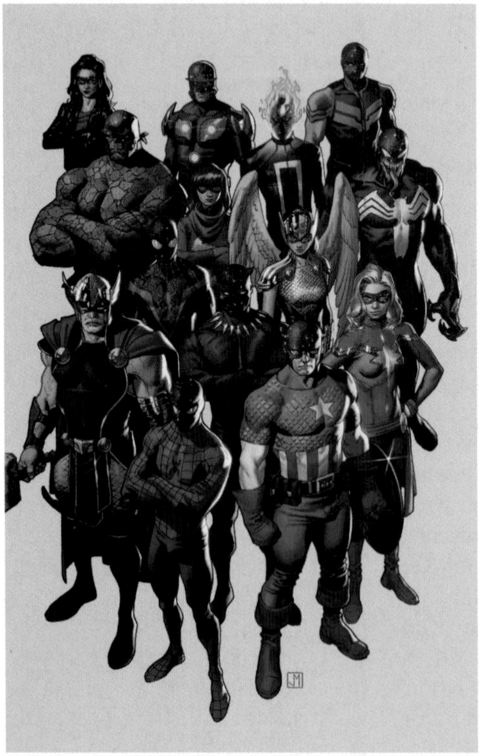

INCOMING! PARTY VARIANT BY
Jorge Molina

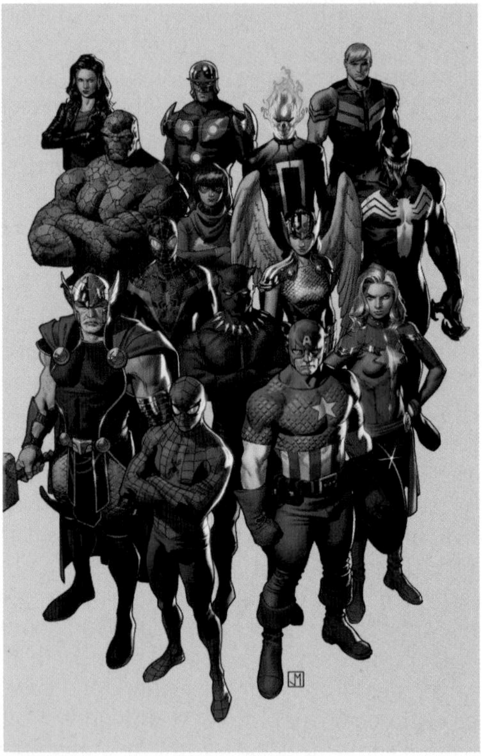

INCOMING! UNMASKED SECRET PARTY VARIANT BY
Jorge Molina

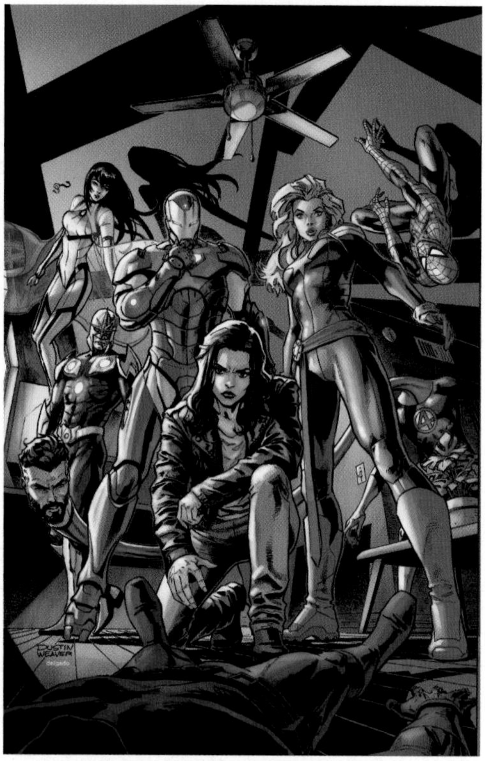

INCOMING! VARIANT BY
Dustin Weaver & **Edgar Delgado**

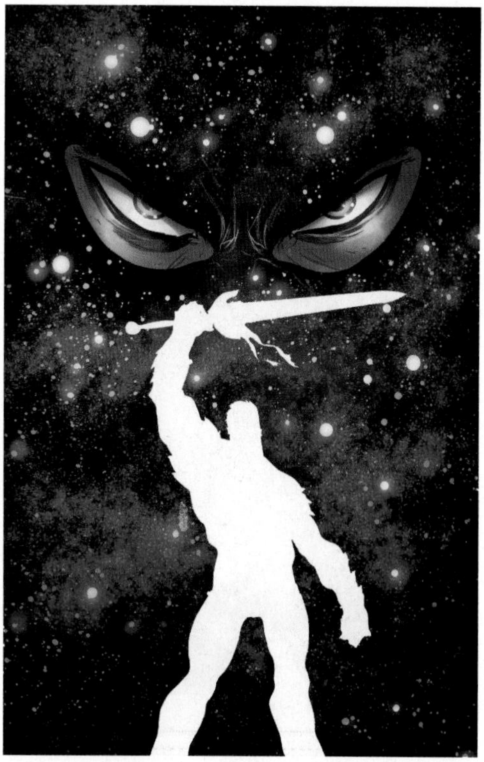

INCOMING! VARIANT BY
Kim Jacinto & **Rachelle Rosenberg**

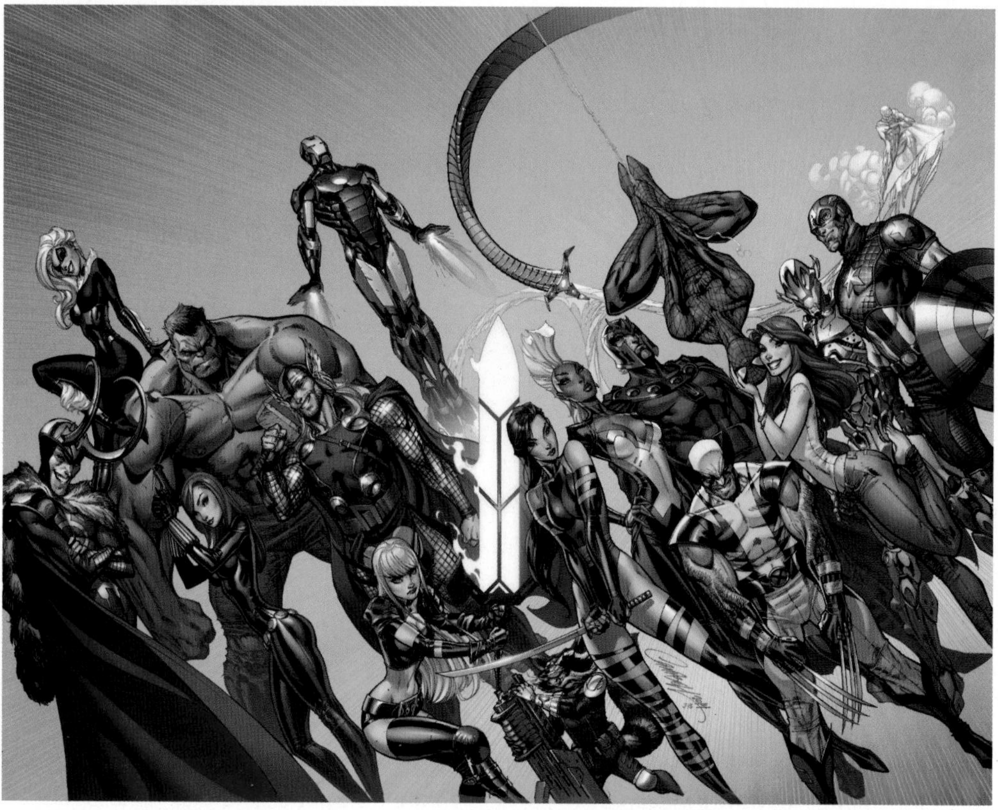

INCOMING! HIDDEN GEM VARIANT BY **J. Scott Campbell** & **Justin Ponsor**

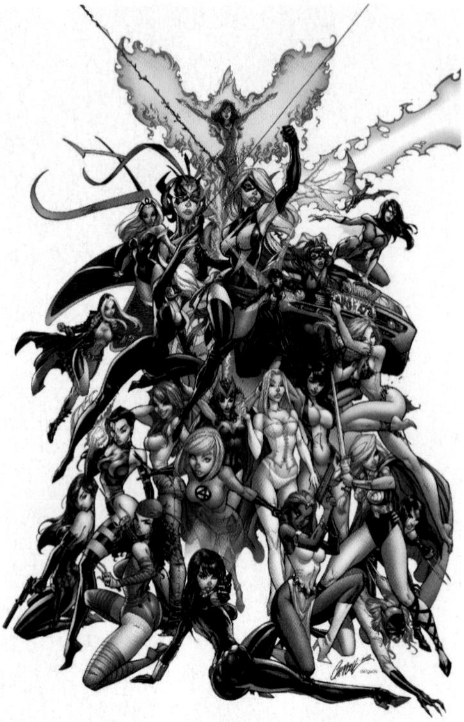

INCOMING! WOMEN OF MARVEL
HIDDEN GEM VARIANT BY
J. Scott Campbell & Edgar Delgado

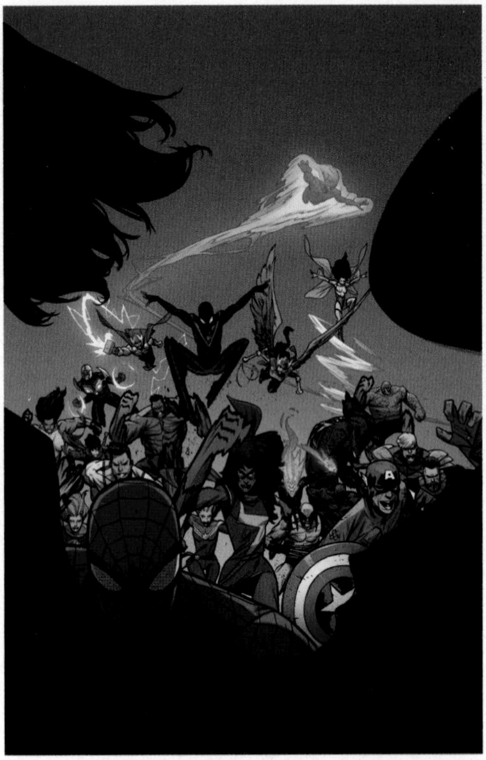

INCOMING! SECOND-PRINTING VARIANT BY
Kim Jacinto & Tamra Bonvillain

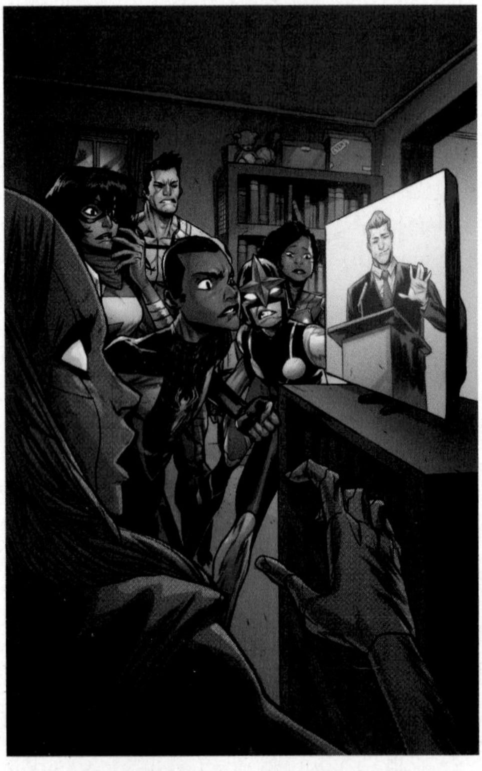

INCOMING! PROMOTIONAL ART BY
Kim Jacinto & Espen Grundetjern

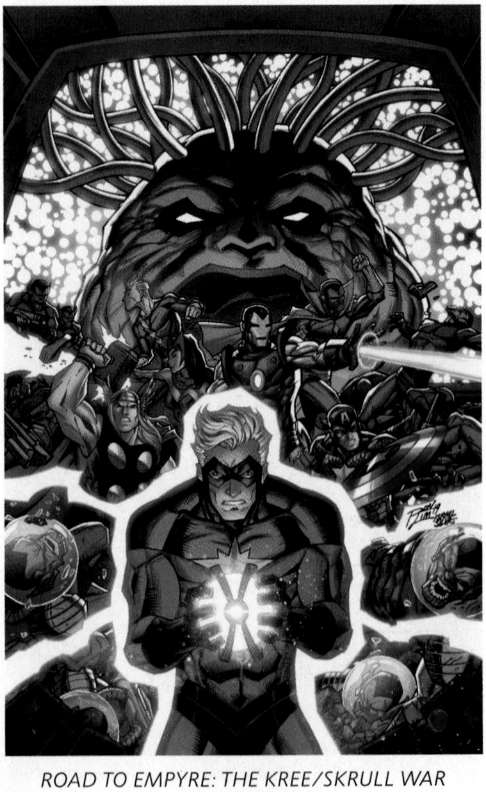

ROAD TO EMPYRE: THE KREE/SKRULL WAR
VARIANT BY
Ron Lim & Israel Silva